INVESTIGATING THE RUSSIAN MAFIA

INVESTIGATING THE RUSSIAN MAFIA

Joseph D. Serio

CAROLINA ACADEMIC PRESS

Durham, North Carolina

Library of Congress Cataloging-in-Publication Data

Serio, Joseph, 1964-
  Investigating the Russian mafia : an introduction for students, law enforce-
ment, and international business / by Joseph D. Serio.
    p. cm.
  Includes bibliographical references and index.
  ISBN 978-1-59460-225-2 (alk. paper)
  1. Mafia--Russia (Federation) 2. Organized crime--Russia (Federation) I.
Title.

  HV6453.R83S47 2008
  364.1'060947--dc22

                                                           2008001758

Carolina Academic Press
700 Kent Street
Durham, North Carolina 27701
Telephone (919) 489-7486
Fax (919) 493-5668

Printed in the United States of America.

For Sasha Gorkin

CONTENTS

Preface		ix
Acknowledgments		xi
About the Author		xv
Introduction		xvii

I. WORDS AND NUMBERS

Chapter 1	Mafia	5
Chapter 2	Russia	31
Chapter 3	Information	43
Chapter 4	Statistics	71

II. ROOTS

Chapter 5	Legacies	97
Chapter 6	The Economy	125
Chapter 7	Vory v Zakone	149
Chapter 8	Accumulation of Capital	175

III. ON THE FRONT LINES

Chapter 9	Groups	205
Chapter 10	Business	229
Chapter 11	Law Enforcement	253

Why Should You Care?	277
Index	283

PREFACE

This book grew primarily out of the enthusiasm of students I encountered in the classroom and the curiosity of law enforcement officers I met in the field. While many of them had heard the dramatic reporting of the 1990s or read textbooks on organized crime in recent years, they understood that there was much more to know, about Russia generally and the context of the development of the Russian 'mafia' in particular.

In undertaking this project, I wanted to present a slightly different perspective from other writers. Earlier works by well-qualified writers presented the Russian 'mafia' without sufficient context for readers. The most popular books produced in the mid-1990s caught the imagination of the public through involved story telling and dramatic use of language, with what amounted to a mere glance at history and culture. Other books, of a more academic nature, were thick with theory or written in an inaccessible style. I have endeavored here to present a broad overview of the so-called Russian mafia through a consideration of language, statistics, culture, history, and Russian realities in a way that ultimately is like my lectures at the university: part investigation, part conversation, and part anecdote. I would encourage you, after reading this book, to explore the topic further. Two excellent, well-written, and detailed accounts are Federico Varese's *The Russian Mafia* and Vadim Volkov's *Violent Entrepreneurship*.

More than anything, I wanted to create an exercise for students, criminal justice professionals, and international businesspeople that challenges the way they consider the world around them. Understanding the function of language, appreciating the way the media functions, and questioning the various versions that are created by a variety of interested parties (such as the media, law enforcement, and others) are some of the first steps in developing a critical-thinking capacity. Ultimately, I may reach similar conclusions as Varese, Volkov, and others, but the kind of journey this book takes, I dare say, is somewhat different.

Investigating the Russian Mafia is divided into three parts. Part I, Words and Numbers, explores issues of language and statistics. The kinds of questions addressed include: What did the Soviets mean by 'mafia'? How were criminal groups counted and what discrepancies do we notice through a careful collection of the statistics? What forces are at work on the media and how do they influence reporting on 'mafia'? In Part II, Roots, I survey some of the key issues repeatedly raised in the 1990s—like the rise of criminal organizations, widespread police corruption, and the nature of business—and cast a net over some 400 years of history to understand the long-term context from which the Russian 'mafia' emerged. Part III, On the Front Lines, involves an examination of the three areas inextricably linked in the volatile struggle for power and property in the 1990s: criminal organizations, business, and law enforcement. It is critical to appreciate that these three spheres of Russian life played their roles on the same stage. Their relationships were far more intertwined in shades of gray than the black-and-white, good guy/bad guy scenario we might prefer.

I am hoping to raise in this book far more questions than provide answers as it is meant as encouragement for you to question what is said all around you in our rapid fire information age.

Joe Serio
November 2007
Huntsville, Texas

ACKNOWLEDGMENTS

Had it not been for the vision and daring of Dick Ward and Gennady Chebotaryov to push forward at a time when few others would, this book would not have been possible. In 1989, Dick was Vice Chancellor for Administration at the University of Illinois at Chicago and Executive Director of the Office of International Criminal Justice (OICJ), when he started exploring the possibility of cooperating with the Soviets on issues of organized crime control. Gennady Chebotaryov, then Deputy Chief of the 6th Department for Organized Crime Control in the Ministry of Internal Affairs (MVD) of the USSR, was very receptive to Ward's overtures. One of the results of that cooperation was a year-long internship that I served in the MVD's Organized Crime Control Department in 1990-91 prior to the collapse of the USSR.

I also owe a debt of gratitude and friendship to three people who were by my side in Moscow at various points in the 1990s. Alexander "Sasha" Gorkin grew from acquaintance to adviser to friend and finally to older brother between 1990 and 1996 as he endeavored to enlighten the poor American who had stepped through the Looking Glass into a land where frequently up is down and black is white. To his credit, Sasha continued patiently peeling back the layers of Russian history, society, culture, and crime after he immigrated to the U.S. in 1996, and all the way up to his untimely death in July 2007. From 1997 to 1999, Andrei Dmitriev and Yevgeny Shagarin were my deputies in the global corporate investigation firm, Kroll Associates, when I was director of Kroll's Moscow office. More than that, they were my brothers who labored long to lift the eternal veil that covers Russia, at least enough for me to have a glimpse at the other side.

Thanks to Erik Hoffmann at The University at Albany whose enthusiasm for the study of Russia set me on the path many years ago and whose friendship I value highly. Thom Shanker, at the Moscow office of the *Chicago Tribune* in the early 1990s and currently of the *New York Times*, was also an important early influence. He graciously gave me access to his files and became a friend whom, unfortunately, I see far too infrequently. Sherry Jones also provided an important window into Russian life for me through her various adventures while creating her numerous award-winning television documentaries. Caimin and Marlene Flannery have been unwavering in their support and enthusiasm for a variety of my projects, including this one. And thanks to Ian Brown for all the assistance he provided working with me in Moscow.

A special thanks to the surrogate fathers in my life. To Norbert Friedman, for his spirit and love of life. As a Polish survivor of the Holocaust, he has shared his hard-earned insights on the realities of that part of the world and more importantly helped me understand the meaning of life. To André Bossard, former Secretary General of Interpol, who over past twenty years has encouraged and supported me. And to Richard Allan, professor of law at Brooklyn Law School, part surrogate father, part brother, part teacher, who continues, twenty years on, to provide invaluable counsel.

From day one, the professionals at Carolina Academic Press expressed great enthusiasm for the project and have steered it to the light of day. Thanks to Jennifer Whaley for her assistance early on and her ongoing friendship. Thanks to Beth Hall for her heroic patience throughout this process. And a special thanks to publisher Keith Sipe for his support, kind words, and most of all for the book you now hold in your hands.

Karen Hitchcock, former President of The University at Albany, made it possible for me to hang my hat in the university's library where I discovered vast and fascinating material about Russia. My thanks to André Bossard, James Phelps, Graham Turbiville, and Emilio Viano for reading the manuscript. At Sam Houston State University, Amanda Farrell, Brett Finn, and Sabrina Hager collected mountains of reference material that was critical to this and future projects. And to the faculty, staff, and students at Sam Houston who have made Huntsville feel more like being at home.

I would also like to make a special remembrance of Ann Rubin, a companion on the hard road in the early 1990s with whom I shared a lot of laughs, some tears, as well as a common frustration and delight at the madness that was (and is) Russia. She passed away far too young and left behind many who miss her terribly.

To my sister, Janine, for taking time from her insanely busy schedule to design the cover.

Finally, this book would not have been possible without the support of my family: my eleven siblings who to this day don't quite know what to make of my international life, and especially to my parents, Jane and the late Dr. Joseph Serio, for their great many sacrifices. They were always supportive of international travel, the study of foreign languages, and hosting international friends. Dad was always quick to invite people in, and Mom, with whom I took my first trip to the Soviet Union in 1986, cooked up meals native to our foreign visitors, wanting to make them feel at home. I'm grateful that our home was always full of books and music, two things that served me well during long, cold winter days in the former Soviet Union. And I'm grateful for all they gave me.

ABOUT THE AUTHOR

As part of a unique internship program sponsored by the Office of International Criminal Justice at the University of Illinois at Chicago, Joe Serio had a desk in the Organized Crime Control Department of the Soviet Ministry of Internal Affairs from September 1990 to June 1991. He conducted groundbreaking research on Soviet organized crime, assisted in the preparation of Soviet police documents for international conferences, and developed a network of law enforcement contacts.

The result of his research was the document, *Soviet Organized Crime*, which served as the first important source in the early 1990s for the FBI, the Italian Ministry of Interior, the Chinese Ministry of Public Security, and other governments as they realized the Russians constituted an important crime threat.

Serio returned to Moscow in 1993 where he worked as a security and media consultant for three years. As a security consultant, he assisted foreign companies understand the pitfalls of operating in Russia and interfaced with Russian police agencies to coordinate problem-solving measures. He worked as a consultant in 1995-96 to Kroll Associates, a leading corporate investigation and business intelligence firm. He also served as co-chairman of the Security Committee of the American Chamber of Commerce in Russia in 1995-96. As a media consultant, he assisted various print and broadcast media, including the *New York Times, Washington Post,* and the *Wall Street Journal,* produce stories related to Russian crime. Serio also helped produce several documentaries on Russian police, prisons, and prostitutes, which aired on the program *Investigative Reports* on the cable television channel, Arts & Entertainment (A&E).

In 1997, he became director of the Moscow office of Kroll Associates. He managed a wide variety of investigations across the former Soviet Union and coordinated with Kroll's American, European, and Asian offices on the many Russia-based cases that had international tentacles. He is the author of the Kroll publication *Guidelines for Safety and Security in Russia,* which enjoyed enthusiastic reviews in European trade and commerce journals.

Serio first traveled to the Soviet Union in 1986 and studied at the prestigious Alexander Pushkin Russian Language Institute in Moscow in 1987. Having lived in Moscow prior to the collapse of the Soviet Union, Serio brings an important perspective on the continuities and changes in the dynamics of Russian crime and the environment in which it operates. He has been interviewed by the *New York Times, Washington Post, Wall Street Journal, Chicago Tribune, The Dallas Morning News,* CNN, NBC News, Fox News, WGN Radio (Chicago), *The European* (UK), *Legal Realm* (China), *Sekai Nippo* (Japan), *Sol de Mexico,* and others. In the late 1990s, he was the harmonica player in a Russian rock-n-roll band.

He is currently Editor in Chief of *Crime and Justice International,* co-author with Robert Kelly and Jess Maghan of *Illicit Trafficking,* and a doctoral student in Criminal Justice at Sam Houston State University.

INTRODUCTION

For some, 'mafia' means a way of life, strong family ties, loyalty. It can also convey notions of organization, hierarchy, discipline, and oaths among thieves. Beyond that, 'mafia' is seen as part of an alternative, 'anti-society' government, a system of rules and punishments that operates independent of traditional government attempting to co-opt official state functions. It might be thought of as a state within a state. For others, 'mafia' is the muscle behind organized crime and is engaged primarily in extortion and protection rackets. For yet others, the 'mafia' doesn't even exist. In the former Soviet Union, the meaning of 'mafia' has cut across an even broader range.

Perception, of course, is in the eye of the beholder. 'Mafia' insiders look on their organization as a positive thing, creating a network of survival through personal relationships. Some outsiders look on it as an insidious cancer spreading through the economy, controlling businesses through violence, and trafficking in narcotics, women, and weapons among other things. Others see it as something to be romanticized, providing a bottomless well of material for Hollywood directors, novelists, and journalists.

Unless you're in a specific conversation and can judge from the context, it's difficult to define 'mafia.' It has become so many things to so many people.

The importance of discussing the post-Soviet criminal world is not merely to dazzle, shock, and amuse each other with titillating anecdotes and lore but to try to take steps, if possible, to do something about it. If we limit the conversation to the traditional understanding of 'mafia,' important characteristics of the post-Soviet system will be missed and certain dangers will go unanticipated. For this reason, the word 'threats' becomes more meaningful than 'mafia.' From where do the potential threats facing Western businesses operating in the former Soviet Union emanate? What can Western law enforcement learn from Russian and Soviet history to help them assess the threat of post-Soviet crime in their local jurisdictions? How can tourists understand the situation in the former Soviet Union better so that media reports won't discourage them from traveling there?

To identify threats posed by the former Soviets we have to be prepared to go beyond our traditional narrow idea of 'mafia' and understand that there are no neat black-and-white, 'us and them' boundaries. It's somehow psychologically comforting to think of the 'mafia' as an external invading force, one that's far removed from us, a kind of alien being. This way we can still read the newspapers and watch the movies without reminding ourselves that the interrelationships among crime groups, law enforcement, politicians, and ourselves are far more numerous and complex than we might be willing to admit. Crime groups or 'mafias' don't function in vacuums. They are intimately connected to the way we live and the values we set for ourselves. It's true in the United States, the former Soviet Union, and virtually everywhere else in the world.

Words like 'invasion,' used to describe either the crime phenomenon in the former Soviet Union or the activities of former Soviets in the West, hinder us from maintaining perspective. The problem is serious enough without using exaggeration, hyperbole, and sensationalism. And we have to look for solutions without making a whole nation, race, or ethnic group the new bogey man onto whom to dump our own cultural insecurities and shortcomings. I've tried to do that in the pages that follow.

None of this can be done, though, without understanding at least in some cursory way the traditions and legacies of the Tsarist and Soviet eras that inform the current behavior of post-Soviet criminals, whether we're talking about professional criminals or the bureaucrats and businessmen who have become criminals. This is not to suggest that history determines what will happen in the future. Rather, this book is an effort to describe some of the typical behaviors of the past so that we have at least a sense of the criminal methods likely to be used in the future.

Over the past fifteen years of talking with a wide array of people from numerous countries, I've found that many assume that the crime groups and corruption of the post-Soviet era were created either by the collapse of the Soviet Union or were exclusively the product of the Soviet regime … that if only the policies of the Communists could be done away with and a moral environment of pre-Soviet Russia could be reborn, all would be fine.

It is clear that crime groups of every stripe inflicted enormous damage on Russia, but it's somehow unsatisfying to let the story enter the annals of history without subjecting it to a kind of analysis that has rarely, if ever, been conducted. It is not my desire to suggest that crime groups, criminal organizations—or even 'mafia,' if you prefer—did not exist in the former Soviet Union in the 1990s. Nor is it my intention to downplay the seriousness of their impact, although in the pages that follow this may sometimes seem the case.

My primary interest is to present a critical view of information we have come to take for granted as fact.

READER BEWARE!

In the course of writing this book I encountered fascinating people, opinions, and intriguing bits of information. The following are typical:

- The country is wracked with fraud and corruption. Connections between the government and 'oligarchs' are getting closer all the time. The president won re-election in 1996 with tens of millions of dollars in his war chest, much of which was contributed by big business outside any meaningful regulation.
- One woman, nearing pension age, described how conditions had deteriorated at her workplace over the past eighteen years. "When I started working in the district government in 1983," she said, "people were hired on the basis of their qualifications and experience. Now, in our department it's all done by where you live and who you know." She went on to lament the decline in talent as well as the extent to which rank-and-file workers were increasingly beholden to the Party. "Incompetence has increased and professionalism has decreased.... We're expected to campaign for a candidate when asked, and contribute money to the Party.... When we want a raise we have to go to the Party, not to our supervisors, to get it approved."
- A law enforcement official was under investigation for his participation in a criminal organization. In the course of working a 'mafia' boss as an informant, the official was swayed to join forces with the thug, turning over classified information, and reportedly even acting as a lookout during the commission of a murder. This came at a time when the number of law enforcement departments under investigation for incompetence, corruption, human rights abuses, and even murder, were on the rise. Local and national politicians were being arrested for embezzlement, fraud, and extortion. And apathy among the population was high.
- A businessman in a major city was blocked for eleven years from obtaining the required permits to open a restaurant because he refused to pay bribes to city officials.
- A newspaper article enumerated some of the more noteworthy offenses committed by members of the national legislature in the second half of the 1990s:

- o 29 members had been accused of spousal abuse
- o 7 had been arrested for fraud
- o 19 had been accused of writing bad checks
- o 117 had bankrupted at least two businesses
- o 3 had been arrested for assault
- o 71 had credit reports so bad they couldn't qualify for a credit card
- o 14 had been arrested on drug-related charges
- o 8 had been arrested for shoplifting
- o in 1998 alone, 84 were stopped for drunk driving but released after they claimed immunity
- • Prior to leaving office, the president granted immunity from prosecution to a drug trafficker, tax evader, embezzler, and others of low repute.

As you may well have guessed, I'm referring to the United States. The woman mentioned above is American, the law enforcement official was an FBI agent, the restaurateur was a New Yorker, the national legislature was the U.S. Congress, and the president was Bill Clinton.

There's little in the former Soviet Union that can't be found in the West including organized crime, extensive corruption and fraud, demoralizing poverty, biased media, and so on. The major differences in many ways appear to be the intensity and scope, and, perhaps more importantly, that the post-Soviet experience is taking place within a legacy of little institutionalized private ownership or rule of law. Without predictable and reliable enforcement methods, this essentially means that everything is up for grabs all the time.

In trying to make sense of the reported lawlessness and criminalization of post-Soviet society and how the so-called Russian 'mafia' fits in that landscape, though, it's useful to reserve an ounce of humility and ask ourselves from time to time, What would we do if we were in their shoes?

Investigating the Russian Mafia

I

WORDS AND NUMBERS

CHAPTER 1

MAFIA

If you wish to understand the Soviet Union, you can make an excellent beginning by going to the movies and seeing 'The Godfather'... because the Soviet system since Stalin may be usefully regarded as a regime of mafioso types who, incredibly, have become the political establishment.

—Irving Kristol[1]

As a well-defined phenomenon, which can be clearly described, measured, compared to other phenomena, the mafia does not exist. But I have met its members. Or some close to them. They look dangerous. *And so they wish.*

—Nils Christie[2]

About a mile from the Kremlin across the Moscow River, Bolshaya Yakimanka Street rose to meet October Square and splintered in various directions. More than just the focal point in a tangled crisscross of roads, October Square offered an analogy of Russia itself where past and present collided in a constant reminder of unrealized potential and stifled ambition.

The Square took its name from the month the Bolsheviks stumbled headlong to power in 1917, leaving them as surprised as anyone at their success. An enormous iron statue of Lenin surrounded by children of the revolution towered in the center of the Square, an unseen wind furling back his coat, his chest pushing confidently into the radiant future that his leadership promised.

Despite whatever promises the diminutive Siberian fashioned in order to manipulate the country he was creating, reality had an uncanny way of interfering. Civil war and Lenin's own backward economic plans set the country on a path of almost unceasing privation and hardship. Rather than glorifying the achievements of a hero, the monument was now a daily reminder of the

---

1. Quoted in Charles Krauthammer, "Communist Mafia on Trial," *The Washington Post*, August 7, 1992, p. A2.
2. Nils Christie, *A Suitable Amount of Crime*, Oxford, Routledge, 2004, p. 43.

person responsible for unleashing a steady rain of social dislocation and political terror, more than seven decades worth. To add insult to injury, this imposing likeness of Lenin was too large to remove, unlike most of the other monuments to the players of the great and tragic Soviet experiment.

The Warsaw Hotel and the Moscow Institute of Metals and Alloys stood in Lenin's line of sight, the former previously a den of shady deals and prostitution, the latter having birthed some of the wealthiest 'oligarchs' in the country. A Lenin frozen for all time unable to shield his eyes from the two ends of the criminal spectrum he spawned seemed worthy of Greek mythology.

Across Leninsky Prospekt from the hotel stood the Children's Library—innocence and wisdom, two things that seemed to be sorely lacking in modern Russia. One building farther was prime office space that had been commandeered by the KGB during the breakup of the USSR. Foreign business partners of the Russian spy agency set up offices here, helping to move millions of dollars to overseas bank accounts, safe from the sticky fingers of Russian tax collectors, the unpredictable economy, and a disintegrating Communist Party.[3]

At the corner of Zhitnaya Street and Bolshaya Yakimanka on the north side of October Square was a great slab of white concrete that took up half a block and stood ten stories tall. The building was originally planned to be twenty floors but, as was often the case, materials ran out in mid-construction and the state decided to cap it at the halfway point. A steady flow of people streamed in and out, while crowds bustled along the sidewalk hurrying to and from the neighboring Oktyabrskaya metro station.

This was the national headquarters of the Ministry of Internal Affairs—MVD by its Russian initials. In its many manifestations it had been one of the most feared government agencies in the history of the Soviet Union, second only to the KGB. Indeed, at times over the past seventy years the two had merged to become a single all-powerful super ministry of oppression.

The MVD was a sprawling mass of bureaucracy, nearly 800,000 strong. It was the administrative equivalent of the FBI, DEA, and all state and local police departments rolled into one. Its primary function was to conduct regular law enforcement work—set policy, conduct investigations, and make arrests. But the Soviets also crammed the administration of the country's prison system, state automobile inspectorate, and fire departments under this same bureaucratic roof. More importantly, it served as one of the buffers between the regime and the populace.

---

3. According to the Deputy Chief of the Organized Crime Control Department, Gennady Chebotaryov, his department uncovered nearly 100 bank accounts in the West that the KGB had set up.

Not simply a paramilitary organization like every other police department in the world, the MVD boasted war-making capability in its Internal Troops branch (*Vnutrennaya Voiska*). Equipped with armored personnel vehicles, tanks, helicopters, and divisions of troops, the VV had been fighting small wars and border skirmishes long before Chechnya entered the world's consciousness.

This was how the MVD looked in the 1990s. Things have changed a bit since then; for example, the prison service has been moved to the Ministry of Justice and new departments have been formed as Russia tries to steady herself under the weight of innumerable and seemingly insurmountable challenges.

I had an office in this building—16 Zhitnaya Street—on the ninth floor in the Organized Crime Control Department in 1990–91. I sat across the hall from the head of the department, the legendary Alexander Gurov, and wandered the corridors much as anyone else in the building, with few restrictions. After weeks of my coming and going, the guards at the main entrance substituted their scrutiny of my identification card and formal salutes with handshakes and laughs. I was the token American—'a real live American' in their words—and they seemed fascinated, puzzled, and, for the most part, glad to have me. I befriended quite a few of the officers, met their families, saw how they lived, and understood their daily challenges. It was here that I first began to see what the Russian 'mafia' was all about.

In early March 1991, while I was sitting in the office of then-Colonel Gennady Chebotaryov, there was a quick knock on the door. Without waiting for permission to enter, one of Chebotaryov's agents rushed in and, on seeing me, stopped suddenly in the middle of the room.

"Gennady Fyodorovich, may I speak freely?" the agent inquired, shooting a glance in my direction.

"What is it?" Chebotaryov asked.

"It's just come to our attention that Ivan Petrovich is connected to the 'mafia.' He's supposed to attend the strategy meeting you're having in fifteen minutes with the deputy minister."

It was a dramatic moment for me. I sat perfectly still, barely breathing, awaiting Chebotaryov's response. He pinched the bridge of his nose as if steeling himself for another frustrating day, and simply muttered an expletive under his breath.

As second in command of the Organized Crime Control Department, Chebotaryov was to devise a plan for getting the thugs off the streets not only in Moscow but also throughout the USSR, across eleven time zones and in 15 distinct republics. Now he was faced with news that the bad guys were apparently coming in the Ministry's front door.

That brief exchange that sent my head reeling would quickly lose its drama and recede in my memory as just another day in Moscow. Only later did it dawn on me that Chebotaryov was relatively unmoved by what I thought was 'shocking' news. The bad guys on the outside weren't invading like an enemy force as I had thought and as had frequently been portrayed by both official-dom and the media; the bad guys on the inside were inviting them in. And it had been going on for some time. Indeed, the very deputy minister Chebotaryov was supposed to meet was the son-in-law of a former Moscow Party boss and thoroughly corrupted himself.

What was it about the word 'mafia' that stirred up such emotion, however brief, in me? Images of *The Godfather*, gangsters, thugs, crime bosses, underworld, machine guns, and shootouts came to mind. Al Capone. The Five Families of New York. Made-men and wise guys. Lifeless bodies slumped over steering wheels or sprawled in pools of blood in back rooms of Italian restaurants in Brooklyn or Queens. Prostitutes, drugs, gambling. Paying off politicians, threatening businessmen. This was a world I knew in the United States only through newspapers and movies where it was larger than life, romanticized, and demonized. For me, it was somewhat removed from reality. The human element had seemingly disappeared. The repetition of the lore turned criminals into both heroes and monsters, something otherworldly. Oddly, they were also regarded as highly organized and disciplined with oaths and codes for their own brand of right living. Civilized monsters, I supposed.

In Moscow, though, it was in my face. It was all over the media, screaming headlines, raw news footage, gangsters roaming freely about town. And 'mafia' became the scapegoat for pretty much everything. But what was it?

No Mafia

Most Soviet police I knew had their own way of looking at it. Rarely did I hear the word 'mafia' uttered inside MVD headquarters. True, there were a few, like department head Gurov, who milked the word for as much shock value as possible. Generally, though, when police used 'mafia' it was almost always to claim that it simply didn't exist. What?! No such thing as the Russian 'mafia'?! But all of Russia was talking about it and by the mid-1990s most of the world would be too. How could so many people be wrong? How could any MVD official say with a straight face that there was no Russian 'mafia'? What was it that Chebotaryov's deputy had referred to?

As far as I could tell, part of the difficulty in interpreting the police meaning turned out to be my own cultural baggage. As a fairly typical American,

I'd grown up negatively predisposed toward the Soviet Union, complete with a healthy knee-jerk reaction that when a Soviet spoke it was probably some kind of deception or outright lie. Moreover, law enforcement was one of the key pillars in sustaining the totalitarian system, only half a step removed from the KGB on the Cold War bad-guy scale. What more could I expect from the Evil Empire?

To my American ear, the police claims that there was no Russian 'mafia' sounded almost like a throwback to that time during the Soviet era when officials denied the existence of crime. Ideologically, crime was to have withered away as a natural result of building Communism. I hardly considered taking them at their word.

It's not as if they never said, "There is no Russian 'mafia.'" They said it quite directly and, by and large, meant it quite literally. But I couldn't hear them because it came across almost as a joke. It sounded like semantic nit picking. They couldn't be serious. "There is no Russian 'mafia'"—I thought it was a stock phrase they didn't believe themselves but said anyway, probably for political reasons. As it turns out, they were serious.

As my circle of police contacts widened and I began to put my American biases in perspective, it became increasingly clear what the police meant. Most I spoke with had a textbook definition of 'mafia' embedded firmly in his or her brain. Mafia is an Italian phenomenon, they said, a product of that society. It's highly structured and organized. Hierarchical. Centralized. Period. End of story.

The police repeated their mantra over and over. "There is no Russian 'mafia.'" They said it to anyone that would listen. To journalists. To scholars. To criminal justice practitioners from abroad. Few paid attention, dismissing it as unsophisticated obfuscation or profound naiveté. Rarely were there follow-up conversations pressing the officials for a deeper explanation.

And it wasn't just foreigners who ignored them. The Soviet media had been fanning the flames of Russian 'mafia' as much if not more than anyone else had. Gorbachev's *glasnost'* encouraged people to talk about almost anything under the sun, and for years 'mafia' had been at or close to the top of the list.

Glasnost' candor served up with a generous helping of sensationalism had only increased after the dismantling of the Soviet Union in December 1991 as newspapers learned what it was to live without state subsidies. Requesting anonymity at the time, the powerful editor of a top Russian newspaper told me in August 1994, "We write about 'mafia' because it sells." That's an explanation anyone raised in the West could understand, I thought.

By April 1995, the MVD was so frustrated by what it considered the obvious ignorance of the media and their apparent conspiracy theories about the rising global threat of the Russian 'mafia' that the police called a press conference to slap the wrists of the journalism community. Playing the self-ordained defender of Mother Russia, the Ministry of Internal Affairs rounded up both local and foreign media representatives and rolled out some of its big guns to deliver a stern linguistic reprimand.

Yuri Melnikov, then Chief of Russia's National Central Bureau of Interpol, fired the first salvo, a literal cross-cultural shot across the bow. "The term Russian 'mafia' is rubbish," he said with a scowl of impatience. "It would never occur to you to use the expression 'the Smolensk Triad' or 'Mozdok 'Ndrangheta.'"[4]

Aside from the clear distinction in his mind that 'mafia' was Italian, triads were Chinese, and so on, Melnikov carried a kind of ethno-nationalistic grudge. Like many others, he'd always been sensitive to what he considered the simplistic and unfair adjective 'Russian,' when the problem—whether it was really 'mafia' or not—was, in fact, 'Soviet.'[5] He had a point. Many in the criminal world were Ukrainians, Lithuanians, Georgians, Armenians, Chechens, Dagestanis, and others. But, to the chagrin of ethnic Russians, the world had adopted the word 'Russian' for convenience sake.

At that same press conference, Alexander Dementiev, Chebotaryov's successor as Deputy Chief of the Organized Crime Control Department, echoed Melnikov's assertion, emphasizing the structural aspects. "There is no classical 'mafia' in Russia. The 'mafia' is a very centralized organization with a rigid hierarchy. Here in Russia, thank God, we do not have a single center that would coordinate all these criminal groups. We will not allow this to happen."[6]

Dementiev's word choice was almost comical. For the three and a half years since the dismantling of the Soviet Union, the MVD had been in administrative, bureaucratic, and political disarray. It was being slapped around and spit on by the criminal world, and more than a few of its own officials had their hands in the cookie jar, running gangs, taking bribes, controlling prostitutes, stealing weapons, smuggling natural resources, and a whole lot

---

4. "Press Briefing by the Interior Ministry Regarding the Activities of the Russian Mafia Abroad," unpublished transcript, April 1995, p. 4.

5. I first came to know Melnikov through telephone conversations in 1989. At the time, he was a foreign affairs liaison officer for the MVD and I was International Representative at the Office of International Criminal Justice (OICJ) at the University of Illinois at Chicago. We coordinated some of the first visits of high-ranking police officials from the USSR to the United States, in 1989 and 1990, and Chicago Police Department officials to Moscow in 1990.

6. "Press Briefing by the Interior Ministry," p. 9 (note 4).

more. Whether Russian officials would *allow* a criminal brain trust to form wasn't the point at all. The MVD wouldn't have been able to stop it if the underworld had wanted to organize itself like the traditional 'mafia.' It was the sheer size of the country and profound distrust among the population as much as anything and *not* some heroic vigilance by the MVD that ensured there would be no "single center," as Dementiev called it. The gangsters were more apt to steal from each other before they successfully cooperated on such a grand scale.

Chebotaryov had made the point six years earlier that, with the exception of a relatively small number of powerful groups, was still true at the time of the press conference in 1995. "Our evidence is that no such large groups exist with a recognized leader. Our bureaucracy here would work against them; it wouldn't be to their advantage to act in such a way. *These groups are probably more dangerous because they are mobile*"[7] (emphasis added).

Although it's tempting to dismiss police claims as politically motivated, hypersensitive, or simply whining, it seems they actually characterized the situation as fairly as could be expected. While powerful groups existed, there was no concerted effort at that time by a single group or even a small number of 'mafia' groups to control the post-Soviet criminal world. There was no small group of crime 'families' or a 'commission' that formed the nucleus of 'mafia' activity in the country. Anyway, the post-Soviet style of 'mafia' wouldn't need an intricate, nationwide organization to enrich itself. There were plenty of opportunities for everyone to rip off the system at every level.

Ten years down the road, post-Soviet Russia was still fighting what would appear to be a losing public relations battle. In June 2005, law enforcement authorities in Spain conducted operations targeting criminal groups from the former Soviet Union, arresting 22 people. Apparently, those apprehended were from Russia, Georgia, and other former Soviet republics. The Russian Foreign Ministry immediately urged Spain to "refrain from creating a negative image of Russian citizens and to be careful using the phrase 'Russian mafia.' "[8]

However technically correct the MVD officials may have been on that April day in 1995 or the Foreign Ministry in 2005, the energy expended about semantics appeared absurd as thousands of small crime groups—made up of professional criminals, novice thugs, bureaucrats, businessmen, and politicians—continued to loot the country. Let's say the media were to satisfy the

---

7. *Reuters*, "Soviet Authorities Battle Increase in Organized Crime," June 13, 1989.

8. *RIA Novosti*, "Russia Calls on Spain to Refrain from Creating a Negative Image of Russians," June 22, 2005.

MVD's linguistic demands, what then? The change would have had little impact on crime levels or on public perception of the problem. So what was the point? Maybe the frustration of knowing they could do little about it urged the MVD to find small victories wherever possible.

The police interpretation wasn't perfect, but they had a point. There really was no Russian 'mafia' as we thought of it in the West. Were there powerful crime groups with developed structures? Of course there were. Whether agreeing or disagreeing with the police, it seemed more important to recognize that the law enforcement version was only one of many interpretations of a word that had taken on numerous meanings in changing contexts over the past two decades.

IVAN IVANOVICH AS MAFIA

One notion of 'mafia' had little to do with gangsters and shootouts. It stemmed from the so-called time of stagnation (*zastoi*) of the Brezhnev regime from the late 1960s to the early 1980s, popularly known as a period of an increasingly corrupt bureaucracy and a deepening sense of dissatisfaction among the population. Here the word 'mafia' conveyed an idea of access rather than traditional criminal organizations and their structures and activities. It had become, in part, the cry of powerless consumers—a form of limited private protest of the inequities visited upon them daily. The targets of their vitriol were usually individuals or institutions perceived as exercising any kind of power or advantage over the average person: retail sales managers and clerks, doctors, auto mechanics, and so on. Sounds strange, I know. That such ordinary occupations and professions would even be thought of in the same breath as 'mafia' seems incongruous.

In Soviet stores across the country retail sales managers and clerks controlled the inventory and sale of goods. Whether foodstuffs, clothing, or textiles, goods of highest quality were stashed under the counter or spirited out the back door by employees to sell through personal channels or to exchange with their friends. Their friends would reciprocate with scarce items they were able to acquire through their own positions or networks. It was all state property anyway so no one much cared. Low-quality goods were left for the consumer who lacked contacts at the store. In the early 1970s, the Soviet satirical magazine *Krokodil* summed up the situation:

> Dear customer, in the leather goods department of our store, a shipment of 500 imported women's purses has been received. Four hun-

dred and fifty of them have been bought by employees of the store. Forty-nine are under the counter and have been ordered in advance for friends. One purse is in the display window. We invite you to visit the leather department to buy this purse.[9]

The 'mafia' in this case was the store administration and employees. The meaning of 'mafia' could change on a daily basis depending on contacts and experiences with the system. If one were unable to afford an appropriate gratuity (say, a bottle of vodka) to offer a doctor of the free medical system to receive adequate and timely care, the doctor might be said to be 'mafia' on that particular day. When I visited the dentist in Moscow with a Russian friend from the MVD, he was always sure to bring a bottle of the best whiskey available even though the care was supposed to be 'free.' Getting access to the whiskey frequently required trading his own goods or services with his friends who had access to the whiskey. As the journalist Yuri Shchekochikhin noted in 1989, "We apply 'mafia' to practically anything—shops, creative unions, hospitals, diplomats, prostitutes, butchers, chess players, cities, regions and republics."[10]

I've had countless experiences with this 'mafia' although as an American I never would have given it that name. More often than not I just marveled at how screwed up the system was. In 1987, during the six months I was studying at a Russian language institute in Moscow, one of the activities that consumed a considerable amount of time was the hunt for food, or more precisely, good food. The dormitory cafeteria, or *stolovaya*, offered suspiciously gray hot dogs and jars of eggplant, along with chocolate bars, stale bread, and glasses of tea served at boiling temperature in metal holders. Motivation was high to take the search to the streets.

One afternoon while wandering downtown, three of us stopped at a restaurant in the 3000-room Rossiya Hotel. A gargantuan eyesore built in the finest tradition of late-Soviet drab, the Rossiya sat on the edge of Red Square, its very presence insulting to the oddly beautiful kaleidoscope of St. Basil's domes against the backdrop of the mighty Kremlin walls.[11] At the restaurant we found the doors shut tight, padlocked from inside. We banged on the glass until one

---

9. Hedrick Smith, *The Russians*, New York, Ballantine Books, 1976, p. 117.

10. Yuri Shchekochikhin, "Mafia," *Soviet Life*, March 1989, p. 5. I'm indebted to the late Yuri Shchekochikhin for his assistance during my early days in Moscow. See also Konstantin Maydanyuk in Lev Timofeyev, *Russia's Secret Rulers: How the Government and the Criminal Mafia Exercise Their Power*, New York, Alfred A. Knopf, 1992, p. 75.

11. The Rossiya Hotel officially closed its doors for the last time on January 1, 2006, and was demolished.

of the waiters who had been in plain view unlocked the door. "Ten rubles," he said. "What?" "Ten rubles," he repeated, keeping the door open only the width of his body.

It cost us ten rubles—nearly ten percent of our monthly student stipend— just to cross the threshold. Entering, we saw that the vast dining room was completely empty, not a single patron.[12] Other wait staff sat at a table in the corner, bored stiff. This happened throughout the city with annoying regularity. To get into an empty restaurant, grease the wheels. To avoid long lines at a store, grease the wheels. To obtain scarce items, grease the wheels. As I would experience time and again, the gatekeeper—whether a lowly waiter or a top Party official—had the power.[13] If you didn't pay the going rate or successfully re-negotiate the asking price, you were out of luck. If you didn't have the relationships to get access, you were forced to go through the system rather than around it. At the time, this was considered a type of 'mafia,' an idea of 'mafia' predicated on bribes and favors. These practices of manipulation and scamming to get access were not rare exceptions to the rule but the rule itself and were embedded in the popular wisdom.

> A Georgian went to Moscow to sell his mimosa flowers. Upon his return home his neighbors all came to see him, asking: "Dear, did you go to the Mausoleum while you were in Moscow?" "Of course," came the response. "You saw Lenin?" "Absolutely," he said. "Didn't you have to wait in line for a long time? We've heard that you should expect to waste as much as half a day!" "Ha!" cried the Georgian. "I didn't have to wait at all. I just gave the sentry some money for a bottle of vodka, and he brought the body right out to me!"[14]

In the late-Soviet era and throughout the 1990s with the release of price controls and somewhat greater freedom of movement within the country, this idea of service providers as 'mafia' only grew. The thousands of merchants from places like Azerbaijan, Armenia, Georgia, Chechnya, Ingushetia, and

---

12. With the average monthly Soviet salary at that time at about 200 rubles, it's little wonder that the restaurant was empty.

13. The notion of gatekeepers controlling access to goods and services obviously is not exclusive to the former Soviet Union, of course. The most striking aspect was how thoroughly developed it was throughout the society. Relationships—whether acquaintances or those developed through bribe giving—were far more important in obtaining creature comforts and avoiding clashes with officialdom than in places like the United States or Western Europe.

14. Emil Draitser, *Forbidden Laughter*, New York, Kensington Publishing Corporation, 1980, p. 39.

Dagestan, who regularly hawked their goods in Moscow marketplaces were seen by many as the source of the capital's, and indeed the country's, woes. Most of the markets were controlled by crime groups, using the merchants as conduits through which to move narcotics and cheap imitation liquor, among other things. The merchants, though, weren't part of any core membership of a criminal organization, and, anyway, they were busy committing their own petty fraud and theft, part of the proceeds from which went to pay the 'rent' demanded of them by the crime groups. The 'mafia' label hung on them, primarily by ethnic Russians, was mostly a popular reaction to high prices, petty crime, and filthy streets surrounding the marketplaces. These southerners were quickly assuming the role as the primary scapegoats for many of Moscow's problems, and this would only intensify over the years.

CRIME GROUPS AS MAFIA

Toward the late 1980s and into the 1990s, the numerous crime groups and gangs operating in the former USSR became the favored candidates for the 'mafia' label as the media became free to report such things. Virtually all groups, regardless of structure, activities, or membership were regarded as 'mafia,' giving the impression that all groups enjoyed equal status, power, and influence. So when it was reported, for example, that there were more than 8,000 crime groups, it sounded as if traditional organized crime had indeed taken over the country. As a result, significant misconceptions about the nature of post-Soviet crime were created, like the one that the 'mafia' was omnipresent and omnipotent. To be sure, crime groups understood this very well and exploited it whenever possible.

In reality, of course, the 'mafia' label was purely subjective and was paraded around whenever someone—almost anyone—had an interest to do so. It could have been the result of a single dramatic criminal act or the whim of a newspaper headline writer. For example, after the murder of Russian parliament deputy Andrei Aizderdzis in April 1994, several deputies seized the opportunity to denounce the act as an attempt by the 'mafia' to gain control of the parliament. This was a typical ploy—to paint the 'mafia' (whether Russian, Chechen, or whatever) as an invading force threatening the security of all Russians. All of Russia's problems could be conveniently laid at the feet of 'gangsters.'

Of course, it was never that simple, and in the Aizderdzis case it was obvious from the beginning that the deputies were grasping at straws. Several other more likely explanations had to be considered. Aizderdzis owned a bank, several companies, and had published a Who's Who of the criminal world, any one of which carried its own special risk. The investigation into the murdered deputy, in fact, found something that had the ring of truth to it. Holding the murder weapon in his hand, the senior investigator on the case told me that the enterprising deputy had been caught by his business partners trying to skim several hundred thousand dollars from a deal in which he had been acting as middleman. Aizderdzis simply had been punished for his transgression.[15]

Thugs who had become highly visible in the early 1990s with their pastel-colored blazers, leather jackets, Italian designer shoes, leather hand purses, and ubiquitous mobile phones also became a convenient target for the average Muscovite to castigate (from a distance) as 'mafia' members. That such attire soon became fashionable among young people with no criminal connections whatever didn't seem to interfere with the opinion of the casual observer. They were all branded 'mafia.'

Federico Varese is one author who favors use of the word 'mafia' to describe these more or less traditional criminal groups. In his excellent book, *The Russian Mafia*, Varese explains that the central function of 'mafia' is to provide protection and generally is "a species of a broader genus, organized crime, and various criminal organizations—including the American Cosa Nostra, the Japanese Yakuza, and the Hong Kong Triads—belong to it."[16] Varese sets for himself the task of exploring whether the Russian mafia fits in this group. He concludes that the Russian 'mafia' shares crucial similarities with the Sicilian Cosa Nostra, specifically the existence of criminal leaders who underwent an initiation process to gain their vaunted position in "an honorable and distinguished tradition."[17]

Varese hastens to add, importantly, that the Russian 'mafia' of the 1990s, as he defines it, was only one set of actors among many in the vast and complex struggle for power in Russia, and it was far from being the most powerful. "[O]ne should not exaggerate its role. It has not dominated the transition to the market." Instead, he says, the economic actors—the 'oligarchs,' government ministries, and other institutions—played the leading role in the transition period.[18] Relying on mass media as the sole source of information, however, one could easily conclude that the Russian 'mafia'—meaning 'gangsters' of the traditional sort—had overrun the country.[19]

---

15. Author conversation with senior investigator Boris Uvarov, August 1994.

16. Federico Varese, *The Russian Mafia: Private Protection in a New Market Economy*, Oxford, Oxford University Press, 2001, p. 4.

17. Ibid., p. 188.

18. Ibid., p. 189.

19. Mark Galeotti agrees with Varese's caution to maintain perspective when assessing the influence of the 'Russian mafia.' "There is a danger in overstating the power and unity

THE STATE AS MAFIA

Notions of 'mafia' were not reserved exclusively for these small fry. They extended to the state as well, portraying managers in industrial and agricultural sectors as members of some of the strongest 'mafias' in the country. Directors of large state ministries and factories as well as managers of state agricultural enterprises controlled the exploitation of natural resources and wealth from the country as well as the production and distribution of goods. Bribery and connections were the tools of the trade in achieving position and acquiring wealth. In the words of the late Zviad Gamsakhurdia, former president of Georgia, poet, and himself a generally roguish character,

> They extract all the money and resources out of the peasants ... in the form of bribes and by inflating production figures. In Georgia, the flow of these millions or billions of rubles was managed by the Party boss [who was] the deputy chairman of the Council of Ministers. He purchased his position. He was Shevardnadze's man—you can say that Shevardnadze legalized this mafia. He has a reputation for fighting the mafia, but in reality, he's in with them.[20]

To the average post-Soviet citizen it was no coincidence that many of the most powerful politicians and businessmen had served in key government posts, production and distribution positions, and wholesale food and consumer goods depots during the Soviet era. Many saw privatization and other 'reform' measures as merely Soviet-era 'mafia' behavior transformed, called by a new name, wearing different clothes, but, in the end, the same people with the same corrupted Soviet mentality. Meet the new boss, same as the old boss. The deeply embedded pre-1917 Russia- and Soviet-era notion that doing business was to be frowned upon and making 'excessive' profit was somehow morally reprehensible—and at times outright illegal—had not dissipated with the dismantling of the Soviet Union. Thus, post-Soviet businessmen together with many of the so-called 'reformers' and 'democrats' had become for many the biggest 'mafia' in the country.

---

of the *mafiya* and the extent to which it is an external parasite on society rather than part of it and the transition it is undergoing." See Mark Galeotti, *Russian and Post-Soviet Organized Crime*, Aldershot, Ashgate Publishing, 2002, p. xiv.

20. Zviad Gamsakhurdia in Timofeyev, p. 47 (note 10).

Communist Party as Mafia

The 'mafia' interpretation that Westerners found most astounding as the USSR disappeared and Soviet reality became somewhat clearer was the Communist Party as 'mafia.' Most of the sensitive positions in the government were held by Party members—and it couldn't have been otherwise. It was the Party that took precedence over the government, particularly since Stalin's death in 1953 and the end of the 'cult of personality.' Stalin's successor, Nikita Khrushchev, and his Party cronies wanted to ensure that such staggering power never again became concentrated in the hands of a single leader. One way to do this was to strengthen the Party.

Since its founding, the Party was a bizarre collection of conscientious hard-working rank-and-file members, entrepreneurial black marketeers, career politicians, corrupt bureaucrats, and common criminals. Of course, not all of its members (nearly 20 million at its height in the late 1980s) were invited to partake in the spoils of pillaging society. It was the Party elite that held real power across the country and made up what many Soviets believed was the ultimate 'mafia.' And this was no passing whim or fad that simply swept over the population at one time and disappeared. For at least the past thirty years people believed that the real 'mafia' sat *na verkhu*—at the top—with the Kremlin housing the *capo di tutti capi* of the criminal pyramid, the General Secretary of the Communist Party. While strolling across Red Square over the years, my Russian friends would point to the Kremlin and say to me, " ... but that's where the real 'mafia' lives."

In the late 1960s, when journalist Yuri Brokhin put the question, "Is there a Soviet mafia?" to Zhora 'the Engineer,' a professional pickpocket, he reportedly responded,

> There certainly is a Soviet mafia. And it's organized a hell of a lot better than the American mafia. But it has another name. It's called the Communist Party. We wouldn't dream of trying to compete with it.... Professional thieves like me aren't organized at all, not in the sense of controlling some kind of business, like a black market, or gambling.[21]

Zhora wasn't alone in his opinion but the most spirited declarations would have to wait some twenty years until the advent of *glasnost'* when people were

---

21. Yuri Brokhin, *Hustling on Gorky Street: Sex and Crime in Russia Today*, New York, The Dial Press, 1975, pp. 110–111.

given license to say publicly what everyone already knew privately.[22] In many cases, elements in the Communist Party used 'mafia' tactics in maintaining control over the country and in fighting their own internal political struggles. The lines between the criminal upperworld and the criminal underworld were blurring rapidly and, in many cases, would be erased outright (See Chapter 10).

> The Communist Party of the Soviet Union was an apparatus designed for the seizure and control of power and property. Its closest parallel in the West wasn't a political organization or even a special-interest group but a mafia family. If the CPSU had existed in the United States, it would have been prosecuted for racketeering. Communist officials claimed ownership of everything they could steal, and a *nomenklatura* of Party leaders and their families took full advantage of their status, giving themselves access to apartments, schools, and stores that were strictly off limits to ordinary Soviets.[23]

Three long-time observers of Soviet society offered strikingly similar perspectives suggesting that the Soviet brand of 'mafia' was a basic system of relationships and access among various sectors of society with the Party in the dominant role and the traditional criminal world playing a relatively minor part.

In one model, the journalist Yuri Shchekochikhin wrote that in the 1970s and 1980s the top tier of the criminal pyramid included bureaucrats and the *nomenklatura* Party elite who had access to and control over the distribution of goods, services, promotions, and favors. The second tier was made up of underground businessmen interested in developing their capitalist tendencies. Local criminals who ran protection rackets and began forming their own groups constituted the third tier.[24]

In the view of noted sociologist Tatyana Zaslavskaya, there wasn't even room for petty traditional criminals in the hierarchy. Corrupt Party and government officials, she said, occupied the first tier. The second level consisted of the workers and employees of the retail trade "who are obliged to pay money to the chain that kicks back to the *apparat*." The third tier "made it possible for the

---

22. According to V.S. Ovchinskii, the term 'mafia' as used to characterize the criminal situation in socialist countries first appeared in official documents in 1981. See V.S. Ovchinskii, *Strategiya Bor'by s Mafiei*, Moskva, SIMS, 1993, p. 190.

23. Bill Thomas and Charles Sutherland, *Red Tape: Adventure Capitalism in the New Russia*, New York, Dutton, 1992, p. 30.

24. Yuri Shchekochikhin, "Roots of Russia's Mafia," *The Moscow Times*, September 1, 1993, p. 8.

entire system to function": the militia [police], prosecutors, courts, judges—
"all the law enforcement people are bought by the trade people."[25]

The third model, by Soviet émigré lawyer Konstantin Simis, featured two
components consisting of Communist Party officials to whom all others were
subordinate. First was the Party leadership, the *nomenklatura* elite, members
of the district executive committees that decided virtually all questions of life
on their territory. The second component, the vast majority of which were
Party members, was made up of store and restaurant managers and directors
of state enterprises, institutions, and collective and state farms. A defining
characteristic of the system was that the "ruling district elite acts in the name
of the Party as racketeers and extortionists of tribute, and that it is the criminal world *per se* who must pay through the nose to the district *apparat.*"[26]

One day in spring 1991, I met an Azerbaijani MVD captain at the home of
a senior MVD official. The man had packed up his wife and two children and
took the three-hour flight from Baku to Moscow for what he'd characterized
as a family vacation. It was the safest way to mask his real intentions. The main
objective of his trip was to get the MVD official's advice about how to raise
250,000 rubles. At a time when the captain was making a maximum of 2,000
rubles a month, this enormous sum was the price demanded for his next promotion. The captain was merely one small link in that "chain that kicks back
to the *apparat,*" as Zaslavskaya described it. Not only did payment guarantee
promotion, it also ensured perpetuation of the system. The captain would be
on the hook. There would be no way for him to repay the sum, wherever it
came from, without becoming a fully active link in that chain, i.e. demanding bribes himself.

These models fairly described a piece of Soviet reality and demonstrated
the thoroughly ingrained and systemic nature of its corruption. They also revealed an important point about the concept of 'mafia': in both the Soviet and
post-Soviet understanding of 'mafia,' the state in various forms was a *central
player*, not peripheral or incidental. The most significant change to this picture after the dismantling of the Soviet Union was, of course, that traditional

---

25. Gail Sheehy, *The Man Who Changed the World*, New York, HarperCollins, 1990, p.
315.

26. Konstantin Simis, *USSR: The Corrupt Society*, New York, Simon & Schuster, 1982,
p. 95. Anatoly Volobuyev, a pioneer in the study of organized crime in the former Soviet
Union, basically agrees with these three sketches when he says, "Criminal groups are nothing but the unskilled workers of organized crime, the foothills of its pyramid. It's that
sphere in which law enforcement is allowed to interfere." Author conversation with
Volobuyev, January 1996.

criminals became something more than bit players, at least for a few years. As Anatoly Volobuyev, one of the MVD's pioneers in the study of the Soviet 'mafia,' summarized the situation as it looked in the mid-1990s, "The majority of scholars and lawyers understood that the system of the Soviet 'mafia' represented the *closest alliance* of criminal circles and power structures at the very highest levels."[27]

THE ALL-UNION MAFIA

At the opposite end of the spectrum from the law enforcement rejection of the word where we began was the all-embracing version, classifying the entire Soviet structure as 'mafia.' The most vocal proponent of this point of view, journalist Arkady Vaksberg, stated very adamantly in his book, *The Soviet Mafia*, that

> the whole political regime of the country—in all its guises—for the last seventy years is itself a mafia: a despotic totalitarian regime cannot be otherwise. Thus, those structures and phenomena which we call 'mafia-like' today, which we recognize as illegal, criminal, anti-state, are in fact very simply the natural outcome of a system of this type, expressing itself in various ways at various stages of its existence.[28]

Vaksberg didn't stop at saying that merely the 'political regime' was a 'mafia.' His point was that the Soviet Union consisted of many different 'mafias.' The entire system functioned in a certain 'mafia' mode. 'Mafia' here indicated methods more than groups: use of networks of contacts to control the economy, politics, and society; criminal exploitation of state resources for personal gain; monopolization of the use of force, and active use of violence against the population when necessary to reach the Party's goals.

Vaksberg's list of the seemingly contradictory explanations of 'mafia' gives an idea of the incredible breadth of the Soviet view of 'mafia':

- "The whole political regime of the country—in all its guises—for the last seventy years is itself a mafia: a despotic totalitarian regime cannot be otherwise."[29]

---

27. Anatoly Volobuev, *Mafiya—po-Sovetski*, 1996, unpublished manuscript.
28. Arkady Vaksberg, *The Soviet Mafia: A Shocking Exposé of Organized Crime in the USSR*, New York, St. Martin's Press, 1991, p. 18.
29. Ibid.

- " … the mafiosi—directors of shops and restaurants, all kinds of doctors and 'technical personnel' who had forgotten their medicine but knew how to please their patients …"[30]
- " 'They' referred to the mafia, of course. Not to the small fry at the regional level, nor even to the big boys in the capital, but the top brass, the highest leadership level—the 'All-Union' mafia, to use a Soviet expression."[31]
- "The mafia (both the political and the economic—they had long since merged into a united front)…."[32]
- "The railway and airline mafia got rich using aircraft and railway wagons which, against all laws and regulations, were put at the disposal of their brothers in the associated mafias. The fishing mafia poached tons of costly sturgeon; in state factories there existed totally unrecorded underground plants for packing caviar. In association with them worked the export mafia, in league with colleagues in the West."[33]
- "The trading mafia can only survive through the closest links and most harmonious coordination with the transport mafia: otherwise it would not obtain goods wagons and transport planes for the timely delivery of goods to the place where it can obtain the best price for them. Even a normal ticket for a passenger train or a scheduled flight is, as a result, difficult to obtain. The transport mafia in turn would not survive without the hotel mafia. Tens of thousands of hotel rooms in Moscow, Leningrad, and other places lie empty, whereas thousands of foreign visitors currently pouring into our country are turned away. The hotel mafia ignores the opportunity to earn foreign currency, because foreign currency goes to the government, not to the director or the administrator of the hotel, and keeps rooms free for 'their customers' who can have them at a moment's notice."[34]
- "But … it is very important to enter one caveat. I feel that I may have yielded on this key issue to a common temptation to use the word 'mafia' too carelessly. *It is widely used in Soviet conversation, and in the Soviet media, to cover everyone including those who are making a living in a not entirely legal way as well as those operating in an entirely illegal way.* It is precisely against the so-called 'black marketeers' that the people's entirely spurious anger has been aroused, while the real mafia which gave birth

---

30. Ibid., p. 34.
31. Ibid., p. 70.
32. Ibid., p. 145.
33. Ibid., p. 181.
34. Ibid., p. 235.

to these 'black marketeers,' and is both inseparably attached to them and dependent on them—i.e. the political mafia—escapes from public scrutiny, remaining undamaged"[35] (emphasis added).

As police official Vyacheslav Komissarov noted just months before the USSR disappeared, the ultimate expression of Soviet-style 'mafia' was the "*merging of the criminal community with corrupted responsible officials of the organs of power including law enforcement*"[36] (emphasis added). Komissarov was talking about people like the underground millionaire of the late 1970s, Babunashvili, who, not satisfied with his illicit multi-million-ruble income, had been able to order for himself the post of Minister of Light Industry. "He had decided to cap his career by combining in a single person (himself) both sides of Soviet 'mafia': the corrupter (underground business) and the corrupted (government)."[37] Relatively tame stuff in Soviet and post-Soviet reality, but it illustrated the 'mafia' concept that existed across the country well prior to the breakup of the Soviet Union.

In *Violent Entrepreneurs: The Use of Force in the Making of Russian Capitalism*, Vadim Volkov opts for a broad interpretation of 'mafia,' indeed to the point of rejecting use of that word and drawing a detailed account of the various players resorting to violent means in pursuit of economic ends. Volkov casts his net across a wide spectrum, including in his discussion traditional criminal groups, private security firms, the power ministries, and others who played important roles in the resurrection of Russia after the dismantling of the Soviet Union. Volkov also rejects the use of the term 'mafiya' (Handelman's inventive spelling discussed below), saying it's a convenient mechanism for putting a disproportionate amount of responsibility for the rise in criminal groups on the legacy of Communism while letting off the hook the ill-conceived reform policies of the Gorbachev and Yeltsin administrations.[38]

---

35. Ibid., p. 250. Western reviewers of Vaksberg's book noted his inconsistency with the word 'mafia'—a wide-ranging notion Soviets had been comfortable with but was new to the Western observer—and saw it as a weakness in Vaksberg's argument. See Peter Gumbel, "Graft, Back in the USSR," *The Wall Street Journal*, March 10, 1992; John Quigley, "Government Corruption in the Soviet Union," *Criminal Law Forum*, vol. 4, no. 3, 1993, pp. 567–572.

36. Vyacheslav Komissarov in *Bor'ba s Organizovannoi Prestupnost'iu: Problemy Teorii i Praktiki*, Moskva, Ministerstvo Vnutrennikh Del SSSR Akademiia, 1990, p. 48.

37. Simis, p. 53 (note 26).

38. Particularly as used by journalist Stephen Handelman. See Handelman's book, *Comrade Criminal: Russia's New Mafiya*, New Haven, Yale University Press, 1995. See also Vadim Volkov, *Violent Entrepreneurs*, Ithaca, Cornell University Press, 2002, p. 18.

In *Russian Mafia in America,* Finckenauer and Waring appreciate the semantic challenges in objectively addressing such an emotion-laden issue.

> The word *mafia* is a handy, catchall label used by journalists, moviemakers, and popular fiction writers because it conjures up images that require no further elaboration in the minds of readers and viewers. Because the term *mafia* is used regularly to refer to different things, in unknown or dubious contexts, sometimes as a noun and sometimes as an adjective, it often ends up conveying more confusion than enlightenment.[39]

They suggest that, as a concept, 'mafia' is a "method or modus operandi of a criminal endeavor that can exist anywhere." As such, Russian social and economic conditions of the 1990s certainly fostered the development of 'mafias.' But, contrary to Varese, Finckenauer and Waring are careful to point out that the Russian 'mafias' were not like the Sicilian 'mafias.' True, both were motivated by money and power, they say, but "the Soviet mafia was not associated with honor and respect and should not be confused with the real thing."[40]

One of the dominant understandings of 'mafia,' of course, refers to traditional crime groups involved in what are widely believed to be typical 'mafia' activities such as extortion, kidnapping, contract killing, and so on. But, at the end of the day, 'mafia' has become a totally inappropriate word to apply to the post-Soviet situation if our primary interest is to get beyond gangsters and shootouts to understand the problem in its fullest extent.

Part of the difficulty for the West in characterizing the situation in the former Soviet Union as 'mafia' was the temptation to decide who qualified as 'mafia' and who didn't. It's clear that many of the activities categorized as 'mafia' in the Soviet era have become or are in the process of becoming normal business practices. But if large-scale corruption remains extensive (as it will) and state officials and businessmen continue to inhabit the crime world along with professional criminals (as they will), then making a distinction between 'mafia' and 'non-mafia' elements seems to be a pointless exercise. It dulls our senses to what the threats are and from which direction they are likely to come. If our mindset prepares us to fear the Western type of 'mafia,' we miss the threats from the non-traditional, post-Soviet type of 'mafia.'

---

39. James O. Finckenauer and Elin J. Waring, *Russian Mafia in America: Immigration, Culture, and Crime,* Boston, Northeastern University Press, 1998, p. 18.
40. Ibid., p. 94.

Of course, this is precisely what happened throughout the 1990s. Many companies operating in Russia stayed vigilant against extortion attempts by gangsters, for example, but never bothered to conduct background checks on their employees or monitor them after they were hired. Frequently, it was the actions of the employees that created the threat rather than the supposedly external 'invading' force of the 'mafia.' Likewise, in numerous countries outside the former Soviet Union, law enforcement, media, and others were concerned about the Russian 'mafia' operating on their territory but failed to appreciate the range of activities traditional 'gangster' crime groups engaged in. They were unprepared for the massive white-collar activities carried out by both the traditional and non-traditional, 'non-gangster' post-Soviet groups.

In their 1996 book, *The Coming Russian Boom: A Guide to New Markets and Politics*, Richard Layard, a professor at the London School of Economics and a former adviser to Boris Yeltsin, and John Parker, a journalist for the magazine *Economist*, speak about 'mafia' in the following terms:

1) "The 'real mafiosi': thugs in sharp suits with bulging armpits; the violent enforcers that collect protection money, run prostitution rings, peddle drugs, and sell weapons";

2) "Small businessmen who own shops or sell goods from a kiosk on the street. Customers call them mafia even though in reality they are more often victims of gangs than members of them";

3) "Big businessmen with large Mercedeses and troops of 'assistants' with bulges under their left arms. Their business methods are rough; they avoid paying taxes when they can and make liberal use of bribery. But their business itself is usually legal. They resemble the robber barons of late nineteenth century America, the Rockefellers and Vanderbilts, rather than outright gangsters like Al Capone";

4) "State mafia, corrupt officials who sell licenses to import or export at controlled prices, licenses that bear with them the chance to siphon off goods for sale at uncontrolled and highly profitable prices. They are perhaps the most deadly of the four groups, because they are mainly responsible for the corruption that is becoming pervasive in Russia."[41]

The authors say that "use of the blanket term ['mafia'] to cover all these groups leads to some exaggeration in the scale of the problem of organized

---

41. Richard Layard and John Parker, *The Coming Russian Boom*, New York, The Free Press, 1996, pp. 151–154.

crime." They're partly right; 'mafia' is a bad label. However, determination of the *scale* of the problem depends on what one calls the problem in the first place. If it is called 'mafia' that will yield a certain kind of picture. If it is 'organized crime' that will be a different picture. If 'gangs' that's something else. There's not likely to be agreement any time soon about the definition of 'mafia.'

The crux of the matter is this: In the 1990s, the former Soviet Union was not experiencing a 'mafia' problem in the sense that the West understood it. The real problem—far more dangerous and destructive than a narrow interpretation of 'mafia'—was the socioeconomic and political nature of the former Soviet Union that necessarily included all four of the groups mentioned above. What we usually think of as 'mafia' was merely one manifestation in the wake of the decline and dismantling of the former Soviet Union. This is why it was crucial to examine 'threats' and not simply neatly packaging a traditional 'mafia' concept and separating it out as a distinct and independent force.

For example, the activities mentioned in point 1 above (collect protection money, run prostitution rings, peddle drugs, sell weapons) were in some form engaged in not only by the "real mafiosi" thugs, but those groups represented in points 2, 3, and 4 as well. Police, businessmen, bankers, and state officials were all known to perform some function in prostitution, collecting protection money, the trafficking and sale of narcotics, or arms dealing. When kiosks were part of a street narcotics network or knowingly trafficked in deadly counterfeit vodka, should they have been considered part of a 'mafia'? When shops or kiosks were financed and protected by crime groups should they have been considered part of a 'mafia' or seen as simply using 'mafia' services? When bankers and businessmen worked together with traditional crime groups to traffic weapons, were they or were they not part of the 'mafia'?

In point 3 above, businessmen are all but excused from culpability, as the authors suggest that their 'rough' practices were similar to those of 19th century American capitalists. The assumption is that the post-Soviet businessman was really a 'robber baron' laying the foundation of an industrial society. Throughout the 1990s that was rarely true of the so-called oligarchs—that group of top businessmen who were so enthusiastically adopted by media and business and promoted as the new Vanderbilts and Carnegies. At best, the 'oligarchs' were in the process of creating mechanisms for the use of capital but weren't building new railroads or engaging in massive infrastructure projects.[42]

---

42. If anything, the oligarchs had more in common with thugs than with the robber barons of 19th century America. See Mark Ames writing in *The Consortium for Independent Journalism* on March 11, 1999, at http://www.consortiumnews.com/c031199a.html.

The added temptation of the 'robber baron' label is to assume that the maturing process will create an environment in Russia roughly similar to that of the United States with regard to development of a free market system. In other words, that everything's going to turn out just fine. It's still far too early to know how it will turn out, and there's currently no reason to expect that everything's going to be fine in the foreseeable future. We'll have to wait another ten or twenty years to find out if, ultimately, the 'oligarchs' do turn out to be robber barons, but the odds are not in their favor.

Layard and Parker assign vague and arbitrary values to the various groups: corrupt officials are "mainly responsible" and "the most deadly"; businessmen's activities are "usually legal"; thugs running prostitutes and guns are "the real mafiosi"; retailers are "more often victims of gangs." The authors provide little empirical or even anecdotal evidence. In more than seven years of living in Moscow, conducting investigations, talking with law enforcement officials, and advising Western businesses, I've seen that the neat lines the authors draw to delineate the players, isolate them, and treat them individually were actually thoroughly entangled.

In reality, the vast majority of businesses in the late-Soviet and post-Soviet periods, whether joint ventures, small enterprises, banking institutions, import-export firms, distribution companies, and others were players in the crime world, either directly or peripherally, by necessity or design. For example, throughout the 1990s, thousands of fake companies had been created to commit illegal activities like trafficking in stolen automobiles or weapons, or to carry out otherwise legal activities in an illegal manner such as the sale of counterfeit foreign consumer goods. Countless Party officials, black marketeers, smugglers, and career criminals capitalized on their proximity to power (notably their long-standing relationships with the KGB and MVD as well as with traditional crime groups) to become some of the top bankers, real estate developers, and politicians looting state coffers. Deciding who was part of the 'mafia' and who was not was fraught with difficulty. To single out some as 'mafia' and excuse others was never a realistic approach, even at the height of criminal tensions in the early 1990s, since the goal was always to determine what steps could be taken to counter the threats regardless of what conventional wisdom called them.

So, do we use the word 'mafia' as understood in the West and focus primarily on the 'thugs with bulges'? The primary problem with this approach, as mentioned earlier, is blinding ourselves to dangers from other quarters that may not fit neatly into our concept of 'mafia.' Do we make a distinction by players? If the 'thugs' were government employees or businessmen committing crime in an organized fashion on an on-going basis for the sake of turning a profit, and never had any connection to the traditional criminal world, were they 'mafia'? Is 'mafia' to be defined by the types of activities engaged in, the quality of its internal organization, or the pedigree and actions of its members?

There's been no real success in finding a substitute word for 'mafia' that would be as attractive and readily recognized in pop culture. In his book, *Comrade Criminal: Russia's New Mafiya*, Canadian journalist Stephen Handelman described the crime phenomenon as 'mafiya,' altering its spelling to signal to the reader that, while the contours may have approximated the Western experience, there was clearly something different about the post-Soviet brand. While the spelling change caught on widely, the essence of that 'mafiya' never really penetrated popular consciousness. Handelman's title, *Comrade Criminal*, was in many ways a better indicator of the real situation: Comrades—state and Party officials—became criminals, and criminals became comrades. But as we will see in later chapters, the intermingling of officialdom and the underworld was not an innovation of the post-Soviet world.[43]

Unfortunately, much of the world's media and academic sources that reviewed or cited Handelman's book focused attention on this word 'mafiya' with its new-fangled spelling. This did little but confuse an already uncertain public. Ask ten people their understanding of 'mafia' and you'd likely get ten different answers. Then to throw 'mafiya' with a 'y' into the mix seemed only to muddle the issue further. It's an indicator of something having to do with the Russian brand of organized crime but what? It's been repeated countless times across the world and seems no clearer to people today than it did in 1995 when Handelman's book came out.

In its broadest sense, the word 'mafia' didn't represent specific groups but rather an idea of control, monopoly, exclusivity, influence, relationships, an inside track, access to goods and services, all for the purpose of making money and accumulating power. In the former Soviet Union of the 1990s, it was all of these things—an expression of the raw power struggle at every level of society.

My preference is to avoid using the word 'mafia' altogether because it simply failed to do what language is meant to do: communicate specific meanings through words. When conducting investigations in Russia in the second half of the 1990s on behalf of Western corporations, our team was required to look at a case as objectively as possible, to determine if the subject under

---

43. Vaksberg had expressed this notion four years earlier in his book (see note 28, p. 77): "Thus was prepared fertile soil for the cultivation of politicians and criminals, the former quickly turned into the latter and the latter into the former. It became impossible to tell one from the other."

investigation represented a threat to the Western partner. Using the word 'mafia' raised more questions than it answered. If a field operative reported that the subject, Ivan Ivanovich, was 'mafia' or connected to the 'mafia,' it didn't mean anything. If I had told a client that his or her potential partner was 'mafia,' I could expect a string of clarifying questions. In the final analysis, it was always critical to get into the details of any given situation because in the former Soviet Union sometimes business people with close ties to the traditional criminal world were the safest people to do business with. Other times they weren't. And this was independent of whether they were called 'mafia.' The word 'mafia' in the former Soviet Union represented a phenomenon far broader and more diverse than that understood in the West, and, ultimately, is meaningless. By the way ... in the May 2000 issue of the Delta Airlines in-flight magazine, *Sky*, an article about English gardens carried the title, "The Horticultural Mafia."

CHAPTER 2

RUSSIA

Not with the mind is Russia comprehended,
The common yardstick will deceive
In gauging her: so singular her nature—
In Russia you must just believe.

—Fyodor Tyutchev[1]

How can you expect a man who's warm to understand a man who's cold?

—Alexander Solzhenitsyn[2]

The phrase 'Russian mafia,' the shorthand of a new phenomenon on the global crime landscape in the 1990s, had been bandied about and parroted by media, law enforcement officials, politicians, and others. It's understandable that the word 'mafia' could be confusing, overused, and ultimately meaningless. One might expect at first glance, though, that the word 'Russian' would be devoid of interpretation problems. It seems straightforward. Most Westerners, though, have only a sketchy knowledge of Russia at best, probably not unlike my first thoughts many years ago: cold weather, abundant vodka, fur hats, and Red Square. The Soviets were godless, atheistic Communists, and they were the enemy. If they had the chance to experience freedom and democracy, surely they would embrace it and turn away from their system that seemed to represent much that was wrong with the world.

The process of starting to think differently about the Soviet Union and Russia began in the United States in 1984, though I couldn't have known at the time that the road would continue for more than twenty years. I remember very clearly a discussion in Soviet politics class being led by Erik Hoffmann,

---

1. Fyodor Tyutchev, 1886, cited in Avrahm Yarmolinsky, *Russians Then & Now: Selected Russian Writings from Early Times to the Present*, New York, The Macmillan Company, 1963, p. 85.
2. Alexander Solzhenitsyn, *One Day in the Life of Ivan Denisovich*, New York, E.P. Dutton & Co., Inc., 1963, p. 34.

a political science professor at the State University of New York at Albany. He posed the following question: If the Soviet Union were to open its borders, what percentage of the population would leave? Various figures were called out around the room. All but one of the estimates exceeded 50%. We, of course, had little sense of the practical, logistical demands necessary to carry out what we were suggesting. But the point was larger than that. Our assumption was that anyone in his or her right mind would opt for freedom and democracy in the West than remain shackled to a totalitarian system. That was our impression at least. Never mind that we knew next to nothing about the realities of Soviet life. Remember, we were still in the throes of the Cold War. Our perception of the Soviet Union was dramatically influenced by the U.S. propaganda machine as much as theirs. We couldn't imagine—*looking through our own lenses*—that there was anything to stay for. In the same way, authors invite readers to explore the horrors of the Russian 'mafia'—as seen through our own lenses—without first introducing some basic features of Russia and the former Soviet Union. It seems reasonable to know at least a little about what's at stake in a country that was said to have been overrun by the 'mafia.'

Even today uncertainty about the difference between Russia and the Soviet Union seems to linger. It's important to make the distinction. The Soviet Union was established on December 30, 1922 (not immediately after Lenin's Bolsheviks came to power in November 1917). Its official name was Union of Soviet Socialist Republics from which we get the shortened version, USSR. In Russian, the name was S̲oyuz S̲ovetskikh S̲otsialisticheskikh R̲espublik. The Latin abbreviation was SSSR, but the more familiar version was the Cyrillic CCCP, which we saw so often on the uniforms of the Soviet Union's Olympic athletes and on the side of Aeroflot jets.

The USSR consisted of 15 different republics. The best known of these was the Russian Soviet Federated Socialist Republic (Rossiiskii Sovetskii Federativnyi Sotsialisticheskii Respublik), better known simply as 'Russia.' Each republic of the Soviet Union had its own array of regions. For example, Chechnya, Dagestan, and Ingushetia, among many others, were regions within Russia. (They still exist today as part of the Russian Federation.)

Although inaccurate, the terms 'Soviet Union' and 'Russia' were frequently used interchangeably in the West. There were several likely reasons for that:

- Russia was by far the largest of the fifteen republics by area, and its population accounted for slightly more than half (52%) of the entire Soviet population of approximately 300 million people;
- the official language of the Soviet Union was Russian in a land of nearly 100 distinct national groups;

- the majority of government and Communist Party positions in the Russian Republic, and indeed throughout the Soviet Union, were occupied by ethnic Russians. Consequently, much of the West's exposure governmentally, socially, and culturally was with ethnic Russians.

The 14 other republics of the Soviet Union were:

Latvia	
Lithuania	Collectively these are the Baltic States.
Estonia	
Ukraine	Ukraine is known as Little Russia. Byelorussia, or White Russia, became known as Byelarus and Moldavia's name changed to Moldova with the dismantling of the USSR.
Byelorussia	
Moldavia	
	These are frequently referred to as the Caucasian republics because they are situated in or near the Caucasus Mountain Range. The label has nothing to do with skin color. In fact, they generally have a darker complexion than ethnic Russians.
Armenia	
Azerbaijan	
Georgia	
Kazakhstan	Collectively, these republics are referred to as Central Asia. Some people include Kazakhstan in this grouping, others do not. These states are still popularly referred to as 'the stans' by foreigners.
Uzbekistan	
Turkmenistan	
Kyrgyzstan	
Tajikistan	

In the Russian language (*russkii yazyk*), there are two different adjectives for what appears in English as a single word, 'Russian.' For some Russians, understanding the distinction between the two meanings was important in drawing a correct understanding of the *Russian* 'mafia.' The two adjectives are *russkii* and *rossiiskii*. The first—*russkii*—is a word that so many of us became familiar with (as a noun) during the Cold War, referring to 'the Russkies.' The word is believed to come from *Rus*, which traditionally has been used to indicate the nascent states of Kiev and Muscovy from the 10th to the 13th centuries. *Rus* was said to be "humble, homely, sacred and definitely feminine," the source of Russian humanity and soul. It's the ancient *Rus* of the pre-imperial era that the Russian calls upon for his or her connection to the land and the language.[3] It's the world of late-night sessions around the kitchen table with a bottle of vodka or a samovar. It's passionate hugs and kisses. It's poetry and music. When the movie *Dr. Zhivago*, starring Omar Sherif and Julie Christie, was shown in Moscow for the first time, the Muscovite movie-going audience giggled and guffawed their way through the picture. It didn't seem Russian at all. Scenes at the frozen train station should have been filled with vapor streaming from the mouths of everyone present and the good-byes should have involved passionate, desperate kisses and grasping, suffocating bear hugs. This strikes me of what *Rus* should be.

The second word—*rossiiskii*—is in many ways almost the opposite of *russkii*. *Rossiiskii* is believed to derive from *Rossiya*, a Latinized version thought to have been used first in Poland. The word is believed to have penetrated the Muscovite consciousness in the 16th century and became common in the 17th century, at the very time when the empire was being formed. In contrast to the humility and sacredness of things *russkii*, *rossiiskii* is "grandiose, cosmopolitan, secular, and masculine."[4] It's formal, administrative, and bureaucratic; it's power and control. It is associated not with the village or the commune but with expansive territory encompassing everything. Its world is not that of the ethnic Russian alone but of the hodgepodge of cultures that had been beaten into submission by the strong hand of the Tsars—Russian and Soviet alike.

As the culturologist Georgii Gachev distinguished, "*Rossiya* is the fate of *Rus*. *Rossiya* is attraction, ideal, and service—but also abyss and perdition. *Rossiya* uprooted the Russian people, enticed them away from *Rus*, transformed the peasant into a soldier, an organizer, a boss, but no longer a husbandman."[5] This sense of loss, confusion, and contradiction in the essence of Russia is widespread and profound to this day.

In the history of Russia, empire building took priority over all else, beginning with the 16th century reign of Ivan the Terrible, and was confirmed in dramatic fashion by Peter the Great in the first quarter of the 18th century. The concerns and needs of the people stood a distant second, a powerful and recurring theme throughout the Russian and Soviet periods and again in the current post-Soviet era. In order to build an empire, first and foremost a military needed to be manned, equipped, supplied, and maintained. This came at the expense of building communities and allowing civic organizations to grow and develop organically. Take careful note of that point—military de-

---

3. Geoffrey Hosking, *Russia: People & Empire, 1552–1917*, London, Fontana Press, 1998, p. xix.
4. Ibid.
5. Ibid.

mands superseded the needs of the people. This theme recurs throughout Russian and Soviet history and will become one of the central underlying reasons for the rise of criminal groups in the former Soviet Union (see Chapters 5 and 6).

In large measure, the ethnic aspect of nationhood (common language, culture, traditions, history, economy, and territory) was manufactured. Russian, as the common language, was imposed on non-Russian peoples conquered over the centuries. Mutual disdain, if not outright hatred, between the Russians and minority ethnic groups has been a feature of the system, at some times more intensely felt than at others.[6]

The civic aspect of nationhood also suffered significantly during the building of the empire and throughout the Soviet era. The lack of political parties, interest groups, voluntary associations, and other institutions of civil society minimized the participation of the citizenry in their own governance. One simple conclusion with profound implications that we can reach is that Russia was and is a very different country in its development and path than the United States or Western Europe. Many of the institutions that form the infrastructure of society—that we have taken for granted in the West for hundreds of years—existed in Russia and the Soviet Union to serve the state and not the people. Not coincidentally, it is frequently noted that Russia missed crucial aspects of Western development such as the Renaissance, the Enlightenment, the benefits of the French Revolution, and other major events. "Significantly, there is little trust between the governmental authorities and general population, little lawfulness in the relations among state institutions and social units, and little balance of the disparate interests throughout the state and society."[7] And, in the 1990s, these institutions, such as law enforcement, social welfare, even the military, joined in the free-for-all struggle created by economic, social, and political chaos. This provided another profound impetus for the rise of criminal groups, coming on a centuries-old backdrop of autocracy, not democracy.[8] There is little reason in expecting or even demand-

---

6. See Janet M. Hartley, *A Social History of the Russian Empire, 1650–1825*, London, Longman, 1999; Lindsey Hughes, *Russia in the Age of Peter the Great*, New Haven, Yale University Press, 1998; Ezra Mendelsohn and Marshall S. Shatz, (eds.), *Imperial Russia, 1700–1917: State, Society, Opposition*, DeKalb, Illinois, Northern Illinois University Press, 1988.

7. Erik P. Hoffmann, "Conceptualizing State-Society Relations in Russia," in Gordon B. Smith (ed.), *State-Building in Russia: The Yeltsin Legacy and the Challenge of the Future*, Armonk, NY, M.E. Sharpe, 1999, p. 142.

8. Hosking, p. xx (note 3).

ing that Russia develop an American- or Western-type democracy—it is an impossible request to fulfill. As Erik Hoffmann notes, "Briefly put, disintegrating authoritarian or totalitarian regimes are not necessarily emerging democracies, and disintegrating centrally planned economies are not necessarily emerging markets."[9]

The tension between *Rus* and *Rossiya*, between organic nationhood and empire building, has traveled through history and remains a defining characteristic of Russian society today. As scholar Vera Tolz summarizes, "In December 1991, the Russian Federation was transformed into an independent state as a *historically formed regional entity*, not as a nation-state. Scholars argue that the Russian empire was built 'at the cost of Russia's own sense of nationhood'"[10] (emphasis added). Political, economic, and cultural institutions were never given the time and nurturing necessary to develop into strong agencies supporting the needs of the people. "As always, the trouble with Russia is that the state develops, but society doesn't. The good of the people is sacrificed for the good of the state."[11] Complicating this was the deep-seated sense in Russians that they should sacrifice their own freedoms for the greatness of the state. At the same time, though, the state was unable to attract the deep loyalty of even its Russian, let alone its non-Russian, subjects. This dichotomy—what might be called 'official' Russia (*rossiiskii/Rossiya*) and 'soulful' Russia (*russkii/Rus*)—was a kind of schizophrenia, worlds which the average citizen of Russia would learn to move between effortlessly.

An apt illustration of this profound dilemma was found in the aftermath of the 1996 presidential election. President Boris Yeltsin "asked his staff to consider 'what kind of idea, what kind of ideology is most important for Russia' and to articulate a 'national idea' that would 'unify all Russians.'"[12] A major Russian newspaper even launched a public contest for the best essay outlining a new national idea or ideology.[13] Once again, Russia had embarked on the search for national unity, for an identity. And, once again, it appeared to take the form of a quick-fix artificial overlay rather than an organic development nurtured by wise leaders.

---

9. Hoffmann, p. 149 (note 7).

10. Vera Tolz, "Conflicting 'Homeland Myths' and Nation-State Building in Post-Communist Russia," *Slavic Review*, vol. 57, no. 2, Summer 1998, p. 267.

11. Nina L. Khrushcheva, "Russia's Dream of Greatness: The Gulag of the Russian Mind," *Bangkok Post*, August 19, 2006, accessed in Johnson's Russia List.

12. Hoffmann, p. 134 (note 7).

13. Ibid., pp. 134–135.

This struggle to *create* an identity and force unity after the dismantling of the Soviet Union seemed to justify the writer Alexander Solzhenitsyn's comment years earlier that these attributes were clearly missing during the Soviet era. "The word *Russia*," he said, "can serve only to designate an oppressed people denied the possibility of acting as one entity or to denote its suppressed national consciousness, religion, and culture. Or else it can point to a future nation liberated from communism."[14]

The territory between *russkii* and *rossiiskii* was occupied by the intelligentsia, trying to create an 'imagined community,' to blend imperial culture and ethnic community. The intelligentsia usually found itself on the losing end, crushed between two unyielding and contradictory forces. One of the results was the failure to form a 'normal' society with a strong middle class and an independent entrepreneurial culture.

> What is striking is not that Russia was economically backward in the 16th, 18th, or 20th century, but rather that every attempt at reform and modernization tended in the long run to reproduce that backwardness. The economic policies deemed necessary to sustain the empire systematically held back the entrepreneurial and productive potentialities of the mass of the people.[15]

The autocratic power of the throne, lack of independent political parties, a non-existent middle class, failure to create a business class, an underdeveloped consumer society, and the long-standing tension between *Rus* and *Rossiya* contributed to the formation of a Russia that was incapable of creating civil society based on rule of law as we understood it.

So, what did any of this have to do with the *Russian* 'mafia'? It begins to answer an important question and acts as a prelude to many other questions that will be addressed throughout the book. That first basic question is who constituted the *Russian* 'mafia'? The distinction needs to be made at the outset that, ethnically speaking, the so-called *Russian* 'mafia' (however you define 'mafia') had a vastly diverse ethnic composition. It was not exclusively ethnic Russians. Rather than the popular Russian-language version, *Russkaya* 'mafia,' a more precise translation, if less pleasing to the ear and more challenging to the tongue, would be *Rossiiskaya* 'mafia.' The latter is inclusive of

---

14. Alexander Solzhenitsyn, "The Mortal Danger," in Erik P. Hoffmann and Robbin F. Laird, *The Soviet Polity in the Modern Era*, New York, Aldine Publishing Company, 1984, p. 7.

15. Hosking, pp. xxvi–xxvii (note 3).

the numerous ethnic nationalities that inhabit the Russian Federation such as Russians, Chechens, Dagestanis, Ingushetians, Kalmykians, Tatars, as well as ethnic groups from other former Soviet republics who call Russia home such as Ukrainians, Georgians, Lithuanians, and others. While on the one hand it is convenient shorthand to refer to the Russian Federation and even the former Soviet Union as 'Russia,' on the other hand it is necessary to appreciate the complex ethnic mosaic of the Russian Federation and the former Soviet Union.

In the post-Soviet period—for almost a decade prior to September 11, 2001, and the rise of Islamic terrorism as the new threat—the Russians had been singled out as the new threat in the organized crime world and the enemy to the West. But if you were Russian, it would have been humiliating to have your country's name and reputation reflexively related to 'mafia.' Consider the outrage of many Italian-Americans through much of the 20th century who could not tolerate being stereotyped as 'mafia.' Or take the case of 'Americans' generally. At the beginning of a lecture at the International Law Enforcement Academy in Roswell, New Mexico, to a group of criminal justice practitioners from South America, I apologized for my carefree use of the word 'Americans' in identifying citizens of the United States. I knew this was a sensitive issue for many of them since they, too, were Americans. Their reactions told me it was an even more sensitive issue than I had thought.

In the Russian case, we were dealing with an entire country being painted with broad-brush strokes. This was what the former chief of Russia's National Central Bureau of Interpol, Yuri Melnikov, referred to during that April 1995 MVD press conference mentioned in Chapter 1. Just as every other people in the world, Russians had tremendous pride in their country for many reasons and grew weary of the constant criticism throughout the 1990s and into the new century. Letters to the Editor had been printed in a variety of newspapers over the past 15 years registering complaints specifically regarding this issue. For example, *The Toronto Star* printed this letter:

> It is high time that someone stood up for the Russian-speaking community of Toronto. Yes, it is the 'Russian-speaking' community, and not, as you call it, [the] 'Russian community,' since it consists of representatives of different ethnic origins united by the common language that was the mother tongue of the majority of them under Soviet rule.... [T]he authors, as well as the headline editor, managed to convey a clear picture of yet another Russian gangster operating right under the very unsuspecting noses of innocent Canadians.... Are there drug dealers, con artists, and other crime figures in the Russ-

ian-speaking community of Toronto? Indubitably, as much as in any other community in any other city.[16]

The California Chapter President of the Congress on Russian Americans struck a similar chord in a letter to the FBI. "The Russian-American community and our National organization continue to be very concerned about the serious negative 'Russian bashing' that the media is propagating every time some adverse political or criminal events take place."[17]

For our purposes, it is important to appreciate the diversity of the former Soviet Union for reasons that are directly applicable to law enforcement. A small example: Consider the California Highway Patrol officer who read a Ukrainian suspect his rights in Russian only to have the case thrown out of court when the accused stated that his native language was Ukrainian and claimed not to have understood the *Miranda* warning in Russian.[18]

Beyond issues of language and ethnicity, one important aspect of Russia that should be discussed in the context of organized crime is natural resources. In short, the question is what was there to steal? This question goes to the activities of organized crime groups, corrupt bureaucrats, and businessmen in the country. A few basic facts about the natural resources and geography of Russia and the former Soviet Union would help shed light on what was at stake.

To say that the former Soviet Union was rich in natural resources would be a gross understatement. It was believed to be the only country on the face of the earth that could more or less sustain itself. The USSR had the world's second largest reserves of oil, and the Russian Republic answered for more than 80% of the country's output. From 1965 to 1981, the Soviet Union nearly doubled its oil output, to 600 million tons a year. And in 1974, it began to out-produce Saudi Arabia and the United States to become the largest producer of petroleum in the world.[19]

---

16. Marsha Gershtein, "Russian Mafiya Not Typical Here," *The Toronto Star*, July 20, 1996, p. C3. See also George B. Avisov, California Chapter President of the Congress on Russian Americans, letter to FBI Agent George Grotz, March 29, 1998, http://www.russian-americans.org/CRA_Art_FBI.htm: "Today, as the Soviet Union no longer exists, the media has conveniently substituted 'Russian Mafia' for the former Soviet Union's criminal element that was able to slip into the U.S. under the special 'Refugee act.' (This legislation allows annually up to 50,000 refugees, predominantly ethnic Jews, to enter this country under very favorable condition.)"

17. Ibid., Avisov letter to Grotz.

18. Author conversation with California Highway Patrol officer, April 1999.

19. Marshall Goldman, *Gorbachev's Challenge: Economic Reform in the Age of High Technology*, New York, W.W. Norton & Company, 1987, pp. 17–18. See also Leslie Symons (ed.), *The Soviet Union: A Systematic Geography*, London, Hodder and Stoughton, 1983.

Due to the rapid development in oil production, obviously refineries and transportation routes sprang up around the country, predominantly in the Russian Republic. In the 1990s, with the decline in Russia's law enforcement effectiveness, this network provided countless points of opportunity for criminal organizations. These included extorting oil executives, stealing supplies, influencing management of refineries, creating their own oil companies, buying their own gas stations, as well as acting as enforcers for warring oil executives. Some crime groups were paid in oil; others had gotten access to oil through the acquisition of export licenses by bribery, intimidation, or privileged relationships. The real question was did the traditional criminal groups threaten to take control of the Russian oil industry in the 1990s? The answer clearly is no, but it was a source of significant income for some groups.

The USSR also had the world's greatest reserves of natural gas. Russia's exports comprised 35% of the world's total. It became the largest producer of natural gas in 1983.[20] The USSR had 40% of the world's total iron reserves and was the second largest producer of gold behind South Africa. The Soviet Union was also believed to have had the world's largest reserves of diamonds, nickel, cobalt, copper, platinum, palladium, iridium, lead, uranium, osmium, and potassium salt. In addition, the aluminum industry was one of the largest in the world. (The four largest aluminum plants are located in the Russian Federation.) It became the largest producer of steel in 1974.[21] Currently, the Russian Federation is the second largest producer of electricity, copper, cement, and tin, and is the number three producer of coal, fish, and grain.

The Soviet Union had the world's largest ocean-going fleet accompanied by large modern fish-processing ships, which operated in the Atlantic and Pacific oceans. Having one-quarter of the world's forested areas, Russia's production of logs and sawn timber exceeded that of all other countries, despite inefficient and wasteful processing. While traveling along the railroad network through major Chinese cities, I frequently wondered how much of the Russian timber I spotted had arrived legally and how much money in bribes had changed hands.

The Soviet Union had over 100 major maritime and river ports in places like Archangelsk, Astrakhan, Baku, St. Petersburg, Moscow, Murmansk, Odessa, Riga, Tallinn, and Vladivostok. Scattered around the country were 4,530 usable airfields, including 1,050 with permanent surface runways, and about 4,500 major transport aircraft. With the dismantling of the Soviet

---

20. Ibid., Symons.
21. Ibid., Symons.

Union and the drastically reduced state budgets for the military, what became of these airfields? In one of our cases in 1995, we were asked to investigate a charter airline that the client was going to use to visit its factories around the country. The first step was to collect information on the principals, shareholders, and so on. Our initial findings were intriguing. The founding shareholders of the airline were listed as a Russian charitable organization established to help fight drug addiction and drug trafficking, a company in Hong Kong, and more than 60 military air bases around the country. We were unable to confirm our hunches since it wasn't part of the assignment, but given this and other information, there seemed a strong possibility that the airline was part of a widespread drug trafficking network.[22]

The USSR covered 8,582,000 square miles, stretching across 11 time zones and measuring two-and-a-half times larger than the United States. It covered one-sixth of the land surface of the earth. It had the world's longest frontiers, some 12,000 miles shared with other countries (Turkey, Iran, Afghanistan, China, Mongolia, North Korea, Norway, Finland, Poland, Czechoslovakia, Hungary, and Romania), and 25,000 miles washed by the Arctic, Atlantic, and Pacific oceans. Today, all of France can fit in just one of Russia's 89 regions. Most of Russia itself lies at the same latitude as Canada. Moscow, Russia's capital, is at roughly the same latitude as Edmonton, Canada; St. Petersburg is at 60 degrees north latitude which is just south of Anchorage, Alaska.

Pick up a newspaper these days and read about the political and economic implications of Russian gas on Europe and, increasingly, on the United States. In December 2005, Russia dramatically increased the price of natural gas to Ukraine, and in December 2006, the price of natural gas to Belarus. On one level, Russia's actions were seen to be an effort to keep Ukraine in its sphere of influence. On a broader level, Europe was shown quite clearly that it is at the mercy of the Russians as Russia supplies some 25% of Europe's natural gas. Was the natural gas industry at risk to fall into the hands of the 'mafia' in the 1990s? What was the role of criminal groups in the aluminum industry? How was the fish industry affected by the crime phenomenon of the 1990s? What role did the so-called mafia play in exporting timber? In short, what became of these industries when the Soviet Union was dismantled?

Before closing this chapter, a note must be made regarding the Soviet Union as a superpower. Anyone older than 35 will likely remember growing up in a bipolar geopolitical world when the United States and the USSR seemed poised in a constant state of nuclear showdown. Few of us realized,

---

22. Author investigative information.

though, that the Soviet Union's status as a superpower was limited largely to its military strength. That is to say, few of us realized that much of the Soviet Union *in terms of infrastructure* was what we might have referred to as a Third World country or a 'banana republic.' It had a rich culture of music, literature, and so on, but in terms of infrastructure, paved roads, well-constructed buildings, indoor plumbing, etc., the country was largely lacking. The quality and reliability of distribution networks for goods were lagging especially as compared to the United States and most other Western countries, and forces of supply and demand worked somewhat differently in the Soviet command economy than in the West (see Chapter 6). Failure in the United States and other Western countries to appreciate this made the dramatic events of the post-Soviet world that much more unexpected.

CHAPTER 3

INFORMATION

Today, many excited, even frenzied observers plunge into this now-accessible present and imagine that it is self-explanatory. The openness and accessibility of the ex-Soviet territory, as compared to the previous restrictions, do not automatically deliver clear and self-evident explanations about the past and the present.

—Moshe Lewin[1]

It has become a sarcastic proverb that a thing must be true if you saw it in a newspaper. That is the opinion intelligent people have of that lying vehicle in a nutshell. But the trouble is that the stupid people—who constitute the grand overwhelming majority of this and all other nations—do believe and are moulded and convinced by what they get out of a newspaper, and there is where the harm lies.

—Mark Twain[2]

We live in an information age, a period in history of the greatest quantity and variety of news and information delivered at unprecedented speed. Cable news networks monitor happenings around the world twenty-four hours a day, seven days a week, challenging each other to deliver information to market first. Even on old-fashioned network television, news and entertainment information can be found on any given station for more than sixteen hours most days of the week. The Internet brings information from the four corners of the globe into our homes, and we have the power to purchase and receive almost anything we want without ever leaving the house. Stock markets rise and fall on news from Washington, New York, London, Frankfurt, Tokyo, Hong Kong, and Singapore. Trillions of dollars are transferred electronically

---

1. Moshe Lewin, *Russia/USSR/Russia: The Drive and Drift of a Superstate*, New York, The New Press, 1995, p. 2.
2. Mark Twain, "License of the Press" speech, at http://www.twainquotes.com/Newspaper.html.

around the world on a daily basis. The decisions we make are based on impressions and perceptions derived from the information that swirls around us: what to buy, where to shop, how to think, what to believe. Like it or not—realize it or not—we're information junkies.

On the surface it may seem that I've strayed from the topic at hand. But in many ways, this is the topic at hand. What we know—or think we know—about the Russian 'mafia' is intimately connected to the business of the production and consumption of information.

Observers frequently use stories to convey a representation of an event, a change in trends, the shifting of society's sensibilities, the failure of a government policy. These snapshots are used to illustrate a larger point, generalizable to a larger population, applicable to the bigger picture. We frequently make judgments based on these snapshots, sometimes failing to understand the context in which the events are taking place. After we have put together a string of these snapshots, we make certain conclusions and we come to *know*. Or at least we think we know.

I was reminded of this many times in Moscow and during my travels around the former Soviet Union. One particular episode—a very simple illustration—serves as our first example. Two of us wandered the streets of Moscow at night in the fall of 1991. A friend of mine, an older American man, had been to the Soviet Union only once before and with the exception of a handful of the most common words didn't understand Russian. We came upon a street and then an overpass where numerous trolleybuses were lined up, pushed nose to back, tightly packed together. All was dark. There was no sign of any people, no passengers, no drivers.

On another day, as we entered Red Square, we saw an animated woman pacing the cobblestone plaza outside the Kremlin, barking into a megaphone.

My friend's interpretation of these two snapshots was interesting. He linked them together in his mind under the influence of other events that were occurring in the country. Earlier in the year there had been demonstrations and protests, some with hundreds of thousands of protesters. In this context, his preliminary assessments were totally understandable, but absolutely misguided. His conclusion was that the trolleybus drivers had gone on strike. Indeed, it looked as if they had. He didn't know that virtually every night the trolleybuses were parked in such a manner; they were simply finished for the day. He also noted that the woman with the megaphone was protesting the government, trying to rile up passersby and get them to join her. In actuality, she was selling lottery tickets.

The point is that much of what we see and how we interpret it will depend in part on how long we've been watching. For example, one evening I was walking from the Bolshoi Theatre toward Tverskaya Street, the main thoroughfare that starts at Red Square and runs to the north of Moscow. As I turned the corner onto Tverskaya, a car raced up to the curb and came to an abrupt stop. Four men jumped out. The middle-aged and elderly men and women who had been lined up against the wall selling knick-knacks to earn some survival rubles scattered quickly. The men emerging from the car found their target and subdued him. If someone were visiting Moscow for the first time and had this experience, it would have conformed very neatly to the impression that had been created by the media around the world—that life was like this all the time, a high level of constant danger. Far too many people I spoke with in the West believed that there were gangs everywhere and at any moment on any street corner one could spot them.

I don't mean to imply here that extortion (*vymogatel'stvo*), shootouts (*perestrelki*), and settlements of accounts (*razborki*) weren't occurring across the country or that gangs were not a serious problem. They were—and a lot of people suffered because of it. But the frequency and scale of the events *on the streets* could not justify the disproportionate fear that resulted, both in Russia and around the world. Each episode generally occurred in a very small physical location or geographic territory and generally involved very few people. It has always interested me that, on the one hand, stories of 'mafia' and 'gangland shootings' splashed across the world's newspapers and television screens creating a profound fear in people. On the other hand, many people living in Russia claimed—in newspapers, in academic articles, in conversation—that Moscow, St. Petersburg, and other parts of Russia felt safer than other major cities in the world.

> One of the biggest obstacles to tourism in Russia today is the widely held perception, fueled almost daily by the Western media, that it is a dangerous place to be. True, urban street crime levels have skyrocketed since the fall of the Soviet Union, but they have skyrocketed from a level of practically zero and still remain well below levels in corresponding North American cities.[3]
> Crime rates have increased since 1991, but even today street crime is lower in Moscow and St. Petersburg than it is in most American cities. A survey of American business people conducted by an American security company showed that nearly all of the respondents disagreed

---

3. Scott McDonald, "Relax But Be Vigilant: Safety in Russia," *Russian Life*, February 1996, vol. 39, no. 2, p. 20.

with assessments given in the media regarding the level of personal danger in Moscow.[4]

Russia is not the totally lawless land that mainstream American media would have you believe, that wild west of nations languishing in a 1930s Chicago dreamscape. I'd sooner walk the streets of this city of 15 million [Moscow] late at night than say Philadelphia or Detroit. You follow a few simple rules of personal safety, like you would in any large city.[5]

Several weeks of vacation in the United States—and watching the news—always made me apprehensive about returning to Moscow. By the time I landed at Sheremetievo Airport, though, I realized that nothing had changed for the worse; it was still the same Russia I had left.

Here's another simple illustration of observing a situation—or, in this case, a person—over time. When I was working in the Ministry of Internal Affairs of the USSR in 1990–91, I had an office across the corridor from Alexander Gurov, at that time Chief of the Organized Crime Control Department. We occasionally ate lunch in the officers' dining room, chatted in his office, and attended meetings together.

Some years earlier, Gurov had been a relatively low-level police officer without particularly broad or deep experience in policing. Later, as a criminologist, he wrote a book called *Professional Criminality* that had raised his profile in certain circles. It had been well received and even police practitioners—not known for their tolerance of academics—hailed the book as a real contribution to the field. Gurov had been plucked from academe to head up the new Organized Crime Control Department at a particularly sensitive and difficult time in Soviet history. The existence of organized crime was finally being acknowledged. Until then it had been ideologically impossible to countenance the problem in a country where, officially, organized crime was recognized as a manifestation of the illnesses of capitalism.

It's the portrayal of Gurov in the West that is of interest to us here. In his book, *Comrade Criminal*, Stephen Handelman acknowledges the debt he has to Gurov for providing the underlying theme for the book. "What Gurov told me that afternoon inspired this book, and continues to form the intellectual

---

4. "The American Chamber of Commerce White Paper on Security Issues in the Russian Federation," unpublished report prepared by the Security Committee of the American Chamber of Commerce in Moscow, 1998.

5. Tim Goodwin, "Crime in Russia: Bitter Fruit of Capitalism and Democracy," *Synapse*, no. 34, Winter 1995, at http://www.traverse.com/conprof/center/synapse34/goodwin.html.

underpinning of its argument. The scrappy general believed that the criminal order that enveloped Russia in the aftermath of Communism was not accidental. He was convinced that powerful interests had a stake in its success."[6] Handelman proceeds to tell Gurov's story, how he had been given the directorship of the new department and developed and expanded it. The department was Gurov's legacy, Handelman says. "Thanks to Gurov's efforts the federal MVD set up an organized crime squad. The Moscow City government followed suit." But along the way, according to Handelman, Gurov had somehow raised the ire of the senior bureaucracy; they hadn't welcomed Gurov's appointment as chief of the department. "His enemies didn't give up: after only a few years on the job, Gurov was suspended and then fired.... Like their Kremlin counterparts, however, the city Party authorities at first demonstrated little faith in Western-style law enforcement concepts and tactics."[7]

By 1992, Gurov had gone from an office on the ninth floor in the national police headquarters to "a paper-strewn cubbyhole of an office in the Lubyanka," headquarters of the former KGB. Commenting on the dark, grim, and depressing environment in the Lubyanka, Handelman says, "It was an appropriately symbolic place to find the man who was both the pioneer and the pariah of modern Soviet criminology." Gurov had fallen from considerable heights to end up in what Handelman characterizes as essentially a nothing job. More than that, the "assignment to the old KGB prison and torture chamber was a kind of punishment for Gurov, who, for reasons he would not explain, was trapped in a dead-end job there, handling the security ministry's relations with the press."[8]

The language, the images of the KGB torture chamber, and the dramatic decline in Gurov's luck paint a picture of yet another unjust outcome in the land of dictators and secret police. It pits the underdog, "the scrappy general," as Handelman calls Gurov, against the lingering dictatorial machine and, once again, as for centuries, reason and justice suffered, the machine won, and democracy lost. This is the undercurrent that rises from those paragraphs on Gurov and works well as part of the underlying theme of the book: the system, the Communist Party, was responsible for all bad things that happened. But what if the things that happened to Gurov in Russia would have also occurred in a 'normal' country? What if the things that did occur were simply following the rules of bureaucracy instead of as part of a dark scheme by the

---

6. Stephen Handelman, *Comrade Criminal: Russia's New Mafiya*, New Haven, Yale University Press, 1995, p. 55.

7. Ibid., pp. 47–48.

8. Ibid., p. 55.

powers-that-be to rid itself of a pesky maverick? What if the things that did occur represented the best outcome? I wonder if the fact that Gurov wouldn't explain why he was "trapped in a dead-end job" spurred Handelman to find the answer elsewhere. There's no indication that he looked.

Here's the point: Handelman's account is but one version of that particular story, giving the sense of Gurov as pioneer, if not crusader, laboring mightily to bring to life the new department. For his troubles, Gurov ends up, essentially, in the broom closet, defeated by 'anti-democratic forces,' or something to that effect. A different version might conclude that Gurov was an ineffectual leader in the corridors of power, failing to understand fully the bureaucratic labyrinth of Soviet politics at a time when sharp political instincts were needed more than ever. Ironically, and in contrast to Handelman's portrayal, Gurov was perfectly suited for the Lubyanka job as press liaison for the former KGB and essentially ended up in an appropriate position. He loved to talk to people and to impart his perspective on the nature of the Russian 'mafia.' He was a natural at public relations. Had Handelman raised questions with others about Gurov's fate, he might have heard a story that challenged his own version. Interestingly, Handelman had also interviewed Gennady Chebotaryov, who was Gurov's deputy. Chebotaryov was the real driving force behind the department, the linchpin providing the leadership and navigating the treacherous political waters in a disintegrating empire. He had the respect of his troops, his political enemies, and even some of the crime bosses who couldn't help but tip their hat to a worthy adversary.[9] (Prior to the collapse of the Soviet Union, Gurov's other deputy, Mikhail Yegorov, had already left the Soviet department to head up the Organized Crime Control Department of the Russian Federation.[10]) Ultimately, Gurov came full circle back to academe, becoming director of the Russian Institute of Security Problems in 1993.[11]

---

9. I'd spent a considerable amount of time with Chebotaryov from 1989 to 1999, and witnessed the respect with which friends and enemies alike addressed him. I spoke with numerous subordinates inside the MVD as well as Russians and foreigners who had interactions with him. For example, Thom Shanker, then of the *Chicago Tribune* and currently with *The New York Times*, interviewed Chebotaryov for his series called "Glasnost Gangsters" that ran in October and November 1991 in the *Chicago Tribune*. Shanker called Chebotaryov the most professional and impressive law enforcement official he'd met in his five years in the former Soviet Union (personal communication). Also, I was with Chebotaryov on several occasions when our paths crossed those of influential underworld figures. Their respect for him was obvious.

10. Mikhail Yegorov would become best known in the U.S. for his testimonies before U.S. Congressional committees on the threat level of Russian organized crime.

11. Handelman, p. 352, n5 (note 6).

It's tempting to dismiss this episode as too insignificant to matter. But consider all of the various versions that accumulate over time to create an understanding of Russia and the Russian 'mafia.' We end up with a picture that is skewed, the image a bit blurry, and, more important, our focus perhaps trained too closely on one phenomenon at the expense of others. Russian history in the 1990s can almost read 'All Mafia, All the Time.' While, of course, organized crime (as well as not-so-organized crime) played a large and important role on the Russian stage, media coverage of it helped to develop a reflex of blaming the 'mafia' for most of the negative things that occurred in the country (see Chapter 4 for more details).

It is the case with the study of Russian 'mafia,' organized crime, criminal groups, and crime in general that snapshots or strings of snapshots can dramatically influence how we look at that phenomenon as it developed after the dismantling of the Soviet Union. It's important to keep in mind that what we are dealing with, what we are investigating, are versions of situations, varying representations of reality. Writers, journalists, analysts, politicians, and academics may often portray a situation as if there is definitive knowledge. Some things can, of course, be known as fact. But how those facts are interpreted and strung together may vary greatly.

In addition to Handelman's book, we've seen abundant offerings of versions time after time with the release of each new book about Soviet and post-Soviet crime. These books—like Robert Friedman's *Red Mafiya*, Paul Klebnikov's *Godfather of the Kremlin*, Arkady Vaksberg's *The Soviet Mafia*, and many others—are interpretations driven by combinations of numerous factors. These factors include the authors' personal views of the world, the shape of their professional careers, the influence of their editors, whom they succeed in interviewing, and, perhaps above all, their personal experiences. There are many more factors that influence what gets written which we'll mention below. Bear in mind again, though, that all these accounts are merely versions of what may have occurred.

In 2000, *Forbes* journalist Paul Klebnikov wrote a book called *Godfather of the Kremlin: Boris Berezovsky and the Looting of Russia*.[12] The cover photo depicted a sinister-looking Berezovsky, cast in dramatic front lighting, an exaggerated shadow towering behind him. His sleazy countenance sealed the deal: this was evil incarnate.[13] How else could the Kremlin insider look, a so-called

---

12. See Paul Klebnikov, *Godfather of the Kremlin: Boris Berezovsky and the Looting of Russia*, New York, Harcourt, Inc., 2000.

13. Berezovsky had earlier been the focus of one of Klebnikov's *Forbes* articles called, "Is He the Godfather of the Kremlin?" December 30, 1996.

oligarch who allegedly rose to the commanding heights of Russian business on a pile of human bones? Berezovsky seemed straight out of central casting. For good measure, his name was printed on the cover in red, the color of danger. Beware of this character, it seemed to say. Read the cover and examine the photograph keeping in mind two things: 1) the publisher's primary interest is in selling books, and 2) in the Russia of that time there were more than a few major players in the game, Berezovsky was not the only one. To my mind, he didn't deserve to be the only crocodile singled out of the whole swamp.

Shortly after the book was published, Klebnikov called me requesting a lunch meeting. We got together at a Japanese restaurant on the Upper West Side of Manhattan, near his apartment. His problem was simple: Berezovsky was suing him and *Forbes* and Klebnikov needed help documenting what sources had told him in interviews. He had conducted interviews with police investigators, state security officials, and others, but apparently didn't collect sufficient documentation to corroborate fully what he had been told and basically wanted me to get it for him. It seemed at the time like a last-ditch effort on his part, trying to justify his approach to his publishers and the judge. Having been well versed in the Russian environment, he should have known that what he was asking was not going to happen.

In the course of our conversation, Klebnikov lamented the fact that Berezovsky had become so well known both internationally and domestically. I reminded Paul that he himself nearly single-handedly created Berezovsky's infamy, at least at the international level. Klebnikov's article in *Forbes*, "Is He the Godfather of the Kremlin?" predecessor to the book, was responsible for much of rise in Berezovsky's name recognition in the West. Paul fell into an awkward silence, seemingly wanting to get past the moment.

With a title as provocative as the one he chose, Paul's book should have been billed as a criminal investigation, not a piece of investigative journalism. While he claimed that "many of the key elements of this story are documented—from publicly available annual reports, registration documents, or investment banking analyses, to more closely held copies of contracts and boardroom minutes,"[14] apparently his documentation of events would not be enough to satisfy a London court. The simple fact is that his book rested in very large part on interviews and newspaper articles as reflected in his Notes (pp. 361–390).

Klebnikov's version made Berezovsky the central character in what was in reality a well-populated tragedy. After he enumerates a litany of activities and

---

14. Klebnikov, p. xii (note 12).

events swirling around Berezovsky—bankrupting companies, suspected in violent deaths, siphoning cash out of big companies, and others—I wonder who among the so-called oligarchs in Russia had not been involved in such activities. Assassinations here, 'accidental' deaths there ... and then Klebnikov's phrase that rings in my ears: "There is no evidence that Berezovsky was responsible for any of these deaths."[15] Accused, tried, and convicted in the court of investigative journalism without a fair trial.[16] If a high-ranking police official who was in a position to know had said to me in an interview that he believed Berezovsky was guilty of murder, it still wouldn't be enough to write about.

A year after the hardcover book was published the paperback version came out under a different name: *Godfather of the Kremlin: The Decline of Russia in the Age of Gangster Capitalism.* This time the cover was adorned with a photo of the Kremlin clock tower.

Here is the essential problem with media versions: often there is little solid evidence—in a legal sense—that journalists will get access to and that points conclusively to an individual and demonstrates his or her participation in certain acts, especially ones of a violent nature.

In the very first sentences of the very first paragraph of the Preface of his book, Klebnikov writes: "Whenever I met important Russians over the past decade I always taped our conversations. Unless otherwise noted, the assertions made in this book are based on tape-recorded interviews with the businessmen and politicians who ruled Russia in the 1990s."[17] I had to wonder why those two sentences must begin the book. Was it to suggest that since a tape recorder was running, capturing every word, the interviewee would have been more inclined to honesty? It brought me some comfort regarding the *accuracy* of what was said but didn't bring me any closer to believing what the speaker said. In fact, it took me further away, for a couple of reasons.

First, social scientists, journalists, and anyone else who has done interviewing with a tape recorder know that its mere presence changes the dy-

---

15. Ibid., p. 4.

16. Several years before meeting Paul I'd seen some of the contracts he was writing about. When it comes to 'proving' Berezovsky's guilt in these matters or in cases of physical violence and murder, if there's no physical evidence that has been recognized by the authorities and found credible by a court (i.e., conviction), there's no guilt. I'm no fan of Boris Berezovsky but until a court finds him guilty of specific charges, I'd just as soon leave him in the hands of law enforcement investigators and out of the versions about what he might have done. Berezovsky dropped his lawsuit in early 2003.

17. Klebnikov, p. xi (note 12).

namics of a discussion. Respondents are somewhat less natural, slightly more guarded, and engage in more self-censorship than would otherwise be the case. It inhibits conversation and promotes performance.

Second, anyone in Russia who was willing to be recorded on tape discussing with a journalist as sensitive a subject as the looting of Russia was very unlikely to have said anything in that meeting that they wouldn't have said elsewhere, didn't have anything of great value to say, or provided a partial or biased account. Information that had real consequences was a valuable and very tightly-guarded commodity in Russia. Let's say that our journalist managed to get ten extremely juicy interviews on tape, what then? It still was not 'evidence' of anything.[18]

The same holds for documents and reports. In a place where passports, diplomas, raincoats, laundry detergent, liquor, automobile parts, compact discs, and countless other products were forged, counterfeited, duplicated, and compromised, what was the value of documents and reports—as evidence—that had not undergone a forensic examination by an expert? The process of collecting documents and reports seemed by many to be the equivalent of having evidence. It may have been somewhat easier to substantiate claims if the documents were formal contracts, for example. But it must be said that many of the documents and reports that circulated were simply additional versions that didn't necessarily prove anything. This applied to law enforcement and government documents as well (or, perhaps, especially).

American journalists frequently used police intelligence documents, particularly those of the FBI, and attributed the information to a 'secret' or 'classified' report, without having identified it by its title. Part of the reason for doing this, certainly, was that the journalist didn't want to risk losing the contact in the FBI or other agency. At the same time, it helped journalists bring to their work a certain aura of access to hard-to-get information. The general effect was to lead the reader to conclude that they were reading something that was true.

In the case of the Russian 'mafia,' naturally a vast majority of the information in FBI documents came directly from Russian MVD sources. That's interesting since there was never a high degree of trust by Americans in Soviet

---

18. In that part of the world, the saying "A word spoken is a shot fired" is deeply ingrained in the psyche of the nation. For another example of a failure to make their case, see "Mafia Power Play," a 1999 *Frontline* documentary on Public Television in the U.S. Little evidence is offered to support the numerous declarations made about the relationships of NHL hockey players and the Russian 'mafia.' See Walter Goodman, "Television Review: Hockey Suspicions and Time Fantasies," *The New York Times*, October 12, 1999, p. E4.

statistics or information, so why should there be now? Likewise, there wasn't a particularly high degree of trust between the FBI and MVD.[19] In addition, it had been repeated countless times that Russian police were notoriously corrupt. But the information was used, added to intelligence reports, and the reports frequently ended up in the hands of journalists. For example, in his book, *Red Mafiya: How the Russian Mob Has Invaded America*, Robert Friedman frequently attributed information that formed the backbone of his version of the Russian 'mafia' in the United States to 'secret' or 'confidential' FBI reports. Unfortunately, he never provided the names or dates of the documents. Interestingly, I could identify much of the information as coming from specific FBI documents that I had obtained through non-law enforcement sources in Europe. I know one Russian investigator who was even able to buy a 'confidential' FBI document in Moscow for a couple of dollars.

These reports had their uses, of course. They were indicative of what the authorities were thinking, the directions they were pursuing. But even this didn't prove anything. All too often journalists and readers took the information in these reports to be gospel. Good journalists collected additional information to corroborate the intelligence information, but ultimately they were still only constructing versions. I'm not suggesting that such information was never right, merely pointing out the importance of collecting information from multiple sources and weighing them accordingly.

Here's a small example. In one case, our sources in the field reported back on specific questions we had posed during an investigation for a European company. Two of the sources, with different backgrounds and from different agencies, came to us with identical reports. They didn't simply contain the same information; they were exactly the same reports. The origin of the reports was the FSB, the successor of the KGB, and neither of the sources was an FSB agent. Nor did the sources know each other. Was it simply the case that the two investigators went to the same source for the information? Or was it that the KGB/FSB controlled all meaningful information about Russian companies, oligarchs, businessmen, and 'mafia'? If the latter, then the FSB had it within their reach to influence greatly how the world saw the Russian 'mafia.' Not unrelated, they also would have played a major role in determining who succeeded in business and who didn't.

As another illustration of the use of multiple sources, consider the following example. In the early 1990s, an article appeared in a major Russian news-

---

19. This is according to Russian police officials and FBI agents I've spoken with on this question in addition to first-hand experience.

paper about the death of a *vor v zakone*, or thief in law, an influential leader in the underworld. (For more on *vory v zakone*, see Chapter 7.) Buried deep in the article was mention of one individual, let's call him Evgeny, whose role reportedly was to assist *vory* in getting visas to travel abroad to settle in the United States and set up their criminal enterprises. The article indicated that Evgeny had done time in a Russian prison.

Two years later I received an FBI intelligence report from a professor in Europe. In it Evgeny was listed as a drug trafficker and it noted that he had connections with several *vory v zakone*. In 1997, his name came up again in relation to contracts he had signed with a high-ranking Russian government official for the delivery of goods to Russia from the United States. Part of the deal was that the goods Evgeny was selling were marked up nearly 100% and a bank account was opened overseas for the government official into which $150,000 was deposited. I had copies of the contracts and held meetings with Evgeny's business competition and with law enforcement to learn more about him. Several newspaper articles had featured Evgeny and his high-level contacts.

Two years later, in 1999, in the course of an investigation for a client, Evgeny's name came up again. It turned out that he had begun selling British widgets in Russia, acting as one of the British company's representatives. The British company was our client. I went to the Russian office of the British company and requested that the head of the office go for a walk with me. (It was generally assumed that the walls had ears in Russian buildings, especially in the offices of a foreign company.) We walked around the block while I gave the client a rundown about his representative. In this particular case, the client chose to ignore it and continued on with plans to have the president of the British company come to Russia to meet with Evgeny. As was usual in our investigations we didn't need to prove anything, but I felt comfortable that we had a pretty good idea of Evgeny's story.[20] When I met Evgeny face to face, he looked like an ordinary, upstanding businessman. In fact, as a representative for a major British company, he was already well on his way to becoming known as a businessman. Whether he abandoned his contacts in the underworld or the activities that he'd apparently been involved in for years was another question entirely.

---

20. In this case, it is wise not to supply the title of the newspaper article, its publication date, or the newspaper it appeared in. Likewise, the title of the FBI document will remain unnamed. The obvious reason is that 'Evgeny' is still an active player in the underworld, is powerful, wealthy, and has business interests on several continents. In addition, as in the Berezovsky case, he has not been found guilty of anything. In the case of the book *Red Mafiya*, Friedman spoke about specific individuals throughout his book. That is not my interest in the present book.

In another example of versions, in the June 1994 issue of *Atlantic Monthly*, veteran investigative reporter Seymour Hersh jumped on the global bandwagon saying the "criminal element in Russia is … hijacking the state.…" Hersh was writing about the theft and smuggling of nuclear material. Martin Morse Wooster offered an analysis of the Hersh piece saying, "Hersh cites no evidence that a Russian has sold nuclear material.… Nor does Hersh find any evidence that Russian mobsters have seized control of any major portions of the Russian economy."[21] Articles like Hersh's were usually based on the information of 'unnamed sources,' making it impossible to judge the qualifications of the speaker and difficult to weigh the value of the information. Hersh never defines what, exactly, a Russian 'mobster' might be. Wooster opines, "If a Russian mobster is someone who hires bodyguards, routinely pays protection money, and avoids taxes, then most of the honest entrepreneurs in Russia are mobsters. While the people they are paying protection money to are genuine mobsters, the honest businessmen still outnumber them."[22]

Again, my emphasis is not to insist that all of these assessments are wrong. Rather, I urge you to look at them with a critical eye, to determine what is missing, what additional information is necessary, and what the ability is of writers of articles or interviewees to know what they are claiming. How does he or she know that? Where did that information come from?

Let's consider the following example. In her review of Friedman's book, *Red Mafiya*, Johanna Granville states that Friedman "actually received death threats from at least two mafia bosses for his own exposés of their activities in the United States: Budapest-based Semion Mogilevich and Vyacheslav Ivankov from his prison cell."[23] She uses the word 'actually,' establishing that she has accepted Friedman's claims at face value. That word 'actually,' though, should give pause, raising one fundamental question: how does she know? In all likelihood she is in a position to know only what Friedman himself had written in his book. In the case of the Ivankov threat, Friedman received a threatening postcard supposedly signed by Ivankov who was believed by many to be a top Russian *vor v zakone*, an underworld godfather of sorts. If Ivankov were serious about having Friedman killed, is he likely to have telegraphed it? What evidence do we have that the postcard is actually from Ivankov? Why did Friedman think it was actually from Ivankov? We have to take claims like these

---

21. Martin Morse Wooster, "Russia's Roaring Twenties," *reasononline*, December 1994, at http://reason.com/9412/col.wooster.shtml.

22. Ibid.

23. Johanna Granville, "Crime that Pays: The Global Spread of the Russian Mafia," *Australian Journal of Politics and History*, vol. 49, no. 3, 2003, p. 451.

with a grain of salt, believing in the possibility that they are true but not jumping too quickly to accept them without question.

The second instance is that of Semion Mogilevich who reportedly put a $100,000 contract out on Friedman. This threat is somewhat more credible since, as Friedman reports, the FBI had warned him that the Mogilevich threat had been intercepted on an electronic wiretap. The Granville review all but accepted Friedman's reporting on the contract without question. I met with one of the FBI agents who was involved in that investigation. He knew first-hand about the telephone intercept and believed the threat, making it much more credible. But we're not done yet.

As we comb the mountains of documents, news reports, and other sources, we keep our eyes open for additional information. We find some, a brief commentary, in "Russian Organized Crime Exposé Doesn't Make Its Case," a review of Friedman's book by Roger Gathman.[24] Among other criticisms of Friedman's book, Gathman reminds us that the going rate for a contract murder was $2,000 in the Russian émigré community. Friedman himself had reported this in his book, Gathman says. If that were the case, why would Mogilevich, the so-called Brainy Don, offer $100,000 to have the job done? Again, it is possible, but Gathman's comment at least raises the possibility for doubt or alternative explanations. After going into hiding in Vermont for a brief time, Friedman decided that he wasn't going to run and returned to his apartment in New York City. On the one hand, if Mogilevich were serious, one would expect Friedman to be killed. On the other hand, perhaps Mogilevich knew that Friedman had suffered from a rare blood disease and would die in a relatively short time, and that the risk of murder wouldn't be worth it. Perhaps Mogilevich was just trying to scare the journalist and simultaneously enhance his reputation as a mobster. The point is that much of what we read and hear shouldn't be accepted at face value. Raise questions until an explanation with the ring of truth to it becomes evident.

Another example comes from the world of law enforcement. Of the many instances in which information about the strength and dangerousness of a criminal organization was accepted without question, the story of the rise of the Chechens was received in one neat package and disseminated by Russian and Western media and academia. The closest thing to a challenge I've been able to find is the following: "There are legends about the Chechen mafia in Moscow. In short, few people have any real understanding about those groups

---

24. Roger Gathman, "Russian Organized Crime Exposé Doesn't Make Its Case," *APB-news.com*, May 22, 2000, at http://www.apbnews.com/media/reviews/books/2000/05/22/red0522_01.html.

which are united in the consciousness of Russians under this widely used catchphrase."[25]

Those legends about the Chechen mafia were the result of a couple of factors. First, for centuries the Chechens had been the on-again off-again enemy of Russia and the Soviet Union. Various Tsars attempted to bring them to heel during the formation of the empire. Stalin punished them, along with other ethnic groups in the region, for collaborating with the Nazis during World War II, uprooting the entire population and shipping them in cattle cars to Siberia and Central Asia. As the Soviet Union weakened, they once again became convenient targets for discrimination in the capital and other cities. Some people, including MVD officers, parroted the popular notions of the late 1980s and early 1990s that the Chechens were to blame for much of the country's crime problem, which was a ridiculous claim.[26] Once the Chechens made it known that they wanted to secede from the Russian Federation, they became public enemy number one. By the end of 1994, Russia attacked Chechnya, a struggle that has continued in one form or other until today.

The second factor, and more important for our purposes, is that the vast majority of reporting on the development of the so-called Chechen mafia in Moscow derived from a single report produced in 1991 by the MVD. Called "The History of the Appearance and Development of the Criminal Organization 'Chechen Community in Moscow,'" the report laid out in very neat terms the rise of three Chechen organized crime groups in Moscow. The main point here is that the information in that report was lifted virtually verbatim by Russian journalists and repeated by journalists and academics around the world. At no time does any journalistic or academic account repeating the MVD's details question the veracity of the information or indicate that they have even attempted to corroborate the information.[27]

---

25. "Chechenskaya OPG v Moskve," *FreeLance Bureau*, http://www.flb.ru/bd0006-01.html.

26. Author conversations with MVD officers.

27. The MVD report on the Chechens was called "Istoriya Vozniknoveniya i Razvitiya Prestupnoi Organizatsii 'Chechenskaya Obshchina v Moskve,'" prepared in 1991. For an account of the three Chechen organized crime groups that derived from that report, see Guy Dunn, "Major Mafia Groups in Russia," in Phil Williams (ed.), *Russian Organized Crime: The New Threat?* London, Frank Cass & Co., Ltd., 1997. Dunn's account was cited in James O. Finckenauer and Elin J. Waring, *Russian Mafia in America: Immigration, Culture, and Crime*, Boston, Northeastern University Press, 1998, p. 123. Finckenauer and Waring do make the point that great care must be used in the handling of Russian law enforcement information, see p. 129. See also "Chechenskogo Cherta Maliuiut Strashnee Vsekh," in *Kommersant Daily*, February 4, 1995, p. 20. Material from the *Kommersant Daily*

It should be kept in mind when considering this material that the Chechens and other ethnic groups in the Russian Federation are exceedingly difficult to penetrate. They close ranks when necessary. They speak languages that bear no resemblance to Russian, which makes monitoring them problematic.

I eventually came upon Alex Soldatov, the MVD official who ran the anti-Chechen unit in the Organized Crime Control Department. He told me that it was very difficult to tell how large the Chechen criminal community was and who were its members. The group took advantage of their homeland as a kind of black hole, a safe haven, he said. "It was impossible to track them because there would always be somebody new who'd come up from Grozny [the Chechen capital], participate in a job, and head back to Grozny. Once they were down there, we couldn't get to them. Many times they were juveniles used for a single job. We couldn't tell who was who."[28]

In 1993, I received a phone call from a friend who had been in law enforcement in the United States. He asked me to meet him at a rundown bar in a dying town outside Philadelphia. In the dimly lit place he passed me a file that contained what looked to be an organizational chart. By this time I had already developed a reflex about organizational charts and crime, especially crime in the former Soviet Union. Charts had a way of bringing too much order to what were frequently tenuous relationships. I'd come to believe that, at least in part, charts were tools for law enforcement to try to make sense of relationships, but were not necessarily accurate representations of reality.

I remembered a conversation I'd had with Joel Campanella, formerly of the NYPD and U.S. Customs. Joel had been investigating the Soviets in New York in the early 1980s. He told me how he approached his supervisor about the growing crime activity of the Soviets—the 'Russian mob'—in New York. His supervisor's response was, "Show me the structure." Joel realized that he wasn't going to be able to persuade his leadership of the real threat. He understood early on that there wouldn't be an expansive structure including hundreds of people, there wouldn't be the equivalent of the five Italian 'mafia' families in New York. Apparently, the supervisor thought that no traditional structure meant there was no problem. End of discussion.

Around 1993–94 in Russia there weren't large, sprawling, intricate structures of organized crime syndicates or a commission that ran the crime world across the country. So when I saw the intricate organizational chart that afternoon in Philadelphia, my experience told me to take it with a grain of salt.

---

article was also cited in Federico Varese, *The Russian Mafia: Private Protection in a New Market Economy*, Oxford, Oxford University Press, 2001, p. 178.

28. My conversations with Alex Soldatov took place in April 1995.

The heading on the chart was 'Chechen Mafia.' In some ways the chart was of limited value almost immediately. My friend couldn't tell me where it had come from or how the information had been collected. I knew that he had received it at a law enforcement conference in Canada, and I could surmise that it originated either with the FBI, the NYPD, the Royal Canadian Mounted Police, or perhaps a joint task force. Topping the structure was the leadership called 'Five Godfathers,' four of whom were based in Moscow and one in the Chechen capital, Grozny. Next there were four different cells identified geographically: two in the United States, one in Germany, and one in Saudi Arabia. Each was believed to have fifty gang members.

Fanning out around this basic structure was a hodgepodge of individuals and companies believed to be involved in criminal activity. I noticed three main things on the chart immediately. First, it was a fairly detailed account; each box contained a name, sometimes an address, current disposition, sometimes an arrest date, company name, and so on. Second, there were familiar names in the chart, people that could never conceivably have been 'members' of the 'Chechen Mafia.' At best, some of these people may have done business with Chechen groups, but nothing more than that. In their book, *Russian Mafia in America*, James Finckenauer and Elin Waring note that "two major criminal organizations made up of ethnic Russians—Solntsevskaya and Podolskaya—are in constant conflict with the Chechens."[29] Interestingly, though, one of the names in the Chechen chart was a very well known influential individual with roots in the Solntsevskaya group.

The third thing was that the three main individuals who served as links between the executive level and the forty individuals and companies mentioned above were listed as having been killed in 1992. There was no way to know what had become of the relationships among the people and entities after those murders. And yet, the chart had been circulated at a law enforcement conference as depicting the 'Chechen Mafia.'

At around the same time, a brief intelligence report attributed to the FBI's New York office, dated March 2, 1993, said the following about the Chechens:

> CHECHENIANS—individuals from the Republic of Chechen-Ingush on the Caspian Sea. In Moscow the CHECHENIANS control prostitution, extortion of persons from the shadow economy. Were Enforcers for the Russian Exiles in Germany, until they realized the amount of money to be made. Currently working for themselves. Involved in the smuggling of Opium and Hashish from the FSU.

---

29. Finckenauer and Waring, p. 124 (note 27).

Besides the fact that the Chechen-Ingush Republic is not located on the Caspian Sea, statements about a single group 'controlling' a criminal enterprise, like prostitution or extortion, always made me uneasy. Chechens controlling prostitution in Moscow? No way. Chechens running some of the prostitution in Moscow? Easier to believe.[30] Reading the document, I now understood that the 'Chechen Mafia' chart mentioned above had been attached to it, increasing the odds that the chart had originated with the FBI. The analysts working this situation gave the Chechens a sense of organization that they may or may not have had.

There was no information regarding actual proof of guilt of a crime, no documentation about the activities of these people. The problem is not that law enforcement agencies have such documents. They're a necessary part of the job. Our concern here is the dissemination of the information. Do the journalists that gain access to this information have histories of specific bank account transactions, bills of lading, invoices, lists of beneficial owners of companies? Have they dug into the background of the companies to find out if the name of the owner is the person making the decisions? It's easy to construct a picture of the Russian 'mafia' as a monolithic monster, particularly if putting together the interconnections into a single organization. Speaking about the attitude of the newspaper business in producing these stories, *Kommersant* journalist Svinarenko notes that "*Kommersant* is only writing about what sells. These Chechens and Ingush are the most popular heroes of our publication. I don't choose it. I only take the most interesting cases. It's not my fault that the most interesting cases involve the Ingush and the Chechens."[31]

---

30. Just as the FBI asserted that it was the Chechens who controlled prostitution, Layard and Parker claimed it was the Lyubertsy. "As with most other aspects of life in the Soviet Union, the underworld was planned, organized, and cartelized, with one group having a monopoly on one form of criminal activity, and other groups. In Moscow, for example, there were about twenty big gangs. The Lyubertsy ran prostitution; the Dolgoprudny controlled big protection rackets; the Ingush gangs controlled smuggling; the Azeris ran drugs. In addition to this professional specialization, there were also regional monopolies, usually for smaller-scale protection racketeers. The city was divided into some dozen regions, each controlled and coexisting in a symbiotic relationship with the bosses of the Communist Party." (Richard Layard and John Parker, *The Coming Russian Boom*, New York, The Free Press, 1996, p. 159).

31. *Insight*, August 26, 1991, p. 17. Or take, for example, the comment of Guy Browning writing in his column for the British newspaper, *The Guardian*: "Most of what you read in newspapers is exaggeration. In fact, it's surprising there isn't a paper called The Exaggerator.... Exaggeration is a lot like inflation, in that it erodes the value and credibility of what you had in the first place," quoted in Michael R. LeGault. *Think: Why Crucial Decisions Can't Be Made in the Blink of an Eye*, New York, Threshold Editions, 2006, p. 152.

In a July 2003 posting on Johnson's Russia List, a daily compilation of news stories, reports, and commentaries on Russia and the former Soviet Union, veteran journalist Gideon Lichfield sums up the problem of marshaling evidence and grappling with versions:

> You sit down with your various versions to construct the definitive, analytical, weighed, and balanced account of what really happened. But a strange thing occurs. Again, the story becomes like the quantum superposition state: once you start analysing it, it dissolves in your fingers. You cannot make all the bits and pieces quite fit together. What's more, you don't have the evidence to prove three-quarters of the things you think you now know. And indeed, if you think about them hard enough you realise you don't know them at all; some of your so-called facts are themselves just interpretations....[32]

I suspect that Lichfield captures at least some of the frustration that Paul Klebnikov and countless other journalists and analysts had experienced when encountering Russia. One of the primary difficulties of working in that environment was that the ground was constantly shifting under one's feet. A criminal yesterday was a businessman today. What was illegal yesterday was now legal today.

Alexander Gorkin, a former detective in the Criminal Investigation Department of the Moscow City Police, always began an investigation with one of the key questions at the front of his mind: Who benefits? In the midst of all this version building—in the 'creation of criminal Russia' as Tawnia Sanford calls it[33]—we can pose the same question. Who benefited from a powerful Russian 'mafia'? Some Russian government officials benefited from the existence of the mafia as a diversion while the officials were looting the state. Some Russian officials benefited by getting crime groups to do their bidding for them. The U.S. government benefited from the rise of a new, post-Soviet enemy to replace the old enemy. The print and broadcast media could file sexy stories as a way to attract eyes to their products; advertisers in print and broadcast media benefited in the same way. Law enforcement and intelligence agencies, both Russian and foreign, could justify increases in annual budgets. Criminals benefited by having a potential pool of victims that had already been

---

32. Gideon Lichfield, "How a Journalist Gets at the Truth," Johnson's Russia List, July 13, 2003.

33. Tawnia Sanford, "The Creation of Criminal Russia," *Canadian-Slavonic Papers*, Sept–Dec 1999, at http://www.findarticles.com/p/articles/mi_qa3763/is_199909/ai_n8864829/print.

prepped by the media to cooperate ... or else. Security companies operating in Russia used the 'mafia' threat to attract new clients. Journalists who made their careers on the backs of the 'mafia' benefited as well as academics and analysts who had written countless articles about the 'mafia.' And, quite frankly, I benefited by having been gainfully employed in Moscow and by being able to write this book. Ultimately, we the consumers play a large role in driving the demand for entertainment, including 'mafia' stories. Of course, it's far more complicated than this, but the point is that there were many people and organizations poised to capitalize on the threat, having little interest in undermining it or questioning it.

> A kind and peaceful enemy is not a good enemy. Evil and dangerous is what the enemy ought to be. And strong. Sufficiently strong to give honour and homage to the hero home from war. But not so strong that the hero is not returning. The pictures of the enemy are important elements in the preparation for war. Concepts with high use-value in our connection are such as 'mafia' and 'organized crime.' Their exceptional lack of precision makes them useful as slogans for most types of evil forces. They are useful words in a war fought by a suitable weakened state.[34]

A prime example of a 'mafia' godfather whose existence, according to Scott Anderson, benefited many is Vyacheslav Ivankov, also known as 'Yaponchik.' "Ivankov was a mafia godfather because it served everyone's interest that he be one. It gave the media a frame, a way to personalize stories about a complex issue. It gave the FBI a symbol to take down, a tool with which to convince the Russian émigré community that justice would prevail."[35] Not surprisingly, Ivankov essentially agreed with that assessment. Finckenauer and Waring report,

> In a recent interview from prison, Yaponchik accuses the FBI of feeding the myth of a Russian Mafia to prove the usefulness of their Russian section. They are, he says, 'only tilting with windmills.' According to Yaponchik, there is no myth about organized crime in Russia because everyone knows that 'Russia is one uninterrupted criminal swamp.' The criminals are in the Kremlin and the Duma (the legisla-

---

34. Nils Christie, *A Suitable Amount of Crime*, London, Routledge, 2004, p. 40.
35. Scott Anderson, "Looking for Mr. Yaponchik," *Harper's*, 291/1747, December 1995, pp. 40–51.

ture), and anyone who thinks that someone like him is the head of all these 'bandits' is delirious.[36]

We might reject Ivankov's comments out of hand as self-interested. After all, he really was a dangerous criminal, according to courts in both the Soviet Union and the United States. But it's difficult to disagree with his assessment that "Russia is one uninterrupted criminal swamp," which brings us back to where we started in Chapter 1. Who was the meaningful 'mafia' in the former Soviet Union? The Communist Party? Traditional criminals? Was 'mafia' best understood as groups or as methods? Was it conceivable that Ivankov, as a single individual up against the power of the Communist Party during the Soviet period, could have been the all-powerful leader of the Soviet underworld? Who benefited from his existence back then in what was commonly called a 'police state'? Who benefited from his early release from Soviet prison? He left Russia shortly after the USSR disappeared and the major publicized crime he committed and was convicted of in the U.S. was extortion in the amount of about $3.5 million. It doesn't seem like much of a crime résumé when compared with the crimes committed by Soviet officials against their own people. As I've said from the outset, this book is not an effort to negate the existence of crime in Russia or to mitigate the harm that has been done by criminal organizations there. It is an attempt to consider alternatives to popularly accepted versions.

When it comes to media, a close examination of headlines and stories is telling. In one article, for example, the headline in bold typeface read: "Extortions a Fact of Business Life in Moscow."[37] The August 1994 article was published at what seemed to have been the height of the extortion phenomenon in Russia. (The most often cited report on extortion in Russia had been released earlier that year and the statistics cited in it appeared in every kind of publication around the world. See Chapter 4 for more details.) Interestingly, the article dealt more with the *fear* of extortion and the need for security to counter the approaches by crime groups. While the headline led one to believe that there were no alternatives to succumbing to extortion attempts, the article itself carried a different message. Speaking about the experiences of a Moscow restaurant, the article says, "The restaurant handles the problem in the same way as many other businesses faced with a criminal 'shakedown': they ask their own security guards to see them off." It went on to say that "busi-

---

36. Finckenauer and Waring, p. 114 (note 27).
37. Adam Tanner, "Extortions a Fact of Business Life in Moscow," *The Moscow Times*, August 26, 1994, p. 3.

nesses preempt the threat of so-called mafia problems by hiring their own guards from the day they open shop. 'When they know you have security, they do not come by.'" Toward the end of the article, the author conceded that "despite the threat of criminal extortion, many businesses and experts say that some have exaggerated the danger."

Another dramatic headline contributed to the image of Moscow and Russia during this period: "Prostitutes Drug, Rob Clients, Doctors Say."[38] "Russian and Western health officials say that Moscow prostitutes are slipping a dangerous blood pressure drug into clients' drinks to knock them out and steal their valuables." The American Medical Center, the main medical facility for foreigners in Moscow, reported having seen 10 poisoning victims in a 3-year period. There were likely more cases in that time frame; still, the number reported was hardly alarming and didn't seem in proportion to the attention given by the media. In a city of 15 million people and thousands of foreigners, the hue and cry in this case didn't seem warranted.

Headline writers played as great if not greater a role than the journalists themselves on occasion. Their job was to attract the eye, get the reader to look at the article. In one story printed in *The Moscow Times*, for example, the headline read, "Petersburg Mafia Targets Foreigners."[39] The article opened up with a dramatic hook. "Criminals in St. Petersburg are better armed, better organized and more arrogant than ever before. For the first time, many of them are targeting foreigners for violent attacks." It then gave an account over the next six paragraphs of the apparent burglary of a British businessman's hotel room. Emerging from the shower, the businessman answered his hotel room door at 8 a.m. A man standing there held out a candy bar. The baffled businessman accepted it and returned to the bathroom to dry off after his shower. Having finished in the bathroom, he found that his briefcase containing $15,000, 6 million rubles, plane tickets, credit cards, and contracts from business deals had been stolen. This was unfortunate for the businessman, but not quite 'mafia' material. Not surprisingly, articles with headlines like "Local Bankers Claim They Don't Feel Threatened by the Mafia" didn't get a lot of attention.

Then there were headlines like "Russian Mafias Replace Soviet Thieves with Evil Criminals." Is there a suggestion here that Soviet thieves were not evil? In the piece, author Venora Bennett claimed that "there was honor among thieves

---

38. Stacey Anderson, "Prostitutes Drug, Rob Clients, Doctors Say," *The Moscow Times*, March 19, 1994, p. 3.

39. Matt Bivens, "Petersburg Mafia Targets Foreigners," *The Moscow Times*, April 19, 1994, p. 4.

in the Soviet Union. But the superpower's collapse has destroyed its underworld hierarchy, as savage new criminals kill off the one-time Politburo of crime."[40] There seemed to be little evidence to back up the claim of honor among thieves, which we'll examine in more detail in Chapter 7.[41]

Think about the various layers of interpretation being introduced in the creation of a story, the different interests and agendas—personal and professional—that were being served by the Russian 'mafia' story. There was the journalist on the ground that may or may not have had solid knowledge of Russian language or the country. There was the interpreter whom the journalist was likely relying on for a portrayal of the scene. There was the editor back home that had never been to Russia but needed to sell newspapers. There was the headline writer who had to grab the reader's eye. What was the stake of the people being interviewed? What was their stake in portraying the country a certain way? Consumers of information had their own interpretations of what was happening or, more likely, didn't know what to think and were left to rely on media for all of their information. How readily did we cast aside or at the very least hold in suspension our own beliefs that define us as individuals, a community, or a nation, to consider a perspective that didn't accord with the way we see things? The differences in meanings and concepts behind the words further complicated the situation as we saw in Chapter 1. Words like 'mafia,' 'police,' 'law,' 'democracy,' and many others had their own peculiarities on the backdrop of Russian and Soviet history.

None of this is to say that 'journalists are bad.' The larger point is to appreciate the complexity of a phenomenon such as the Russian 'mafia' and to realize that journalists were presenting merely the first draft of history. And they did so largely by telling stories. That is, "constructing narratives is what the press does, and by necessity reporters often simplify the story for the sake of time and style. But to parrot a facile storyline when the issue is obviously more complicated does the reader—and history—a disservice."[42]

The first series on Soviet organized crime, which appeared in the *Chicago Tribune* in October and November 1991, was a good example of balancing the

---

40. Venora Bennett, "Russian Mafias Replace Soviet 'Thieves' with Evil Criminals," *The Moscow Tribune*, November 18, 1994, p. 6.

41. Interestingly, *The Times* carried the headline, "Shocking Crime in Russia," on October 4. The only real difference from the other headlines cited above is that the year was 1867. Or see "Crime in Soviet Russia: Recent Big Increase," from *The Times* on January 6, 1926.

42. Paul McLeary, "Stubbornly Clinging to 'Stubborn' Storyline," *CJR Daily*, October 28, 2005, at http://www.cjrdaily.org/politics/stubbornly_clinging_to_stubbor.php.

forces at work on a journalist with the need to tell a good story in a way digestible by the readers. The author, Thom Shanker, interviewed organized crime figures, victims, and Soviet police officials, putting a face on an otherwise anonymous problem. Shanker brought five years of in-country experience, knowledge of Russian, a keen intellect, and an understanding of the connections between organized crime at the street level and that found at higher social and political levels to his series, making it one of the best-informed accounts. And he interviewed people who hadn't been interviewed before. Many journalists wrote about the Russian 'mafia' typically missing one or more of these important pillars.

The former Soviet Union—with its difficult language, xenophobic tendencies, and misunderstanding of the West—has always been a tough place for a foreigner to gain access. In many cases, journalists were casting their lines into the same waters, interviewing the same people, and hearing the same stories. As Lydia Rosner put it, "Round and round they went. The same reporters, speaking to the same sources, validated the other's conceptual framework of Russian crime and its 'mafia' connections."[43]

The engine driving crime stories was the mutual need for all parties to get exposure. This was an extension of the question raised several pages ago: Who benefits? 'Exposure' was the answer to the question of how they benefit. The producers needed to fill time. The journalists needed to get air time or column inches. Law enforcement, like any bureaucratic entity, needed to justify its existence. Politicians had to demonstrate to their constituents that they were effective leaders and were leading the charge against a perceived threat. Writers had to sell books, companies their products. Scholars who were interviewed got to demonstrate their expertise and translate that into value to their institutions as they fought for tenure or extensions on consulting contracts. They all needed exposure.

Journalists on the front lines of an issue faced numerous challenges and competing interests in the course of getting a story into print or on the air

---

43. Lydia S. Rosner, "The Sexy Russian Mafia," *Criminal Organizations*, Fall 1995, p. 30. This was not an issue only during the post-Soviet period regarding the Russian 'mafia.' A quick survey of books written in the 1970s and 1980s shows that by and large journalists interviewed the same set of dissidents and the same set of officials. As Matthew Robinson notes, "An alarming realization is that the media tend to cover the same crime repeatedly as it processes through the criminal justice network. With any recent development in a case, the details of the original crime are rehashed, fostering an impression that the crime occurred more than once.... The effect is a general feeling that there is much more crime out there than there really is." *Justice Blind? Ideals and Realities of American Criminal Justice*, Upper Saddle River, New Jersey, Pearson Prentice Hall, 2005, p. 119.

waves. As mentioned above, first and foremost the name of the game was getting air time or column inches. With an ever-expanding number of television channels, the job of the company was to get the viewer to stop on their channel. In order to do that, the stories broadcast had to be attractive, appealing, eye-catching, and, in many cases, have something of a sensational spin to them.[44]

At a party in Moscow one evening, several of us were speaking with a well-known U.S. reporter based in Russia. He explained that the competition he faced came not only from his external competitors but internally as well. Everyone was fighting for exposure.

> In a typical broadcast I have about two, maybe three minutes to tell a story. I'm competing with other reporters from London, Paris, Los Angeles, and all over the world for that same two-minute slot. And that's just the competition within my own network. So in order to increase my chances of getting on the air, I have to find a story that's attractive, that people are going to care about, and I have to put it together in such a way that will make it sexy.

Competition between networks was natural enough but it was easy for the outside observer to overlook internal competition as a motivating factor. Each of the network news programs, for example, had stations all over the world which meant that even before they got to compete with their market competition they had to catch the eye and imagination of their own producers. An added layer of complication was that they were vying for the attention of executives back at headquarters in, say, New York or London, who may not have had Russia as a priority or may not have thought it was 'sexy' enough for their viewers.

Another issue was the nature of people who get into the information business. They're competitive and love the thrill of the chase and scooping the competition. In an article for *National Journal*, William Powers notes, "An old-timer at *The Washington Post* once told me that if he didn't have a byline roughly every other day, he'd get a knot in his stomach, and it wouldn't go away until he scored another story."[45] David Krajicek worked the crime beat

---

44. There is the additional complicating factor regarding media in Russia: newspaper editors frequently decide which stories to print based on the amount of money that passes hands. See Alla Startseva, "Russian Journalism's Dirty Little Secret," *The Moscow Times.com*, June 9, 2001.

45. William Powers, "The First Shall Be Last," *National Journal*, November 4, 2005, at http://nationaljournal.com/scripts/printpage.cgi?/powers.htm.

for years and notes that "the peer culture among journalists is as intense as that at any junior high school. Reporters and editors look to one another— both colleagues and competitors—to determine what is appropriate. If everyone else is doing it, that deserves an affirmation."[46]

The need to get the story—especially one with a sexy edge—could encourage journalists to lose their sense of perspective. When a U.S. network news producer learned that I had gotten a film crew inside Russian prisons, she excitedly asked me to do the same for her, adding, "I want grim, grim, grim."[47] Apparently she didn't appreciate that pointing a camera in any direction in a Russian prison would produce 'grim' on its own; there was no need to orchestrate.

In one of the more interesting and dismaying examples, a well-known American investigative journalist strolled into Moscow in preparation for his journey to Siberia to investigate 'mafia' activities. Meeting him, I thought I had detected a crack in his bravado prior to his departure but brushed it aside, reminding myself that this was a big-time investigative reporter. After the trip the journalist returned to his chic New York lifestyle, his occasional television appearances, and his seven-figure income. The only problem was, as his interpreter informed me, the writer was so scared that he refused to leave his hotel room in Siberia. That didn't stop him from filing a sexy story on the 'mafia' for his magazine, which graced newsstands across the country.

There were countless other forces at work on journalists in the field. Consider the following enumeration of just a few of the additional factors: frequent rotation and relatively short-term assignments; herd mentality; flagrant careerism; pressures from senior editors; tight deadlines; high pressure; Russia as first posting; overriding need to satisfy corporate headquarters; the need to produce entertainment; lack of resources; little language ability, and generally not knowledgeable of crime and criminology.

Dale Herspring, a former diplomat in Moscow and an academic who has dealt with journalists, sums up this aspect of the information process.

> Most [journalists] work their butts off with deadlines in the middle
> of the night and editors who always want something difficult if not
> impossible—and they want it yesterday. On the other hand, like

---

46. David Krajicek, *Scooped! Media Miss Real Story on Crime While Chasing Sex, Sleaze, and Celebrities*, New York, Columbia University Press, 1998, p. 35.

47. The producer had learned that I was part of a team that filmed inside Russian prisons for a documentary for "Investigative Reports" on A&E. As soon as I heard her desire for 'grim,' I decided not to work with her. She already had her mind made in advance about what she wanted to depict.

many diplomats sent to Moscow, few of them know Russian or Russia. They are simply dropped into the country and told to become an expert. The result is that their knowledge of what is happening is uneven and they often get close to this or that local (usually the elite) which has its own ax to grind.[48]

For example, what do we make of the journalist from a major newspaper who was reporting on one of the 'oligarchs' and also sleeping with him?

In the early 1990s, there were reports of gunshots often shattering the evening quiet. I heard the sounds on occasion from my apartment. In the newspapers Russian officials attributed it to fireworks. Of course, such an explanation was not to be believed. One day while walking in Moscow I heard the same sound just around the bend. When I turned the corner of the building I saw a couple of kids setting off fireworks. On another day in Moscow an explosion shook the building I was in. Around the corner a car bomb had gone off, shredding a Mercedes and reportedly incinerating a top crime boss. Sometimes fireworks were just fireworks and sometimes not.

One foreign businessman concluded that the media had blown the crime monster entirely out of proportion. "Organized crime here has been highly over-emphasized in the press. I don't think Moscow is any different from any other big, urban center. I don't feel any different than I do in New York."[49]

The point of this chapter was to begin to generate an appreciation for the complexity of the Russian 'mafia' issue in terms of processing information. As I mentioned earlier, in providing a contextual framework the intention is not to deny the existence of danger in Russia in the 1990s, but merely to appreciate the forces at work that helped shape the essence of the danger. To borrow David Krajicek's phrase, the majority of crime coverage can be depicted as "drive-by journalism—a ton of anecdote and graphic detail about individual cases ... but not an ounce of leavening context to help frame and explain crime."[50] The work of journalists is one of the major forces that influence how we see the world around us. Those working in journalism decide what is important enough for the public to know about. And we should at least have a general understanding of how they function.

---

48. Dale Herspring, Johnson's Russia List, November 30, 2005.

49. Natasha Mileusnic, "U.S. Security Firm Joins War on Crime," *The Moscow Times*, April 7, 1995, p. 10.

50. Krajicek, p. 7 (note 46).

CHAPTER 4

STATISTICS

More statistics. They are all about you in your life. They explain something here, offer a more or less convincing excuse there, rouse you to dreaming—to enthusiasm, perhaps—elsewhere. Now they lure you on, now they hold you back. It is hard to guess at such things, but it is possible you might miss statistics if they were abolished from the Soviet scene. They are like an old friend who is somewhat disreputable, but you have become used to him. You do not mind so much that he is something of a liar now and then. You have become used to that, too.

—Leonid Vladimirov[1]

As they say, there are white lies, black lies, and statistics. It would be impossible to dream up a bigger lie than Soviet statistics.

—Unknown

After the breakup of the Soviet Union in December 1991, the reputation of the Russian 'mafia' as an external force, 'penetrating' and 'invading,' grew by leaps and bounds. During the so-called Great Mob War of 1992–94,[2] the reported number of crime groups nearly doubled. Armed clashes between criminal groups seemed a daily occurrence as the struggle for territory shifted into overdrive.

Throughout this period, hundreds of entrepreneurs were gunned down, stabbed, or blown up. In 1992, the MVD recorded 100 contract murders, a number that increased two-and-a-half times the following year. In 1993, more than ninety bankers and entrepreneurs were killed 'gangland style.' By 1994, *nayomnye ubiistva*, or contract murders, had reportedly reached 500, claiming at least thirty-five more bankers and even some of Moscow's alleged crime bosses.[3]

---

1. Leonid Vladimirov, *The Russians*, New York, Frederick A. Praeger, 1968, p. 30.
2. See Paul Klebnikov, *Godfather of the Kremlin: Boris Berezovsky and the Looting of Russia*, New York, Harcourt, Inc., p. 21, for references to the 'Great Mob War.'
3. See *Rossiiskaya Gazeta*, "Murders for Hire are Becoming an Industry," May 13, 1994,

With newspapers to sell and eyeballs to attract to television screens, the media ratcheted up its coverage of the tension in the criminal world. Screaming headlines like "Mafia's Attempts to Establish Control Over Major Banks Pose Threat to Russia's Economy," "Mafia Threatens Economic Takeover," and "Mafia's New Order," instructed us how to think about the times we were living in.[4] The typical practice of both Russian and international media as well as academia and policy makers was to provide neat summarizing statements of the situation, such as the following:

- "Many Russian bankers have been killed in apparent criminal efforts to seize control of commercial banks; city and regional officials have been assassinated...."[5]
- "At least 35 Russian bankers were murdered over the past year [1994], and many banks have assembled their own security forces, made up mostly of former KGB officers, who provide protection for banks and bank employees."[6]
- "In 1993, ninety-four entrepreneurs were murdered, presumably in connection with extortion at the hands of organized crime."[7]
- "Assassins have targeted hotel bosses, restaurateurs, sports figures, businessmen, politicians, journalists and Afghan war veterans."[8]

Most stories were similar to those excerpted above, consisting of just a few basic components. First, 'bankers' and 'businessmen' were being killed. Second, gangsters, organized crime, and 'mafia' were killing them. Third, the

---

interview with then Minister of Internal Affairs, Viktor Yerin; Nikolai Modestov, "Russia: Contract Murders Increase 10-Fold in 5 Years," interview with Major General Leonid Vtyurin, Deputy Chief of the Main Criminal Investigation Department of the MVD, quoted in FBIS-SOV-96-138-S, July 17, 1996; *Moskovskiye Novosti*, "Russia: Rising Professionalism of Killers Noted," interview with crime expert Mikhail Slinko, in FBIS-SOV-96-044-S, March 5, 1996; Yegor Shemetov, "Nayomniki," *Sevodnya*, date unknown; Matt Taibbi, "Grim Catalog of Banker Slayings," *The Moscow Times*, August 17, 1995.

4. The first headline is from *Izvestia*, July 24, 1993, p. 4; the second is from *Moscow News*, date unknown; the third is from *Stolichny Kriminal*, no. 2, 1993, p. 1. See also Sarah Koenig, "True Crime, All Too True, on TV," *The New York Times*, July 24, 1997, p. C11.

5. Congressional Research Service Report for Congress, "Crime in Russia: Context and Implications for U.S. Interests," September 9, 1994, p. 1.

6. Bill Gertz, "Most of Russia's Biggest Banks Linked to Mob, CIA Report Says," *Washington Times*, December 5, 1994.

7. In Thomas C. Owen, *Russian Corporate Capitalism from Peter the Great to Perestroika*, New York, Oxford University Press, 1995, p. 154.

8. *BBC Online Network*, "The Rise and Rise of the Russian Mafia," November 21, 1998, at http://news6.thdo.bbc.co.uk/hi/english/special_report

stated or implied reason for the killing was to get 'control.' Fourth, extortion was the most common approach, and when targets resisted, they got dead.

It's not that the facts were totally wrong, but the cumulative effect of these stories was to reinforce the impression that the 'mafia' was the new Mongol horde, an unmatchable, omnipotent, invading force—simply put, 'the bad guys.' Their targets were 'bankers' and 'businessmen'—words that in the West, for the most part, indicated 'the good guys.' It was presented in fairly black and white terms, making it easy to know which side to take.

Just in case there was any uncertainty about what was occurring, the CIA issued a 'secret' report ... that just happened to be quoted in the media. Post-Soviet crime groups, it said, were engaged in "a fierce campaign to penetrate Russia's banking sector." According to James Woolsey, former director of the CIA, crime groups in Russia were using bribery, kidnapping, and murder to gain control over many of Russia's 1,800 banks.[9] The enemy had been identified. The CIA also concluded that "more than half of Russia's 25 largest banks are linked to Russian organized crime groups or involved in other illicit financial activities."[10] This was one of those typical statements that, on its own, said almost nothing at all, particularly in the post-Soviet context. Were banks being targeted and overrun or not? A "link" sounded far less nefarious, if no less ambiguous, than "control." But the basic questions remained. What was the nature of the link? Were the banks and the gangsters working together? And to talk about "illicit financial activities" in a country where 'normal' financial transactions had been illegal for decades and tax evasion and other machinations were a prerequisite for commercial survival was patently absurd.

Of course there were relatively honest bankers and businesspeople (or perhaps I should say less crooked) who were killed for resisting efforts by crime groups to infiltrate their businesses and influence decision-making. They simply refused to make loans, funnel money through their accounts, or pay extortion demands. But to suggest that such a clear-cut scenario was the sole or even primary reason for the murders would be to oversimplify a highly complex situation. In reality, throughout the 1990s, bankers and businesspeople were killed for a wide variety of reasons.

In some cases, these banker-entrepreneurs took the offer presented them by the crime group and were eventually killed because they came to know too much about the operations of the group, how money was moved out of the country, through which companies, and to which accounts. (It must be re-

9. Gertz (note 6).
10. Ibid.

membered that the security departments of companies and banks sometimes killed their own entrepreneurs and bankers, with traditional organized crime nowhere in sight.)

In other cases, bankers and businesspeople paid the ultimate price for dipping their fingers into someone else's pot of gold.

Some bankers and businesspeople were in fact bona fide gangsters who found themselves in conflict with other gangsters. (In the first years after the collapse of the Soviet Union a bank could be established for the price of a new Mercedes Benz. There were more than a few gangsters who owned banks.)

Bankers and businesspeople had been known to call upon the traditional criminal world to help resolve disputes among themselves by having their partners killed. In such cases, the gangsters were just the middlemen.

Some bankers and businesspeople willingly invited local crime groups to protect them from the advances of other crime groups.

It's important also to note that, in many cases, there was a partnership. The bankers and businessmen were friends with the gangsters and went into business with them voluntarily.

Part of the reason for killing businesspeople that resisted extortion attempts was to send a message to others, to make the gangsters' prospective victims as pliable and accommodating as possible.

One temptation in all of this was to think of banks in the former Soviet Union as equivalent to banks in the West. Bear in mind that during the Soviet era many entities that would be thought of as private businesses in the West, for example factories, shops, banks, and so on, were all owned by the state. There were no private banks, as we knew them. The Soviet State Bank, Gosbank, covered the entire Soviet Union and its function was to support the economic system of central planning. (See Chapter 6 for more on the Soviet economy.)

Toward the end of the Soviet era, Gosbank was split into three branch state banks, for industry, construction and utilities, and agriculture. As the Soviet Union was carved up, the remainder of Gosbank became the Central Bank of Russia responsible for monetary policy, commercial bank supervision, and facilitating interbank settlements. Other state banks were re-formed into joint-stock banks owned by enterprises, government agencies, and government-connected private groups. All of these commercial banks, however, remained dependent on subsidized credits from the Central Bank.[11] For example, the

---

11. See Michael S. Bernstam and Alvin Rabushka, *Fixing Russia's Banks: A Proposal for Growth*, Stanford, Hoover Institution Press, 1998, p. 9. See also Jerry F. Hough, *The Logic of Economic Reform in Russia*, Washington, D.C., Brookings Institution Press, 2001, p. 3, and Hans-Henning Schröder, "El'tsin and the Oligarchs: The Role of Financial Groups in

Oil Industry Bank (Neftprombank) and the former Russian State Agriculture Bank (Rosselkhozbank) were closely tied to their sectors and had little interest or ability in providing loans to new entrepreneurs. Loans to their industries weren't collectible; it was impossible to sue defaulters, and western-style credit-worthiness checks, monitoring, and collateral requirements didn't exist. In their 1998 book, *Fixing Russia's Banks*, Bernstam and Rabushka rightly note that *"Russian banks are not really banks at all.*... [T]hey have served since 1991 as financial arms of the government and the Central Bank of Russia, distributing and reallocating resources to favored individuals, companies, groups, and industries."[12]

So while there were bloody battles for control of some banks, those banks were not the kind of traditional lending institutions we think of in the West and they were not the kind of major state-controlled banks mentioned above. And with the former KGB forming the security departments of many banks, can we consider that these were being taken over by 'mafia'? But this was lost on Western consumers of media information. The die had been cast; the mafia was taking over banks.

It's probably safe to conclude that the media coverage of the Great Mob War of 1992–1994 would have been sufficient to confirm the place of the Russian 'mafia' in the annals of history as an external, invading force sweeping across the country, leaving unspeakable devastation in its wake. But it was the Russian government itself that ensured that the 'mafia' legacy would endure.

In a report issued in late 1993, the MVD claimed that "criminal gangs controlled 40,000 businesses including 1,500 in the state sector, over 500 joint ventures, and more than 1,800 banks."[13] For some reason, the profound distrust of statistics from the Soviet Union seemed to vanish in the post-Soviet years. These figures spread like wildfire throughout the world, repeated verbatim as 'proof' of the dramatic inroads the 'mafia' had made in the country, threatening to suffocate Russia's new 'democracy.'

If this report wasn't enough to create a sensation, in January 1994, the Analytical Center for Socio-Economic Policy issued one of its own, stating that "every, repeat every owner of a shop or kiosk pays a racketeer." It continued,

Russian Politics Between 1993 and July 1998," *Europe-Asia Studies*, vol. 51, no. 6, 1999, pp. 957–988.

12. Bernstam and Rabushka, ibid., p. 2.

13. This information appeared again three years later in *Annual Statistical Report, 1995*, Russian Ministry of Internal Affairs, 1996 (unpublished). See Maryanne Ozernoy and Yuri Voronin, "Russian Organized Crime: Trends and Political Implications," September 25, 1996, p. 9, n13.

"nearly 80% of private enterprises and commercial banks in the country paid up to 20% of their earnings in 'taxes' to racketeers."[14]

This English version of the institute's name sounded innocuous enough—just another think tank conducting social science research. Most commentators, however, either didn't realize or felt it wasn't important that in Russian the institute's name was rendered as Analyticheskii Tsentr po Sotsialno-Eko-nomicheskoi Politike *pri Prezidenta Rossiiskoi Federatsii*. The English translation is telling: The Analytical Center for Socio-Economic Policy of the President of the Russian Federation. The Kremlin's own think-tank. That fact alone put a different spin on an assessment of the information.

Interestingly, the report was issued only three months after Yeltsin had ordered military tanks to fire on the parliament building in October 1993 and one month after extremist Vladimir Zhirinovsky made a strong showing in the December 1993 parliamentary elections.[15] Was the report a way to divert attention from the bloody October episode and a response to the December elections? It wouldn't have been the most ridiculous guess.

It wouldn't have taken a lot of imagination to speculate that the report was one of the first steps in Yeltsin's campaign strategy toward the 1996 presidential election. The title of the report, "Organized Crime and the Prospect of National-Socialists Coming to Power in Russia," left little doubt that it was a political document. The findings of the report were carried in countless newspapers around the world, sprinkled in numerous scholarly publications, and entered into the U.S. Congressional Record through individual testimony, with little explanation. The problem wasn't that the figures were being reported but

---

14. Piotr Filippov, "Organizovannaya Prestupnost' i Perspektivy Prikhoda k Vlasti v Rossii Natsional-Sotsialistov," Administratsiya Prezidenta Rossiiskoi Federatsii, Analitich-eskii Tsentr po Sotsialno-Ekonomicheskoi Politike, January 17, 1994. Cited in, among many others, FBIS-SOV-94-033, February 17, 1994, "Think Tank Addresses Fight Against Mobsters," p. 19; Richard Layard and John Parker, *The Coming Russian Boom: A Guide to New Markets and Politics*, New York, The Free Press, 1996, p. 155, and Stephen Handelman, *Comrade Criminal: Russia's New Mafiya*, New Haven, Yale University Press, 1995, p. 160.

15. As has been pointed out, in its report the Analytical Center took the opportunity to encourage the adoption of extraordinary measures and powers for President Yeltsin. "Only the formation of specialized units, well equipped and responsive directly to the President, will provide the means to effectively combat organized crime. The units should be stationed outside the cities and should have access to criminal information kept by the Interior Ministry," cited in Leonid Maximenkov and C. Namiesniowski, "Organized Crime in Post-Communist Russia—A Criminal Revolution?" in Commentary No. 48, published by the Canadian Security Intelligence Service, September 1994, at http://www.csis-scrs.gc.ca/eng/comment/com48_e.html.

that they were taken at face value as 'proof' that the Russian 'mafia' was taking over the country. It seemed exactly what the Kremlin would have wanted.[16]

Perhaps most unbelievable was that it took just two sentences to enshrine
in history the reputation of the 'mafia' as an invading force sweeping across
the country:

> "Criminal gangs control 40,000 businesses including 1,500 in the
> state sector, over 500 joint ventures, and more than 1,800 banks,"
> and
> "70–80% of private enterprises and commercial banks pay
> 10–20% of their turnover to the mafia."

One might have expected these figures to be news for a few months and
possibly reappear from time to time when journalists wrote their accounts of
the Wild East and the Great Mob War. After all, the world keeps turning and
new figures would be churned out. Not this time. These numbers, and with
them the impression about the Russian 'mafia,' tenaciously maintained their
place over the years. At the end of 1997—a full four years after the figures

---

16. For examples of Congressional Testimony, see the statement of James Woolsey, then
director of the CIA, in 1994, stating that "of the 2,000 banks in Russia today, a majority
are controlled by organized crime, according to the Ministry of Internal Affairs." See also
the statement of Rick Palmer, former CIA station chief in one of the Baltic States prior to
the dismantling of the USSR, repeating the MVD estimate that criminal groups controlled
more than 400 banks and 47 currency exchanges. Cited in Palmer's statement is Professor
Lydia Krasfina, head of the Institute for Banking and Financial Managers, estimating that
70% to 80% of private banks in Russia are controlled by organized crime. In academic circles, see Russian sociologist Olga Kryshtanovskaya's citation of the Russian newspapers
Izvestia (October 21, 1994, p. 5) and *Argumenty i Fakty* (1994, no. 48, p. 10) in her article, "Illegal Structures in Russia," in *Sociological Research*, July–August 1996. "At present,
40% of entrepreneurs and 66% of all commercial structures have been drawn into criminal relations. The mafia has established control over thirty-five thousand entities engaged
in economic activities, including four hundred banks, forty-seven stock exchanges, and fifteen hundred enterprises in the state sector." In the mass media, see *Economist*, February
19, 1994, "Crime in Russia: The High Price of Freeing Markets," p. 57, cited in Thomas C.
Owen, *Russian Corporate Capitalism from Peter the Great to Perestroika*, New York, Oxford
University Press, 1995, p. 154. See also "Russian Mafia: Organized Crime is Big Business
for the KGB," in *The New American*, by William F. Jasper, February 19, 1996, vol. 2, no. 4.
Jasper quotes Hans Graf Huyn, German expert on Soviet deception: "The Russian mafia
has direct control over 40,960 commercial enterprises, among them 449 banks, 37 stock
exchanges, 678 markets and 566 joint ventures with Western participation." In journalistic
books, see, among others, Timothy Harper, *Moscow Madness: Crime, Corruption, and One
Man's Pursuit of Profit in the New Russia*, New York, McGraw-Hill, 1999, p. 144.

were originally issued—the MVD presented nearly identical data: 40,000 economic subjects, including 1,500 state enterprises, over 500 joint enterprises, and over 500 banks were said to be controlled by criminal groups.[17] And well past the turn of the century the same unquestioning acceptance of the same numbers continued. In *Organized Crime and its Control in Central Asia*, published in 2004, Slawomir Redo quotes an article called, "The Appearance of Corruption in the Kazakh Economy." Amazingly, the article's author writes that "the mafia exercises control over 35 thousand legal entities among which are 400 banks, 47 stock exchanges, and 1,500 state enterprises." It would seem that the author of the article applied Russia's figures to the situation in Kazakhstan.[18]

The single word that packed the biggest punch and was common to nearly all reports and articles was 'control.' Everyone seemed to be in agreement that the 'mafia' 'controlled.' Again, that sense of an external force invading and penetrating was unmistakable.

The obvious question that needed to be answered in order to give some perspective to what had been treated largely as a black-and-white issue was: What did 'control' mean?

Gennady Chebotaryov, the Deputy Chief of the MVD's Organized Crime Control Department, knew the reaction the MVD and Analytical Center reports were generating, though, frankly, the MVD wasn't exactly bending over backwards to clarify its position publicly. In November 1994, as I prepared to leave Moscow to deliver a speech in Washington D.C., Chebotaryov suggested I take care with the word 'control.' According to the MVD usage, he said, 'control' didn't necessarily mean that an enterprise would be wholly subservient or 'taken over' by a crime group. It covered a wide range of possible relationships between a crime group and bank or business, he explained.

It could be a low-level extortion by a crime group that never came to the attention of the top echelon of management in the enterprise.

A group may simply 'get' (*poluchat'*) a cash tribute or payoff (*dan'*) from a business in return for protection, without any further consequences to the integrity of the enterprise's management.

---

17. See Vadim Volkov, "Violent Entrepreneurship in Post-Communist Russia," *Europe-Asia Studies*, vol. 51, no. 5, 1999, pp. 747–748. See also Joseph Blasi, Maya Kroumova, and Douglas Kruse, *Kremlin Capitalism: Privatizing the Russian Economy*, Ithaca, ILR Press, 1997, pp. 116–119.

18. O.E. Alakhunov, "Proyavleniye Korruptsii v Ekonomike Kazakhstana," *Preduprezhdeniye Prestupnosti*, no. 2, 2001, p. 15, cited in Slawomir Redo, *Organized Crime and its Control in Central Asia*, Huntsville, Office of International Criminal Justice, 2004, p. 103.

It could indicate a high-pressure extortion/blackmail attempt by a crime group with the goal of affecting the decision making of the enterprise management.

It could be a hostile takeover by a crime group, an effort to oust the leadership of the enterprise outright.

'Control' could even mean the cooperation of the administration of an enterprise with a crime group to facilitate the looting of that enterprise.

Ultimately, though, it could also mean that the crime group was invited in by the management to function in both a security and management advisory capacity.[19]

In this light, the MVD statement that "criminal gangs controlled 40,000 businesses including 1,500 in the state sector, over 500 joint ventures, and more than 1,800 banks" would have to be reassessed.

There are other issues for economists, social science researchers, and historians to explore in order to arrive at a more fully developed explanation of 'control' and the impact of the 'mafia.' This includes reconciling seemingly problematic if not outright contradictory statements made by Russian officials, media, and analysts. For example:

- Numerous post-Soviet companies were established with the involvement of the KGB.[20]
- "Several powerful organized criminal groups exercise control over the national economy."[21]
- "Organized criminal groups participate in every lawful and unlawful deal."[22]
- About 55% of Russian capital is in the hands of the 'mafia.'[23]

---

19. Author conversation with Chebotaryov, November 1994. See also Volkov (note 17).

20. Conclusion reached by the author as a result of conducting investigations in Russia and interacting with police officials and KGB agents.

21. Statement by Richard L. Palmer, on the infiltration of the western financial system by elements of Russian organized crime before the House Committee on Banking and Financial Services on September 21, 1999, http://www.house.gov/banking/92199pal.htm, p. 1.

22. Ibid., p. 9.

23. "O Sostoyanii i Merakh Usileniya Bor'by s Ekonomicheskoi Prestupnost'iu i Korruptsiei v Rossiiskoi Federatsii," unpublished report of the Ministry of Internal Affairs, November 1996, p. 2, citing the Analytical Center of the Russian Academy of Sciences. See also Huyn in Jasper (note 16). Razinkin cited in Tanya Frisby, "The Rise of Organised Crime in Russia: Its Roots and Social Significance," Europe-Asia Studies, vol. 5, no. 1, 1998, p. 35. In some cases, 40% has been the figure cited. See Mark Galeotti, Russian and Post-Soviet Organized Crime, Aldershot, Ashgate Publishing, 2002, p. xvi: "Of course, organized crime does not 'own' Russia. The Interior Ministry routinely claims that it [organized crime] controls 40% of the Russian economy, but this figure must be treated with considerable caution since not only has it remained suspiciously static for the period 1992–2001, but the 40

- Roughly two-thirds of Russia's economy is under the sway of the crime syndicates.[24]
- The 'oligarchs' control 50% of the Russian economy.
- 30–50% of all entrepreneurs work for the criminal fraternity.[25]
- Thousands of registered companies have no commercial function whatever, and exist only on paper as 'stand-bys' to be used in tax evasion, moving money, or smuggling goods.[26]
- Many post-Soviet commercial enterprises are unprofitable, and the 'mafia' is not going to bother with companies that have no prospects of turning over a profit.[27]

Were KGB-backed companies being 'controlled' by crime groups or 'mafia'? Was it conceivable that they could have been? How did you look at this issue if you were a citizen of the former Soviet Union and considered the KGB itself to be 'mafia'? Was the MVD calculation of the number of companies controlled by crime groups based on an extrapolation using the number of officially registered companies in Russia? If so, what allowance was made, if any, for all those dormant and 'stand-by' companies that essentially were nothing but mailboxes? Surely crime groups couldn't have targeted these phantom companies. And it wasn't necessarily the case that crime groups had established all of those shell companies.[28]

How many Russian companies were profitable so that targeting them actually made sense? As Joseph Blasi, et al., pondered in their book, *Kremlin Capitalism*, "It is hard to imagine why organized crime would want to control weak firms that are cutting employees, reducing capacity, confronting serious cash flow problems, and struggling to supply the kindergartens, housing, and hospitals their employees need."[29]

---

per cent figure also seems interchangeably applied to the proportion of firms under criminal control, proportion of GDP, and proportion of the economy operating in the 'shadow sector.' However, what organized crime does not control outright it can influence."

24. Center for Strategic and International Studies Task Force Report, *Russian Organized Crime: Global Organized Crime Project*, CSIS, Washington, D.C., 1997, p. 2.

25. Razinkin cited in Frisby, p. 35 (note 23).

26. Conclusion reached by the author as a result of conducting investigations in Russia and interacting with police officials and KGB/FSB agents.

27. Volkov, pp. 747–748 (note 17). See also Blasi, et al., pp. 116–119 (note 17).

28. The figure 40,000 businesses referred to in 1994 was four times the number of medium-size and large enterprises that were privatized at that time and twice the number of large enterprises in existence.

29. Blasi, p. 119 (note 17).

Further, if the 'mafia' was said to control 55% of Russian capital and the 'oligarchs' controlled 50% of the Russian economy, how do we reconcile these numbers?

Like Blasi and his co-authors, former chief of the Moscow Regional Organized Crime Unit, Vladimir Rushailo, had a difficult time swallowing the Analytical Center's conclusions that 70–80% of privatized enterprises and commercial banks were forced to pay extortion money.

> It would be stupid to deny it—such things exist, but to say that the absolute majority of enterprises are under the heel of criminal groupings is irresponsible at best. We know that this kind of information used to be disseminated by the criminal groupings themselves so that potential victims would reconcile themselves to paying them off without making a fuss.[30]

For some, like Russian scholar Vadim Volkov, 'to control' (*kontrolirovat'*) meant that a crime group not only provided physical protection to an enterprise but also introduced its own bookkeeper or regular auditor into the enterprise. The auditor reported back to the group information about business transactions and their value, while the group supervised and secured major contracts and transactions for a fixed share of the profits. At this point, Volkov says, the activity of the group turned from racketeering into "enforcement partnership."[31] When this arrangement was made by mutual agreement, it seldom rang alarm bells. It was when this 'control' was begun surreptitiously that the management of the enterprise ran a high risk of being driven from its own company.

Thinking in terms of 'mafia,' many businesses failed to anticipate threats from directions other than stereotypical 'gangsters.' For example, a potential extortion situation or a quest for outright 'control' did not necessarily begin with an approach from a traditional crime group. In many cases, individuals, such as a company's own manager, secretary, driver, or landlord, who didn't

---

30. Vladimir Rushailo, Chief of RUOP and then Deputy Minister of Internal Affairs, was removed by President Putin in March 2001, and made a member of the National Security Council, cited in Galina Odinokova, "Who Will Fight the Mafia? MVD Workers are Confident that Professionals Can," *Moskovskii Trud*, March 29, 1994, p. 3, reproduced in FBIS-USR-94-037. It is possible that the article was commissioned by Rushailo himself or other MVD officials. At the time of the article, Odinokova served as an MVD officer responsible for media relations for the Organized Crime Control Department.

31. Volkov, p. 743 (note 17).

raise immediate suspicion, collected important information about the commercial activity of a company. That is, people who had access to company files, computers, client lists, and other important data may have been either actively working for a crime group or may have approached a crime group with the information in an attempt to get a piece of the action. This happened throughout the 1990s in part because many businesspeople operating in the former Soviet Union were attuned to direct approaches by 'gangsters' but were less aware of other threats.

One foreign businessman was surprised and more than a little scared in 1995 when he was approached by a local crime group and was told in detail about his company's operations not only in Moscow but in several other Russian cities with a high degree of accuracy. Investigation revealed that the businessman's landlord had approached the local crime group and had been feeding it information about the tenant-company.[32]

In 2001, a group, in what apparently was a straightforward extortion attempt, approached a foreign company that had been operating successfully in Russia for nearly a decade. The group knew not only about the operations of the company and the locations of all its branches around the world, it also knew the home addresses of the top management in the United States as well as the names and ages of their wives and children. In this case, too, there was an insider providing information.[33]

When a crime group, or "violent entrepreneurs" as Volkov calls them, that "solves questions" (*reshat' voprosy*) for a business enterprise invested its money in an enterprise and introduced its representative onto the board of directors, it became a shareholder and increased its share of income (*byt' v dole*). For reasons mentioned above, this did not necessarily have to be interpreted as an aggressive move by the group.[34]

Making the distinction was critical when foreign companies were evaluating the pros and cons of getting involved with an enterprise in the former Soviet Union. If it was the case that a crime group was working on a cooperative basis with the management of an enterprise, it then had to be determined if the group was supportive of a commercial relationship with a foreign company.

For example, in 1999, an American company had identified a distributor in Siberia with whom it had reached a certain comfort level. The Russian distributor had met all the commercial requirements. The only remaining task for the American company was to initiate a due diligence investigation to: 1)

---

32. Author investigative information.
33. Author investigative information.
34. Volkov, p. 743 (note 17).

confirm the identity of the distributor and his claims of ownership; 2) identify shadow decision makers, if any; 3) determine how the Russian company was being financed; and 4) determine what measures the Russian company had at its disposal to protect itself in the sometimes bloody, always delicate Russian business environment.

Preliminary information revealed that the Russian company was 'controlled' by a crime group. Upon closer inspection, it was determined that the regional crime boss 'controlling' the company had a fifteen-year friendship with the distributor and had invested a considerable sum in the business. In this case, there was little, if any, threat to the distributor from the crime group.

Then it was necessary to check the other side of the fence. If there was no threat to the distributor from the crime boss, what about a threat against the two from law enforcement? It was learned that there were no pending law enforcement or tax inspection investigations targeting either the distributor or the crime boss. Law enforcement knew of the long-term relationship between the two and considered it to be a stable business partnership. It was then left to the American company to decide if it could live with those facts or if it would pass on the deal.[35]

Extensive reporting about 'mafia' groups 'controlling' enterprises led to the questionable conclusions that: 1) the figures reported by the MVD and Analytical Center were fact; 2) criminal groups were always the aggressors; 3) the 'mafia' became the owner of the enterprise; 4) the enterprise itself had become criminal by virtue of the fact that criminal groups 'controlled' it, and 5) doing business with these enterprises should have been avoided at all cost.

As seen above, many of the conclusions reached by a wide variety of observers around the world were driven by statistics issued by law enforcement and reported by the media. We're not quite finished with the impact of statistics on our impression of the realities of the Russian 'mafia.' What was the nature of the crime groups that were supposedly 'invading' the country? Were they as numerous as reported? What could we surmise based on the figures that were made public?

One Sunday afternoon in 1987, while I was wandering around Red Square, I came upon an artist named Vladimir. Looking over his shoulder and at the collection of oil paintings lining a nearby wall, I could see that St. Basil's Cathedral was his specialty. Anxious to make a sale, Volodya (the familiar version of Vladimir) struck up a conversation and soon succeeded in selling me one of his paintings.

Volodya painted as much as possible to supplement his meager salary. Like most people, he had been forced to make extra money on the side, as he

---

35. Author investigative information.

couldn't survive on his salary alone. During the week he worked as resident artist at the mighty Hammer and Sickle Metal Works in Moscow. His job was to draw posters, charts, and graphs showing how the factory had been meeting and exceeding its production quota.

After knowing each other for a few weeks, he offered to smuggle me into the factory. The very suggestion made me nervous. After all, it was still the Soviet Union. Gorbachev had been in power for only two years. We foreigners were still instructed by our Soviet hosts not to speak English in staircases of apartment buildings for fear of nosy informant neighbors. It would still be several years before the society's overt paranoia began to subside. Worst of all, Hammer and Sickle was a premier industrial concern in the city, one of those 'sensitive objects' that was off limits to foreigners. The Soviet Union had a long list of seemingly mundane things like factories, bridges, and trains that they classified as 'secret' and couldn't be photographed or visited—in many cases, ironically, things that could be seen easily in high resolution detail by satellite reconnaissance. But I've long surmised that the secretiveness was as much about embarrassment and inferiority as concern for national security.

Volodya gave me his ID card, instructing me to hold it up with my hand over his photo and walk right through the main entrance. "Don't look at the woman in the booth. Don't stop if she says anything to you."

We arrived by metro and crossed the wide boulevard in front of the factory, Volodya beaming with a boyish laugh, "Ok, Joe, here's where we act like spies!" As Volodya had anticipated, the guard in the booth yelled as soon as I passed through the turnstile. I shot a glance to make sure she wasn't pursuing and pushed my way into the factory yard. My anxiety only intensified from there. The men in uniform who eyed me suspiciously made me exceedingly nervous.

It wasn't until we reached Volodya's studio that I began to relax, although the pressure wasn't totally gone. Volodya's boss, a staunch Stalinist, kept looking over his shoulder at me in my Western blue jeans, sneakers, and wire-rimmed glasses, probably thinking that he should turn me in. He eventually decided that having this intruder so obviously from another planet was more a curiosity to him than a threat.

The two of them proceeded with their business. Volodya had to draw a chart showing the quarterly increase in output for the factory. They rummaged through documents, checked industry newspapers, and discussed it for a good half-hour. Failing to find any official figures, they made up a number they both could live with. The increase was 120%. Problem solved.

Of course, industry wasn't the only one playing fast and loose with statistics. In October 1991, I was one of five outsiders permitted to attend the

United Nations-MVD conference on international organized crime control held 145 miles outside Moscow in the ancient town of Suzdal. I met with Anatoly Volobuyev, the former MVD researcher whom I'd known for two years already. He had become a freelance journalist and succeeded in obtaining a special invitation to the proceedings. During one of the coffee breaks, he and I talked about crime groups. He said the official number of crime leaders (the so-called *avtoritety*) in the country at that time was reported as 20,000. "But, it could just as easily be 10,000 or 40,000," he added with a smirk. "No one knows."

It's no secret that the Soviet system was notorious for fudging data and cooking the books in virtually every sector of society. And it was understandable for reasons to be discussed in Chapter 6. Anyone who had any contact with the Soviet Union knew that all numbers were assumed to be, let's say, imperfect. (Part of this, of course, was simply due to the malleable nature of statistics and part to the ideological nature of the USSR.)

That's not to say that statistics in other countries were without their shortcomings. But it's important to note two things. First, throughout the 20th century, numbers fueled the Soviet economy. Bonuses, awards, and Orders of Lenin were awarded based on numerically fulfilling and exceeding the plan. Shortfalls in production output were disguised. Ideological victories were proclaimed based on fraudulent information. It was an administrative-bureaucratic system in which in many cases reports mattered more than reality.

Second and closer to our subject matter, official MVD statistics supposedly demonstrated the apparent dramatic increase in the number of crime groups operating in the country. This is important because these figures—like those discussed earlier—were taken uncritically for the most part, by journalists, policy makers, and scholars, and disseminated throughout the world. We discussed in Chapter 3 how this happens. Articles frequently reported both the current MVD official figures and ones from the previous several years to show the supposedly clear and indisputable rise in the number of groups. It's worth taking a few minutes to look at the numbers as presented by law enforcement and the media.

In a typical example, a *USA Today* article reported that "in the period from 1990 to 1995 the number of organized crime groups rose from just under 2,000 to around 5,000." Or from the BBC: "In 1994, the number of organized crime groups in the former Soviet Union had grown from 785 during Gorbachev's reign to 5,691. By 1996, this estimate had grown to 8,000 groups."[36]

---

36. *BBC Online Network*, "The Rise and Rise of the Russian Mafia," November 21, 1998, at http://news6.thdo.bbc.co.uk/hi/english/special_report.

In this way, police and media created the impression that there had been a steep, straight-line increase in the number of crime groups. But what did the numbers mean? The article didn't say. And most articles didn't.

As a first step in making at least some sense of all this, it has to be recognized that so many labels had been used to describe post-Soviet crime groups that it had become difficult to know what actually was being counted. The labels included criminal groups, organized groups, organized criminal groups, organized groups of criminals, active organized criminal groups, bandit groups, group formations, criminal groupings, criminal associations, criminal communities, criminal societies, brigades, gangs, mafia, mafia clans, mafia gangs and others.

In a closed seminar at the National Police Academy of the Soviet MVD held in January 1990, Vyacheslav Komissarov cited an interesting figure from MVD research. He said that, in 1987, police uncovered 12,000 criminal groups that displayed 'signs of organization'[37]—this coming a full three years prior to the dismantling of the USSR.

Such a high number might come as a surprise to the Western observer for two reasons. First, from my conversations in the U.S. and Europe, it was clear that many people generally assumed that criminal groups were primarily products of the social, economic, and political confusion *after* the breakup of the USSR. There had not been a lot of public sense that crime groups had such a presence during the Soviet era. Second, observers who tracked MVD and media reports had never seen any indication that criminal groups in the former Soviet Union could have been that numerous. More interesting was that only two years later, in 1989, the number of groups reported by the MVD's Organized Crime Control Department was only 3,000—some 9,000 *fewer* than that cited by Komissarov.[38]

There's no clear explanation for the discrepancy but some reasonable guesses can be made. There may have been a significant difference in the way each of the sources counted groups. We don't know if their concepts of 'criminal groups' were the same or if there were variations in the type and amount of information collected. One source hailed from academia and the other from police operations suggesting that their general orientations toward the subject matter likely were different.

---

37. Vyacheslav Komissarov, "O Nekotorykh Problemakh Bor'by s Organizovannoi Prestupnost'iu," in *Bor'ba s Organizovannoi Prestupnost'iu: Problemy Teorii i Praktiki*, Moskva, Ministerstvo Vnutrennikh Del SSSR Akademiya, 1990, p. 48.

38. G. F. Chebotaryov, "Questions of Cooperation with Foreign Countries," *CJ International*, vol. 5, no. 6, November–December 1989, p. 16.

One contributing factor in varying approaches could very well have been the instability of the MVD in the late Soviet period and throughout the post-Soviet era. High turnover of personnel at all levels, from Minister to researcher, from police chief to neighborhood inspector, affected policy approaches, implementation, priorities, and department morale.

Moreover, the Organized Crime Control Department of the MVD was created in 1988. There may have been a decision on the part of the department to start its information collection from scratch, ignoring any research that had been conducted up to that point. During my time in the Ministry in 1990–91, researchers in the MVD's institute frequently complained that the operational arm of the Ministry didn't pay sufficient attention to their findings.

The figure 12,000 may have been inflated somewhat as a result of *glasnost'* enthusiasm. We don't know if that number was based on police records or included media accounts. If the latter, this raised the potential of duplicate reporting. For example, on March 28, 1990, in a story titled "The State Security Committee Reports," the Soviet news agency TASS reported that the 'Kuntsevo group' that had its start in 1988 extorting fledgling private enterprises was 'seized.' Five days later, an identical story appeared under the headline, "Dangerous Mob Seized in Moscow." This time TASS called the group 'Orda.' Was 'Orda' a sub-unit of the 'Kuntsevo group' or another name for it? Was the 'Kuntsevo group' still in existence? Was anyone arrested and held, or just 'seized'?

Related to this, the police researcher may have included every petty gang showing 'signs of organization' while the Organized Crime Control Department pursued only what it deemed to be *organized* crime. (At the time, the Department defined organized crime as "a stable, hierarchical, organized group of people, having at least a two-level organizational structure of administration, created for the systematic commission of profit-oriented crime and corruption."[39])

It may simply be that crime groups could not be counted accurately.

It's well known that crime groups, however defined, had done considerable harm to Russia and had increased in number between 1985 and today. But it's not the official statistics that will conclusively bear this out. The figures offered a degree of convenience since they were concrete, easy for police and media to report to the public, and seemingly demystified a largely under-stud-

---

39. "Organized Crime Survey Response" prepared by the Sixth Department for Organized Crime Control of the Ministry of Internal Affairs of the USSR, 1991, for the United Nations-MVD Conference on International Organized Crime Control, October 21–25, 1991, held in Suzdal, Russia, pp. 1–2. The Survey Response was translated into English by J. Serio for the Sixth Department and can be found in *Interpol International Review of Criminal Police*, 1992, 434, pp. 29–35.

ied phenomenon. In the end, though, they should have been used with caution, at least in the form presented by police and media. This doesn't mean, however, that they were totally useless. Looking closely at the numbers as reported, we might begin to draw conclusions about the general nature of these groups, how they operated and, ultimately, the implications for Western law enforcement facing post-Soviet crime at home as well as companies engaged in business activities in the former USSR.

In 1990, the Organized Crime Control Department prepared a report on the state of organized crime in the Soviet Union for the October 1991 UN-MVD conference in Suzdal mentioned earlier. It said there were between 3,500 and 4,000 criminal groups operating in the Soviet Union. This was already a jump of 500–1,000 over the figure reported in 1989.[40] Likewise, Russian police expert and historian Mark Galeotti reported that there were 3,500 groups in 1990.[41] But in comments before the U.S. Permanent Subcommittee on Investigations, Mikhail Yegorov, then chief of the Organized Crime Control Department of the Russian Republic (not the Soviet Union), reported that in 1990 785 'organized crime groups' were operating in Russia.[42] Even allowing for the size and population difference between the USSR (280 million) and the Russian Republic (150 million), it's unlikely that less than one-quarter of all *Soviet* crime groups were operating in Russia.

In 1991, some in the Soviet academic community pegged the number at a precise 952.[43] By 1992, figures ranged from the MVD's estimate that 3,000 'criminal structures' were operating on the territory of Russia (by this time an independent country),[44] to then Security Minister Barannikov's estimate that there were more than 6,000 'criminal groups,' from "armed gangs of bandits in the borderlands through to the well-organized 'mafia' groups of the cities."[45] By July that year, the MVD pinpointed the number at 3,296 'organized groups of criminals.'[46]

---

40. Ibid., p. 1.

41. Mark Galeotti, "Organized Crime in Moscow," *Low Intensity Conflict and Law Enforcement*, vol. 1, no. 3, p. 249.

42. Mikhail Yegorov, "The Growth of Organized Crime in the Russian Federation and the Republics of the Former USSR, and its Effect on International Security," comments to the Permanent Subcommittee on Investigations hearing on International Organized Crime and its Impact on the United States, May 24, 1994.

43. Figure originally found in A. Dolgova, ed., *Prestupnost' i Reformy v Rossii*, Moskva, Kriminologicheskaya Assotsiatsiya, 1998, p. 254, cited in Volkov, p. 753, n11 (note 17).

44. Larisa Kislinskaya, "The Investigation is Concluded. Forget It?" *Rossiiskiye Vesti*, November 11, 1992, p. 5.

45. Galeotti (note 41).

46. *TASS*, "Regional Officials Cite New Figures on Organized Crime," July 16, 1992.

To add confusion to the uncertainty, geographically diverse and structurally different categories were being added to the discussion. "Today it is estimated that there are probably some 5,000 'mafia clans,' as the individual *crime syndicates* are sometimes known, operating within the territory of the *Commonwealth of Independent States (CIS)*. Probably as many as 3 million people are involved in their activities"[47] (emphasis added). At the same time, journalist Larisa Kislinskaya reported the number of 'active members' in Russia to be 15,000.[48] By the end of 1992, chief of department Yegorov announced that there were "about 3,000 criminal organizations, with tens of thousands of members" operating in the Russian Federation.[49] Other estimates said that total active gang membership in Russia was less than 100,000 people[50] while Yegorov himself offered another estimate, saying the figure had reached 100,000.[51]

At the beginning of 1994, 5,691 groups had reportedly come to light. Leading these groups were almost 3,000 criminal 'leaders' (*avtoritety*), among them 279 'thieves in law' (*vory v zakone*). According to police intelligence, 926 groups were united in 155 'associations' with an average membership of 70–300 persons, in what was said to be a continuing effort by the criminal world to consolidate.[52] At the same time, *The Washington Post* reported that "exactly 35,348 mobsters belonged to 8,059 criminal gangs in Russia."[53]

By 1996, the number of groups was still in flux with some researchers putting it at an exact 6,743 while others indicated that it had passed the 8,000 mark.[54] By the end of the decade, the figure had reached 10,000. Oddly enough, though, an article appeared in 2003 under the headline, "About 100 Criminal Gangs Operating in Russia."[55] The most recent figures include a 2005

---

47. *Intersec*, "The Eastern Mafia," vol. 2, issue 4, September 1992, pp. 115–119.

48. Kislinskaya, p. 5 (note 44).

49. Oleg Shchedrov, "Police Commandos to Get Tough with Mafia," *The Moscow Times*, December 30, 1992, p. 3.

50. Stephen Handelman, "The Russian 'Mafiya,'" *Foreign Affairs*, March/April 1994, vol. 73, no. 2, p. 83.

51. Mikhail Yegorov comments to the Permanent Subcommittee on Investigations hearing on International Organized Crime and its Impact on the United States, May 25, 1994.

52. Ibid. Remember that three years earlier it was being reported that there were 20,000 *avtoritety* in Russia.

53. Lee Hockstader, "Gangsters Targeting Russia's Businessmen," *The Washington Post*, August 16, 1995.

54. A. Dolgova in Volkov, p. 753 (note 43). Guy Dunn cited the same figure in "Major Mafia Groups in Russia" in Phil Williams (ed.), *Russian Organized Crime: The New Threat?* London, Frank Cass & co., Ltd., 1997, p. 64, rightly qualifying it by stating that the number is "alarming, but essentially meaningless."

55. *Pravda.ru*, "About 100 Criminal Gangs Operating in Russia," August 5, 2003, at http://newsfromrussia.com/accidents/2003/08/05/49079.html.

estimate by the Ministry of Internal Affairs that there were at least 116 'criminal organizations' consisting of about 4,000 members operating in the country,[56] and a 2007 estimate that there were approximately 450 'organized criminal formations' involving around 12,000 people.[57]

The numbers for Moscow are just as murky. In 1987–88, 29 criminal
groups were reported in Moscow alone.[58] Five years later, in 1992, this figure
was said to have jumped by a factor of eight. According to a Moscow police
official, 228 'criminal groupings' were identified. That same year, Moscow's
law enforcement agencies were said to have exposed 131 organized criminal
groupings.[59] Reporting varied constantly. In September 1993, it was reported
that "about 100 major organized criminal groups are now operating in
Moscow,"[60] while a year later there was said to be "12 large criminal entities in
Moscow, each with about 200–300 members. Another 30 groups with 20–30
members are also on the streets."[61]

Perhaps one of the most reasonable presentations of statistics regarding
criminal groups in Moscow was found in a November 1995 *Sevodnya* newspaper article. Quoting police sources, the article outlined seven ethnic crime
communities (*obshchina*) (Georgian, Azeri, Armenian, Chechen, Ingush,
Dagestani, Ossetian) consisting of 116 organized crime groups. There were
approximately 2,000 active members. The article went on to say that for the
first nine months of 1995, 101 criminal groups were 'liquidated' in which there
were 335 active members. Among the 'liquidated' groups were 16 Chechen (58
people), 12 Georgian (47 people), 12 Armenian (41 people), 11 Dagestani (28
people), and 6 Azeri (14 people).[62]

There were still shortcomings with these last numbers, not the least of which
was that they said nothing about ethnic Russian crime groups. But at least they
began to illustrate the fluidity and relatively small sizes of the groups as well as
the non-monolithic, but increasingly organized, nature of the criminal world.

---

56. *United Press International*, "Russia Knows of 116 Operating Mafias," March 23,
2005.

57. "Mafiya Bessmertna? Eto Mif," February 4, 2007, at http://www.rususa.com/news/
print.asp-nid-24092.

58. Komissarov, p. 48 (note 37).

59. *Interfax*, "More than 200 Criminal Groupings Operate in Moscow," February 3,
1993.

60. *TASS*, "Some 100 Criminal Groups Operate in Moscow," September 16, 1993.

61. Paul Norton, "Crimewise," *Moscow Tribune*, November 10, 1994, p. 8.

62. *Sevodnya*, "Kavkazskaya Prestupnost' v Moskve Ustupaet 'Slavyanskoi,'" November
16, 1995, p. 6.

Hopefully your head is spinning; it's a confusing state of affairs. Laying all the numbers out, it becomes somewhat easier to see that the increase in the number of crime groups—at least as reported—did not happen quite as neatly and precipitously as we would think. The numbers that many observers relied on to show the 'obvious' explosion in crime groups raised more questions than they answered.[63]

Summary of Crime Group Estimates

1987	12,000 'crime groups'
1988	3,000 'crime groups'
1989	3,500 'criminal groups' (in USSR)
1990	785 'organized crime groups' (in Russia)
1991	952 'organized criminal groups'
1992	3,000 'criminal structures'
	6,000 'criminal groups'
	3,296 'organized groups of criminals'
	5,000 'mafia clans'
1994	4,300 'criminal groups'
	5,691 'crime groups'
	8,059 'criminal groups'
1995	5,000 'organized criminal groupings'
1996	8,000 'crime groups'
1999	10,000 'criminal groups'
2003	100 'criminal gangs'
2005	116 'criminal organizations'
2007	450 'organized criminal formations'

Number of People Involved

1992	3,000,000

---

63. Much of this information was originally presented by the author at the Second Annual Convention of the Association for the Study of Nationalities (ASN), "Towards Europe or Eurasia? The Future of Post-Communist States," held at Columbia University, April 25–28, 1997. It also appeared in edited form in Joseph D. Serio, "Counting the 'Mafia' in the Former Soviet Union," *Criminal Organizations*, 11(1,2), 1998.

	15,000
	less than 100,000
	100,000
1994	35,000
	40,000
1995	20–25,000
2005	4,000
2007	12,000

The basic question that needed to be asked, of course, was what did these numbers mean?

First and foremost, they appeared to indicate that no one had any idea how many crime groups there were in post-Soviet Russia in the 1990s.

Second, although the reported increase in criminal groups had been characterized as "reflecting the growing decay and lawlessness within the Soviet Union and its successor," it's clear that these figures weren't the best indicator of the state of the Russian crime world.[64] The discussion above shows that it's exceedingly difficult to rely on these figures to determine the pace at which the Russian crime world was expanding or lawlessness was growing. And yet these were the numbers that had been bandied about in both the former Soviet Union and the West to demonstrate the 'rise of the Russian mafia.' Until a standardized definition of 'criminal group' and 'organized criminal group' is agreed upon and a methodology for measuring those groups is devised, there is little chance of gaining any confidence in the statistics.

As depicted in Russian-language sources such as law-enforcement intelligence reports and newspaper articles, criminal groups were constantly 'exposed,' 'seized,' 'arrested,' 'broken up,' or 'liquidated,' making it difficult to understand the exact disposition of the groups. For example, it was reported that 70 crime groups had been 'liquidated' in the period from late 1989 to early 1991.[65] For 1991, this number was reported to be 943,[66] while one of the Deputy Ministers of the Ministry of Internal Affairs noted that "the activities of 600 organized criminal groups have been stopped in the first six months [of 1991] alone."[67] The following year the number of groups 'arrested' reached

---

64. Cited in Galeotti, p. 249 (note 41).

65. N. Zhelnora, "Those Who Have Joined the Gang … Are Sentenced," *Argumenty i Fakty*, no. 50, 1991.

66. T. Kolganova, "Russian Mafia," *Shchit i Mech*, no. 13/14, 1992, p. 3.

67. Statement of Victor Yerin, First Deputy Minister of Internal Affairs of the USSR,

1,684.[68] Figures reported for the first eleven months of 1995 claimed officials 'neutralized' about 3,500 criminal groups.[69] By 1996, police officials indicated that some 4,000 groups had been 'broken up.'[70] According to an internal report of the Moscow Regional Organized Crime Control Department, from 1993–1998, the department (covering Moscow city and region) 'broke up' 2,827 organized crime groups which included 9,511 people.[71]

There are several possible explanations for the reported increase in the number of crime groups in Russia. First and most obvious is that the number of groups increased. There is little doubt that criminal groups in the former Soviet Union became much more active as the USSR was dismantled and that their numbers increased. By how much they increased is anybody's guess. A second and, to me, more interesting explanation for the increase in the number of crime groups as well as the increase in the number of groups 'liquidated' is that throughout the 1990s greater resources were being directed toward the problem. As the MVD's Organized Crime Control Department matured, it added thousands of officers to its rolls across the country specifically to analyze, expose, and fight crime groups. Beginning in 1992, Regional Organized Crime Departments (RUOPs) were established throughout Russia where in 1988 there were none. The former KGB established a unit to focus on the problem. Groups were being exposed through the Economic Crime and Drug Enforcement Units. Some 19,000 'commandos' backed by helicopters and armored vehicles were deployed to deal with the 'mafia.'[72] It seems that an increase in the number of criminal groups was inevitable. Third, perhaps the statistics reflect the confusion within the criminal world itself as groups fought over territory and, over time, attempted to consolidate their holdings. As groups moved into legitimate business, such as private security, and as they were absorbed into larger entities, it would make some sense that the overall numbers would decline.

The structure of crime groups and their interaction with each other made it difficult to distinguish one from another, further complicating attempts to

---

October 21, 1991, at the United Nations-MVD Conference on International Organized Crime Control, Suzdal, Russia.

68. Joanne Levine, "Beneficiaries of Reform Becoming Targets of Crime," *The Moscow Times*, April 21, 1993, p. 3.

69. Alexander Zhilin, "Russian Organized Crime—A Growth Industry," December 22, 1995, at http://www.amber.ucsf.edu/home/ross/public_html/russia_/ruscrime3.txt.

70. Author conversation with Yuri Melnikov, former Chief of the Russian National Central Bureau of Interpol, May 1996.

71. "Rezul'taty Deyatel'nosti RUOP po Moskvy pri GUOP MVD Rossii za 1993–1998," unpublished report of the Moscow Regional Organized Crime Control Department, p. 2.

72. Shchedrov, p. 3 (note 49).

record their total number. For example, the Izmailovo group in Moscow, which was very closely connected to the Solntsevo group, consisted of the Golianov and Perov groups and engaged in extensive sharing of members. Was this considered one, two, three or four crime groups? Or was it simply one 'criminal community' or 'organized criminal formation'?

It may have been that the situation defied simple statistics and required exhaustive research and explanation. However, it seems reasonable to conclude from looking at the numbers alone that the underworld was really a hodgepodge of loose-knit associated groups that were highly flexible and mobile for most of the 1990s. They had small core memberships and cooperated with one another when mutual interests were involved. The groups were difficult to extinguish fully, and fragments of broken groups likely found new associates with whom to work. The statistics seem to suggest that consolidation took the entire decade and only after 1999 did the criminal world stabilize. It's interesting that organized crime and 'mafia' are rarely even spoken of today in cities like Moscow and St. Petersburg, and most assessments conclude that 1) the gangster era of the large-scale struggling for territory, property, and influence is basically over, 2) many of the crime groups have transformed themselves into private security agencies and other companies, and 3) the business of providing protection and battling for territory, property, and influence is now undertaken by government agencies (see Chapter 11). The latter suggests that Vaksberg's Soviet 'mafia' and the traditional criminal world have become thoroughly intertwined and have ceased to exist in their 1990s form. In any case, the 'invasion' of the 'mafia' that was spoken of so often was really a cancer that grew from within the rotting body of the host organism. And it is this characteristic that made crime coming out of the former Soviet Union so dangerous.

II

ROOTS

CHAPTER 5

LEGACIES

The Tsar, pitying the peoples of his realm, zealous to root out unjust, disastrous, general burdens and crafty thefts from the State treasury, having ascertained that great falsifications and thefts are increasing the public burdens and injuring the interests of the State, and that by this many people of every station, but most of all the peasants, are becoming impoverished and ruined....

—From a decree of Tsar Peter the Great, 1713[1]

Communists did not invent the criminal underworld, just as they did not invent the repressive institution of the secret police. Both were legacies of Tsarist Russia. Autocratic government was a structure Lenin adapted to his 'revolutionary' purposes. The criminal underclass the Bolsheviks inherited had long experience in surviving in a police state.... This does not absolve the Communist era from culpability. The worst legacy of the Soviet Union is that it warped the Russian's everyday concept of what is criminal and what is not.

—Robert Fleet[2]

In 1994, the head of the National Central Bureau of Interpol for Russia, Yuri Melnikov, said to me, "I don't know what the fuss in the West is about the Russian 'mafia.' We've always been this way. It's just that you're finally finding out." That comment never left the back of my mind. After spending much of the 1990s in Russia, I arrived in the United States with two questions.

Since I had been a consultant to and later director of the Moscow office of a global corporate investigation and business intelligence firm (1995-1999), the first question pertained to business matters. What was the experience of

---

1. Cited in Warren B. Walsh, *Readings in Russian History*, Syracuse, Syracuse University Press, 1948, p. 150.
2. Robert Fleet, "The Underworld in Russia: It's Been There All Along," *Commonweal*, October 20, 1995, vol. 122, no. 18, p. 9.

foreign companies in Russia prior to the Russian Revolution of 1917? I had a general idea that Singer Sewing Company and International Harvester had been active in Russia in the second half of the 19th century.[3] I expected to focus on them. But as I started to dig, I found myself going all the way back to the 16th and 17th centuries, observing some of the challenges experienced by English traders.

And since I had lived through a dramatic and historic period of the golden era of the Russian 'mafia' (1990-94), the second question: Was there any period in Soviet history that resembled the post-Soviet 'mafia' world? I knew that the nascent Soviet state had experimented with a limited market economy in the 1920s, but I hadn't heard much about gangsters. Nevertheless, I suspected that that's where I'd find them if there were any to be found.

Putting the answers to these two questions together provides an interesting backdrop for what is to come in Chapters 6, 7, and 8. As it's impossible to present four hundred years of history in one brief chapter, I've taken certain elements that were frequently discussed in the 1990s in connection with the Russian 'mafia' and have provided illustrations of how they appeared between the 1550s and 1930. These elements include the nature of business in Russia, gangs, realities of Russian policing, and bribery. The goal here is to get a general sense if there was any truth to Melnikov's comment. If there was, it might change the way we look at the 1990s and the issue of group crime both in the former Soviet Union and in its transnational form. As I write this paragraph, the words of my former colleague, Andrei Dmitriev, drift through my mind. When speaking about corruption he would say, "We get this with our mother's milk. It's learned from a very young age." Already I have a feeling that there may be some truth to Melnikov's comment.

My starting point became 1555 as I stumbled onto English traders, under Richard Chancellor, sailing north around Russia in search of an alternate route to the riches of the Orient. Unfortunately for them, one of their ships wrecked near Archangelsk, and they recast their mercenary focus on Ivan the Terrible's Russia (Muscovy).

Ivan the Terrible granted a charter allowing the English Muscovy Company right of internal trade and of free transit to the East. The English merchant ships carried "dyed and dressed cloth, pewter, lead and tin, armaments and munitions, wine and spices to the foreign land. On their return they brought Russian cables and cordage, wax, tallow, flax, train oil, furs, and hides." The

---

3. There were 262 foreign companies recorded in existence in 1914 in Russia. See Thomas C. Owen, *Russian Corporate Capitalism from Peter the Great to Perestroika*, New York, Oxford University Press, 1995, p. 19.

traders remained close to Moscow, maintaining proximity to the Tsar in order to facilitate negotiations and rely on his protection in case of xenophobic outbursts by noblemen or the populace. The nobility and royalty pressured the merchants to extend credit for goods, making trade a hazardous undertaking for the foreigners. Understandably, Tsar Ivan sanctioned the English commercial monopoly in Muscovy only so long as it suited his political interests.[4]

In the book *Of the Rus Commonwealth* (1591) that resulted from his travels in Muscovy, Giles Fletcher, a special ambassador of Queen Elizabeth, conveys his observations of the Muscovites.

> In their manner of government your Highness may see both a true and strange face of a tyrannical state most unlike your own, without true knowledge of God, without written law, without common justice save that which proceedeth from their speaking law—to wit, the magistrate, who hath most need of a law to restrain his own injustice.[5]

In addition to being law-less, God-less, and lacking justice as according to Fletcher, the Russians were already being fashioned a nation of thieves before the close of the 16th century, a theme that has been propagated with striking consistency to this day by Russians and foreigners alike.[6] It's little wonder, then, that the English traders would concur with such a conclusion given their experiences over the next two centuries. In 1633, Charles I wrote to Tsar Mikhail that the English merchants were "dayly wronged & oppressed by your Officers, Ministers & subjects," particularly by the tobacco patentees and Tsarist officials who, "by their rigorous searching of al[l] boats and sled that

---

4. Giles Fletcher (1591), Albert J. Schmidt (ed. 1966), *Of the Rus Commonwealth*, Ithaca, Cornell University Press, 1966, pp. xiv-xv.

5. Ibid., pp. xxiii-xxiv.

6. Ibid., p. 24. See, among many others, Zara Witkin, *An Engineer in Stalin's Russia: Memoirs of Zara Witkin, 1932-1934*, Berkeley, University of California Press, 1991. Marquis de Custine, *Empire of the Czar: A Journey Through Eternal Russia*, New York, Doubleday, 1989. See also Robert K. Massie, *Peter the Great: His Life and World*, New York, Ballantine Books, 1980, p. 789: "Once, after hearing a Senate report listing further corruption, Peter summoned Yaguzhinsky in a rage and ordered the immediate execution of any official who robbed the state of even enough to pay for a piece of rope. Yaguzhinsky, writing down Peter's command, lifted his pen and asked, 'Has Your Majesty reflected on the consequences of this decree?' 'Go ahead and write,' said Peter furiously. 'Does Your Majesty wish to live alone in the empire without any subjects?' persevered Yaguzhinsky. 'For we all steal. Some take a little, some take a great deal, but all of us take something.' Peter laughed, shook his head sadly and went no further."

co[me] laden with their goods betwixt Archangel & Mosco, both hinder their trade & imbezel their goods."[7] One thing had become apparent very quickly: the more I read, the more the problems of the 16th and 17th centuries paralleled those of my clients some four hundred years later.

Toward the end of the 17th century, Peter the Great attempted to normalize the tobacco trade, seeing in it a lucrative source of tax revenue. He permitted the open sale and consumption of tobacco, claiming he was forced into this move by extensive smuggling operations and his missing out on the potential tax revenue. Smuggled tobacco indeed passed through many hands getting to market—including Polish, Swedish, and Cossack—but scarcely through those of the English, who had been given exclusive rights to the Russian tobacco market. The Russia Company, as the Muscovy Company was now called, lost its monopoly contract as it was able to sell only 500 hogsheads of tobacco from a shipment of 5,500.[8] Throughout the country, regional governors and local officials harassed the English traders and permitted smuggling to continue. "The regional monopolists, like Orlyonok and later the industrial magnate Strogonov, had mounted great resistance of the selling of tobacco within their holdings, the former accused of everything up to murder."[9] Elite merchants carried out administrative and fiscal duties for the Tsar and in return were granted special privileges, were exempt from taxation, had the right to trade abroad, and had the right to own land.[10] Understandably, English complaints fell on deaf ears.[11]

These challenges of excessive bureaucracy, lack of predictability, thorough arbitrariness in trade, and extensive smuggling undermining legitimate business would continue for centuries, with varying degrees of intensity, right up until today. Perhaps more importantly, even with the passage of time there was little meaningful development of a corporate commercial culture that would allow for the conduct of business without the direct involvement—or interference—of the crown or regional administrative forces.

In *The Corporation Under Russian Law, 1800-1917: A Study in Tsarist Economic Policy* and *Russian Corporate Capitalism from Peter the Great to Pere-*

---

7. Jacob M. Price, *The Tobacco Adventure to Russia: Enterprise, Politics, and Diplomacy in the Quest for a Northern Market for English Colonial Tobacco, 1676-1722*, Philadelphia, The American Philosophical Society, 1961, p. 18.

8. Ibid., p. 48.

9. Ibid., p. 52.

10. Janet M. Hartley, *A Social History of the Russian Empire, 1650-1825*, London, Longman, 1999, p. 58.

11. Price, p. 51 (note 7).

stroika, Thomas Owen presents detailed histories of the development—or lack of development—of the business environment throughout the Russian era. From Peter the Great to the eve of World War I and the Russian Revolution— from 1700 to December 31, 1913, Owen writes, only 4,542 corporations were chartered with a mere 33 of those coming into existence in the first 120 years. Most had very short life spans.[12] "Particularly ominous was the failure, within two decades of its founding, of the Russian Livestock Insurance Company, the only large corporation specifically devoted to the improvement of agriculture in this predominantly agrarian society."[13]

Despite being called a kind of 'political entrepreneur' who was innovator, inventor, engineer, manager, and mobilizer,[14] Peter the Great was an autocrat who was interested in building a strong state—a military power—on the backs of the people. He was unable to allow a competing center of power and influence in the form of corporate life, a pattern his successors would repeat. This didn't bode well for the future of commerce in Russia, the practice of making money being shackled by suspicion, jealousy, and ignorance.

The system of autocracy created the need for the population to preoccupy itself with survival while relying on someone else, someone higher up the food chain—the Tsar—to act. This was true in all facets of life, including commercial endeavors, alluded to in this illustration: One Russian official confided to a Dutch commercial negotiator frustrated by endless delays, "Between ourselves, I will tell you the whole truth. We have not a single man who understands commercial affairs at all. But I can assure you that the Tsar is now occupying himself with this matter."[15]

In the second half of the 18th century, Catherine the Great mentioned corporations only once, in a decree enumerating the powers of the police to enforce the regulations of each "society, partnership, brotherhood, or similar institution," and to "destroy and ban" any that injured "the general welfare."[16] Given the profound negative orientation toward business, one can imagine

---

12. Owen, p. 18 (note 3).

13. Ibid., p. 19.

14. Blackwell in Gregory Guroff and Fred V. Carstensen (eds.), *Entrepreneurship in Imperial Russia and the Soviet Union*, Princeton, Princeton University Press, 1983, pp. 21-22. See also Lindsey Hughes, *Russia in the Age of Peter the Great*, New Haven, Yale University Press, 1998.

15. Walsh, p. 152 (note 1). See also in Walsh, p. 147: "In Russia, if the Tsar were away for a year or less, the administration became thoroughly disorganized. So far Peter had succeeded in pulling down better than in building up."

16. Thomas C. Owen, *The Corporation Under Russian Law, 1800-1917: A Study in Tsarist Economic Policy*, Cambridge, Cambridge University Press, 1991, p. 9.

who fell among the targets of the police. This trend continued throughout the 19th and 20th centuries.

Although more corporations were chartered in the 19th century than in the previous, the difference, given the size of Russia, was insignificant. During the thirty-year reign of Nicholas I, 136 new companies were founded and only 18 held capital amounts in excess of one million rubles.[17] In any event, a critical characteristic of Russian merchants of the day was that they relied more on intuition and the aid of loyal friends and relatives than on rational calculation and an understanding of trends in the world market.[18]

> English and American merchants in Russia in the early nineteenth century marveled at the skill of illiterate Russians in the use of the simple abacus, but they noted also the merchants' reliance on secrecy, cheating, and evasion in dealing with strangers. One British merchant noted the pride with which Russian merchants turned a dishonest profit: 'A dextrous theft in the way of overreaching is regarded by them as the very triumph of their genius.'[19]

Both of these characteristics—reliance on intuition and friends rather than planning and employing what the West defines as underhanded methods—are still very much in evidence today.

For foreigners, the size of Russia, its poverty, and inadequate infrastructure increased the cost of doing business, as International Harvester and Singer learned in the run up to the Russian Revolution. According to Fred Carstensen, International Harvester found doing business in Russia two to three times more expensive than in the United States. Singer had nearly two times as much capital tied up in Russia relative to some other countries where it was operating.[20]

The market presented endless frustrations for foreign businesses in the last decades of the 19th century, but as for native entrepreneurship, companies in the city centers of Russia were finally beginning to show promise. As Owen notes, "The proliferation of factories, the increase in the number of hired workers, the emergence of industrial cartels, and the financial involvement of the major banks in giant manufacturing corporations provided some evidence that Russian capitalism was approaching maturity on the eve of World War I."[21]

---

17. Owen, p. 19 (note 3).
18. Owen, p. 2 (note 16).
19. Ibid.
20. Carstensen cited in Owen, p. 25 (note 3).
21. Thomas C. Owen, "Doing Business in Merchant Moscow," in James L. West and Iurii A. Petrov (eds.), *Merchant Moscow: Images of Russia's Vanished Bourgeoisie*, Princeton,

However, with World War I, the Russian Revolution, and subsequent Civil War rapidly approaching, this relatively anemic Russian version of capitalism would not be given a real chance to reverse centuries of overbearing control from above and underdevelopment below. The Communists would ultimately do away with formal business practices, and in any event entrepreneurship still didn't enjoy support among the population. Commercial operators were held in low esteem; 'tradesperson' was a synonym for "narrow-minded, vulgar, uncultured, and Philistine...."[22]

In 1905, a spokesman for Russian iron producers summed up the sentiment of the people toward big business: "In the 'cultured' language of our dear country, employed by former owners of serfs, the word 'industrialist' has somehow become a synonym for 'swindler,' 'bloodsucker,' 'exploiter,' and other, no less flattering, definitions."[23] In the southern port city of Odessa, for example, business was blamed for the absence of 'normal civic consciousness' and was seen as representing 'moral defects.'[24] Again, not an exclusively Soviet perspective, anti-capitalism had deep roots among the Russian peasantry, working class, intelligentsia, and bureaucracy long before the Bolshevik Revolution of 1917. And it has not fully disappeared from the contemporary Russian landscape.

Generally speaking, Russian businessmen suffered from many powerful negative forces including low social and political standing, a tough and arbitrary tax regime, a lack of experience, severe punishments, state favoritism in protecting certain merchants, and the issuance of tax breaks and other advantages to favored nobles.[25]

While business was held in check by autocracy and tradition, the same cannot be said of crime, which was omnipresent through much of Russian history. In the 16th and 17th centuries, entire villages of 'thieves and brigands' existed around the country. And here the matter was not simply one of 'stealing.' As Esipov notes, "Bandits embodied in themselves the ideal of freedom

Princeton University Press, 1998, p. 29. See also Jonathan A. Grant, *Big Business in Russia: The Putilov Company in Late Imperial Russia, 1868-1917*, Pittsburgh, University of Pittsburgh Press, 1999.

22. Cyril E. Black, "Russian and Soviet Entrepreneurship in a Comparative Context," in Guroff and Carstensen, p. 7 (note 14).

23. Owen, p. xii (note 16).

24. Daniel R. Brower, *The Russian City between Tradition and Modernity, 1850-1900*, Berkeley, University of California Press, 1990, p. 61.

25. See Abby M. Schrader, *Languages of the Lash: Corporal Punishment and Identity in Imperial Russia*, Dekalb, Northern Illinois University Press, 2002, and Richard Hellie, *Slavery in Russia: 1450-1725*, Chicago, The University of Chicago Press, 1982.

of the Russian commoner in the 17th century...." This is an idea encountered time and again in Russian history including in the rhetoric of street children, gangsters, and *vory v zakone* of the 20th century[26] (see Chapter 7).

Moscow of the 17th and 18th centuries was notorious as a crime center of the country. Masses of thieves and juvenile delinquents gathered in Zariad'e, a dark and dirty corner in Kitaigorod in central Moscow. Students from a nearby school were recruited and taught how to pick pockets.[27] On the outskirts of Moscow alone there was said to be more than 30,000 thieves. Robbery and theft of personal property as well as physical assaults committed by groups were rife.[28]

In tones familiar to 20th century observers, 18th century foreigners spoke of the audacity of Russian thugs and the emptiness of the dark streets, the habitat of thieves and armed beggars. "These villains," writes an Austrian visitor, "place themselves at the corners of streets and throw swinging cudgels at the heads of those that pass by, in which practice they are so expert that these mortal blows seldom miss."[29] Peter the Great tried to dictate law and order through threats and drastic measures. In a 1718 decree, he instructed that any able-bodied people found roaming the streets were to be "beaten with rods and returned to their village; if caught again they were to be knouted and the men given hard labor and women and children sent to factories."[30]

Already during the 18th century, levels of organization of crime gangs were believed to be increasing as indoctrination into groups, financial contributions as a membership requirement, use of nicknames among criminals, and a distinct argot (*fenia*) came into greater use.[31]

Perhaps the best known criminal archetype of the Russian empire was Vanka Kain. The story goes that from 1731-1749 Kain was a kind of detective-robber (*syshchik-grabitel'*). When he was young, Vanka was always stealing from family members and relatives. One day, one of the men from whom he stole introduced him to a real thief, Pyotr Romanov, who went by the nickname Kamchatka.

On the night of their introduction in Moscow, Vanka and Kamchatka stole goods from Vanka's master and retreated to a dark place under Stone Bridge

---

26. S. Ya. Lebedev, *Antiobshchestvennye Traditsii, Obychai i ikh Vliyanie na Prestupnost'*, Omsk, MVD, 1989, p. 14.

27. Ibid., p. 16.

28. Ibid., p. 14. See also M. Dikselius and A. Konstantinov, *Prestupnyi Mir Rossii*, Sankt Peterburg, Bibliopolis, 1995, pp. 42-43; Massie, pp. 5, 281-282 (note 6).

29. Ibid., Massie, p. 5.

30. Hartley, p. 104 (note 10).

31. Lebedev, p. 16 (note 26).

where Vanka was inducted into the criminal society. Accounts claim that there were two main parts to the ceremony: the first was giving money over to the group and the second was the offering of a speech by one of the thieves in thieves' jargon. (We will meet these characteristics of the underworld again in Chapter 7.)

Vanka, like many thieves of the time, specialized in picking pockets. After several successful operations, he was arrested. But he didn't receive severe punishment because Kamchatka came to his rescue. A note written in thieves' argot said, "Here is the key to open the shackles." After his escape, Kain continued his criminal career and was involved in several groups.

Quite unexpectedly, Kain denounced his criminal life in 1741 and became a detective. The authorities gave him 14 soldiers to fight crime and on the first night he detained 32 thieves. Over a period of two years in Moscow, Vanka and his team caught 109 swindlers, 37 thieves, 50 thieves who were in hiding, 60 fences, and 42 AWOL soldiers. He was given no reward for his service or even compensation for his own money that he spent in search of criminals. Kain then reportedly went to the opposite extreme. He turned to extortion, extracting payoffs from his former criminal associates for protection. In 1749, Kain's police career came to an end when a new chief had him arrested for the kidnapping of a 15-year-old girl with the intention of forced cohabitation.[32]

Robber gangs, like Vanka Kain and his criminal brethren, were prevalent throughout the century. Travel was so hazardous that in 1735 the Senate ordered that all the trees along one of the roads leading from St. Petersburg be cut down so that bandits could not hide in them. Reports from around the country decried the threats from the underworld. As today, the dangers were real but many of the stories grew into legend. A Cossack, I.G. Melnikov, "was terrifying for all travelers … they said that he had cast a spell on guns so that it was impossible to kill or wound him with a bullet."[33]

---

32. A. I. Gurov, *Professional'naya Prestupnost': Proshloe i Sovremennost'*, Moskva, Yuridicheskaya Literatura, 1990, pp. 59-61. See also Lebedev, p. 15 (note 26). Lebedev notes that this story has been told by other writers, citing M. Komarov, *Ostoyatel'nye i Vernye Istorii Dvukh Moshennikov*, Moskva, 1788; G.V. Esipov, *Tyazhelaya Pamyat' Proshlogo: Rasskazy iz Del Tainoi Kantseliarii i Drugikh Arkhivov*, Sankt Peterburg, 1885. For an English-language version of the story, see "The Tale of Vanka Kain," in James von Geldern and Louise McReynolds (eds.), *Entertaining Tsarist Russia: Tales, Songs, Plays, Movies, Jokes, Ads, and Images from Russian Urban Life, 1779-1917*, Bloomington, Indiana University Press, 1998, pp. 23-31.

33. Hartley, p. 109 (note 10).

With so much criminal activity afoot, it's little surprise that by the end of the 18th century the criminal world had developed a professional nucleus (*yadro*) and specific divisions of labor with the first signs of a criminal 'boss' emerging.[34]

At this time and throughout the 19th century, theft of cattle, horses, and grain, and the burning down of houses were widespread practices by so-called bandit groups.

> A survey of 'ordinary' rural crime exposes the very serious dangers that communities faced from outside assaults upon their property and, at times, their persons as well, and that created widespread insecurity as the century wore on. The networks of organized horse thieves who mercilessly preyed upon peasantry, clergy, and nobility alike are by far the best example here, although robbers, bandits, arsonists, escapees from prison or exile, swindlers, confidence men and women, and vagrants made up sizable portions of rural Russia's little-known criminal underworld.[35]

And it was not unknown for lords and property owners to engage in the organized theft of peasants' property.[36] Some noblemen would force the villagers into supplying them with equipment and grain. And little justice was brought to those arrested. "In the never-ending hierarchy of Russia, poorer nobles could suffer in much the same way as the villagers at the hands of more powerful nobles. The strongest took the best land using armed serfs. The poorer of the nobles couldn't afford to start legal proceedings."[37]

By the second half of the 19th century peasants started hiring den owners (*pristanoderzhateli*) who would guarantee the safety and security of the peasants from horse thieves for a specific fee.[38] Like today, it was the organized bandits, horse thieves, and others who captured the imagination, but crime was primarily a local affair, between acquaintances. In the rural areas crime remained an 'intrapeasant phenomenon' and swirled around the typical array of offenses: "pilfering from a neighbor's barn or field; drunken brawls on the

---

34. Lebedev, p. 20 (note 26). See also Mikhail Dyomin, *The Day is Born of Darkness: A Personal Account of the Soviet Criminal Underworld*, New York, Alfred A. Knopf, 1976.

35. Stephen P. Frank, *Crime, Cultural Conflict, and Justice in Rural Russia, 1856-1914*, Berkeley, University of California Press, 1999, p. 12.

36. Dikselius, p. 43 (note 28).

37. Hartley, 102, (note 10).

38. Valery Chalidze, *Criminal Russia: Crime in the Soviet Union*, New York, Random House, 1977, p. 54.

village street; familial animosities; arguments over land use; jealousies aroused in any number of situations ranging from infidelity within marriage to hostility toward a well-to-do fellow villager."[39]

Regarding crime generally, the population at that time, as in the 1990s, was uncertain as to what actually constituted a 'crime.' There were sets of confusing and contradictory laws, and judges usually determined the reality of crime and justice. People from all strata of society had to somehow divine the boundaries of the permissible and the forbidden. This was a complicated undertaking at a time when anxiety over public order was rising steadily, fueled in large part by news accounts of crime that were disseminated widely by the end of the 19th century.[40] Part of the result of this confusion was for the population to 'work the system,' bending the laws and the judicial system in their favor.[41] The people lived in constant survival mode, everything was negotiable and every obstacle could be sidestepped, whether through connections, bribes, or threats. As a result, shadow systems of justice, disparate sets of rules, and varying approaches to punishment developed independently in the state and upper class, the peasantry, and the criminal world. Each would take matters into their own hands observing their own sets of rules.[42]

In the 1890s, journalist Vladimir Gilyarovsky wrote of a kind of anti-society that contained a hierarchy, rituals, and honors that were "a gruesome caricature of respectable society." He portrayed a hierarchy that included lowly beggars and 'fences' at the bottom and 'the lords of the land'—thieves—at the top.[43] This world continued to grow and gather strength throughout the 20th century, coming to a dramatic climax in the 1990s with the intermingling of the *vory v zakone*—the lords of the anti-society—into the "respectable society" (see Chapter 7).

---

39. Frank, p. 11 (note 35).

40. Ibid., p. 5; see pp. 6-7: "[T]he official and narrowly conceived definition of rural crime would remain closely bound up with the state's fiscal needs and its fear of disorder—a definition clearly reflected in the criminal statistics."

41. Ibid., p. 13.

42. "It should be noted that most of Russian society continued to live outside and below the law, according to traditional customs and dependent on local centers of power, as did much of the rural population of Europe at the time. But in Russia the situation was exacerbated by two factors. Firstly, serfdom meant that nobles acted as judges and tax collectors for the state and their serfs, with the result that the largest social group was in effect isolated from the jurisdiction of the state. Secondly, peasants—serfs and state peasants—were governed by customary law and not the law of the land on the matters which concerned them most, that is, inheritance and property law." Hartley, p. 111 (note 10).

43. Brower, p. 149 (note 24).

The presence of extensive criminality may seem somewhat counterintuitive in a place like the Russian empire, presumably ruled by iron-fisted autocrats in a 'police state' environment. It's convenient to think of Russian autocracy— and later the Soviet system—in terms of 'absolute control' and 'police state,' as a place that had a police officer on every street corner, threatening to cart a person off to some black hole never to be heard from again for the smallest of transgressions. But the realities of Russian administration and law enforcement could not support such an image.

In 17th century Muscovy, the bureaucracy was so poorly trained and educated and suffering from the eternal Russian problem of inadequate salaries that "favoritism, incompetence in the collection of taxes, and above all endemic corruption" were already features of the system. For example, the military governor (*voevoda*) exercised authority over both town and countryside in his province. The primary obligation of local communities was the material support of the *voevoda*. The community provided food and goods to the *voevoda* in an established system of 'feeding' (*kormlenie*): grain, food, wood, alcohol, and so on were provided as was money to cover the expense for the *voevoda* to move to the province once assigned there. Interestingly, an uprising broke out in 1635 in one city not because of the system but because the local *voevoda* demanded five hundred rubles to pay for his moving expenses rather than the typical three hundred.[44]

At a time when the coffers of the state were often low, the *voevoda* system of *kormlenie* was essentially a tax that frequently went directly into the governors' pockets. The system was maintained and developed by the Tsar at a time when he was also issuing threats of punishment for bribery. But it was often difficult to distinguish between the taxes and the bribes.[45] For example, in Siberia *voevody* would increase the levy through tax-like 'gifts' in return for turning a blind eye to certain types of illegal activity. ("In the capital too it was impossible to achieve anything without money and above all connections, a system that naturally struck foreigners as particularly repugnant."[46]) A large part of the problem with the system of *kormlenie* was that it was open to abuse. The further from Moscow, the less forceful the influence of the Tsar. Some officials took double and more than they should have while others simply took 'gifts' without performing the requested favor.[47] In one investigation, Peter the

44. Hans J. Torke in Ezra Mendelsohn and Marshall S. Shatz (eds.), *Imperial Russia, 1700-1917: State, Society, Opposition*, DeKalb, Illinois, Northern Illinois University Press, 1988, p. 6. See also Hartley, p. 115 (note 10).

45. Ibid., Torke, p. 6.

46. Ibid., p. 7.

47. Hartley, p. 115 (note 10).

Great was told of a provincial governor who had embezzled more than a million rubles from the state treasury.[48] At points during Peter's reign, government officials were paid in furs and other goods instead of money. One of the Tsar's decrees said that "when money is absolutely necessary, and when no other way of raising it is found, the sum must be deducted proportionally from the salaries of the officials, spiritual as well as temporal, except foreign artisans and soldiers and sailors."[49] Little wonder, then, that bribery was widespread. This depiction of the challenges facing the regime hundreds of years ago is strikingly similar to the delays in payment of salaries and the extensive bartering system in the 1990s.

Generally speaking, the lack of resources to administer the enormous empire properly was a fundamental problem. As Janet Hartley notes, as late as 1763, Russia employed 16,500 officials in central and local administration, while Prussia, with less than one per cent of Russia's land area, employed about 14,000 people in a far more structured and coherent civil service in the same period.[50] There was a profound shortage, for example, of clerical staff, their salaries were low—as little as 10-30 rubles a year, and were paid only three times a year. In 1797, a provincial governor reported to the Procurator General that he had dismissed several officials for bribery the previous year and now asked if they could be reinstated since he was short of trained personnel.[51]

The lack of order, discipline, and sufficiently trained and compensated officials in the administration of the empire fueled an eternal corruption in Russia that exists in the very roots of the system and continues to this day, widespread and indeed systemic. The German pastor, Johann Gottfried Gregory, reported to the Brandenburg Elector at the end of the 1660s that "the Germans must often give the boyars presents, as a result of which some things are then put right...." People were accustomed to the fact that they could not successfully do business in Moscow unless they gave the requisite presents.[52]

Bribery has been a concern throughout Russian history. Peter the Great's decree of December 24, 1714, on bribery and corruption (*likhoimstvo*) was

---

48. Andrei Platonov, "The Epifan Locks," *Collected Works*, Ann Arbor, Ardis, 1978, p. 236.

49. Walsh, p. 152 (note 1). See also from ibid., pp. 223-224: "Tsar Peter is a very powerful man, for all his empty shouting and undisciplined behavior. His nature is like his country, superficially as undisciplined as a creature of the wild, but underneath all this abundantly capable."

50. Hartley, p. 111 (note 10).

51. Ibid., pp. 116-117.

52. Torke, p. 7 (note 44).

aimed at "rogues whose only goal is to undermine all that is good and to fill their insatiability." Offenders were to undergo corporal punishment and confiscation of property, and to be disgraced and expelled from the company of good people, or even executed.[53] But attempts to legislate away such behavior inevitably and understandably were ineffective. Even one of Peter's closest associates had actively embezzled from government grain delivery contracts, took massive bribes, and shipped million of rubles abroad at a time when the average monthly salary was 18 rubles.[54]

In response to the shortfall in administration staff in the 19th century, merchants were pressured into municipal service. Understandably, this became another opportunity to bribe. A sufficient bribe ensured that "a person with power could bypass all laws and regulations so that [he] would not be disturbed and would not be called to serve." With the exception of chiefs, the police received a pittance for pay. Because of their low salaries they often took advantage of their considerable powers to ensure themselves immediate personal profit. Town traders and artisans, surrounded by administrative "unpleasantness that can trap them at every step," had the habit of "bribing everyone who shouts at them." In 1862, a municipal commission found that, not surprisingly, the police "violate the urban peace and order that it is their duty to enforce."[55]

Even after reforms in the middle of the 19th century, police remained underpaid and understaffed. The ratio of police officer to citizenry was one to 700 or less. In the late 1860s, a provincial governor complained that the province's urban police forces were "inadequate and insufficient in relation to the number of inhabitants and to the local conditions." Police salaries rarely climbed above 150 rubles a year, and the police force frequently attracted former soldiers whose only training was "exposure to the draconian regime of military command and their habit of obedience." Not surprisingly, the police experienced a high turnover rate; in one city in 1887, resignations were handed in at the rate of almost one per day. In that year, three hundred new policemen had to be appointed to maintain a force of just sixty. Frequently, police work was interrupted by other more lucrative opportunities, such as work on the docks in port cities.[56]

Throughout the system, officials lived on bribes and other sources of income. One provincial officer estimated that police clerks "lived on their [ille-

---

53. Lindsey Hughes, *Russia in the Age of Peter the Great*, New Haven, Yale University Press, 1998, p. 132.
54. Massie, pp. 786-788 (note 6).
55. Brower, pp. 15, 16, and 19 (note 24).
56. Ibid., p. 191.

gal] income from passport registration, earning 30 rubles a month." An important observation to note is that this kind of situation was not out of the ordinary; it was a fact of life. An inspector in southeastern Russia acknowledged that the police were zealous in enforcing regulations for "the external cleanliness of the central parts of the city, [and] filling out forms for official registers."[57]

Building code violations, sanitation code violations, fire code violations, residency violations, obtaining internal passports, and a host of other obstacles could be resolved with the careful placement of a bribe. In some urban areas toward the end of the 19th century police were responsible for more than forty-six thousand official orders. There was no way to deal with all of these regulations, which provided sufficient fuel to keep the fires of bribery burning. Importantly, the police did not need to rely on the presence of a violation to extract a bribe. The excessive number of regulations encouraged the police to judge criminality according to customary practices as well as personal convenience and administrative statute. Equally important to note is that the rural areas rarely ever saw representatives of the police and lived largely according to their own traditions and customs without much police interference.[58]

Throughout Russian history there have been ambiguities and contradictions in law to the point where informal arrangements carried significant weight.[59] No clear distinction existed between a law (zakon) and an administrative ruling (razporyazhenie); any decree (ukaz) issued by the Tsar had the force of law, requiring "no special procedures or prescribed channels." The Tsar's laws grew increasingly weaker the farther from the center one traveled. In the countryside, nobles and landowners laid down the law over their serfs, properties, and inheritance in a kind of feudal relationship. And the serfs weren't necessarily looking for fairness under the law but rather officials sympathetic to their particular needs.[60]

In the 19th century as in the 20th, it was not the fact of bribery that caused consternation among the population. After all, this was part of life, understood by all. As my former colleague Andrei Dmitriev had noted, it came with their mother's milk. Authority had frequently been seen in personal terms; problem solving was largely through informal networks or informal arrangements within the formal system. It was when the system of bribing became

---

57. Ibid., p. 196.
58. Ibid., pp. 196-197.
59. See Hartley at note 42.
60. Hughes, p. 132 (note 53).

unpredictable that real dissatisfaction arose. The population wanted the person in charge to be strong and consistent. They wanted the comfort of knowing they could bribe one person and get what they required. If they didn't know whom to bribe or if the number of people to bribe became too great, confusion would result.[61] A remarkably similar sentiment was expressed innumerable times when the Soviet Union was dismantled.

From the very beginning of the new regime after the Russian Revolution in 1917, survival was first and foremost in the minds of virtually everyone. World War I and the ensuing Civil War left the country in utter chaos. Illegal and semi-legal free markets flourished as the official economy failed to satisfy basic needs.[62] Armed bands roamed the countryside, "seizing what they could, killing whomever they pleased."[63] One sociologist reported that during the Civil War years, "hundreds of bands are stopping trains, robbing everyone they meet, pillaging hamlets, villages, and small towns."[64]

To exacerbate the situation, the new regime attacked symbols of non-Communist morality. Churches were demolished or sealed up, turned into prisons or dumping grounds for garbage. In the months after the Revolution, fourteen bishops and hundreds of priests were tortured, shot, hanged, drowned, or burned.[65]

During the Civil War, the Bolsheviks introduced a new initiative called War Communism which, in a sense, was Lenin's declaration of war on the economy to ensure the survival of the fledgling state. In keeping with well-established patterns, the regime felt it necessary to pursue its economic agenda through the use of violence. War Communism consisted of the seizure of grain and other foodstuffs from the peasants, frequently by armed force. Virtually all industry was nationalized, private trade was banned, and central planning policies inherited from the Tsarist regime were expanded. As the Bolsheviks were still fielding an army, most resources went to the soldiers rather than the peasantry, despite that the peasantry constituted the vast majority of the population. There were deep shortages in food, shelter, and warm clothing; peo-

---

61. Ransel in David Ransel (ed.), *Village Life in Late Tsarist Russia by Olga Semyonova Tian-Shanskaia*, Bloomington, Indiana University Press, 1993, pp. 157-158, 166.

62. R. W. Davies, *Soviet Economic Development from Lenin to Khrushchev*, Cambridge, Cambridge University Press, 1998, p. 19.

63. Alan Ball, *And Now My Soul is Hardened: Abandoned Children in Soviet Russia, 1918-1930*, Berkeley, University of California Press, 1994, p. 5.

64. Sociologist Pitirim Sorokin in Alan Ball, *Russia's Last Capitalists: The NEPmen, 1921-1929*, Berkeley, University of California Press, 1987, p. 9.

65. Zigurds L. Zile (ed.), *Ideas and Forces in Soviet Legal History: A Reader on the Soviet State and Law*, New York, Oxford University Press, 1992, p. 113.

ple took to eating animal feed and, consequently, many animals perished, exacerbating an already critical situation. According to Davies, by 1921, prices were running an estimated 16,800 times above 1914 levels.[66]

More than 17 million people remained unsettled with many millions more uprooted during the next few years. Large towns were essentially depopulated. Between 1917 and 1920, the combined populations of Moscow and St. Petersburg fell from 4.3 million to only 1.8 million. Over two million people emigrated, and the famine of 1921-22 sent many more refugees fleeing in search of food; an estimated 13 million civilians died prematurely, mainly as a result of the famine and other epidemics that tore through the country. More than 3 million soldiers were killed or died of wounds or disease. The population of the Soviet Union, at its lowest point in January 1923, was 6-9 million less than in January 1914.[67]

Faced with such a staggering set of circumstances, by 1921 Lenin had little choice but to reconsider the path the Revolution had taken. The choice was relatively easy because it had, in fact, already been made for him. Networks of traders and private markets were springing up, operating extensively on a barter system and turning significant parts of Russia into a market society.[68] As Lenin later admitted, "The private market proved stronger than us."[69]

Forced food requisitioning was no longer a viable option. The peasantry was exhausted and their resources nearly depleted. Lenin's priority of getting Russia back on its feet economically was totally untenable without a robust agricultural sector to support the needs of the urban industrial workers.

As a result, the New Economic Policy (NEP) was introduced in March 1921 and granted peasants the right to market their goods, within certain parameters established by the state. Private and cooperative trade, private manufacturing, and service enterprises were revived to facilitate the process.[70] The state maintained control over what was called the 'commanding heights': major industry, military production, and so on.

The concept of speculation at this time, however, could be stretched to ban nearly all private trade. A July 1921 law declared that anyone who conspired

---

66. Davies, p. 19 (note 62).

67. Ibid., p. 22.

68. Alan Ball, *Russia's Last Capitalists: The NEPmen, 1921-1929*, Berkeley, University of California Press, 1987, p. 7.

69. Davies, p. 24 (note 62).

70. Robert V. Daniels, *A Documentary History of Communism in Russia: From Lenin to Gorbachev*, Hanover, University Press of New England, 1993, pp. 112-113. See also Zile (note 65).

to raise prices or withhold goods from the market was to be imprisoned or have property confiscated, or both. The law forbade peasants to store their grain until prices improved and made it a crime for a private middleman to offer peasants or any other producers a higher price for their products than that offered by the state. Like most everything else in Russia at the time, there was no uniform enforcement against speculation. But police cracked down enough to make the very definition of speculation confusing. As one Russian put it:

> There was a very fine dividing line between permissible profit and illegal speculation. From time to time the GPU arrested a dozen or a hundred enterprising traders; this was called 'skimming the NEP.' The cook knows when to skim the fish-soup, but I doubt whether all the Nepmen understood which they were: the scum or the fish.[71]

In 1921 and 1922, a wide variety of activities was made legal: individuals could buy, sell, and own municipal buildings; private publishing houses were established, as were private hospitals and clinics; and the private trade in medicine was now allowed. The state monopoly on the sale of agricultural tools and equipment was repealed. Restrictions on freight shipments belonging to the so-called Nepmen were eliminated. Horses could be bought and sold freely, and it was no longer a crime to own foreign currency, precious stones, gold, and silver. By 1923, private trade in nearly all items was permitted with the exception of those few that were officially banned.[72]

From the outset of the policy, the regime had every intention of trying to control the development of the state-sponsored market activity while simultaneously undermining the ability of private interests to operate in this relatively relaxed atmosphere. The overarching approach in attempting this, as Nikita Khrushchev notes in his memoirs, was not through administrative measures but to train members in the state sector to engage in business, hence, the appearance of the slogan 'Learn Commerce.' But, the future Party leader reports, "We did not have much success."[73]

In such an environment the necessity for personal contacts only increased. That the regime relied somewhat less on violence and executions in the 1920s as a primary policy tool and eased its restrictions on private trade and other business practices did nothing to encourage the population to adhere to the rule of law. Arbitrariness was still the mainstay of the criminal justice system.

---

71. Ball, p. 33 (note 68).
72. Ibid., p. 23.
73. Zile, p. 143 (note 65).

Confusion and contradictions in legislation meant that virtually any person could be reeled in for virtually any crime. The Bolsheviks affected changes that had nothing to do with building a legal foundation or ensuring the rights of individuals or of supporting commercial interests. Their policies had nothing to do with fostering the trust critical to a normal functioning business environment and everything to do with retaining and strengthening their own power base.

NEP—within the environment described above—had the effect of forcing the private dealers to devise methods of deception in order to circumvent the obstacles placed in their path by the state. Much of the behavior was simply fraud, taking advantage of the conditions of the day. In a typical scenario, for example, Alan Ball tells the story of a man named Vitkun who had arrived in Moscow from Siberia with only a hundred rubles in his pocket.

> Along with his wife and some friends, he announced the formation of a joint-stock gold mining company. Shortly thereafter, one of the 'partners' was dispatched to the Urals, whence he sent back telegrams describing the work in the fictitious gold fields in glowing terms. Armed with these cables and exploiting the desire of the state to increase the output of gold, Vitkun obtained provisions on credit from various state agencies, allegedly to supply workers in the gold fields. In reality, the goods were resold. The ploy even worked for a fourteen year old boy in Leningrad, who proclaimed the organization of a producers' cooperative, the Detskaia artel imeni t. Lenina. The Commissariat of Finance gave him eight thousand rubles to get started; the Commissariat of Communications provided free travel tickets for the use of the cooperative; and the Leningrad Soviet donated seventy-two hundred pounds of clothing. Actually the cooperative was just a front, and the youth (who may have been a front himself) used the money and various resources he had been given to open a movie theater.[74]

The poet Mayakovsky summed up the importance of having well-placed trusted contacts throughout the system: "*Nevesta v treste, kum v GUM, brat v narkomat.*" ("A fiancee in a trust, a godparent in GUM [the major state store], and a brother in a People's Commissariat.") In 1922, for example, an agent of the state trading store, Gostorg, at the Nizhnii Novgorod Fair delivered supplies at low prices to the private firm, Transtorg, whose director happened to

---

74. Ball, p. 119 (note 68).

be his brother. A member of the board of directors of Transtorg was also the head of a division of Gostorg, and the founder of Transtorg was at the same time an agent for Gostorg.[75] Note well that the story of Vitkun and the poetic observations of Mayakovsky are presented here not as historical curiosities in a transition period in Russia. They are examples of widespread patterns of behavior that were relied on daily across 11 time zones in the former Soviet Union throughout the 1990s, by some as a way to quick wealth and by others as a means of surviving.

Some of the first private stores opened in 1921 were owned by former state employees who had used their official positions to acquire goods they then sold on their own. Other people remained in state service, registering their shops under someone else's name (often a close relative), and then supplied the stores with products they controlled (stole) as state officials.

Occasionally a private contractor or supplier for a state agency who was also an official in that agency could buy and sell goods to and from himself, on rather unattractive terms for the state. One Nepman even wrote a letter to himself proposing transactions to himself in his other capacity as an official in a state farm. Seventy years later, with the dismantling of the Soviet Union, the restoration of business as a legal activity brought a torrent of exactly these types of deceptive practices.

As at the end of the 20th century, the NEP era was characterized by widespread theft of state property, manipulation of documents, extensive reliance on personal contacts, and well-placed bribes to access goods of all kinds. For example, for years after the Russian Revolution, officials of the new state failed to take inventory of the equipment and supplies in the Leningrad naval yard. Entire warehouses, listed as empty in the naval yard's books, were actually full of valuable commodities, much of which found its way to the open market largely thanks to the numerous bands of thieves who populated the city's underworld. An example from the naval yard bears a striking resemblance to shady deals that would become a daily occurrence after the dismantling of the USSR. A Nepman, representing a private firm with virtually no capital, contracted to supply a state factory with nine hundred tons of oil in return for some steel pipe. After promising the steel pipe to another enterprise in exchange for some roofing iron, he stole the oil he needed from the naval yard. He then carried out all of the transactions, leaving himself with a supply of roofing iron, which he sold. Part of the proceeds went to certain naval yard employees who had helped him steal the oil.[76]

---

75. Ibid., p. 114.
76. Ibid., p. 115.

Throughout the NEP period the state and the merchant-traders were in a constant struggle over the extent to which private business would be tolerated. Using the tax regime as a sledgehammer, the state would squeeze the merchants in an attempt to drive them out of business. Arbitrary assessments and outright confiscation of merchandise or cash were popular approaches. The Nepmen, in turn, maintained their flexibility in maneuvering through the bureaucracy. Some simply closed their enterprises or scaled down to activities less scrutinized by the state. More often they resorted to the kind of manipulation that later became a hallmark of Soviet and post-Soviet business. This included the outright concealment of a business or misrepresentation of the business's operations. Businesses retreated underground so that their existence wouldn't be discovered. Other times they represented their activities as one type of business in order to fall into a lower tax bracket. A third approach was the outright bribing of local tax and regulatory officials.[77]

One episode illustrates the typical heavy hand of the state in action. Walter Duranty, a reporter for *The New York Times*, witnessed a raid on some Nepmen in the apartment building where he lived. A man and his relatives were arrested for making stockings without a license and selling them without paying taxes. Another individual, in possession of foreign currency worth $20,000, was also arrested. Three others who were in the apartment had already retired from business. Nevertheless, the next day they were told that a new, retroactive tax had been levied on sales made during their last year in business. The tax happened to coincide exactly with the value of all their possessions. As Duranty notes, "Within three days they were out in the streets with little more than the clothes they wore and some bedding."[78] All of these activities were quite common in the 1990s and are still practiced in Russia today.

Not unlike the days of Ivan the Terrible and Peter the Great, smuggled goods crossed Russia's western border from Estonia, Latvia, and Poland as well as Central Asia. Markets in many towns were reportedly well stocked with contraband and a large portion of imports was illegal. A report at the end of 1922 by the Central Commission in the Struggle against Contraband, noting that "our most important markets, not only in border regions but also in the largest urban centers, are flooded with contraband," concluded that the influx of smuggled goods "far exceeded" legal imports.[79]

---

77. Ibid., p. 63.
78. Walter Duranty, *I Write as I Please*, New York, Simon & Schuster, 1935, pp. 275-277.
79. Ball, p. 123 (note 68).

Two things were happening at this time as a reaction to economic conditions. First, the relative flourishing of a trading class, not to mention swindlers, smugglers, and thieves, meant that there was money to spend on the high life and, second, given the economic hardships for most of the population, thousands of bands, gangs, and criminal groups formed around the country. Many of the trends and anecdotes of that time bear a strong resemblance to the events of the late 1980s and 1990s.

In the 1920s, casinos and racetracks, nightclubs, gaming parlors, and brothels opened up around the major cities. Bootleg liquor flourished and cocaine and heroin, the drugs of choice, were relatively easy to come by. As Duranty reports of the casino life,

> banks at baccarat frequently ran as high as $5,000, a dozen different currencies were used, from bundles of Soviet million notes to hundred dollar bills, English five- and ten-pound notes, and most surprising of all, no small quantity of gold, Tsarist ten-ruble pieces, English sovereigns, and French twenty-franc coins. As in France, there was an 'inner cercle prive,' where only baccarat was allowed and play was higher, with banks of $25,000 or $30,000.[80]

Hotels, bars, and restaurants were the focal points of high society, with the unseemly side of the criminal world lurking in the wings. According to Victor Serge, "The sordid taint of money is visible on everything again.... What would you like—a dose of 'snow'? At the Europa bar thirty girls show off their paint and cheap rings to men in fur-lined coats and caps who are drinking glasses brimming with alcohol...."[81]

In the kind of scene that had been repeated numerous times in the 1990s, the GPU (secret police) burst in on a lavish New Year's Eve party being held at Moscow's Hermitage Restaurant in 1923. They arrested the host at each table if he was a state or cooperative employee and announced that a check would be made to determine if all the Nepmen present had been paying their taxes. The restaurant was owned by Nepmen and had been recently renovated. The lease was revoked.[82]

The high life wasn't limited to the high rollers; inhabitants of the street life played games of chance, especially cards, where the stakes could be dramatic.

---

80. Duranty, pp. 145-146 (note 78).
81. Ball, p. 42 (note 68).
82. Ibid., p. 40. See also Duranty, pp. 210-211 (note 78).

Clothing was thrown in the pot, while some played for the right to inflict blows on the loser. In extreme cases, the losers "agreed to undergo sodomy if their reversals continued, just to stay in the game."[83]

Games of chance were just a small part of the underworld life. We get a good sense of the underworld generally through Alan Ball's *And Now My Soul is Hardened: Abandoned Children in Soviet Russia, 1918-1930*, invaluable research about the 7 million homeless youths, called *besprizorniki*, in the 1920s. The youth largely adopted the ways of the adults, taking on their behavioral and organizational characteristics, and often operating at the direction of adult criminals.[84] From the adults, for example, juveniles were able to obtain cocaine, opium, morphine, and hashish, which was one way to get closer to the adult crime groups. Cocaine was most popular, partly because it was widely available and easy to take.[85] Since the youngsters largely emulated the adult criminals, for our purposes we can draw some conclusions about the adults from the behaviors and attributes of the juveniles as reported by Ball.

As three hundred years before during the reign of Peter the Great, *besprizorniki*, alongside their adult counterparts, saturated the Kitaigorod section of Moscow near the Kremlin and fanned out across the city. With at least 20,000 homeless children in the capital, the town squares, train stations, and markets became their operating territory.[86]

Like adults in the underworld, the children adopted nicknames and many, with the passage of time, actually forgot their original surnames and identified themselves only with street names. They took their names from their physical attributes (One-Eyed, Cross-Eyed, Pock-Marked), from place names where they traveled to often (Odessit, Sevastopolskii), and so on.[87] Homeless youths had their own argot of several hundred words much like the adults. The use of nicknames, argot, and tattoos helped to create a new identity for both the *besprizorniki* as well as the adults. They were perpetuating that antisociety written about by Gilyarovsky in the 1890s.

This is an important point to emphasize. Professional criminals in Russia used language, tattoos, nicknames, songs, punishment systems, and other attributes—behavioral norms—to separate themselves from mainstream soci-

---

83. Ball, p. 74 (note 63).

84. Ibid., p. 70.

85. Ibid., p. 76. See also Mary Schaeffer Conroy, "Abuse of Drugs Other Than Alcohol and Tobacco in the Soviet Union," *Soviet Studies*, vol. 42, no. 3, July 1990, pp. 447-48.

86. Ball, p. 30 (note 63).

87. Ibid.

ety.[88] They looked on 'outsiders' with suspicion; they were distancing themselves from the larger society, creating their own world, and enjoying their own version of freedom. A teenage girl, working as a prostitute since the age of thirteen, stated bluntly: "When I have money, I like to take a little cocaine and smoke a bit. I like this life and will never change it." A twelve-year-old boy, living on his own declared: "It's better to live free like this. I eat what I please and don't starve. It's cold here, yes, but I like it better than in an orphanage. I can go wherever I please."[89]

As in groups of the past and the future, gangs in the 1920s had a leader (*vozhak* or *glavar*) and sometimes more than one. Their authority was based as much on intimidation and domination as charisma, resourcefulness, and intelligence, characteristics we'll see later in the *vory v zakone* of the 1960s-1990s (see Chapter 7). "Some groups depended so entirely on a leader's initiative that they crumbled when arrest or other misfortune removed him from the scene."[90]

As Ball reports, out on the streets groups as large as ten to thirty children swooped in lightning fashion on individuals, knocking them down and making off with their purses, bags, or packages. While gangs generally preferred to ambush women and the elderly, even healthy men found themselves stripped of belongings on occasion, stunned by the suddenness of an assault and swarmed over as if by a school of piranhas. This tactic had changed little as youths descended on foreigners in several parts of Moscow and in other cities 70 years later. The assaults had escalated in the 1990s to the point where the Moscow mayor's office had to take special measures to force the youths out of the downtown area.[91]

In the 1920s, thousands of children turned sooner or later to prostitution. As one author inquired, "Who among the inhabitants of Moscow is not fa-

---

88. "A study of 146 juveniles in the Moscow Labor Home discovered 37 with at least one tattoo in 1924, and a later investigation reported such decorations on 'nearly all' the residents. Popular motifs included nude figures, the sex organs, and emblems signifying membership in a gang. Nearly any part of the body might carry a design, including locations chosen to allow the characters a semblance of animation. A naked man on one shoulder blade, for example, and a naked woman on the other, or a cat and mouse on the buttocks, could be moved in provocative or amusing fashion." See Ball, p. 39 (note 63).

89. Ibid., p. 81. It should also be obvious that these behaviors were not unique to the Soviet Union.

90. Ibid., p. 42.

91. If one was attuned to the occurrence of these assaults, it was possible to spot the telltale signs in advance and prevent an attack. Once in St. Petersburg and once in Moscow I was able to identify the early stages of an attack and take appropriate measures.

miliar with the figures of rouged and curled adolescents, flooding every evening the sidewalks of Tverskaya? Who has not seen the disheveled, ragged inhabitants of the Smolenskii, Trubnyi, and other markets? They are all a juvenile 'commodity,' awaiting its customer."[92] In 1920, a survey of 5,300 street girls up to the age of fifteen found that 88% had engaged in prostitution.[93]

With prostitution came the young girls' exposure to underworld jargon, learning the fine art of stealing, and imbibing in cocaine. While markets and stations may have been their points of greatest concentration, homeless children also worked as prostitutes in abandoned buildings, vacant lots, taverns, restaurants, squares, public baths, movie theaters, parks, and other outdoor locations, especially in the summer.[94] In many respects these scenes differed little from those of the 1990s.[95]

One policeman summed up to an investigator in Omsk the general attitude toward the homeless youths.

> Here's how it is, comrade. Officially, I have nothing to say to you. Unofficially, my opinion is this: the sooner all your *besprizorniki* die, the

---

92. Ball, p. 56 (note 63).

93. Ibid., p. 57. Prostitution was by no means a new problem. Laurie Bernstein notes that "as early as the 17th century an order lumped 'whoring' with fighting and robbery, stipulating that 'streets and alleys should be strictly patrolled day and night' to prevent such occurrences." Punishment for 'lecherous relations' between men and women was a beating from a knout, according to the Law Code of 1649. In 1716, Tsar Peter the Great proclaimed that "no whores will be permitted near the regiments." Women who violated his order ran the risk of being taken under guard and driven out of the area—naked. In 1718, Peter directed the police chief of St. Petersburg to stamp out "all suspicious houses, namely taverns, gambling parlors, and other obscene establishments." Empress Anna ordered all 'debauched' women kept by 'freethinkers and innkeepers' to be beaten with a cat-of-nine-tails and thrown out of their homes. See Laurie Bernstein, *Sonia's Daughters: Prostitutes and Their Regulation in Imperial Russia*, Berkeley, University of California Press, 1995, pp. 13-14. In 1853, St. Petersburg had 148 registered brothels. By 1880, the city had more than 6,000 prostitutes. See Irina Titova, "City Crime Not What Once Was—Author," *St. Petersburg Times*, January 20, 2004.

94. Ball, pp. 58-59 (note 63).

95. Plus ça change.... Prostitutes gathered at the markets once again in the "Wild East" of the 1990s. My walk home from work took me through the area where Sukharevskii market once stood. Occasionally one could see 20, 30 prostitutes in full flight, like cockroaches in a suddenly lit room, racing for cover from the police. Ironically, they also gathered at night in a vacant lot at the end of Bolshaya Spasskaya Street, directly across from, of all things, the MVD's Organized Crime Control Department. Clients would angle their cars toward the sidewalk, their headlights illuminating the girls lined up in what looked like a bizarre fashion show.

better. I have to deal with them daily, and I tell you sincerely that they are a hopeless bunch, soon to be bandits. And we have enough bandits without them. Is that clear?[96]

Even the chairman of the Baku Juvenile Affairs Commission—whose organization was entrusted with the very task of placing delinquents on the road to recovery—once remarked: "When all is said and done, you will not make a human being out of a *besprizornyi*. They are all toughs, hooligans, and murderers."[97]

Among the colorful adult figures that emerged in the criminal world in this period, Misha Kultyapnyi made a career of strong-arming the Nepmen in the years following the Revolution and Civil War. Called 'the blood poet' and 'Robin Hood of the Twenties,' Kultyapnyi used what was known as the daisy method in extorting the traders of their new-found wealth: laying hostages down in a circle and chopping off their heads until the Nepman paid the sum 'willingly.'[98]

Kultyapnyi wasn't the only Robin Hood of the era and Vanka Kain of the 17th century wasn't the only one who lived a double life. News of Leonid Pantelkin, 'Lyonka the Lucky,' first appeared in the newspapers of Petrograd (later St. Petersburg) in 1922. Over the course of his career he was charged with 11 murders (though some say it could have been as high as 89), making him one of the most feared gangsters of the time.[99] After serving in the army, he joined the Cheka, the forerunner of the KGB, in a small provincial town. He used his Cheka identification to enter homes and commit robberies and burglaries against lawyers, jewelers, and speculators.[100] When his regional bosses discovered him, he was dismissed. Lucky Lyonka traveled to Petrograd, Cheka ID in hand, and continued his thefts from wealthy city residents. He had gained a reputation as a sort of Robin Hood, since it was rumored that he gave

---

96. Ball, p. 83 (note 63).

97. Ibid.

98. R.E. Rodgers, J.L. Albini (eds.), "Report No. 9," Novosibirsk, 1990, prepared by the Joint Russian-American Academic Committee to Promote the Study of Comparative Criminal Justice, p. 5. In the 1990s, 'soft extortion' (*miagkoe vymogatel'stvo*) was sometimes used. Similar to the daisy method, extortionists would take a homeless person from the streets, give him shelter and food for a few days, and then execute him in front of the businessman, convincing the businessman to cooperate.

99. Molly Graves, "80-Year Bandit Headhunt Ends," *St. Petersburg Times*, March 6, 2001, no. 650(17) at http://www.sptimes.ru/index.php?action_id=2&story_id=14664.

100. Anna Malpas, "The makers of a new television series plan to explore the little-known history of the Soviet Union's criminal underworld," *The Moscow Times*, January 20, 2006, at http://context.themoscowtimes.com/stories/2006/01/20/101.html.

some of his ill-gotten gains to street children.[101] According to Leonid Kesselman, a political analyst at the Russian Academy of Sciences, Pantelkin's heroic
image changed to terror when his thefts began to include murder. Pantelkin
was eventually shot and killed on Feb. 13, 1923, by an 18-year-old police
rookie during a stakeout set up as part of a citywide sweep of 20 criminal
gangs.[102]

While there are important differences between the events of the 1990s and
those of Russian and early Soviet history, there are also many commonalities.
Vaksberg's Soviet 'mafia' and the traditional criminal world were influenced
not only by the events of the day but by behavioral patterns, attitudes, and
beliefs that developed over hundreds of years. The similarities between now
and then are no accident. It is important to note that this legacy did not cause
the events of the 1990s, but strongly influenced the avenues open to Russia by
the time the 1990s arrived. Next we'll see how the Soviet era, particularly in
terms of the economic system, represents a more recent legacy that strongly
influenced the intertwining of the upperworld and the underworld.

---

101. This is according to Malpas, although Graves reports that he robbed from the rich
but never quite got around to giving to the poor.
102. Graves (note 99).

CHAPTER 6

THE ECONOMY

A totalitarian regime has no use for society as an independent arena where different individuals, groups, institutions, and forces co-exist and interrelate. It consequently seeks to absorb society, and where this fails, to destroy it.

—F.J.M. Feldbrugge[1]

The *Homo Sovieticus* emerging in the 1930s was a species whose most highly developed skills involved the hunting and gathering of scarce goods in an urban environment.

—Sheila Fitzpatrick[2]

The tolerance of the Soviet regime toward market forces didn't last long, and by the end of the 1920s the Nepmen were a thing of the past. Stalin had emerged victorious in the drawn out succession struggle after Lenin's death in 1924, and the country was about to undergo a horrible transformation. While a measure of capitalism may have been important for stabilizing the economy, it was incapable of providing the industrial growth needed to modernize the country. Vestiges of private business were crushed as the Soviet Union adopted a two-pronged approach to rapid industrialization: Five Year Plans and the collectivization of agriculture. The reckless and persistent pursuit of industrialization using these approaches would cost millions of lives and exacerbate the Russian empire's legacy of deception, corruption, and theft to the point where the possessors of the emerging complex psychology could commit crimes, justify them, and ignore them all at the same time. The system would create what was known as *Homo Sovieticus*, a new Soviet Man.

---

1. F.J.M. Feldbrugge, *Russian Law: The End of the Soviet System and the Role of Law*, Dordrecht, The Netherlands, Martinus Nijhoff Publishers, 1993, p. 13.
2. Sheila Fitzpatrick, *Everyday Stalinism: Ordinary Life in Extraordinary Times: Soviet Russia in the 1930s*, New York, Oxford University Press, 1999, p. 2.

The basic challenge facing the Soviet Union heading into the 1930s was finding a way to industrialize an agricultural land inhabited by a population that was still largely made up of peasants. This meant providing an infrastructure—food, housing, and so on—for the millions of people who were migrating from the countryside to the rapidly growing cities. At the same time, though, agricultural output had fallen dramatically short of its goal. The Soviet government opted to force the peasantry to turn over their harvests.

The first step undertaken in transforming the face of the Soviet Union was the collectivization of agriculture. Stalin ordered the forced consolidation of peasant fields as a way to quickly modernize the agricultural sector and maintain control over the countryside.[3] He decreed that the peasants had to turn over their land, livestock, and equipment to the newly formed collective farms (*kolkhozy*).

Not surprisingly, many peasant families did not surrender their holdings willingly, in which case police and soldiers were used to forcibly wrest control of the property. Bearing the sharp end of this policy were the so-called kulaks, or 'wealthy' peasants, who had more to lose than others. It should be noted, however, that the 'wealth' that stood the kulaks apart from other peasants could frequently be measured by just a handful of cattle or horses, for example.

The process of eliminating the kulaks, which came to be called dekulakization, carried a high price both in terms of human lives and livestock. More than a million kulaks—five million people including their families—disappeared, often having been sent to labor camps in Siberia and Central Asia. Initially, the process of collectivization was to have been limited in scope. However, in an effort to prevent the state from benefiting from the seizure of land and animals, peasants slaughtered their cattle, horses, and other livestock rather than bring them into a *kolkhoz*, further deepening the agricultural crisis. According to Nicholas Riasanovsky, from 1929 to 1933, the number of horses in the Soviet Union declined from 34 million to about 16 million. Cattle declined from 68 million to 38 million, sheep and goats fell from 147 million to 50 million, and the number of hogs fell from 20 million to 12 million. Droughts in 1931 and 1932 added to the horrors of the transition from private to collectivized farming. In a little over four years, 68% of all cultivated land in the Soviet Union was under the collective farm system (*kolkhoz*) and 10% was under the state farm structure (*sovkhoz*) while only 22% remained for independent farmers.[4]

---

3. Marshall I. Goldman, *Gorbachev's Challenge: Economic Reform in the Age of High Technology*, New York, W.W. Norton & Company, 1987, pp. 9–10.

4. Nicholas V. Riasanovsky, *A History of Russia*, New York, Oxford University Press, 1984, p. 498.

In theory, collectives were to have been self-governing cooperatives. In fact, the peasants were driven onto the collective farms which were taken over completely by local bureaucracies whose role was to extract maximum production with minimum remuneration. Administrative pressure became the sole method of drawing labor out of a reluctant population. The state deprived them of their status as free producers, deepening the lack of incentive to produce. This led to a dramatic decline in agriculture and in some places, like Ukraine, outright famine.

In order to put the resources taken from the peasants to work as quickly as possible, the state introduced central planning as embodied in the Five Year Plans. The first Five Year Plan was initiated in 1928, setting in motion what in theory was supposed to have been a highly disciplined, centralized approach to managing the economy. Ironically, the First Five Year Plan lasted only four years and three months which immediately brought into question the very notion of a having a 'plan.'

Under the Plan, the central government established quotas for each production unit, instructing enterprises what to produce, on the basis of what inputs of materials, finance, and labor, at what prices, and to which receiving enterprise they should deliver their product.[5] In other words, production was determined not by economic laws of supply and demand, but by the dictates of a political and ideological machine. Centralized administration of economic activity would dictate pace, parts, and productivity.

The Plan fulfilled Stalin's short-term goals of rapid industrialization and militarization. Entire cities rose up artificially to support the massive factories that were being built to fuel the industrialization drive. The Siberian industrial city of Magnitogorsk, for example, acquired in just a few years a population of a quarter of a million.[6] Not surprisingly, some 86% of all industrial investment during the First Five Year Plan went to heavy industry. New branches of industry sprang up: chemical, automotive, agricultural machinery, aviation, machine tool, electrical, and others.[7]

In actuality, chaos reigned supreme. Zara Witkin, an American construction engineer who spent several years working in a construction ministry of the Soviet government in the early 1930s, marveled at the disorganization that

---

5. Ronald J. Hill, *Politics, Economics, and Society*, Boulder, Colorado, Lynne Rienner Publishers, Inc., 1985, p. 151.

6. See Stephen Kotkin, *Magnetic Mountain: Stalinism as a Civilization*, Berkeley, University of California Press, 1995.

7. Riasanovsky, pp. 496–497 (note 4). See ibid. as well as John Scott, *Behind the Urals: An American Worker in Russia's City of Steel*, Bloomington, Indiana University Press, 1942.

accompanied the centrally planned economy. Witkin observed that production at the numerous new industrial plants wasn't coordinated with production at the older ones. "As an instance," says Witkin, "half a dozen different types of wall blocks might be sent to the same building. The strength and insulating value of the finished walls were consequently highly variable. Door and window frames did not fit."[8] While overall quality had improved over the decades, construction was still shoddy sixty years later, as only a brief walk around Moscow would reveal. In a conversation in 1993, a retired middle manager from the State Planning Agency (Gosplan) told me that it was frequently the case in her sector, industrial piping, that several different types of pipes would be used in a single line. Over the years, managers used whatever materials they had at their disposal. Some of the pipes, she confessed, were not appropriate for the job and would corrode and collapse over a relatively short time. The piping was not fitted properly and the system generally looked like a hodgepodge of parts collected from anywhere and everywhere.[9]

It should be clear that the experiences in the construction sector were not an anomaly and, indeed, were repeated in every sector of production throughout the Soviet period. Soviet journalist Leonid Vladimirov relates a story about the impact of the Plan on the automobile sector in the 1960s.

> The production of tires for the Moskvich had been planned with no thought of the voracious appetite of its faulty front suspension. In addition, the factory did not dare to report to the government that it was producing poorly designed cars and therefore needed an increase in the output of tires. As a result, prices for the tires shot up to fantastic levels in the regular shops (about $50.00 each). On the black market, as might be expected, the price was three times as high. But even at such prices, few spare tires were available. Six years after the appearance of the problem, engineers managed to correct the problem.[10]

It is clear from this example that the notion of a Plan was untenable. An unforeseen consequence of production—a faulty front suspension in this

---

8. Zara Witkin, *An Engineer in Stalin's Russia: Memoirs of Zara Witkin, 1932–1934*, Berkeley, University of California Press, 1991, p. 99.

9. I had numerous conversations with Lyudmila, a retired Gosplan manager, between 1993 and 1996.

10. Leonid Vladimirov, *The Russians*, New York, Frederick A. Praeger, 1968, p. 51. A typical joke about cars went, "The new model Lada had a rear-window defroster—so the owner could keep his hands warm while pushing it."

case—meant that output would have to be increased. This was not part of the Plan and would serve to create new opportunities in the black market. Across the economy instances like this were countless.

Generally speaking, machinery was unreliable, of poor quality, and poorly maintained. Because planning did not adequately provide for spare parts, broken machinery sat idle thus further affecting production output levels. Combines broke down after 6-8 hours of operation even though according to specifications they were built to last 300 hours. In late 1981, there were only 2.4 million tractors in working condition, 100,000 fewer than the number produced in the USSR from 1976 to 1981. Much of the farm machinery (as well as trucks, cars, airplanes, and other machines) was cannibalized for spare parts.[11]

The distribution system was woefully inadequate. The system of roadways was severely underdeveloped causing damage to vehicles, which then sat idle for lack of spare parts. Production priorities were not focused on the domestic economy, and there was little incentive to devise a system to deliver goods to market efficiently. Crops lay rotting in the fields for want of effective harvest methods and modes of transport. According to Marshall Goldman, by the 1980s, still only 40% of all farms had storehouses. This was a leftover effect from the famines of the 1930s when peasants looted the stocks; the government was subsequently determined to keep reserves out of the hands of peasants. "In many cases, farms were 200 to 300 miles from grain storage and 140 to 150 miles from meat packing centers. The few refrigerated trucks that existed had to travel axle-busting roads that turned to impassable mud with the spring thaw and few roads led directly from the farms to storage."[12]

It's little surprise, then, that the Soviets lost one-fifth of their gross annual harvest of grain, vegetables, and fruit during harvesting, transporting, storing, and processing. "During winter storage, reportedly 25% of the potato crop, 20% of the grain and sugar beets, and 18% of the fruit crop was ruined, never making its way to the consumer."[13] There was little need to anticipate consumer demands so that when supplies of food or products were exhausted there was frequently no stockpile for immediate replenishment, thus contributing to shortages. A common banner draped on factory walls encouraged, "Fulfill and Surpass the Plan!" (*Vypolnim i perevypolnim plan!*), but in reality quotas frequently went unmet for lack of parts.

---

11. Goldman, p. 37 (note 3).
12. Ibid.
13. Ibid.

In an effort to augment their meager salaries, workers and managers alike were essentially forced to steal labor, materials, food, goods, and equipment from their workplaces and from other enterprises and industrial sectors to use for personal goals or to sell on the black market.[14]

> The closer one was to actual product control the more there was to steal. Whereas a doctor could receive 'gifts' for quicker appointment privileges, a painter could water down his paint and take some home to sell to friends. A director of a car factory was able to sell preferences to those who were willing to pay for the limited number of cars produced. Control of the rationed gasoline supplies and distribution to favored drivers provided an even better income.[15]

Over time, official fulfillment and over-fulfillment of the Plan brought cash bonuses, creating a powerful reason to perpetuate widespread deception and fraud. High-level officials, directors of enterprises, factory managers, and many others throughout the system perfected the art of the lie, kicking glowing statistical reports of production output up the bureaucratic chain. However, the statistics contained in these reports were the fanciful imaginings of those in charge, frequently done with the full knowledge—and the wink of an eye—of their superiors in the state apparatus.[16] It is worth listening to Zara Witkin's eyewitness account of how all of this looked on the ground in the early days.

> At that time [May 1932], the Kharkov Tractor Plant had been in operation several months. Production was claimed to be above capacity, which was one hundred tractors per day. An air of confusion clung to the plant. Finished machines were scattered about the loading yards. Completed tractors were lined up awaiting shipment, exposed to the weather with their wheels already rusted.... Near the factory a group of large apartment houses had been built to house the workers, engineers, foreign mechanics, and consultants employed at the plant. We asked to see them. The recent rains had converted the

---

14. Recall the example of the Leningrad naval yard and other instances in the 1920s mentioned in the previous chapter. These types of fraud were widespread throughout the country for the entire 20th century and became a dominant characteristic of the system.

15. Lydia Rosner, "The Sexy Russian Mafia," *Criminal Organizations*, vol. 10, no. 1, Fall, 1995, p. 18.

16. Maria Łos, "Economic Crimes in Communist Countries," in I.L. Barak-Glantz and E.H. Johnson (eds.), *Comparative Criminology*, Beverly Hills, CA, Sage Publications, 1983, p. 41.

dirt roads into mud, through which our car wallowed. This condition prevailed right up to the buildings. There had been no grading or drainage around them. Mud and dirt had been tracked into the buildings. The staircases and walls were soiled. Though the houses had been 'completed' the previous year, rubbish and waste material remained in disorderly piles on the site.... Among other serious defects, there was little critical inspection or proper manufacturing standards. Much spoilage resulted and many defective machines were sent out which should have been rejected.... Several days afterwards, the Kharkov Tractor Plant and several of its managers received the Order of Lenin, the highest Soviet decoration for outstanding performance and meritorious work![17]

The net effect of businesses engaging in such illegal activities was further intensification of shortages, bottlenecks, waste, and low productivity throughout the system. This, in turn, led to long queues and consumer hoarding. When products did appear on store shelves, they were quickly bought and the supply depleted. These realities made even the simplest tasks a challenge. While living in Moscow as a student in 1987, I went to the supermarket one day and came across oranges. I had never seen them before. At that time there were no brown bags, plastic bags, or canvas bags offered by the stores. Shoppers brought their own *avoska*, a homemade string bag whose name meant 'maybe' or 'just in case,' as in 'just in case I find something to buy.' I didn't have one and left the store with oranges shoved in every one of the eight pockets in my winter jacket. I never saw oranges again after that. Consider also that a product as simple as a plastic bag could become a source of revenue for the underworld (see the story of Viktor in Chapter 8) and, likewise, because of the shortages in goods across the board, all major consumer goods could be controlled by a combination of Vaksberg's Soviet 'mafia' and traditional crime groups.

Another example from Witkin's time in the Soviet Union: Telephone lines were not grouped into central exchanges. They were run separately to the desk of each important official. "If one left his desk for a few moments, or went on a trip for a few days, or a vacation for a month, or was sent to prison for several years ... work simply stopped."[18] Likewise, the tempo of work, often touted by Soviet propaganda as 'feverish,' was more accurately compared with that of Mexico, Chile, and India, Witkin argued. "It is almost impossible to

17. Witkin, pp. 53–54 (note 8).
18. Ibid., pp. 96–97.

obtain appointments with responsible officials before ten in the morning or after four o'clock in the afternoon."[19] Sixty years later, it was still common to search for an official in vain by telephone, and the pace of work did not appear to have increased much. At the Ministry of Internal Affairs National Police Academy where I spent a considerable amount of time in 1990–91, we passed many hours drinking tea and engaging in small talk. On occasion, a colleague would announce that a truck was down at the corner full of deficit goods like sweaters or sausage. Everyone would vanish to buy those rare commodities and I'd suddenly find myself alone. Understandably, these were difficult times and consumers had to be ready to take advantage of unforeseen purchasing opportunities. But it also spoke to Witkin's point about levels of production and progress. It should be understood that these events were not just annoyances; they were features of the system that required the development of vast survival skills.

The fact that the Five Year Plans were given the force of law dramatically complicated the overall situation. Implementation of the Plan was mandatory. Workers found themselves in an impossible situation: failure to fulfill the Plan was labeled 'anti-state' activity—one of the most serious offenses one could commit—and could result in criminal sanctions. Having to rely on unpredictable state suppliers and shortages of raw materials, enterprises faced the practical impossibility of fulfilling the Plan independently, forcing them to buy, barter, and steal parts, resources, and even finished output from other enterprises in order to fulfill their own quotas. Strict punishments were imposed on those guilty of shirking work, carelessly handling machinery, or stealing 'socialist property.' For example, according to a law in 1940, any worker or employee who was twenty minutes late for work was to be dismissed and criminal charges were to be filed.[20] Where were law breakers to be sent?

The Gulag system, that vast network of prison camps across the former Soviet Union, was developed out of the forced labor camps created during collectivization and the dekulakization period. These were not simply prisons and they were not institutions of punishment *per se*. Forced labor camps were primarily political and economic entities. Stalin realized that it would not be possible to industrialize the economy without a massive pool of cheap labor.[21] At the same time, he realized that he could dispense of his enemies—real and imagined—by having them shipped off to Siberia or some equally harrowing

---

19. Ibid., p. 97.

20. Fitzpatrick, p. 6 (note 2).

21. Galina Mikhailovna Ivanova, *Labor Camp Socialism: The Gulag in the Soviet Totalitarian System*, Armonk, New York, M.E. Sharpe, 2000, p. 190.

and desolate fate, that is, if the fate of the unfortunate were not determined by a bullet.[22] One eyewitness account of conditions in the infamous Solovki camp, written in 1931, told of the horrors of punishment as a means to keep productivity high.

> In the summer, for failing to accomplish one's task in time, they often put those guilty out to mosquitoes. It means that a fully naked man is tied up to a tree, so that he cannot move hand or foot, for one or two hours, until he passes out. In the winter, they put naked men on a tree stump. Depending on the temperature, a man becomes frozen in about thirty minutes. He falls down and then they warm him up by the fire and repeat the same operation or make him work. Those who failed to accomplish the task were left in the forest for the night. There were cases when a man didn't get to his barracks for a whole week. Guards changed, and he worked nonstop. The task was such that even strong and experienced woodcutters couldn't accomplish it in less than twelve hours. Many had to work for sixteen, eighteen hours. To evade work that was beyond their strength, many hacked off their fingers or froze their hands.[23]

A substantial part of the economy was being run on the backs of slave labor; the vast majority of inmates had committed no crime whatever. Ironically, many of those who became inmates had actually been willing to cooperate with the regime, supporting its efforts at work and in their professions. The system, though, wasn't predicated on rational penal policy but on the economic and political demands of the day. Locations of the camps were determined by economic necessities and production needs. Camps would come and go, close and then open again in a different locale, all of which happened outside the logic of punishment. Imagine, in 1949, the Ministry of Internal Affairs—the agency of law and order—"accounted for over 10% of the country's gross industrial production."[24]

The most dangerous part of the system was that virtually anyone could be entrapped by it. Anyone could be hooked and reeled in at a moment's notice since virtually everyone was breaking the law in order to survive. Worse, the regime wasn't particularly concerned about rule of law. Labels such as 'enemy of the people,' 'class enemy,' and 'members of the wrong families' could justify

---

22. Oleg V. Khlevniuk, *The History of the Gulag: From Collectivization to the Great Terror*, New Haven, Yale University Press, 2004, p. 332.

23. Ibid., pp. 40–41.

24. Ivanova, p. 189 (note 21). See also ibid., p. 330.

any arrest. A simple phrase summed up the attitude of the state toward due process and rule of law: If you've got the person, you can find the article to pin on him (*Byl' by chelovek, stat'ya naidyotsya*). That article frequently was Article 58 of the Russian Penal Code, introduced in 1927, at the decline of the NEP period and just in time for collectivization and dekulakization. Article 58 contained wide-ranging justifications for arrest including the highly elastic notions of treason, sabotage, counterrevolutionary activity, and terrorist acts against representatives of Soviet power. Supporting any of these activities or failing to report them carried a prison term.

The mere probability of guilt was sufficient. "It is pointless," said Andrei Vishinsky, the chief procurator during the show trials of the Great Purge period of the 1930s, "to repeat [in court] without particular need what has already been established in the preliminary investigation."[25] The great Russian writer Alexander Solzhenitsyn was sentenced to eight years in a labor camp followed by permanent internal exile for criticizing Stalin in a personal letter to a friend.[26] "The overwhelming majority of so-called political prisoners had committed no actual illegal acts and consequently could not be considered criminals. They were innocent victims of class struggle, lawlessness, tyranny, and terror."[27]

The number of people fated to the Gulag was impressive. According to Michael Jakobson, pre-revolution prisons never held more than 184,000 inmates. The figure remained below 300,000 until 1928. After the collectivization of 1933, their numbers exceeded 3 million.[28] By 1937, there were 35 clusters of camps with each cluster containing about 200 camps of around 1200 inmates each.[29] Many millions of citizens who were not in the Gulag at the start of World War II had already been in and millions more had been indicted. Between 1930 and 1941, 20 million convictions were handed down, about 3 million people were exiled and deported, and relatives and families of those charged with crimes were harassed and discriminated against. This at a time when there were only 37.5 million families in the country, so most families had a relative or knew someone who had been sent to the camps or killed.[30] Think of it this way: the Black Marias, those patrol wagons that carted

---

25. Robert Conquest, *The Great Terror: A Reassessment*, New York, Oxford University Press, 1990, p. 285.

26. For his account of the Gulag, see Alexander I. Solzhenitsyn, *The Gulag Archipelago, 1918–1956*, New York, Harper & Row, Publishers, 1985.

27. Ivanova, p. 185 (note 21).

28. Michael K. Jakobson, *Origins of the Gulag: The Soviet Prison Camp System, 1917–1934*, Lexington, The University Press of Kentucky, 1993, p. 139.

29. Conquest, p. 309 (note 25).

30. Khlevniuk, pp. 328–329 (note 22). See also Ivanova (note 21).

people off to jail, were already well over capacity during the Tsarist era when they carried 48 men. In the Soviet period, 100 men were forcibly packed into the wagons and brought to railway stations to be shipped off to their destinations in cattle cars.[31]

The Gulag has been characterized as a state within a state, "a colony with its own laws, customs, moral standard, and social groups."[32] More than that, the Gulag was a zone within a zone. 'Malaya zona,' used by many to depict prisons in the Soviet Union, was 'the small zone.' That label was used to differentiate it from 'bolshaya zona,' or 'the large zone,' meaning the country as a whole. Jacques Rossi, a Frenchman who spent more than twenty years in Soviet prisons and camps, said, "The Soviet Gulag was not only the most durable concentration camp system of this century, with a life span of seventy-three years, but also the most precise embodiment of the state that created it. It was not a mere slip of the tongue to say that a freed *zek* had been transferred from the 'small' zone to the 'large' one."[33] As a mother wrote to her imprisoned son, "My dear beloved son, you know that all Russia is a big concentration camp."[34]

As with prisons around the world, most of the inmates (those who weren't murdered by the state, that is) returned home. This was a vast collection of rehabilitated innocent victims of the Stalinist era and common criminals freed under various amnesties. All had been placed together; they lived day by day, cheek by jowl, influencing each other in various ways. After Khrushchev released a large number of prisoners in 1956, "the population lost its fear and ceased to be obedient and industrious."[35] More than this, people who were guilty of absolutely nothing had spent years learning the ways of the criminal. They had graduated from 'the academy,' as prison was commonly called. They were changed and could not 'unknow' what they had been exposed to. The writer, Varlam Shalamov, who had spent years in some of the most horrific camps, noted, "Hundreds of thousands of people who have been in the camps are permanently seduced by the ideology of these criminals and have ceased to be people. Something criminal has entered into their souls forever. Thieves and their morality have left an indelible mark on the soul of each."[36]

31. Conquest, p. 311 (note 25).

32. Donald J. Raleigh's introduction to Ivanova, p. xiv (note 21).

33. Ivanova, p. 185 (note 21).

34. Pishet synochku mat': "Synochek moi rodnoi, Ved' i Rossiya Vsya—Eto kontslager' bol'shoi" (in Jakobson, note 28).

35. Jakobson, p. 144 (note 28).

36. Varlam Shalamov, *Kolyma Tales*, London, Penguin Books, 1994, p. 411.

Concepts like 'guilt,' 'innocence,' 'law,' and 'justice' lost their meaning. The prison mentality together with the need to skirt the requirements of the Five Year Plans meant that economic planning became, in many senses, a scam writ large. As mentioned earlier, bureaucracy became a force unto itself and the circulation of paper—glowing reports of Soviet achievement, as in the case of the Kharkov Tractor Plant—replaced the circulation of real products.[37] Even inside the Gulag, production output figures were manipulated to put the best face possible on the state's despicable practices.[38]

In a scathing indictment of the system as a whole, Moshe Lewin summarizes the Stalin era, which continues to influence Russian reality, as nothing less than "a gigantic industrialization effort coupled with a loss of freedom, a cultural and political counterrevolution, and the making of a barbaric system built on the ruins of a great emancipatory ideal."[39]

It is out of this environment that *Homo Sovieticus* emerged. Sheila Fitzpatrick gives a classic description of the complex and contradictory nature of Soviet Man. He spent his time, she writes,

> 'getting' goods legally and illegally, using patrons and connections, counting living space in square meters, quarreling in communal apartments, 'free' marriage, petitioning, denouncing, informing, complaining about officials, complaining about privilege, enjoying privilege, studying, volunteering, moving up, tumbling down, confusing the future and the present, mutual protection, self-criticism, scapegoating, purging, bullying subordinates, deferring to officials, lying about social origin, unmasking enemies, hunting spies ... hours wasted in queues ... to the endless bureaucratic rudeness and red tape and the abolition, in the cause of productivity and atheism, of a common day of rest. [I]t was a hard grind, full of shortages and discomfort. *Homo Sovieticus* was a string-puller, an operator, a time-server, a freeloader.... But above all, he was a survivor.[40]

According to Oleg Khlevniuk, campaigns against 'enemies of the people' left a lasting legacy of aggressiveness, extreme intolerance, lack of initiative, xenophobia, nationalism, and anti-Semitism in a predominantly Russian pop-

---

37. Los, pp. 39–40 (note 16).
38. Ivanova, p. 189 (note 21).
39. Moshe Lewin, *Russia/USSR/Russia: The Drive and Drift of a Superstate*, New York, The New Press, 1995, p. 16.
40. Fitzpatrick, p. 227 (note 2).

ulation.[41] Added to that as mentioned earlier, the centralized command economy created perpetual shortages of goods, justification for hoarding, stealing, cheating, bribing, and a general lack of legal recourse in the face of commercial disputes. Understandably, the shadow economy came to account for nearly half of the national economy and "trained large parts of the population in illegal activities, creating human capital specific to illegality and a social morality supportive of activities outside formal legality."[42]

Let's take a very simple example to illustrate the extent to which activities we took for granted in the West became delicate, if not dangerous, in the former Soviet Union and helped to shape the mindset. In 1987, the involved process of purchasing a *matroshka*, the famous Russian wooden nesting doll, on the Arbat, the outdoor pedestrian shopping mall in downtown Moscow, would have been comical if the potential consequences weren't so serious. The young merchant said the doll would cost ten dollars. I reached into my pocket for the cash, U.S. dollars, and he stopped me. "No, not here." He instructed me to walk down a nearby alley leading into the courtyard of an apartment building behind the mall and wait for him on a bench. A few minutes later he came along with the *matroshka*. There on the bench we exchanged the money for the doll. I felt like I was in the middle of a drug deal. At that time it was still illegal for a Soviet citizen to possess foreign currency. Getting caught, the merchant could have gone to prison or, perhaps more likely, would have paid a bribe in dollars to the police. The system made the easiest transactions illegal, driving home the idea on a daily basis that deception, bribery, dishonesty, and maintaining the closest of relationships with a small circle of trusted friends were necessary tools in one's survival kit to the point where their illegality became meaningless.

This idea of the necessity of a small circle of trusted friends was a new concept for me. In the mid-1980s, friends warned me not to speak English in the stairwells before reaching their apartment. Friends warned me not to speak about them to others. Friends warned me that not all is always what it seemed. Friends warned me that some of the people from the MVD that I was socializing with were in fact working for the KGB. "A word spoken is a shot fired," they said.

And so it was—an atomized society huddled in countless small groups for mutual protection for a variety of reasons. The inadequacy of salaries to meet

---

41. Khlevniuk, p. 343 (note 22).
42. Richard Lotspeich, "Crime in the Transition Economies," *Europe-Asia Studies*, vol. 47, no. 4, 1995, p. 571.

ordinary daily expenses, combined with the frequent shortages of goods, forced consumers to rely on their own network of friends and contacts in order to acquire daily necessities. They watched out for each other, bought shoes, meat, and toilet paper for each other when possible, and even bought things they didn't need. It could always be traded for a desired product. Obtaining goods was done *nalevo* (on the left), *po znakomstvu* (through a contact), *na chyornom rynke* (on the black market), and *po blatu* (through pull).[43] "Not to have *blat*, that's the same thing as having no civil rights, the same as being deprived of all rights.... Come with a request, and they will all be deaf, blind, and dumb. If you need ... to buy something in a shop—you need *blat*. If it's difficult or impossible for a passenger to get a railroad ticket, then it is simple and easy *po blatu*."[44] Everyone was always making a deal to survive, and everyone was always guilty of something.

An extra layer of complication was that all of this activity took place in an environment rich with KGB informants. Whom to trust? Entering a social network as a trusted partner could take time. In the Soviet Union, people tended to make friends slowly and keep them for a long time. They didn't use the word 'friend' casually in an environment where talking with the wrong person, trusting the wrong person, could land them in a labor camp.

It must be clear by now that we are talking about a mode of living that was not an anomaly, was not restricted to certain pockets in particular parts of the economy, but rather was a systemic, deeply rooted, psychological state of being. For me the most apt reminder of the effect of this transformation was the way Tamara Epifan, a professor at Norwich University's Russian Summer School, characterized it in 1985: "The Russian will think one thing, say something else, and do something entirely different." The mode of survival was one of deception and theft. Access, sleight of hand, and fraud were the operative tools for survival in that environment across the whole 20th century as well as today. There are countless examples, great and small, of the fraud practiced throughout the society. For example, in the 1960s, one enterprising character made fake boots out of cardboard. Decent boots cost 300 rubles at the time on the open market, and a good pair was the only gear that could withstand the muddy, unpaved Soviet roads. He dipped his cardboard products in a pail of black paint, dried them out, and polished them with wax. Shortly before

43. See Mary Fish and Lynn Edwards, "Shadow Trading by International Tourists in the Soviet Union," *Journal of Criminal Justice*, vol. 17, 1989, p. 420.

44. Cited in Fitzpatrick, p. 62 (note 2). See Alena Ledeneva, *Russia's Economy of Favours: Blat, Networking, and Informal Exchange*, Cambridge, Cambridge University Press, 1998.

selling, the boots were dipped in water to make them soft to the touch, like fine leather. When the state increased boot production, the fraudster would move on to another scam.[45]

Toward the end of Stalin's reign and after his death in March 1953, there was reportedly a significant growth in illegal businesses. And since that world was illegal, "it was easy prey for the police, the prosecutors' offices, and the judges, who were all trading in justice just because it was impossible for them to live a decent life on their salaries from the state—and who, or what, could stop them?"[46] At roughly the same time, exposure to the West increased through a variety of avenues, many of which lent themselves to the pursuit of black market activities. For example, sailors and merchant seamen visiting foreign ports brought with them Russian goods such as caviar, furs, and souvenirs, which they could sell for foreign currency. Simultaneously, they could acquire Western goods to sell on the growing black market back home.

The state, too, was anxious to lay its hands on valuable foreign currency and began to open its doors to foreign visitors. Tourists, students, and business people were a welcome sight for cabdrivers, waiters, hotel clerks, and others who would entice the visitors to exchange their foreign currency through them rather than at official currency exchange points.[47] It was also an opportunity to further develop their negotiating skills in getting the foreigners to part with anything that would command a good price on the black market such as blue jeans and shirts with English-language logos or sayings on them. Having been through an exhausting and costly war, both in terms of material goods and human lives, people began to grow weary of the system. Forty years had passed since the revolution, and the promises of the 'bright future of Communism' remained unfulfilled.[48]

In the 1950s, the state began to acknowledge that regular crime and fraud were becoming problematic. Regardless of ideological claims that crime could not exist in the Soviet Union, the government passed measure after measure to fight this 'non-existent criminality.' In August 1953, the Council of Minis-

---

45. Yuri Brokhin, *Hustling on Gorky Street: Sex and Crime in Russia Today*, New York, The Dial Press, 1975, pp. 71–72.

46. Konstantin Simis, *USSR: The Corrupt Society*, New York, Simon & Schuster, 1982, p. 100.

47. Brokhin, p. 45 (note 45).

48. These mechanisms of commerce were largely still in place in the second half of the 1980s. During my first trips to the Soviet Union, in 1986 and 1987, I frequently used packs of cigarettes and other Western goods as currency. The Russian Federation still functions in large part on barter.

ters of the USSR adopted a resolution called, 'On Measures for Strengthening Public Order and the Fight against Crime' and in October 1956, 'On Measures for Improving the Performance of the MVD USSR.' In the middle of the 1950s, the state went on the offensive against the numerous criminal gangs that had been roaming the country for years. In addition, interestingly enough, in spring 1961, the Central Committee of the Communist Party and the USSR Council of Ministers approved a document called, 'Measures for Preventing Fraud and for Strengthening Control over the Reliability of Reports on the Carrying out of Plans and Obligations.' This cut right to the heart of the command-administrative system and acknowledged that all was not well in the central mechanism that was guiding the economy.

By the 1960s, it was being acknowledged that the system had created in essence a vast society with a system of morality that was determined largely by the situation in which people found themselves. At that time a letter appeared in the newspaper *Izvestia* that went as follows:

> As I understand it, there are two separate sets of morals. On the one hand, there is nothing more disgraceful than stealing. A person would not take even a sliver of wood from his neighbor, let alone a bundle of logs. A housewife will say: 'Even if we leave the washing in the street for a week, no one will touch it.' On the other hand, it is not considered shameful to steal a bucket of potatoes or a sack of cabbage from the collective farm.[49]

The author of the letter may not have been aware that the idea of competing sets of morals was far more profound than she had expressed. At around the same time the letter was written, journalist Yuri Brokhin, in his book, *Hustling on Gorky Street*, described the extensive bribery practices of the head of a Soviet coal factory. Brokhin said he thought the factory head accepted bribes just so he would 'live and let live.' Enlightening his Western readers, Brokhin indicated that this actually meant 'steal and let steal.'[50] And here we must appreciate once again that this was not simply a literary device or clever turn of a phrase by a journalist. It was part of the unwritten rules of the game: steal if you have access as long as it's not done in a brash, public way or to excess. Don't be greedy and don't forget to share.[51]

---

49. Vladimirov, p. 128 (note 10).

50. Brokhin, p. 96 (note 45).

51. The title of an article bore a classic attitude of the Russians, Soviets, and post-Soviets toward bribery. See Åse B. Grødeland, Tatyana Y. Koshechkina & William L. Miller, "'Foolish to Give and Yet More Foolish Not to Take'—In-depth Interviews with Post-Com-

There were two very different codes at work in Soviet society; one was an official, idealistic and ideological code, and the other a road map of how to survive in Soviet political and economic reality. The first, the well-established Communist Party code of devotion to building Communism, included the following tenets: 1) Be devoted to building Communism; 2) Love the socialist Motherland and other socialist countries; 3) It is the concern of each individual to maintain and increase common property; 4) Possess a strong understanding of the role of society; 5) Display an intolerance for any infringement on society's best interests, and 6) Honesty, justice, and strong 'moral purity' are the cornerstone of society.[52]

But, in 1962, during the investigation of an embezzlement case, law enforcement authorities reportedly were told of a different kind of code called, 'The Morals and Ethics of Trade.' The tenets were a striking contrast to the ideals of the Communist Party code. 1) Idealism is nonsense. Philosophize less frequently. Remember, money makes the world go round; 2) Everyone steals. Honesty is ridiculous and no one values it. The state will not get poor; 3) Conscience is old fashioned and dangerous. One's conscience must be flexible and always serve its master and no one else; 4) Never show thievery for what it is. And always find a polite way to explain it as 'a mistake' or 'a misunderstanding'; 5) 'Bribe' is such an unpleasant word, better not to use it. Give and take bribes but call it 'mutual assistance.' Live and let live! 6) Never admit to anyone that you steal—it is unethical. Talk more often about honesty and hard work in life. Cry out loudly about it in public—it will make an impression. However, never put yourself on display. Try to stay in the shadows. It is one of the fundamental rules of security; 7) The more you steal, the more you should raise a fuss about the interests of the state; 8) Operate on the principle: 'You're not guilty if they don't catch you.' Learn well how to cover your tracks. It is important to be seen as honorable, honest, and respected. It helps to mask your real activities as a thief.[53]

This was the reigning mentality throughout much of the Soviet era, wielded by managers and government and Party members as part of the reality of a centrally planned economy. These attitudes developed out of necessity in an environment where the laws of the jungle were always very close to the surface. Rule of law took a back seat to survival and became just another lever in

---

munist Citizens on Their Everyday Use of Bribes and Contacts," *Europe-Asia Studies*, vol. 50, no. 4, 1998, pp. 651–677.

52. Conversation with Anatoly Volobuyev, August 1993.

53. Anatoly Volobuyev, "V Bor'be s Organizovannoi Prestupnost'iu v Rossii Vlasti Dolzhny Nachat' s Sebya, No Oni k Etomu ne Gotovy," 1994, p. 7–9, unpublished article.

manipulating one's way through the treacherous waters of daily life across decades. (As one popular Russian saying goes, "Law is like a front axle: whichever way you turn it, that is the direction it will go. [*Zakon—chto dyshlo, kuda povernul to i vyshlo.*]) In the 1960s, Party leader Nikita Khrushchev asked rhetorically, "Who's the boss, we or the law? We are masters over the law, not the law over us!"[54]

Even this expression of disdain for the rule of law was merely a prelude to what was to come over the next three decades. Khrushchev had rejected the 'cult of personality'—Stalin's domination over the Party—and restored the Party to its supreme position. No individual would again rise above it. Khrushchev learned just what this meant when the Party had had enough of his 'hare-brained schemes' and shuffling of personnel and state agencies. After Khrushchev's ouster in 1964, the new General Secretary of the Communist Party, Leonid Brezhnev, sent an unmistakable message to Party functionaries, essentially saying: Relax, comrades. Your positions are safe. There will be no more shuffling. Go about your business. One senior Party official gushed, "You can't imagine, comrades, what a joy it is for all of us to be able to get on with our work quietly and how well everything is going under the leadership of dear Leonid Ilyich [Brezhnev]. What a marvelous moral-political climate has been established.... It is as if wings have sprouted on our backs."[55] This 'moral political climate,' of course, was the continuation and furtherance of 'The Morals and Ethics of Trade,' featuring corruption, bribery, theft, and prostitution, among other things. "The 'moral climate' was that of the criminal."[56]

> Beating the system, acting outside the law, and getting away with it *was* the virtue. Black marketeers, underground manufacturers, Party bosses, factory managers, and restaurant directors—all of them were a part of the system by working outside the system, milking the system, and privatizing the benefits of state property years before privatizing became official. The notion of property became blurred. The state property was nobody's property, to be exploited by those who administered it on the state's behalf.[57]

---

54. Simis, p. 30 (note 46).

55. Arkady Vaksberg, *The Soviet Mafia: A Shocking Expose of Organized Crime in the USSR*, New York, St. Martin's Press, 1991, p. 76.

56. Ibid., p. 74. For a thorough treatment of corruption during this era, see William A. Clark, *Crime and Punishment in Soviet Officialdom: Combating Corruption in the Political Elite, 1965–1990*, Armonk, New York, M.E. Sharpe, 1993.

57. Vladimir N. Brovkin, "Corruption in 20th Century Russia," *Crime, Law & Social Change*, vol. 4, 2003, p. 214. See also Alexander Shvarts, "The Russian Mafia: Expulsion

State ownership of all property created a lack of responsibility for its maintenance or security—an ingrained sense that it was acceptable to steal public property—since the property belonged to everyone and therefore to no one. Economic activity that brought benefit to the individual was illegal since initiating such activity necessarily involved the theft of state property. Goods and services illegally diverted from the state were exchanged for other illegally diverted goods and services in vast and complex patterns of theft, bribery, corruption, and blackmail. As the Soviet émigré lawyer Konstantin Simis observed, "Everyone regarded all this as perfectly normal, day-to-day routine that did not deserve any particular attention. Not only did the locals not condemn the system of merchandise payoffs, they fully approved it, considering it unavoidable, since without it a rank-and-file office worker would find it impossible to live."[58]

A favorite example of the Communist Party's slide into an ever-deeper abyss of corruption was Vasily Mzhavanadze, the Communist Party boss of Georgia. In the 1960s, Mzhavanadze exemplified the all-too-typical pattern of finding the corrupter and the corrupted in the same person. In addition to his official Party position, he oversaw a network of secret factories and black market stores in the Georgian capital, Tbilisi. He raked in millions of rubles in profits and millions more in bribes before the Party arrested dozens of his accomplices. Eventually Mzhavanadze, whose involvement was hushed up at that time, was allowed to step down quietly from the Politburo in 1972, and take millions in illegal earnings with him.[59] As with so many other aspects of the system, Mzhavanadze was not an anomaly, but rather one of countless plunderers.

In another interesting case, Yuri Sokolov, the director of Yeliseyevsky's, an exclusive Moscow store that carried Western goods and catered to the high and mighty, was executed in 1984 for accepting bribes, among other things. Sokolov, a relatively small player in the vast network of survival in the upper levels of the Soviet elite, managed to squirrel away some $4 million that he kept in a safe hidden under his apartment floor. The director was brought down in one of the typical struggles between political clans within the Com-

---

of Law," *Contemporary Justice Review: Issues in Criminal, Social and Restorative Justice*, vol. 6, no. 4, 2003. See also Lydia Rosner, *The Soviet Way of Crime: Beating the System in the Soviet Union and the U.S.A.*, Massachusetts, Bergin & Garvey Publishers, Inc., 1986.

58. Simis, p. 70 (note 46).

59. Bill Thomas and Charles Sutherland, *Red Tape: Adventure Capitalism in the New Russia*, New York, Dutton, 1992, p. 168. For more detailed background on Mzhavanadze, see Clark, pp. 152–155 (note 56).

munist Party. And the Party publicized his case as an example of cleaning out 'unconscionable bribe-takers,' not as part of the political struggle that it was and certainly not as an illustration that the entire system was rotten to the core.[60]

But it was no secret that the system attracted "inveterate money-grubbers," which was to say "embezzlers, thieves, and swindlers of one kind and another."[61] Instead of creating a pool of people skilled in entrepreneurship, the Soviet economic system produced a population adept at evading government regulations, at operating proficiently at the intersection of the legal and illegal worlds, at capitalizing on some of the inefficiencies in government regulations for private profit.

All of this made for a dramatic and dynamic underworld throughout the Soviet era. To take a brief look at a very thin slice of that world, gambling was enjoying an explosion both within traditional criminal circles and beyond by the 1960s. According to the journalist and small-time participant in underworld activity, Yuri Brokhin, there were countless hustlers' brigades, as they were called, working day and night across the country running games of chance. The games, which had been played primarily in railroad stations, spread to airports, hotels, public parks, beaches, and even the back seats of taxis.

Brokhin underscored two key characteristics of criminal activity which continue to this day: 1) criminals are highly flexible and 'go where the money is,' and 2) criminal activity frequently attracts non-criminal elements if there is easy money to be made. "Gangsters in neighboring professions put aside their pistols, razor blades, and lock picks and armed themselves with cards. The ranks of card hustlers were also swelled by former university students, tailors, dentists, barbers, and medics. They wore expensive made-in-Finland suits, smiled urbanely, and, in their cultured way, flashed leather attaché cases stuffed with money."[62] Some of the individuals participating in these gambling activities, whether professional criminals or the non-criminal types, would go on to form the core of criminal groups that would become particularly active in the 1980s and 1990s. (For a good example, see Chapter 8 for a profile of Otari Kvantrishvili.)

If Brokhin's reporting is to be taken at face value, the Soviet underworld must have had a certain level of organization and structure, not to mention

---

60. Clark, p. 184–185 (note 56). See also Vaksberg (note 55) for numerous illustrations of corruption among the political elite.

61. Vladimirov, p. 143 (note 10).

62. Brokhin, p. 49 (note 45).

financial success, already by the late 1960s. In gambling alone, Brokhin claims, "the average take of a hustler's brigade jumped to $3,000 a day…. If you consider that all across this vast country, hundreds of brigades worked day and night (and are working even now), their gross income would clearly rival that of any other sector of the Soviet national economy."[63]

The traditional criminal world generally began to interact more frequently with the upperworld, as the so-called shadow economy operators (*teniviki*) and the workshop managers (*tsekhoviki*) were pulling in massive amounts of money by providing the black market with products that should have been going into the state distribution network. They needed protection from the government, from their competition, and from criminals. They sought it through bribing state officials but also by entering into agreements with protectors in the criminal world.

One of the best known groups of this period was that of Gennady Kharkov, nicknamed 'Mongol,' who put together in the late 1960s a group of 31 active members, including seven women. They dealt in narcotics—gradually bringing under their control many of the drug dealers in Moscow and outlying areas—and the extortion and protection of underground businessmen. They were known for their use of extreme violence including beatings and brandings. At the beginning of the 1970s, Kharkov was arrested and, reportedly, one of the members, Vyacheslav Ivankov, known as 'Yaponchik,' filled the void. The crime phenomenon we witnessed in the 1990s had been building since the 1960s in the sense that a number of criminals who were active twenty-five years ago developed into the high profile 'crime bosses' (the so-called thieves-in-law or *vory v zakone*) and criminal 'authorities' (*avtoritety*). Along with his close friend Otari Kvantrishvili mentioned in Chapter 8, Ivankov was one of the most publicized examples of the thread linking the 1960s and 1970s to the post-Soviet crime world.[64]

According to several sources, in the 1950s and 1960s, Soviet law enforcement supposedly believed their own propaganda: professional criminality was disappearing from the Soviet landscape and full eradication of crime was imminent. Ideologically this made sense. It was expected that "as socialism was perfected, the social base for crime would gradually disappear, and crime would disappear as well."[65] Since it was practically impossible to run counter to this belief, law enforcement and much of the justice system stopped talk-

63. Ibid.
64. Dmitry Likhanov, "All Hail the King," *Ogonyok*, No. 19, May 1988.
65. Vadim Bakatin in Stephen Handelman, *Comrade Criminal: Russia's New Mafiya*, New Haven, Yale University Press, 1995, p. 276.

ing about these problems on an official level "since the problems of organized and professional criminality reflected both the social and political inadequacies in the country." According to former MVD organized crime researcher Anatoly Volobuyev, this state of affairs lasted until 1985 when Mikhail Gorbachev came to power.[66] Vadim Bakatin, one-time Minister of Internal Affairs and later Chairman of the KGB, acknowledged that as a result of the ideological stance, "there was no point in spending money on criminal justice, on modernizing the police, on training prosecutors, or even on improving our courts."[67] Of course, this didn't mean that professional criminality actually disappeared; it just wasn't permitted to penetrate the rose-colored lenses worn by the country's leadership. As Volobuyev noted in 1990, "For several decades already law enforcement organs have uncovered organized crime groups with all their inherent attributes (leaders, division of labor, common monetary fund, their own judges)."[68]

All of this brings us back to Yuri Melnikov's comment at the beginning of Chapter 5 that Russia has always been this way. In many ways, of course, he was right. A large part of the fascination and disbelief by outsiders was that we didn't have a good appreciation for what came before. While the last years of the Soviet Union and its subsequent collapse helped spur the development and dramatically increase the influence and power of traditional criminal organizations, the existence of these groups was not a result of the disappearance of the USSR; they did not develop spontaneously or in a vacuum; they were not an invading force. The infrastructure, perhaps in more primitive forms, had existed for decades. The major problem was that the rules of the mafia-like Communist Party and the rules of the traditional criminal world became the rules of the whole society. Rather than being restricted or limited to pockets of the underworld, these tools became available to one and all. Businessmen began using contract murder, extortion, and other underworld methods to carry out what would otherwise be upperworld activities (e.g., commercial law, contract law, etc.) And this is where I think Melnikov's comment falls short. There was something qualitatively different that occurred in the 1990s, especially in the first half of the decade. While many of the factors and characteristics of the underworld can be found in most other countries, the main difference in the case of the Soviet Union after it disappeared was the scope. And this is what I think makes the Russian (*Rossiiskaya*) situation noteworthy. The economic, social, and political chaos of the post-Soviet years,

---

66. Volobuyev, p. 3 (note 53).
67. Bakatin in Handelman p. 276 (note 65).
68. Author conversations with Volobuyev, November 1990.

including the collapse of state regulatory institutions, combined with the dramatic increase in firepower as well as the intensification and institutionalization of corruption meant that the 'law of the jungle' played a far greater role than ever before.

CHAPTER 7

VORY V ZAKONE

It is very important to stress that [*vor v zakone*] is a caste-like rank held by several hundred men dispersed all over the former USSR. It is not a centralized organization, nor even an order. It is an institutional design embedded in local culture and is best suited to survival in the conditions of highly repressive, large states like Tsarist Russia and the Soviet Union.

—George Derluguian[1]

A *vor v zakone* is mostly just a conventional understanding. It's a myth, a legend. Everyone understands perfectly that the old codified customs have already become obsolete.

—Twenty-four year-old Russian inmate[2]

"Yes, we have one of those in our prison. Would you like to meet him?"[3] It was October 1991 in Suzdal, one of the twelve ancient cities of the Golden Ring, where I was attending an international conference on organized crime hosted by the United Nations and the Ministry of Internal Affairs of the USSR. Government agencies had been invited—ministries of justice and interior officials from around the world—and five outsiders had been given special per-

---

1. Georgi Derluguian, "The Invisible Fist: Russia's Criminal Predators against Markets and Themselves," Memo #77 in the series, Program on New Approaches to Russian Security (PONARS), 1999, at http://www.fas.harvard.edu/~ponars/POLICY%2MEMOS/Derluguian77.html.

2. Alix Lambert, *Russian Prison Tattoos: Codes of Authority, Domination, and Struggle*, Atglen, PA, Schiffer Publishing, Ltd., 2003, p.111.

3. This chapter derives in part from the article by Joseph D. Serio and Vyacheslav Razinkin, "Thieves Professing the Code: The Traditional Role of *Vory v Zakone* in Russia's Criminal World and Adaptations to a New Social Reality," *Journal of Low Intensity Conflict and Law Enforcement*, vol. 4, no. 1, summer 1995, pp. 72–88. The article was reprinted in Mark Galeotti (ed.), *Russian and Post-Soviet Organized Crime*, Aldershot, Ashgate, 2002.

mission to attend.[4] As with many other conferences, the most valuable moments happened outside the formal sessions. In those few days I struck up conversations with profoundly bored guards monitoring the corridors outside the conference sessions. Our talk turned to *vory v zakone*, those 'godfathers' of the Russian underworld. Word got back to the organized crime control officials from the nearby city of Vladimir, another gem in the Golden Ring, who were assisting with conference logistics. One of them approached me. "Yes, we have one of those in our prison. Would you like to meet him?"

The imposing prison walls rose up before us in the ancient city. My first thoughts were of suffering. Vladimir, some 150 miles northeast of Moscow, experienced the same breathtaking cold as much of the rest of the region. The cells of the old Tsarist prison became iceboxes in winter and multiple layers of clothing and coats were standard dress throughout the day and night.

After World War II, the regime at Vladimir Central was mild, and Japanese and German generals and other military ranks that had been held there did not have particularly negative memories of the place.[5] But, according to Jacques Rossi, who had been held in Vladimir Central and numerous other prisons and labor camps between 1937 and 1958, by the late 1950s it had turned into "one of the most horrible Soviet prisons for 'especially dangerous recidivists' (*osobo opasniye retsidivisty*) and political prisoners."[6] Swedish diplomat Raoul Wallenberg, arrested by Soviet authorities in Budapest in January 1945, was held there in the 1950s. Janos Kadar, whom the Soviet Politburo sent to Budapest in 1956 as Secretary General of the Hungarian Communist Party, was held there until 1955. And dissident Anatoly Shchransky was there in the early 1980s.

Perhaps the most famous inmate incarcerated for a time within the unforgiving walls of Vladimir Central was Francis Gary Powers, the American Air Force pilot who had been shot down in 1960 in his U2 spy plane during a mission over the Soviet Union. Powers survived the missile that struck his air-

---

4. The conference was closed to the public. Two of the other foreigners in attendance were Dick Ward, at the time Vice Chancellor for Administration at the University of Illinois at Chicago and Executive Director of the Office of International Criminal Justice, and the journalist Claire Sterling, author of *Thieves' World: The Threat of the New Global Network of Organized Crime*.

5. Jacques Rossi, *The Gulag Handbook: An Encyclopedia Dictionary of Soviet Penitentiary Institutions and Terms Related to the Forced Labor Camps*, New York, Paragon House, 1989, p.47.

6. Ibid. At this time, especially dangerous recidivists were individuals previously convicted of any political crimes under Article 60 of the Criminal Code or of planning political crimes, for banditry, counterfeiting money, unauthorized use of currency, robbery, gang rape, theft of state property, and so on.

craft, was arrested, convicted in a high-profile trial, and locked up. One of the staff members in the room with us could barely contain herself. "Show him Powers's cell. Show him Powers's cell." Perhaps there was some lingering Soviet pride at besting the capitalist enemy and embarrassing the United States all those years ago. Her enthusiasm flagged when we opened the cell door only to find the lone inhabitant, pants bunched up around his ankles, startled at the appearance of the unannounced visitors. The cell itself was nondescript—the same cramped space barely tolerable for two as in most other prisons I'd visited.

We moved on quickly, together with the red-faced staffer, to another cell, a dormitory-sized room with more than a dozen inmates bunking together. Here I was introduced to 'Sasha,' Vladimir Central's resident *vor v zakone*. During an earlier meeting the warden informed me quite frankly that Sasha controlled half the population of the prison, some 350 inmates. The *vor* didn't look all that impressive. His build was slight and the sleeves of his shirt ran past his wrists, giving him an even more diminutive appearance. "Kto vy po-zhizniu?" he asked. Who are you? ... with a sense of What is your position in life? "I work at a university." For some reason he and his men were delighted with the response and at that moment I received my nickname from the underworld boss: 'Professor.'

As a *vor v zakone*, Sasha represented an elite world that had grown up in the Soviet prison system and wielded vast influence in that realm. As Alexander Gurov points out, fixing a date of the appearance of *vory* and how they came to be named is difficult. Pre-Revolution researchers apparently did not use the name. By the beginning of the 1930s, however, the name *vory v zakone* was established.[7]

The predecessors to the *vory* developed quickly after the Russian Revolution of 1917. In an effort to create instability, chaos, and panic, the political enemies of the new regime began to draw into their fold traditional professional criminals. It was impossible, however, to unite the political and traditional criminals without some degree of assimilation of the former into the criminal world. As a result, the politicals frequently became heads of juvenile criminal groups and eventually took the name *zhigani*. *Zhigani* borrowed the criminal traditions and customs and adapted them to the new conditions, giving ideological overtones in an effort to disseminate their message to the widest audience possible. This, too, helped the politicals avoid total assimilation into the criminal world. As the 'ideological' opposition to the new state, the *zhigani* developed the following laws:

---

7. Alexander Gurov, *Professional'naya Prestupnost': Proshloe i Sovremennost'*, Moskva, Yuridicheskaya Literatura, 1990, p. 108.

1. Forbidden to work or to take part in the work of society;
2. Forbidden to have a family (*postoyannaya sem'ya*);
3. Forbidden to take up arms on behalf of the state;
4. Forbidden to cooperate with authorities as a witness or victim;
5. Obliged to contribute money for the common good.[8]

Three out of five of the laws pertained to the refusal to cooperate with the state in any form and would become the core of the *vory* tradition. This period was the first stage in the formation of new regulative traditions and customs while traditional attributive elements such as tattoos, jargon, nicknames, and gestures, as well as emotional elements like songs, verses, and sayings, remained more or less constant since bygone days.

Failure to unite internally resulted in conflicting philosophical viewpoints: one that defined 'profession' (traditional criminal) and one that leaned toward a system of subordination (*zhigani*—politicals). Toward the end of the 1920s and into the 1930s, a leadership crisis developed. The lower rungs of the hierarchy began to disobey the *zhigani* and promoted their own leaders, *urki*. Constant conflict between *urki* and *zhigani* created the need to perfect the code of the underworld. Based on pre-Revolution criminal traditions and customs, a single 'law' was accepted to regulate the behavior of top representatives of the criminal world. By this code, the most authoritative criminals became known as the *vory v zakone*, literally 'thieves in law.'[9]

Correctional labor camps—the Gulag system—acted as the medium for further development of thieves' traditions and customs and their swift dissemination throughout prison. Once released from prison, former inmates continued the propagation of the code and attracted greater numbers of adherents, which strengthened the *vor*'s authority and promoted group cohesion.[10]

By the 1930s, according to Likhachev, there had already developed an intricate set of rules prescribing behavior among thieves in a thoroughly hierarchical set of relationships. A thieves' court with its own procedures was in place and "the penalty is always severe and inflicted without delay."[11]

By the time the opening salvos of World War II sounded, *vory v zakone* were a potent force in the Soviet criminal world. The war, however, had a profound effect on the criminal community. Part of the thieves' brotherhood responded

---

8. S. Ya. Lebedev, *Antiobshchestvenniye Traditsii, Obychai i ikh Vliyanie na Prestupnost'*, Omsk, Omskaya Vysshaya Shkola Militsii, 1989, p. 30.

9. Ibid., p. 31. See also Gurov, pp. 107–108 (note 7).

10. Ibid., p. 32.

11. Cited in Valery Chalidze, *Criminal Russia: Crime in the Soviet Union*, New York, Random House, 1977, p. 53.

to the call to defend the Motherland while others elected to remain in prison, true to their oath. At war's end, those who had violated the code by taking up arms in support of the state attempted to reintegrate into the criminal world. Because of their defection from the criminal ranks, however, they were now considered turncoats or 'bitches' (*suki*)[12] and forbidden to reclaim their authority. This tension among the elite led to the so-called bitches' war (*such'ya voina*).[13]

The bitches' war was a battle to the death in prison between criminals adhering to the thieves' law and those who betrayed the code by taking up arms in the name of the state. The bitches supposedly introduced an alternative code at the end of World War II that allowed for collaboration with state authorities during the war in an attempt to regain the authority they had abandoned during the war.[14]

Soviet prison authorities attempted to use the bitches' war to exterminate systematically certain prisoners at the hands of their criminal colleagues. Warring groups were purposely placed in the same facility, and the administration didn't immediately suppress fights that erupted. The bloodletting reportedly became so great that the *vory* were forced to adapt their code to survive. After considerable debate, they settled on an exception to the rules: thieves had the right, in case of extreme need, to become team leaders and barbers in the camps. A team leader could always save and feed several friends at a time. Barbers had access to sharp-edged objects—razors and scissors—a distinct advantage during times of intracamp bitch warfare. It was believed that the prohibition of service to the state also softened as a result of the bitches' war.[15]

In the 1950s, some *vory* began to drift from criminal traditions. Prison administrations frequently supported those they thought to be leaving the ranks of the *vory*, considering their mutiny in a positive light. Using the cover provided by the officials, these criminal elite gathered power in their own hands and began to establish their rule over the criminal world. They once again set down the 'law' and fashioned themselves the protectors of criminal tradition and custom. The *vory v zakone* who left the fold and then reclaimed power (known as *otkoloty*) formed new groups and continued to develop their crim-

---

12. It has been reported that the oath a *vor* was to swear upon his acceptance into the brotherhood began, "I'll be a bitch if ..." Ibid., p. 59.

13. Mikhail Dyomin, *The Day is Born of Darkness*, New York, Alfred A. Knopf, 1976, pp. 20–30.

14. Rossi, pp. 443–444 (note 5).

15. Chalidze, p. 49 (note 11). See also Dyomin (note 13) as well as Rossi (note 5).

inal activity. The initial decline in the number of *vory* was misunderstood by law enforcement officials to be the *vor*'s final destruction, the disappearance of traditions, customs, and the code.[16]

As mentioned in Chapter 6, law enforcement organs were supposedly so convinced that the criminal leaders and their groups had disappeared forever that they practically ceased all work in this area by the 1960s.[17] Despite this belief, there was no evidence that the draconian measures used by the state against the *vory* had been successful. Social and economic conditions of the time actually encouraged an increase in crime and strengthened the role for the *vory*.[18] Special meetings (*skhodki*) were held by the *vory* in various regions of the country—Moscow (1947), Kazan (1955), and Krasnodar (1956), to name but a few—to discuss the development of their criminal activity. At the Moscow and Krasnodar meetings, several *vory* were convicted by their fellow thieves and received the ultimate punishment.[19] Meetings were held primarily to welcome new *vory* into the brotherhood through coronation ceremonies, to discuss discipline among the *vory* and dole out punishment if necessary, and to discuss division of territory and relations with other groups. Much of this secretive elite world of coronations and crime was guided—at least in its ideal state—by the code.

By tradition, *vory v zakone* scorned everything associated with 'normal' society; they were the rulers of the anti-society that Vladimir Gilyarovsky had written about in the 1890s, having their own hierarchy, their own rules, and their own system of punishment. It wasn't surprising to find that prison had been the only place the thief called home; freedom—as the mainstream world defined it—was thought to be temporary.[20] Prison was a place of honor for these underworld bosses and served to strengthen a *vor*'s reputation. Sentence duration and respect seemed directly proportional. Even if sentenced to a lengthy term, the code forbade the *vor* from engaging in prison work,[21] and it was incumbent on the inmates to assume prison duties of the *vor* if necessary. For his part, the *vor* had to accept any punishment given by the prison administration for refusing to work.

---

16. Lebedev, p. 33 (note 8).

17. Ibid., pp. 33–34.

18. See Rossi (note 5).

19. Gurov, pp. 116–117 (note 7). See also Chalidze, p. 67 (note 11). While it is useful to note *vory skhodki*, it's also important to understand that these meetings were a normal part of their policy-making process. The fact of their occurrence should not be met with any great surprise; they had been taking place for many decades.

20. Author interview with 'the Georgian,' May 1991.

21. See Yuri M. Antonyan, *Osobo Opasnye Lidery v ITU i Vospitatel'noe Vozdeistvie na Nikh*, Moskva, Vsesoiuznyi Nauchno-Issledovatel'skii Institut, MVD SSSR, 1989.

There were a number of activities that were looked upon as collaboration with the prison administration and consequently forbidden by the code. These included informing on other inmates, accepting leadership positions in prison with the support of the administration, participating in the construction of isolation cells or compounds, taking up arms, or engaging in any activity that could have been interpreted as cooperating with the government or prison administration.[22] The *vor* was permitted contact with law enforcement officials only if such meetings furthered the *vor's* interests without assisting law enforcement.

One of the most common enumerations of the *vor's* code is as follows:

1. A thief must turn his back on his family—mother, father, brothers, and sisters. The criminal community is family.
2. It is forbidden to have a family—wife, children.
3. It is forbidden to work. A thief must live off the fruits of criminal activity only.
4. A thief must give moral and material assistance to other thieves using the *obshchak* (money fund).
5. A thief must give information about accomplices and their whereabouts (e.g. locations of hideouts) only in the strictest confidentiality.
6. If a thief is under investigation, a petty thief must take responsibility upon himself to give the suspected thief time to flee.
7. When a conflict arises in a criminal group or among thieves, there must be a meeting (*skhodka*) to resolve the issue.
8. When necessary, a thief must attend a meeting (*skhodka*) to judge another thief if his conduct or behavior comes into question.
9. Punishment for a thief decided by the meeting must be carried out.
10. A thief must be proficient in criminals' jargon (*fenia, blatnaya muzyka*).
11. A thief must not enter a card game if he does not have the money to pay.
12. A thief must teach his craft to novice thieves.
13. A thief should keep a gofer (*shestiorka*) under his influence.
14. A thief must not lose his sense when drinking alcohol.
15. A thief must not in any way become involved with the authorities. A thief must not participate in social activities. A thief must not join social organizations.
16. A thief must not take up weapons from the hands of state authority. A thief must not serve in the army.

---

22. See Rossi (note 5), Antonyan (note 21), and Dyomin (note 13).

17. A thief must fulfill all promises made to other thieves.[23]

Several of the prescriptions listed above spoke to the core of the *vory* ideal. For example, 3, 10, and 12 concerned the professional aspects of the *vor*'s life. And many of the items—4, 5, 6, 7, 8, 9, and 17—guided the thief in his relations with his criminal colleagues. 15 and 16 spoke to the refusal to cooperate with authorities. These were the defining items that underscored the purpose of the *vors*' existence. The code was used by the *vory* to maintain power, provide services, act as advisor to criminals, and mediate disputes. According to the late Evgeny Vasin ('Dzhem'), "A thief-in-law they call a person, who can pass the just judgment, who can achieve a resolution without bloodshed. This is what I used to do in prison."[24]

> This law ... prescribes every aspect of the thief's life. Spiritual life, language, prison-camp mores, evaluation of human beings, relations with other thieves in the framework of their own community, judgment and punishment for infraction of thieves' rules, work and leisure, eating and drinking, treatment of their own bodies, attitudes toward sex and women, towards renegades from the thieves' society, relations with common people outside and state officials inside the camps—all these aspects of life are treated in their laws.[25]

As Alexander Gurov summarizes, the two main professional characteristics of *vory v zakone* were "parasitism and organization."[26] First, the thief was never to work. He got his sustenance either by a life of crime or from others whom

---

23. For an enumeration of the thieves' code (*vorovskoi zakon*) as well as lengthier treatments of *vory v zakone*, see D. S. Baldayev, *Slovar' Tiuremno-Lagerno-Blatnogo Zhargona*, Moskva, Kraya Moskvy, 1992, p. 80; Chalidze, pp. 40–55 (note 11); Yuri Glazov, "'Thieves' in the USSR: A Social Phenomenon," *Survey*, 22, 1976, in Mark Galeotti (ed.), *Russian and Post-Soviet Organized Crime*, Aldershot, Ashgate, 2002, pp. 31–46; Gurov, pp. 111–112 (note 7); Georgii Podlesskikh and Andrei Tereshonok, *Vory v Zakone: Brosok k Vlasti*, Moskva, Khudozhestvennaya Literatura, 1994; Joseph D. Serio and Vyacheslav Razinkin, "Thieves Professing the Code: The Traditional Role of *Vory v Zakone* in Russia's Criminal World and Adaptations to a New Social Reality," *Journal of Low Intensity Conflict and Law Enforcement*, vol. 4, no. 1, summer 1995, pp. 72–88; Federico Varese, *The Russian Mafia: Private Protection in a New Market Economy*, New York, Oxford University Press, 2001, pp. 145–186; Vadim Volkov, *Violent Entrepreneurs: The Use of Force in the Making of Russian Capitalism*, Ithaca, Cornell University Press, 2002, pp. 54–63.
24. *Kommersant*, October 5, 2001, p. 12, cited in Volkov, ibid., p. 57.
25. Glazov, p. 34 (note 23).
26. Gurov, p. 109 (note 7). See also Gurov cited in Larisa Kislinskaya, "'Vory v Zakone' i ikh Pokroviteli," *Sovetskaya Rossiya*, March 28, 1992, no. 49 (10748), p. 3.

he advised in their criminal activity. In terms of organization, generally speaking, *vory v zakone* had to fulfill some basic management functions, what Antonyan calls the information function, organization function, normative-regulatory function, and the decision-making function. Actually, these were functions that most effective managers would need to be proficient in, whether operating in the underworld or upperworld.[27]

Vory v zakone were believed to occupy the highest level of the criminal hierarchy. In prison, *vory* were essentially the masters of their environment and, in freedom, they were believed to have influenced criminal groups over vast stretches of territory. The *vor* had a trusted advisor (*sovetnik*) who was adept at working the prison system. The advisor knew the situation in the prison, its internal procedures, and vulnerable points. He aided in the establishment of channels to smuggle forbidden goods into the prison, such as liquor, narcotics, and women, one of the most important functions of the *vor* in prison. His advice was important in the *vor*'s decision making regarding future group activities. This was true outside the prison environment as well. In carrying out his basic functions within prison, the *vor v zakone* had an assistant, frequently referred to as a 'watcher' (*smotriashchyi*) who would scope out new arrivals to the prison and help to determine the newcomer's role in the prison, among other things.[28] This included remaining aware of individuals who might eventually be accepted into the *vory* brotherhood. *Smotriashchye* were used in freedom as they were in prison, as 'watchers' to look after the interests of the *vor* in a certain territory (*sledit' za poriadkom*).[29]

---

27. Antonyan, pp. 19–26 (note 21). See also Vyacheslav Razinkin, "O Rasprostranennosti Prestupnykh Gruppirovok Osuzhdennykh v Ispravitel'no-Trudovykh Uchrezhdeniyakh," unpublished document, 1994. See also Serio and Razinkin (note 23).

28. In one episode of the Russian TV series, *Brigada*, members of the crime group are arrested and brought to jail. The first question the leader asks of the other inmates is, "Who is the *smotriashchyi* here?"

29. The following is an example of a secret note discussing both *obshchak* and *smotriashchye*, reportedly sent by the *vor v zakone* Alexander Zakharov to inmates in Moscow's Butyrsky Prison: "The time has come to talk to you again. We express our deep respect to those who have supported our Russian movement and Leonid Zavadski, one who did not shit out of fear and considered things as they should be considered by an honorable convict. We understand that many people turned out not to be what they claimed—I know about this from our secret letters. We will deal with each of them appropriately. We, and consequently you, are being supported by all Russian thieves. Slava Yaponets is in America now—he stands with us. Rospis is in Poland now and together with our guys he is expanding our movement there. The same is happening in prisons. Do not forget about this. Do not let Russia get screwed. All guests will have our respect as long as they do not touch our interests. We accomplished tremendous work with Zavadski. He will soon come home

The level below the *sovetnik* and *smotriashchyi* was the 'supply group' (*gruppa obespecheniye*). Members of this level carried full responsibility for the organization, storage, and use of general supplies, and in some cases the monetary resources of the group (*obshchak*, see below). They enjoyed close relations with the *vor*. In prison, group members attempted to protect members of the supply group from encroachment by surrounding convicts or the prison administration.

The next level was the 'security group' (*gruppa bezopasnosti*). These individuals were responsible for the more physically challenging administrative activities of the group. They extracted debts and collected money for the support of the *obshchak* as well as protected members of the group. In prison, they oversaw punishment of non-productive convicts who were under the influence of the *vor*. Frequently, former athletes were used because of their strength and were referred to as 'bulls' or 'torpedoes.'

Another person in the *vor*'s orbit in prison was the *shestiorka*, or the 'sixer,' named for the lowest-ranking card in traditional Russian card games. They were essentially lackeys who cleaned the laundry and acted as go-fers for the *vory*, among other things.[30] These members were usually recruited from among those convicts having a material or psychological dependence on the groups.

In prison, hierarchy was generally demonstrated in individual prison cells. The *vor* occupied the most comfortable space in the cell usually near the window, away from the door and the communal toilet (*parasha*).[31] It was sym-

---

to us here in freedom. In prison, there remain men who have proven themselves as brave and honest convicts under the most difficult circumstances. I have appointed these men as 'watchers' responsible for the situation in Butyrski Central, this Moscow prison of ours. From now on, all *obshchak* money will not go where nobody knows, but to these 'watchers.' And from them to all the needy, to all those inmates who are deprived of support by relatives and close friends. And it doesn't matter what his nationality is. All our Moscow guys are working very hard. They have collected and continue to collect money for you. And the vermin that tries to put a spoke in our wheel will be torn apart. These are the men you should go to: Volokha 'Irkutsky,' Shurik 'Graf,' and Volodka 'Sverdlovsky.' These men will be reliable 'watchers' and will deliver all my addresses to you. With sincere respect to all of you, Shurik Zakhar." See Vladimir Yarov, "Istoriya Zakhara," *Sevodnya*, May 31, 1995, p. 7; *Kommersant Daily*, "Na Svobodu s Chistoi Sovest'iu," October 31,1995, p. 14; *Kommersant Daily*, "Pomoshchnik Deputata Ispytyval na Kladbishche Glushiteli," June 20, 1995, p. 15; *Kommersant Daily*, "Vasia–Bandit Razdelil Sud'bu Zakhara," August 30, 1995, p. 14; *Kommersant Daily*, "Militsionery Nashli Ideologa v 'Shamane,'" May 30, 1995, p. 14.

30. Rossi, p. 501 (note 5). Rossi quotes the renowned lexicographer Dal' regarding the definition of *shesterit*': 'to run and back forth often.'

31. Author interview with 'the Georgian,' 1991.

bolically important for the *vor* to maintain his distance from the area around toilet as it was reserved for the 'small fry' and homosexuals, "for this is where same resides."[32]

The cast of characters in the prison also included the downcasts. Sometimes called the 'offended' or the 'residues,' these inmates played the role of a woman in the prison colony. These were the lowest of the low and were relegated to sleeping under the bunks in the overcrowded Russian prisons.[33] The *muzhiki* (peasants) carried out the majority of the mandated work in the prison camps. They were individuals not belonging to any criminal group but who knew the rules of the *vory* and of prison and forced labor camp life.[34] The last group to be mentioned is *frayer*, which has been translated as 'pigeon' and most frequently as 'sucker.'[35] But this was more than simply a sucker as in a 'mark' or victim. A *frayer* was an individual who did not belong to the thieves' world and who was actively preyed upon. Said to come from the German *frei*, or free, a *frayer* was a person belonging to the outside world.[36]

In freedom, frequently a *vor* would wield influence over a region. For example, one *vor* had the head of the local customs service on his team along with two *avtoritety*, influential individuals in the criminal world. The two *avtoritety* controlled the trade in cars and were frequently guests in the home of the customs chief. This relationship easily led to cooperation with the regional customs chief. The *vor* oversaw the region and received massive amounts of money every week. One of his primary functions was to resolve problems that arose with local government authorities and with government officials in Moscow.[37]

One of the most important tasks assumed by the head of a crime group, whether he was a thief-in-law (*vor v zakone*), a criminal leader (*avtoritet*), or some other important figure, was maintenance of a common monetary

---

32. Ibid. See also Dyomin (note 13).

33. See Lambert (note 2). For an additional perspective on prison hierarchy, see Lebedev, pp. 23–25 (note 8).

34. 'Muzhik' ('Peasant')—a convict that belongs to no group. Behind a mask of neutrality, indifference, and non-interference, he hides a fear for his own life. He does not refuse to participate in the prison's work program. See L. A. Mil'yanenkov, *Po Tu Storonu Zakona: Entsiklopediya Prestupnogo Mira*, Sankt-Peterburg, Redaktsiya Zhurnala Damy i Gospoda, 1992.

35. Rossi, p. 239 (note 5).

36. Glazov, p. 37 (note 23).

37. "Organizovannaya Prestupnost' (Regional'nyi Aspekt Bor'by s Orgprestupnost'iu)," 1995, p. 3, unpublished MVD document.

fund, a kind of criminal community chest.[38] The fund was known as the *ob-shchaya kassa*, or *obshchak* for short. It was essentially the bank accounts of the underworld.[39]

The *obshchak* was maintained through profits from traditional criminal activities such as extortion, prostitution, narcotics and weapons dealing, and others. In the commercial sector, profits were made in areas such as timber and fishing industries as well as importing (smuggling) foreign cars, and other activities. Later these were surpassed by the tremendous amounts of money to be made through the sale of oil and gas or a percentage cut from such deals.

The *obshchak* served several purposes. First, the size of the fund gave corresponding authority to the particular *vor* and to the groups he oversaw, both in prison and on the outside.

Second, within prison, *obshchak* funds were used to bribe prison administration officials; outside, the funds were used to buy state officials and others.

Third, funds were used in the acquisition of foodstuffs as well as alcohol and narcotics for the prison community.

Fourth, money was allocated for planning and perpetrating new crimes.

Fifth, the *obshchak* made possible financial assistance to those in prison, to support the families of imprisoned group members, retain lawyers, and finance lavish funerals for those who lost their lives while 'on duty.' For example, in June 1994, the *vor* 'Plotnik' reportedly obtained bedding and mattresses worth tens of millions of rubles for prisons. It was relatively easy to compromise the prison administration at a time when state budgets weren't sufficient to maintain the prisons. In this way, Plotnik strengthened his own position by acting as a patron to inmates.

Sixth, in the post-Soviet era, considerable sums had been directed toward buying luxury automobiles, apartments, real estate, companies, as well as securing the opportunity to stand as a candidate of a political party in elections.[40] In the Russian Far East, the *vor v zakone* Evgeny Vasin ('Dzhem') was said to have had a strong team of emissaries (*polozhentsy*) who controlled the various *obshchaka* in Magadan, Petropavlovsk-Kamchatsky, Yuzhno-Sakhalinsk, Vladivostok, Nakhodka, Ussuriisk, Khabarovsk, Birobidzhan, Blagoveshchensk, and

---

38. Volkov, p. 744 (note 23). See also Derluguian (note 1).

39. *Obshchak* has also been referred to as a 'criminal community,' although I have seen this reference in only one place. See T.G. Tatidinova, "Young People and Organized Crime," *Russian Social Science Review*, vol. 42, no. 5, September-October 2001, pp. 50–63.

40. For a discussion of some of these functions, see Marat Akchurin, *Red Odyssey: A Journey Through the Soviet Republics*, New York, HarperCollins, 1992, p. 46.

Yakutsk. Reportedly Dzhem was presented with a Land Cruiser at his birthday celebration in 1997 courtesy of the Khabarovsk *obshchak*.[41]

Vyacheslav Komissarov estimated the portion of *obshchak* moneys dedicated to some of these activities. Assistance to families of imprisoned group members, for example, consumed some 22% of the funds, 26% went to the preparation of new crimes, and 30% went to loan sharking.[42] Gennady Chebotaryov, the former Deputy Chief of the Organized Crime Control Department, estimated that from 30–50% of *obshchak* funds was used to bribe officials.[43] George Derluguian agrees with Chebotaryov, adding that the figure was even higher than that by the end of the 1990s. "The major expenditures of the [*vorovskoi obshchak*] are now the regular protection payments and one-time bribes to police, state officials, politicians and lobbyists, lawyers, and even journalists—rather than the support of imprisoned comrades."[44] Former Moscow criminal investigator Alexander Gorkin strikes a similar chord when he notes that *obshchak* funds "were redistributed towards the creation of a 'good image'—the brave, sincere, honest, and patriotic *vor v zakone* shown in books, movies, and TV shows."[45]

And the sums in question could be rather high. Many criminal organizations that developed rapidly in the 1990s and survived the Great Mob War were worth hundreds of millions of dollars and more. Russian law enforcement sources noted that the *obshchak* of a large Moscow-based group figured in the tens of millions of dollars, which was kept in accounts in a major Russian bank. One of the individuals who oversaw this *obshchak* maintained a public persona as a businessman and celebrity but was deeply involved with the criminal world.[46] According to Chebotaryov, the organized crime figure that was reportedly killed when a bomb ripped apart his Mercedes (mentioned in Chapter 3) was worth $100 million.[47]

In addition to the *obshchak*, much had been made of the various attributes of the Russian criminal world and particularly of the *vory* tradition. Lebedev notes three basic categories of elements of traditions and customs in the criminal world.

41. Author investigative information.

42. Vyacheslav Komissarov in G. Min'kovskii (ed.), *Bor'ba s Organizovannoi Prestupnost'iu: Problemy Teorii i Praktiki*, Moskva: Akademiya Ministerstva Vnutrennykh Del SSSR, 1990, p. 54. Komissarov does not indicate how he reached these figures.

43. Author conversation with Chebotaryov, November 1992.

44. Derluguian (note 1).

45. Author conversations with Gorkin, July and December 2006.

46. Author investigative information.

47. Author conversation with Chebotaryov, November 1994.

First, regulative elements, which included certain laws (*zakony*) and rules (*pravila*), dictated and regulated the proper criminal conduct for an anti-social way of life, how to conduct oneself in the criminal world, how to commit certain crimes, and how to properly observe rituals of the underworld. Second, attributive elements, including tattoos, jargon, nicknames, and gestures, reflected the type of criminal activity the individual was involved in. Lastly, emotional elements such as songs, verses, sayings, poetry, and folklore, helped attract new recruits into criminal enterprises. These three elements worked in concert to create an alternative life, an anti-society with its own hierarchy, rules, and punishments. This was a closed society that ran parallel with 'normal' society and, in theory, didn't rely on it or interact with it except to victimize it for the thieves' gain. In the creation of the anti-society it was important to promote ideals such as honesty, openness, the love for life, and the breadth of the thieves' soul.[48] Some of this, of course, was simply part of the legend, part of the manipulation, of the underworld.

One of the attributive elements, Russian prison tattoos, received considerable attention and was the subject of several books.[49] After the Communist Party took power, inmates began using tattoos more actively and extensively to express their political beliefs, demonstrate their positions in the complex prison hierarchy, and, most importantly, proclaim their "personalities, 'talents,' and plans."[50]

Tattoos were an integral part of the criminal and prison experience. It was not uncommon to see Russian prison inmates tattooed from head to toe. Tattooing was one way to display dedication to a life of crime and, specifically, a life behind bars.[51]

Tattoos told the story of the criminal history of the wearer, frequently indicating the crime committed, number of times in prison, criminal specialty, level of authority in the underworld, attitudes toward other types of prison-

---

48. Lebedev, p. 9 (note 8). Lebedev calls this the "chestnost', otkrytost', zhizneliubiya, i shiroty vorovskoi dushi."

49. For example, see Baldayev (note 23) as well as D. S. Baldayev, et al., *Russian Criminal Tattoo Encyclopedia, Volume II*, London, Fuel Publishing, 2006; Lambert (note 2); Mil'yanenkov (note 34). See also "Russian Criminal/Prison Tattoos: Research Conducted for the Migration Integrity Unit, Immigration Section, Canadian Embassy, Moscow," June/July 2005, compiled by Graham MacCaffrey. See photographs of Russian tattoos at Foreign Prisoner Support Service at http://www.phaseloop.com/foreignprisoners/exp-russian_tats.html.

50. Ralph Bouhaider, "Body Language," *Financial Times*, November 2, 2004, accessed through Johnson's Russia List.

51. Lebedev, p. 27 (note 8).

ers, if the wearer had ever escaped from confinement, and so on. During the Stalinist years it was popular to have images of Lenin and Stalin tattooed on the chest in the belief that the prison administration would not fire at their portrait to execute an inmate. Illustrations of playing cards or card suits — a spade, diamond, club, or heart — indicated that the wearer was a gambler. A dollar sign meant safecracker. An independent thief who worked without a gang wore a tree branch tattoo. Some tattoos were given involuntarily as warnings or punishment for transgressions. For example, sex offenders were frequently branded with the image of a dagger running across their shoulder blades and through their necks.[52]

The symbols and images inked into the inmates' skin told of the rank and standing of the individual in the complex social system behind bars. Some *vory v zakone*, for example, had minimal tattooing but what they wore spoke volumes to prison inmates. Matching eight-pointed star tattoos on each side of the torso, located just below the collarbone, or on the knees, was one of the marks of a *vor v zakone*. Tattoos in the shape of epaulets on each side, with various designs within the epaulets, identified a criminal within the upper hierarchy.

Understandably, Russian prison tattoos became a subject of interest to various agencies of the U.S. and Canadian governments, among others. According to a U.S. Department of State Memorandum dated September 16, 1993, the U.S. Embassy in Kiev reported that "unsavory appearing visa applicants, sporting tattoos, were presenting suspicious business petitions. Post requested information about one of the sponsoring companies and about Russian criminal tattoos." In the case of the Kiev inquiry, the San Francisco-based company sponsoring the tattooed individual could not be located. The company letterhead had typographical errors and was written in varying typefaces. Apparently the company in question didn't exist, but a Russian representing another company answered the telephone when inquiries were made.

The issue of Russian tattoos as an indicator of "unsavory" types was important enough to the State Department that the Memo was circulated to the capitals of all the former Soviet republics, St. Petersburg, and Vladivostok in Russia as well as Finland and three posts in Poland. Logically, then, it would be expected that the tattoo issue would play some role in enforcement in the United States as well. In 2000, for example, an officer of the U.S. Border Patrol found underworld tattoos on a Russian individual who had been moni-

---

52. For examples of Russian prison tattoos, see http://www.word.com/place/russian _tattoos/.

toring the U.S.-Canadian border with GPS equipment. While they were not tattoos of a *vor*, they suggested that hardened criminals were actively probing the border. A similar event occurred at another part of the U.S.-Canadian border, at the opposite end of the U.S. from the first incident.[53]

Even as the Russian criminal world continues to evolve out of the dramatic 'mafia' era of the 1990s, the subject of tattoos will be of interest to law enforcement agencies in the United States, Canada, and around the world for some time to come. It is less important, though, for law enforcement to become experts at the meanings behind each tattoo but rather simply appreciate that tattooed suspects should be treated with great care as they have likely served time in a Soviet or Russian prison.

Here a brief word about another of the attributive elements mentioned by Lebedev above. Like many communities of thieves around the world, the Russian underworld developed its own jargon, a criminal argot. Indeed, it is considered a subject of such sufficient importance that it was included in the enumeration of the thieves' code (see point 10 in the thieves' code, above).

Although there has been little consensus on where the underworld language (*fenia*) came from or when it developed, it was widely believed to have developed out of *ofenia*, a secret language used by roving merchants for the deception of customers. The criminal world was said to have adapted it for its own purposes.[54] However, Chalidze says that there were other sources for the language including sailors' slang, Yiddish, Romany, and other languages.[55]

Likhachev, writing in 1935, says that the thieves' argot emerged at the end of the 15th century and the beginning of the 16th century.[56] Others have put the era of the development much later, at the end of the 18th century and the beginning of the 19th century. In any case, there did not emerge simply one language that the entire underworld used. Jargon differed among criminal specialties (bribery, speculation, pocket picking, gambling, theft, theft of antiques, drug dealing). It varied by region of the country and changed over

---

53. The Border Patrol officer wrote to me in an email in May 2000: "Here in the northern border area during the past couple of years we have had several encounters with Russian nationals. These encounters seem to be on the rise.... This last encounter which prompted my question about tattoos involved a group of individuals from Rhode Island. One of the individuals in the group had been encountered twice previously with GPS equipment and was apparently scouting the local border area in an attempt to find an illegal crossing spot."

54. Lebedev, p. 16 (note 8).

55. Chalidze, pp. 56–57 (note 11).

56. D.S. Likhachev, "Cherty Pervobytnogo Primitivizma Vorovskoi Rechi," *Yazyk i Myshlenie*, vol. 3–4, Moskva-Leningrad, 1935, in Chalidze, p. 45 (note 11).

time. The language was generally ungrammatical and frequently used words that were known but assigned different meanings to them so that it was incomprehensible to the average person. The language of the criminal went largely unstudied until the last years of the Soviet Union since, ideologically, professional criminality could not exist and, therefore, there was no reason to study its language.[57]

Another major attribute of the *vory* world worth mentioning was the coronation ceremonies and the oath taken by initiates. In order to join the brotherhood, thieves had to be invited based on the recommendation of 2–3 other *vory*, in part determined by the strength of the characteristics noted by Gurov—his parisitism and organizational skill as well as his overall ability, in theory at least, to observe the code. The more recommendations received, the greater the perceived authority of the new *vor*. If there was some debate about the qualifications of a candidate, he was asked to prove his worthiness through the commission of specific crimes.[58] Their selection was confirmed at a coronation ceremony, sometimes referred to as an 'approach' (*podkhod*), at a meeting of *vory* (*skhodka*). The *vor* reportedly was to declare the following oath before his peers: "Being an inmate, I have chosen the thieves' path and swear before equals to be a worthy thief and never fall in (cooperate) with the Chekists."[59]

Federico Varese, author of *The Russian Mafia*, makes the following distinction about the attributes mentioned above:

> A dress code, tattoos, and even a language of their own would not distinguish the *vory* from any other human group that lives in a closed space, such as sailors, soldiers, and ordinary convicts. The *vory* stand out among such groups because they formed a secret criminal fraternity, with its own code of behavior and its own ritual for the ini-

---

57. Lebedev, p. 36 (note 8).

58. Yu. P. Dubyagin and A. G. Bronnikov (eds.), *Tolkovyi Slovar' Ugolovnykh Zhargonov*, Moskva, Inter-Omnis, 1991, p. 6. See also Rossi (note 5) and Gurov (note 7).

59. M. Dikselius and A. Konstantinov, *Prestupnyi Mir Rossii*, Sankt-Peterburg, Bibliopolis, 1995, p. 67. See also the following quote in Edwin H. Sutherland, *The Professional Thief: An Astonishing Revelation of Criminal Life*, Chicago, The University of Chicago Press, 1937, p. vi: "The hypothesis may well be taken that professional thieves constitute a group which has the characteristics of other groups and that these group characteristics are in no sense pathological. Also, the hypothesis may be taken that tutelage by professional thieves and recognition as a professional thief are essential and universal elements in the definition, genesis, and continued behavior of the professional thief. No one is a professional thief unless he is recognized as such by other professional thieves."

tiation of new members. Furthermore, the *vory* created rudimentary yet effective 'courts' where members' misbehavior was judged and wrongdoers punished and which achieved a national dimension.[60]

Toward the end of the Soviet era and into the post-Soviet years, two types of *vory* emerged, simply referred to as 'old' (*starye vory v zakone*) and 'new' (*novye vory v zakone*).

Old *vory* followed customs and traditions from the 1940s and 1950s and usually were more than fifty years old. They had considerable criminal experience, including multiple convictions and significant authority and influence among criminals both in freedom and in prison. These *vory* made their living exclusively on the commission of crime, running groups that committed fraud, speculation, and extortion, and to some degree on relatively small crimes like picking pockets.[61]

Because the old *vor* spent most of his life incarcerated, it was said that he tried to maintain 'thieves' justice' (*vorovskoi spravedlivost'*), the idea that relations with other convicts should have been guided by honesty and those who violated the code of the criminal world should have been punished.

From a managerial viewpoint, the old *vory* followed a comparatively rigid style and generally didn't adapt well to changing social conditions. Their vision was somewhat limited, which restricted the scope of their criminal activity. The information base from which they operated was believed frequently to be missing important facts necessary to attain their goals.

Novye vory v zakone had different views on methods of criminal activity and behavior. The new *vory* appeared in the late 1980s and 1990s with the increase in various criminal activities including various types of theft, speculation, large-scale property crimes, and an increase in bribery. Contrary to the old thieves, the new *vory* appeared to organize and operate on a grander scale and took advantage of an opportunity to make a large sum of money quickly, even if in violation of the thieves' traditions. In the late 1980s, it was estimated that 20% of all *vory* had associations with cooperatives, those independent private or semi-private businesses (restaurants, cafes, and art galleries), operating legally under legislation introduced during the *glasnost'* era.[62]

The leadership style of the new *vory* could be characterized as flexible. They reportedly had a good command of the overall situation and, through

---

60. Varese, p. 147 (note 23).

61. Antonyan, pp. 7–9 (note 21).

62. This figure is according to an MVD internal document, "O Sostoyanii Bor'by s Liderami Ugolovnoi Sredy 'Vorami v Zakone,'" 1989.

more sophisticated intelligence gathering, could make more accurate estimations of other convicts, their abilities, and the level of readiness for illegal activity.[63]

Rafik Bagdasarian (aka Svo, aka Rafik-Svo) was one of the best-known Armenian *vory v zakone* and a good example of an old-style *vor*. He was born in 1930, committed his first crime at age 11, and had already left school by the sixth grade. Between 1944 and 1984, Svo was convicted 15 times for a variety of crimes including theft, robbery, hooliganism, and illegal drug possession. The Armenian crime boss served out his sentences (*sidel' ot zvonka do zvonka*), some 34 years in total. In the tradition of the *vory*, he refused to work, never testified in court, never assisted state authorities, or attempted to escape. In 1972, the *vor's* crown was bestowed upon him.[64]

After the death of the widely respected *vor* Kuchuloria in 1988, Svo stepped up to fill the void, acting as a mediator in disputes, collecting money for the *obshchak*, and gathering information about other groups as well as politicians and businessmen. He was arrested for the last time on December 23, 1992, in the Minsk Hotel in downtown Moscow.

Svo had three passports for foreign travel.[65] The first passport reportedly had been obtained through the police sports organization, Dynamo, on March 13, 1992. The year of birth was the only thing that had been changed. This simple change helped him look as if he didn't have a criminal record when it was checked by the MVD information center. On this passport he traveled to Belgium, the Netherlands, and Germany; the United States had refused to grant him a visa. The two other passports had been obtained through the Russian Ministry of Culture. The second passport listed him as Rafail Sogomonian, the third as Rafail Aleksanian. Like many *vory v zakone* and other influential criminals in the post-Soviet era, Svo traveled abroad several times, becoming well known to law enforcement officials in Germany, Belgium, the Netherlands, and Luxemburg. He was said to have wanted to go to New York to meet with the *vor v zakone* Vyacheslav Ivankov but was denied a visa.

In Germany, the authorities followed him and noted everything he did. During his visit, Svo reportedly met with one individual to negotiate the purchase of a submachine gun. On December 1, 1992, this individual was found murdered in his apartment. Svo was arrested on December 23, 1992.

---

63. See Valery Pakhomov and Lev Fisher, "Novye 'Vory v Zakone,'" *Sovetskaya Militsiya*, 4/1991, p. 2.

64. Author investigative information.

65. According to an MVD source, these three passports were 21No.0531592 (March 13, 1992); 21No.0734273 (August 21, 1992); and 21No.0730787 (September 16, 1992).

On June 18, 1993, Svo began to vomit blood and was sent to the hospital. Five days later, German police visited Moscow, wanting to question him about a string of murders there. They were not allowed access to him and he died later the same day.

One of the important aspects of Svo's biography to note is that he would be one of the last major *vory* of the era who had spent so many years in prison. The dramatic events in the former Soviet Union had changed the *vors'* attitude toward prison. If before it was a badge of honor and legitimacy to have spent most of one's life in prison, now the *vory* attempted to stay out of prison, considering even a single day behind bars unacceptable. The traditional symbols of the *vory*, such as tattooing, were being forsaken. Clean-shaven, donning the finest clothes, driving foreign cars, and owning three or four of the best apartments available, *vory* began to enjoy openly the fruits of their labor. This was in contrast to the traditional code according to which thieves were not permitted to have an apartment or house, among other things.[66]

As in other parts of this book, our interest is in assessing how the so-called Russian 'mafia' looked in the 1990s, trying to get beyond the media hype and, equally important, seeing through some of the self-serving propaganda disseminated by the criminals themselves. The discussion above outlined how the *vory* developed and how their traditions looked during the Soviet period. Now we must recall the words of George Derluguian cited at the beginning of this chapter: "[The vory tradition] is an institutional design embedded in local culture and is best suited to survival in the conditions of highly repressive, large states like Tsarist Russia and the Soviet Union." [67] If we assume that he is correct, then the conclusion we're led to is that during the post-Soviet years we should have noticed a decline in *vory* commitment to the code; the repressive measures of the Soviet state were largely gone after the dismantling of the Soviet Union. Most institutions—such as the MVD and KGB/FSB were caught up in the free-for-all of a suddenly unleashed economy and were redefining themselves in an era of uncertain financial support from the government. What became of the *vory*? And, consequently, what became of the code?

According to the MVD, in January 1989 there were approximately 512 *vory v zakone*: 240 were incarcerated, 272 were in freedom. About 16% of them were under 30 years old, 40% were between 30 and 40, and about 44% were

---

66. Author interview with 'the Georgian,' 1991. Author conversations with Chebotaryov between 1990 and 1998. Author conversations with Gorkin between 1993 and 2006.

67. Derluguian (note 1).

over 50.[68] The following year this number reportedly reached 700.[69] In February 1992, the MVD's Organized Crime Control Department formed a new unit to address the problem of 'particularly dangerous recidivists' (*osobo opasnye retsidivisty*), including *vory v zakone*.[70] In 1993, it was reported that there were about 387 *vory v zakone* based in Russia, 100 of whom were serving prison sentences. A year later this figure had dropped to about 200.[71] More recent figures (2005) maintain that the number has remained more or less steady at about 200.

Several factors accounted for this decline including death due to natural causes, death due to the violent struggle for power particularly during the Great Mob War from 1992–1994, leaving the country to establish bases overseas or to flee from law enforcement, and a reduction in the number of *vory* being counted due to the disappearance of the Soviet Union.

While the number of *vory*, as reported by official sources, may be of interest, the status of the *vory* in the context of the rapidly shifting socioeconomic landscape of the 1990s is ultimately more satisfying as an explanation of their fate. Generally, perspectives on the stature of the *vory* seemed to occupy the extremes of the debate. At one end of the spectrum, the *vory* were seen as the lords of the underworld. They were, as Alexander Gurov characterized them in 1991, "all-powerful mafiosi ... supermen, big-time leaders...."[72] Stephen Handelman had written about the arrival of the *vor v zakone* Vyacheslav Ivankov, "Yaponchik," to the shores of the U.S. supposedly to bring order to the Russian underworld in what Handelman suggested was part of a larger

---

68. MVD internal document (note 62).

69. Author conversations with Chebotaryov, 1990–91.

70. Ibid.

71. Nikolai Modestov, "Zhizn' Vne Zakona," *Sevodnya*, April 23, 1994. It would seem that the MVD had a good idea of where most of the *vory v zakone* were based. Among the Russian-language intelligence documents I'd come across over the years, there were several compilations regarding the *vory v zakone*, including "*Vory v Zakone* Living in Moscow," "De-crowned *Vory v Zakone*," "Major *Vory v Zakone*," and "*Vory v Zakone* Living in the Central Region of Russia," among others. The lists included the *vor*'s name, nickname, year and place of birth, and last known address. There was also the MVD list called, "Leaders of the Criminal World Operating in Moscow Region," which included twenty-six *vory* among the leaders (*avtoritety*) listed, providing full name, date and place of birth, last known residence, and nickname. Not surprisingly, the official reporting on the number of *vory* in the country suffers as much as the numbers of crime groups discussed in Chapter 4. See *BBC Monitoring*, "Russian Police Report on How They Keep Tabs on Top Crime Bosses," December 16, 2003.

72. *Reuters*, "Head of Organized Crime Squad Comments on Banknote Operation," January 26, 1991.

Russian effort to bring vast stretches of territory around the world under their criminal sway. In her book, *Thieves' World*, Claire Sterling outdoes Handelman and Gurov in enthusiasm when she says, "The rise of both [Yaponchik and the Russian mafia] within a few years—their ability to stake out whole blocks of the planet, half a continent here, another there—conveys all the menace of an international crime community in a phase of stunning expansion, threatening the integrity and even the survival of democratic governments in America, Europe, everywhere."[73]

As with most discussions on *vory* specifically and the Russian 'mafia' generally, Gurov's comment would have to be considered within the context of the question: compared to what? Compared to the countless rubles, dollars, francs, marks, and pounds the Communist Party elite wrapped their arms around, Ivankov, for example, was a minor player. Peter Grinenko, a former New York City detective, was adamant that the superman status conferred on Ivankov was pure myth. "He was a car thief who got arrested in Russia when he went to the fellow whose car he stole and tried to sell it back to him. And he wasn't sent here to take over anybody's American organization because there is no such thing. Russian organized crime is anything but organized."[74] In August 1992, Chebotaryov, the Deputy Chief of the Organized Crime Control Department, asked me to get a message back to the FBI that Ivankov was on his way or already in the United States. Never one to sensationalize or exaggerate, he characterized Ivankov as a "dangerous criminal" and nothing more. From that conversation and others about cases and individuals, it was clear that Chebotaryov didn't attribute to Ivankov the same criminal celebrity status that Gurov and others did.

The major impact of the rapidly developing economic situation as concerned the *vory* was the rapid decline in the potency of the code. It cannot be stressed enough that, as Derluguian says, the code was a product of a repressive regime. It was a set of rules, a constitution of sorts, for the parallel world, the anti-society, a response to the totalitarian nature of the regime. As soon as the *raison d'etre* was removed, the code lost its central position as the guiding ideology of the underworld. There were even some who failed to be impressed with the code at all. Zhora 'the Engineer,' a pickpocket in the 1960s, interpreted the code as just another system of law, just another manipulation by "sharp operators in order to bend the world to their inclination." It wasn't

---

73. Claire Sterling, *Thieves' World: The Threat of the New Global Network of Organized Crime*, New York, Simon & Schuster, 1994, p. 13.

74. Grinenko in Jeffrey Robinson, *The Merger: The Conglomeration of International Organized Crime*, Woodstock, The Overlook Press, 2000, p. 119.

the code, he said, that was the appropriate measure of values, but the behavior of individuals.[75]

While Zhora may have been right in his interpretation of the manipulative nature of the code, that didn't undermine the importance of it. Most observers lent credence to the centrality of the code. Nevertheless, it was still merely a social construct and as society changed, so did the code. Just as the old *vory v zakone* during the Soviet era had adopted the code as part of their survival mechanism, the new *vory v zakone* of the late 1980s and 1990s began to forsake the code as part of their survival mechanism. The late-Soviet and post-Soviet eras built their foundations on money as compared to the power, influence, and position that were the currency of the realm in Soviet days.

Understandably, the confusion and ambiguity that gripped society as the Soviet Union disappeared also impacted the thieves' world. Suddenly a *vor*'s decades in prison didn't count for much on the outside world. The mystique of the *vory* started to decline and their vaunted role as the mediators of disputes over property and territory was dramatically diluted as automatic weapons and hand grenades did the talking for a new generation of criminals. The central tenets of the code were weakened. "New *vory* saw the necessity to cooperate with law enforcement, had no problem having families, kids, money, expensive things, property, cars ... unlike the 'classical' vory."[76] According to Anatoly Zhoglo, an MVD colonel who followed the *vory* closely, "Representatives of the new type of criminal world pay no attention to the *vory*. In prison, of course, everyone has to bow his head to the traditions. But outside, if a criminal has money and his own fighters, he can act independently."[77]

Even this perspective as expressed by Zhoglo in the early 1990s would rapidly change. A few years later, a twenty-four-year-old inmate laid it on the line:

> A thief-in-law is mostly just a conventional understanding. It's a myth, a legend. Outside of jail it happens like this: a nineteen-year-old boy with a lot of money just buys the crown of Thief-in-Law. It's the same thing here. Rank is built mostly on personalities and leadership qualities and on how much money, or goods that can be valued in money that someone has.... Everyone understands perfectly

75. Yuri Brokhin, *Hustling on Gorky Street: Sex and Crime in Russia Today*, New York, The Dial Press, 1975, p. 148.

76. Author conversation with Gorkin, December 2006.

77. Stephen Handelman, *Comrade Criminal: Russia's New Mafiya*, New Haven, Yale University Press, 1995, p. 42. Author conversations with Anatoly Zhoglo, 1990–91.

that [the old code] has already become obsolete. The situation has changed dramatically, both in society and in prison.[78]

Even the older recidivists were uncertain of the world as it changed around them. "They were excellent people, those *vory v zakone*. They maintained strict order. Now, the New Russians have come and I don't know if they are real thieves or not."[79]

Former Moscow criminal investigator Alexander Gorkin put an interesting additional spin on the status of the *vory*, raising a rarely-asked, thought-provoking question: Who was using whom? He went on to explain that the operative assumption was that the *vory* were the bosses of the crime groups, that the *vory* in many cases had formed the crime groups. What if, he says, it was the other way around? What if the *vory* were chosen by the crime groups to be their 'leader'? In this way, attention by law enforcement and in some cases by the public would fall on the *vor* and to a lesser extent on the group. The *vor*, in this sense, was a buffer for the crime group, a kind of insurance policy against the police. In this case, the role of someone like Ivankov would also be understandable. The FBI pursued Ivankov for several years in the United States before arresting him in 1995 in New York. How much manpower, time, and money was committed to scoring the first arrest of a 'major Russian crime boss,' diverting attention and resources from other investigations? As Gorkin put it, "It gave group members the opportunity to say, 'It wasn't us, it was him. He was the boss.'" Gorkin's point is worth bearing in mind.

Interestingly, a passage by the great Russian poet Alexander Pushkin hints at this kind of relationship in the story of Emilian Pugachev, a Cossack leader who had stirred the disgruntled population to rebellion toward the end of the 18th century. In addressing the issue of Pugachev's dependence on the community, Pushkin writes:

> Pugachev was not an autocrat. The Yaik Cossacks who originated the revolt controlled the activities of the leader who had come amongst them with no other distinction than his exceptional boldness and some knowledge of the art of war. He did nothing without the Cossacks' approval, whereas they often acted without his knowledge and sometimes against his wishes. They paid him external respect: in public they walked behind him bareheaded and bowed obsequiously; but in private they treated him as a companion, sitting beside him in

---

78. Lambert, p.111 (note 2).
79. Ibid.

shirtsleeves and with their caps on, getting drunk together and singing rivermen's ballads.[80]

One last point for consideration before closing out this chapter:

> The profession of theft is more than isolated acts of theft frequently and skillfully performed. It is a group-way of life and a social institution. It has techniques, codes, status, traditions, consensus, and organization.... In fact, an understanding of this culture is a prerequisite to the understanding of the behavior of a particular professional thief.[81]

At first glance, this is a perfectly reasonable summary of the *vory v zakone* phenomenon. Many *vory*, particularly those of the old traditions, did indeed make their reputations on their ability to excel at thieves' skills. Foremost among these was picking pockets. Not merely stealing, this was art. The *vor* with a good set of hands, *zolotiye ruki*, was praised, admired, and respected. In addition, the code, as we saw, called upon one to forsake family and join the criminal brotherhood in what was a "group-way" of life. The traditions and rituals of the anti-society, as transmitted through the coronation ceremony, tattoos, jargon, songs, poems, and so on, were important parts of forming the culture of the thieves' world (*vorovskoi mir*). It is difficult to argue with the advice in the quote that understanding the culture is critical to understanding the individuals who live that culture.

But ... the quote cited above has nothing to do with *vory v zakone*. It was written by the American criminologist Edwin Sutherland in his introduction to the book, *The Professional Thief*, published in 1937. The book, a transcript of a series of conversations Sutherland had with an American thief, reads very much like the Russian experience. While the comparison is not perfect, I mention it here as a reminder that most aspects of the Russian experience are not new to the world of crime. Their newness, as Melnikov noted at the beginning of Chapter 5, to some degree comes from the fact that the outside world had rarely been exposed to this side of the former Soviet Union. Their uniqueness in many ways comes from the scope and intensity of the criminal world in which they were operating in the 1990s, and the vast interconnections between the underworld and upperworld in a context of globalization. Their violence is in part a response to the violence visited upon them by centuries of repressive governments (the gulag experience, for example). Criminal societies everywhere are a reflection of the larger environment in which they develop.

---

80. Chalidze, pp. 43–44 (note 11).
81. Sutherland, pp. v–vi (note 59).

The maintenance of a common fund (a kind of *obshchak*) to support comrades in prison, the presence of hierarchical relationships in prison, the use of specialized jargon to keep the outside world (especially the police) from penetrating their activities, the emphasis on skill, and many other facets of professional criminality were present in various criminal milieu around the world. Indeed, Russia was not alone in its production of thieves with codes, traditions, and status. For example, descriptions of the London crime epidemic of the 1720s rival those of Moscow. Jonathan Wild and other key players of the underworld shared many of the same characteristics as the 20th century Soviet thief. New York of the 1870s and 1880s also displayed similar dynamics at a time when crime was running rampant. In some respects, professional thief Adam Worth seemed little different from Russian thieves.[82]

One major difference may be that the harshness of the Russian autocracy followed by the murderous Soviet regime in the context of poor economic conditions meant that the Russian underworld would retain its coarseness much longer than the underworld in the West.

---

82. See Gerald Howson, *Thief-Taker General: Jonathan Wild and the Emergence of Crime and Corruption as a Way of Life in Eighteenth-Century England*, New Brunswick, New Jersey, Transaction Books, 1970; Ben Macintyre, *The Napolean of Crime: The Life and Times of Adam Worth, Master Thief*, New York, Farrar, Straus, Giroux, 1997; Paweł Moczydłowski, *The Hidden Life of Polish Prisons*, Bloomington, Indiana University Press, 1992; Gresham M. Sykes, *The Society of Captives: A Study of a Maximum Security Prison*, Princeton, New Jersey, Princeton University Press, 1958.

CHAPTER 8

ACCUMULATION OF CAPITAL

The long and slow chain of centralized command means that anyone who can offer quicker solutions in terms of funding or resourcing, even if clearly as an illegal operation, will have many takers in business and industry.

—Vyacheslav Komissarov[1]

Criminals are highly flexible and 'go where the money is'.... Criminal activity frequently attracts non-criminal elements if there is easy money to be made.

—Yuri Brokhin[2]

In the previous three chapters we looked at the general conditions that created certain mindsets as well as the vast opportunities for theft, fraud, and general criminality during the Russian and Soviet eras. We discussed the *vory v zakone* and essentially how they came to accumulate their power, knowledge, and influence. In this chapter, we take another step forward in looking at the roots of the merging of the criminal upperworld and criminal underworld. Our goal is to get a sense of where the traditional criminal groups came from, how they became interwoven with Vaksberg's upperworld 'mafia,' and how they capitalized on the opportunities presented by the command economy as described in Chapter 6. How did they get their start? How did they accumulate their capital? By capital, we're talking about money of course but, as importantly, the knowledge and experience they gained that they would use to propel themselves to the pinnacle of the crime world as the Soviet Union raced toward its last days. We'll pick up where Chapters 7 left off, in the 1970s.

---

1. *Reuters*, "Soviet Business Mafia Begins to Emerge," October 17, 1990, interview with Vyacheslav Komissarov, at the time the head of academic studies at the USSR Ministry of Internal Affairs Academy.

2. Yuri Brokhin, *Hustling on Gorky Street: Sex and Crime in Russia Today*, New York, The Dial Press, 1975, p. 71.

Despite the ideological belief that crime would not, and indeed could not, exist in the Soviet Union, gangs continued to operate throughout the country in the 1970s and 1980s. The tight control of both information and the movement of foreigners in the country meant that accessing information about these trends was not easy. In addition, the Cold War relationship between the U.S. and the USSR was focused primarily on military issues with special attention appropriately paid to nuclear weapons. Crime didn't figure prominently on the radar. This doesn't mean that scholars weren't paying attention to it; the subject, though, was thoroughly overshadowed by propaganda wars and arms races, among other things.

There was more criminality involving gangs than we in the West appreciated. For example, there was the gang in the Rostov region that had carried out a series of raids on banks, stealing hundreds of thousands of rubles before being caught in 1973. They had manufactured their own submachine guns using primarily a lathe.[3] In another case, counterfeiter Viktor Baranov successfully made 1,249 fake currency notes in 25- and 50-ruble denominations before his 1978 arrest in Stavropol. The popular Soviet movie, *Mesto Vstrechi Izmenit' Nel'zya*, portrayed the famous Moscow Criminal Investigation Department in its struggle with a particularly pernicious gang called 'Black Cat' (*Chyornaya Koshka*). But the presence of a 'Black Cat' in real life was not exceptional; there were 'Black Cats' all over Russia.[4]

Gangs at this time were engaged in many of the activities that we might mistake as new to the post-Soviet era. For example, they sometimes impersonated police—dressed in official uniforms—and staged armed robberies. In 1974, one group, dressed as police and armed with a submachine gun and hand grenades, held up a bank for $163,000 (a considerable sum of money at that time in the Soviet Union), spraying the street with bullets as they left.[5]

Drugs also caused concern to the Party leadership at this time. Long before the Afghan War—which had been blamed for an explosion in the use of narcotics—a growing disenchantment with the system, combined with a burgeoning hippie movement and a large indigenous crop of marijuana and opium poppies, fueled the drug subculture. Already in 1974, the government introduced a sweeping expansion of laws penalizing the theft, growth, pro-

---

3. The theft of parts from factories to build guns as well as the digging up of World War II ordnance was far more widespread than one might expect.

4. Anna Malpas, "The Makers of a New Television Series Plan to Explore the Little-Known History of the Soviet Union's Criminal Underworld," *The Moscow Times*, January 20, 2006, http://context.themoscowtimes.com/stories/2006/01/20/101.html.

5. *International Herald Tribune*, "Russia Tightens Drug Laws, Penalties," May 26, 1974.

duction, sale, and use of narcotics. It also added new crimes including in-
ducing others to use narcotics and failing to report narcotics violations.[6] Rens
Lee, who studied drug policy issues in the former Soviet Union, revealed that
opium was cultivated on state farms in Kyrgyzstan as late as the early 1970s.
As much as 40% of the crop was stolen and sold through criminal channels
to addicts around the country.[7]

Throughout the 1970s and 1980s, factory employees and managers took
over parts of their factories to produce deficit goods earmarked for the black
market (see Chapter 6). They used state materials and infrastructure but channeled the goods into private hands, bribed a wide range of officials, and pock-
eted the profits.[8] As we'll see below in the profile of Viktor, some of the most
powerful people in the post-Soviet era—in both business and organized crime
circles—had accumulated experience in these underground production units
(*tsekh*), frequently referred to as workshops. The shopkeepers, known as
tsekhoviki (along with the *teniviki*, the so-called shadow economy operators),
were making considerable amounts of money, which meant several things.
First, they became targets for existing gangs and *vory v zakone*. Second, they
became targets of the government since they were essentially agents of private
enterprise in an anti-capitalist country and, perhaps more important, they
were undermining part of the state's revenue stream. And, third, they used
some of their ill-gotten capital to finance crime groups.

The *tsekhoviki* had a vested interest in staying out of the government's
crosshairs since stiffer sentences were being pinned on them for their boldness
in challenging the ruling ideology. As part of their effort to do this, it is widely
believed that in 1979 some *tsekhoviki* and *vory v zakone* held a meeting in the
southern Russian city of Kislovodsk to negotiate a business arrangement. Reportedly, the *vory* would take 10–15% of the shopkeepers' illegal income in
exchange for protective services.[9] This is illustrative of the increasingly close

6. Alexander Kudakayev, "Narkotiki," *Sevodnya*, no. 70, April 15, 1994, p. 7. See also
ibid.

7. Rens Lee, "The Illicit Drug Market in the CIS: Scope, Dynamics, and Policy Impli-
cations," at the Conference on Narcotics in the CIS Region, Meridian House, Washington,
D.C., September 11, 1992. In 1990, it was reported that there were approximately 120,000
drug addicts in the Soviet Union. During a drive along the Turkmenistan-Iran border in
November 1990, Gennady Chebotaryov, the former head of criminal investigation for the
Turkmen republic, told me that there were at least 120,000 addicts in Turkmenistan alone.

8. Arkady Vaksberg, *The Soviet Mafia: A Shocking Exposé of Organized Crime in the
USSR*, New York, St. Martin's Press, 1991, p. 181.

9. Komissarov (note 1). See also Boris Z. Rumer, *Soviet Central Asia: A Tragic Experiment*, Boston, Unwin Hyman, 1989, p. 155.

relationship between elements of the underworld and the upperworld. In some respects it was the forerunner of what would later be widely referred to as *krysha*, or roof, generally meaning protective services provided by criminal groups for businessmen.

Interestingly, in his book, *USSR: The Corrupt Society*, published in 1982, Konstantin Simis outlines the structure of an organization created for the sale and distribution of Western goods such as blue jeans, denim skirts, and sunglasses—products of the underground economy. The head of the organization developed thirteen small groups or cells of students and young workers, each group consisting of 5–6 people. Four groups operated in Moscow, seven out in the regions, while two mobile groups traveled the country with their goods in tow. But the head of the whole organization was known only to the leaders of each cell. Only the cell leaders came into contact with him and received the goods for sale, and only they handled the financial end of the business. Neither the sources of supply nor the extent of the operation was known by the members.[10] This arrangement looked very much like other organizations, including traditional crime groups of the 1990s.

Despite claims in February 1983 by the Moscow 'World Service' short wave radio program that "the number of criminal offenses ... has been dropping steadily [and] we have done away with organized crime," gang activity was growing.[11] The World Service claim itself was fascinating since the Soviet Union didn't officially acknowledge the existence of organized crime in their country until the late 1980s. Nevertheless, groups that would play an important role at the end of the 1980s and into the 1990s were forming and rapidly gaining experience in the late 1970s and early 1980s. In addition, police, politicians, doctors, entertainers, and businessmen helped ensure the groups' success, whether by running interference for them or actually being members of the groups.

Already in the middle of 1985 the Deputy Minister of Internal Affairs of Uzbekistan wrote a letter to the Minister of Internal Affairs at MVD headquarters in Moscow, reporting:

> There are currently about 20 criminal clans in the city of Tashkent. They divide their authority among the city and surrounding regions, which is leading to clashes between the groups. In order to make a

---

10. Konstantin Simis, *USSR: The Corrupt Society*, New York, Simon & Schuster, 1982, p. 275.

11. Karl Yegorov from Moscow "World Service," February 16, 1983, excerpt from "Mailbag," answering a question from a listener in India about crime rates in the USSR.

reputation for themselves, the leaders of the clans maintain close contacts with thieves (*vory v zakone*). On the thieves' initiative, special 'cash boxes' (*obshchak*) have been established to help out associates being tried for crimes.... [12]

The following year, a 'bandit' group that had been operating since 1979 was 'exposed.' The 16 members committed at least 99 crimes including 3 murders, 43 thefts of public and state property, 19 auto thefts, and 7 thefts of personal property. Police seized a cache of weapons including various pistols, rifles, carbines, grenades, detonators, and ammunition. Between 1986 and 1988, about 2,600 'organized crime groups' were uncovered by criminal investigation departments. Of them, around 50 were 'deeply conspiratorial' and had operated for three years or more. During this period they reportedly committed around 20,000 crimes, including 218 murders, 785 assaults, 1,469 robberies.[13]

From 1985 to 1987, criminal investigation officials from Moscow region police exposed five interconnected 'organized crime groups.' They had committed 162 crimes including 1 murder, 17 assaults, 11 robberies, 15 thefts of personal property, 7 fraudulent deals, 5 cases of extortion, and others. Weapons, narcotics, and disguises were confiscated. The members of the groups had higher education and were also top-ranked athletes. They were even said to have controlled a specific territory, which is something we in the West didn't hear much about until 1990. During the investigation it was learned that police and other law enforcement officials had provided cover for the groups. Forty victims were located but all refused to cooperate with police.[14]

The existence of the groups mentioned above and the circumstances surrounding their activities (e.g., police complicity, fearful victims) shouldn't come as a surprise. Although the international media started paying close attention to the situation only in 1990–91, gangs and organized crime groups had been active in the country for decades if not centuries. A combination of

---

12. *Pravda Vostoka*, "A Fight for Life," November 10, 1988. See also Rumer, p. 157 (note 9).

13. Vyacheslav Komissarov in G. Min'kovskii (ed.), *Bor'ba s Organizovannoi Prestupnost'iu: Problemy Teorii i Praktiki*, Moskva, Akademiia Ministerstva Vnutrennykh Del SSSR, 1990, p. 47.

14. Ibid., p. 53. See also Mark Galeotti, "Organized Crime in Moscow and Russian National Security," *Low Intensity Conflict and Law Enforcement*, vol. 1, no. 3, Winter 1992, pp. 237–252. See also Joseph D. Serio, "Organized Crime in the Former Soviet Union," unpublished Master's Thesis, University of Illinois at Chicago, 1993, pp. 72–77.

many factors discussed in earlier chapters, including shortages created by the command economy and the expansion of the underground economy, ever-present corruption, and a long-standing criminal tradition, ensured that both the criminal underworld and the criminal upperworld would enjoy endless opportunities.

It was the extent of these opportunities that surprised me. Every nook of Soviet society seemed to play by similar rules, even dormitories and hotels. During my time at the MVD's Organized Crime Control Department, I had access to police intelligence reports. As I leafed through one, the name of the institute in Moscow where I had studied in 1987 jumped off the page. According to the police, the dormitory of the institute was officially part of the growing realm of the Chechen 'mafia.' This was at once surprising and strange. Surprising because I had just graduated from the institute six months prior to the date of the report and there had been no noticeable Chechen presence; strange because I couldn't imagine what an organized crime group could possibly want with a dormitory.

Conditions in the institute dormitory in 1987 were more than adequate, particularly when considering that in only a few short years many dormitories would fall into disrepair and even dilapidation in the financially-strapped post-Soviet era. On occasion, though, personal items would go missing from the foreign students' rooms: a pair of blue jeans, a Walkman, jewelry, makeup. We assumed that the janitorial staff or hall monitors helped themselves to our property. After all, it would have been simple to gain access: as was the practice, whenever we left our rooms we dutifully surrendered our keys to the hall monitor, or *dezhurnaya*, usually a middle-aged woman or grandmotherly type who sat at a desk near the elevators on every floor. I didn't know at the time that dormitories played a role in the development of crime groups. Items were pilfered from rooms and sold on the black market, contributing in a modest way to the start-up capital of the gangsters and 'businessmen' of the future.

A few years later I came to learn that Soviet hotels, even more than dormitories, were in many ways a microcosm of Soviet life. The various and colorful cast of characters operating in hotels represented a cross-section of Soviet life. The state came in the form of police officers who were responsible for maintaining order at these facilities. Naturally, they were well informed about the illicit goings-on and, in many cases, were direct benefactors of the 'hotel mafia's' largesse. The KGB had its share of informants in all Soviet hotels, most commonly believed to be in the person of the doormen, but in reality a variety of people. Like most everything else, hotels were state owned-and-operated, making hotel administrators and employees, strictly speaking, cogs in the state machinery. The traditional underworld was represented by prostitutes, petty crooks, and black marketeers (*fartsovshiki*). The business world had yet to take the overt form we know today. At that time, it consisted primarily of a mix of state and party officials, employees of enterprises and factories, *tsekhoviki*, and others. It was a whirlwind of people manipulating the system in an endless game of deception, bribery, theft, prostitution, and occasionally murder.

Prior to the dismantling of the Soviet Union, hotels served a function we're all familiar with—providing temporary housing to tourists, travelers, and business people (in this case state employees and Party officials). But these places of repose also sheltered migrant workers and roving criminals (*prestupniki na gastroli*) who lacked the official residence permits (*propiski*) required to live in Moscow.

In our Western, business-oriented mentality, we would expect a hotel to maximize corporate profit through good service and maximum occupancy. As we saw in Chapter 6, though, the Soviet economy didn't necessarily function according to Western logic. Since all property was state-owned and salaries were not necessarily tied to performance, there was little concern for improving service. The priority was for individuals to make extra money for themselves in any way possible. In this context, a full hotel essentially meant the same as an empty hotel. (Recall the waiter at the empty restaurant in the Rossiya Hotel in Chapter 1.) But if the hotel directors and staff could earn money for themselves rather than for the state, they would take advantage of the situation. It was possible to find a shortage of hotel rooms for tourists while in actuality there were thousands of rooms available—they were being held by the hotel administrators "for their customers."[15]

Igor Yudin, a former police officer who had been assigned to a Moscow hotel in the 1980s and early 1990s, details the activities inside Soviet hotels in his doctoral dissertation. Much of the information on hotels presented here derives from that study.

Given the restrictions on movement within the Soviet Union, a hotel reservation was required in the destination city in order to obtain permission to travel. As Yudin describes it, there were two basic methods for securing permission from the hotel administration. First, a hotel employee would write a request to a hotel director to accommodate 'my friends,' as a rule for a short visit of 1–3 days, which would then be extended after the arrival of the guests. These requests came primarily from maids and porters since they had the most interaction with guests. The hotel employees would receive from the 'friends'

---

15. Vaksberg, p. 235 (note 8).

a payment which they shared with the administrator who had granted permission. These 'friends'—who were sometimes petty criminals and sometimes people simply taking advantage of an opportunity—directed maids to steal property from the rooms of other guests at the hotel. The visiting 'friends' then sold the goods outside the hotel. The more industrious visitors collected information about specific guests to target for extortion. Some acted as pimps providing prostitutes to foreign businessmen for hard currency.[16]

The second method of gaining access to hotels was as simple as the first. A guest presented to the hotel director a letter from any one of a variety of enterprises, organizations, or associations regarding the accommodation of its worker. As a rule, these people didn't come to Moscow on business but to pursue personal matters. The letter would indicate, for example, that accommodation was needed for '1+3'. That is, there should be accommodation made available for one person from the organization and then three others who may or may not have had any official relationship to it. For example, in August 1990, three people were accommodated according to a '1+2' request in a letter from an Intourist (the state tourist agency) department in the southern city of Rostov-on-Don addressed to a Moscow hotel. The two 'add-ons' had gone to the capital to extort Soviet citizens staying at the hotel and to buy consumer goods and U.S. dollars from foreigners. Since the victims themselves were usually committing illegal acts of one sort or other, complaints were usually not filed with the police.

Some of the characters most commonly found at hotels were speculators and black marketeers (*fartsovshiki*), currency changers, and prostitutes. Thefts were usually committed by those who had been convicted of theft in the past. In fact, there were professional thieves who specialized in theft from hotels. In 1989, a group was arrested committing thefts and robberies against foreigners, with the help of prostitutes and taxi drivers.[17]

A significant portion of the regular 'guests' at the hotel where Yudin was posted were employees of resort area hotels, trade enterprises, cooperatives, and joint ventures. These guests made numerous friends among hotel employees over time, including high-ranking personnel, and were protected by hotel employees. The hotel administrator kept a list of certain people who could use the hotel at almost any time they wanted. For example, in June 1990,

---

16. I. V. Yudin, *Kriminologicheskaya Kharakteristika Prestupnosti i Otklonyaiushchegosya Povedeniya na Otdel'nom Ob"ekte*, Moskva, Moskovskii Gosudarstvennyi Universitet, Yuridicheskyi Fakul'tet, 1991, p. 22.

17. Ibid., p. 15. Criminal case no. 44584 under Article 146 of the Criminal Code of the RSFSR in the Dzerzhinsky district of Moscow.

a secretary from a Baku-based joint venture came to Moscow and stayed at the hotel. She paid 1,000 rubles for protection. During her stay, she engaged in prostitution for foreign currency.

A visitor from Batumi was officially unemployed but still worked as a speculator and foreign currency money changer. In 1990, he stayed at the hotel three times for weeks at a time. This had been going on for nearly ten years and he knew many of the hotel employees very well. He stayed on the same floor and in the same room every time. He contacted foreigners staying in the hotel to engage in foreign currency operations.

In 1990, arms buyers from the Fergana Valley in Central Asia stayed for several days at the hotel to make an arms purchase from the Solntsevo group. Also, some people from Dagestan stayed at the hotel for several days while committing a series of crimes, including murder. Two from the Chechen-Ingush Republic who were arrested for committing several robberies and armed assaults unofficially lived in the hotel in a friend's room.

According to Yudin, practically all of the chambermaids of the hotel were involved in buying and selling with foreign tourists. In 1989, a maid paid 3,000 rubles to racketeers. She had worked at the hotel for 9 years and regularly engaged in prostitution, foreign currency operations, and trading goods. She also went abroad several times for prostitution. Arkady Vaksberg indicated in his book, *The Soviet Mafia*, how much was at stake for the average worker. "Many Moscow hotel workers got a second monthly salary, which in some cases was several times more than their basic pay, from the mafia. It cannot be doubted which of the two salaries they earn by putting their back into it."[18]

There was also a brisk business in the sale of hotel cards. At the time, hotel guests received a card that they showed at the front door in order to get into the hotel. These cards were frequently sold by hotel employees to friends or acquaintances or sometimes to people they didn't know at all. There were cases in the hotel where Yudin was posted when a single room was passed from hand to hand several times. The porters sometimes organized a room for a night if it had just been freed up and had to be cleaned. The cost for the service was 50 rubles. The chambermaids frequently received information from the porters regarding which rooms were about to be freed up for the night, paving the way for prostitution. There was a case in the hotel when one person stayed for ten days moving from room to room. He was not registered to any permanent residence, was unemployed, and was using the hotel to commit theft.

---

18. Vaksberg, p. 236 (note 8).

The criminal activities at the hotel where Yudin was based were run by the Chechens. They were constantly cultivating relationships with officials from the Soviet Ministry of Foreign Affairs which was located across the street from the hotel, sometimes providing rooms and prostitutes for the officials in exchange for brand new blank passports.[19]

In the late 1980s and 1990s, large hotels changed hands frequently as groups fought over territory. For example, in Moscow, one major hotel came under the influence of the Chechens and then the Solntsevo and finally the Dagestanis. The hotel where I had an office had a Dagestani presence. It was not uncommon to see 'gangster-businessmen' huddled in business meetings in the lobbies of major hotels such as the Radisson Slavyanskaya and the Baltschug Kempinski. According to a law enforcement document of April 1996, at least 30 Moscow hotels were in some manner influenced if not controlled by crime groups including Russian, Chechen, Dagestani, Armenian, and Azeri. The restaurants and offices in some of these hotels served as headquarters or meeting places for groups. Shops and boutiques were opened in the bigger hotels, offering outrageously-priced goods for the nouveau riche and convenient channels for laundering money. Generally speaking, hotels played an important role in the development of crime groups.

As with every other aspect of organized crime in the former Soviet Union, traditional 'gangsters' weren't the only ones using hotels for their personal ends. The Oktyabrskaya Hotel (later renamed The President Hotel) had been built for the Central Committee of the Communist Party. It was both an oasis and mirage. A marble staircase dominated the lobby with a bust of Lenin perched on a pedestal at the top. The hotel boasted two bars, a fitness club, a glassed-in sun deck, Cuban banana trees, and a sauna.[20] Black Volgas, the official car of the Soviet government, gained access to the property only by passing through an electronic gate and a KGB sentry post. In the old days, guests were typically Communist Party functionaries from around the world and Third World revolutionaries. During my first stay there in September 1990, a delegation of top Communist officials from Greece was counted among the guests, and Daniel Ortega of Nicaragua had been there just the week before. Some months later, Americans rented several suites from where they dealt in computers and coordinated the smuggling of automobiles from Europe.

But the hotel might as well have been a mirage. While the building certainly seemed to exist, it quickly vanished from peoples' vision. I stopped pedestri-

---

19. Author conversation with a former official of the Ministry of Foreign Affairs, May 1998.

20. See Bill Thomas and Charles Sutherland, *Red Tape: Adventure Capitalism in the New Russia*, New York, Dutton, 1992, for their portrayal of the Oktyabrskaya Hotel.

ans on the street in front of the hotel to ask what the building was. Most had no idea and I had the impression that they didn't want to know. Black Volgas, electronic gate, KGB sentry, no signs on the building, no name marquis anywhere to be seen ... better not to know.

In spring 1991, a top investigator from a major credit card company visited the MVD to meet with officials of the Organized Crime Control Department. Gennady Chebotaryov called me into his office to do the interpreting. The company was interested in developing a working relationship with the police because of the dramatic rise in credit card fraud. The content of the brief meeting was general, followed by shots of lemon vodka (at 10:30 in the morning!). I later came across a letter from the investigator to then-Minister Boris Pugo saying that the company was concerned about a significant credit card fraud ring whose core they had traced to the administration of the Oktyabrskaya Hotel. According to the company, losses were in the millions—a level of damage that could not have been possible without the complicity of elements in the KGB and the Communist Party.

My first glimpse into the accumulation of capital and experience came in 1985. In one of the many historic developments taking place in the early days of the Gorbachev era, for the first time the Soviet Union sent a team of world class wrestlers to a U.S. university for training exercises with the university team. I worked as an unofficial interpreter for the athletes at the welcome reception at a local hotel. Early in the evening Grigorii, one of the star wrestlers, grew impatient with the reception, urging that we forget the social niceties and move on to business. "When can we go up to the room?" he whispered to me. "I need five or six people ... as many as you can.... Get those guys and let's go upstairs." My job was to quietly get word to the men attending the reception that Grigorii's mobile souvenir shop would be open for business—strictly cash. With ten of us assembled in the room, Grigorii unzipped the large duffel bag lying on his bed, revealing a wide variety of items: fur hats, Soviet flags, *matroshka* nesting dolls, fur hats, military belt buckles, and souvenirs—typical fare for Americans enchanted with the fairytale allure of Russia.

My language skills were left unchallenged as the lively bidding called only for spitting numbers back and forth. Grigorii had the Americans outbidding each other and he proved a tough negotiator when it came to haggling. By the end of the session, the Russian was satisfied with his success, stuffing the remaining goods back into the bag to be peddled again in the next city on his tour. This kind of petty dealing was a common route for black marketeers, athletes, and others to get access to extra money. More importantly, this was part of their 'business school' training. Years later, when most Soviets still didn't understand much about business, these individuals already knew how to do deals and, more importantly, had made contacts in the police, KGB, enterprises, factories, and in other countries. And, obviously, they were ideal as soldiers in the armies of organized crime. I found out quite by accident that Grigorii went on to become a close associate of gangster, businessman, member of the legislature, and police wrestling coach, Otari Kvantrishvili.

Kvantrishvili serves as a good example of the merging of the upperworld and underworld. He was said to have got his start in the 1960s in the criminal group led by 'Mongol.' In the early days, Kvantrishvili was a petty criminal, starting his career with gambling and card playing for big stakes at the Sovetskaya Hotel in Moscow. Supposedly he was also involved in foreign currency frauds.[21] In 1966, he was charged with rape but was sent to a psychiatric hospital and then released, diagnosed as a schizophrenic, a common method of shortening one's sentence.[22] He gained influence in part thanks to the vast contacts he made as a wrestling coach for the police team, attracting all types of athletes, in particular boxers, wrestlers, and martial arts specialists. Some of these would fill out the ranks of such criminal groups as Baumansky, Lyuberetsky, Domodedovsky, and Balashikhinsky, over which Kvantrishvili was said to have had considerable influence.

As vice president of a high-profile 'charitable organization,' Kvantrishvili had numerous business and government associates. The organization's president had traveled with Gorbachev to Europe to conclude contracts with Italian companies. They also exported oil, timber, and non-ferrous metal. A Russian business daily published an interview with the president of the organization, during which the journalist presented rumors that the organization "controls the most powerful mafiosi structures in Moscow."[23]

In 1993, President Yeltsin ordered the creation of the Sports Academy, of which Kvantrishvili was to be a director. This 'social organization' was to be exempt from paying import-export tariffs from 1993 to 1995 for exporting aluminum, titanium, fuel oil, and cement and importing vodka, cigarettes, and consumer goods.[24] Kvantrishvili never had an opportunity to fully enjoy his windfall as he was gunned down by a sniper in April 1994.

---

21. Author interview with Kvantrishvili acquaintance, July 1994.

22. Author conversation with Gennady Chebotaryov, October 1990. See also Igor Pankov, Sergei Pluzhnikov, and Sergei Sokolov, "Ya Khorosho Soobrazhaiu v Loshadyakh i Liudyakh," *Komsomol'skaya Pravda*, no. 61 (20834), April 9, 1994, p.1.

23. Oleg Utitsin and Mikhail Mikhailin, "Assotsiatsiya XXI Vek: 'Mafiya—Eto ne k Nam!'" *Kommersant*, no. 45, December 7–13, 1992, p. 29.

24. Yuri Shchekochikhin, "Death of a Mystery Man," *The Moscow Times*, April 9, 1994. Shchekochikhin reports that he once heard Kvantrishvili say, "Yes, sure, it is all true. But my children will be honest." See also Pyotr Yudin, "Professionals Kill Moscow Mafia Boss,"

In his travels in the underworld, Kvantrishvili had reportedly come to influence a number of Moscow groups including the Lyubers who got their start engaging in extortion and fraud at Beriozka stores. These were foreign currency stores that sold deficit goods and souvenirs to foreigners for dollars, francs, marks, etc. Since possessing foreign currency was against the law, Soviet citizens who worked abroad were given vouchers (*sertifikaty*) which they could use in the Beriozka stores.

As retired police investigator Alexander Gorkin tells it, in 1981, several young guys from the suburb of Lyubertsy came to Moscow and went to one of the Beriozka stores. They had managed to get their hands on *sertifikaty* but didn't find what they wanted at the store. Someone outside the store offered to buy the coupons at double their face value. The deal was done. Only later did the young guys from Lyubertsy realize that for their *sertifikaty* they had gotten a 'doll' (*kukla*)—a wad of plain paper with real bills on either end to make it look like a lot of money. When they understood they had been swindled, the Lyubers did two things. They decided to get their money back (which they did by beating up the swindlers) and they got into the business themselves. They hired several other boys from Lyubertsy and went back to the store. They convinced the dealers in front of the shop to pay them for protection. After a short time, the Lyubers started to rob the very people they were protecting, which by 1983 escalated into shoot-outs. They eventually came to run a network of street swindlers working 'three-card monty' and 'thimble' games.[25]

The Lyubers were well known as fanatic weightlifters, ostensibly preparing to join the army. The mere sight of them on the streets dressed in their baggy

---

The Moscow Times, April 7, 1994, and Stephen Erlanger, "A Slaying Puts Russian Underworld on Parade," *The New York Times*, April 14, 1994.

25. Author conversation with former Moscow criminal investigator, Alexander Gorkin, July 1994. One article cites the beginning of the movement to be around the end of the 1970s when special sports schools sprang up in the town. They also began working out in self-equipped gyms, mostly basements of apartment buildings. *Sobesednik*, "Lyuberites under the Street Light—Stepsons of the Capital," no. 7, 1987, pp. 10–15. According to the *Ogonyok* article that brought the Lyubertsy into the spotlight, the Lyubertsy began coming to Moscow in 1984. "And they are not just pumping iron and then looking for something to test their strength on because they are bored. They are in training to fight." Vladimir Yakovlev, "The 'Lyuberi' Office," *Ogonyok*, no. 5, 1987, pp. 20–21. The roots of the Lyubertsy were fairly typical of gangs and organized crime groups in Russia. For example, the Solntsevo group got its start by extorting taxi drivers and shell game operators, among others. See "Obzornaya Spravka v Otnoshenii t.n. 'Solntsevskoi' Mezhregional'noi Prestupnoi Gruppirovki," 1996, material labeled 'Secret' received by the author from a Russian intelligence source.

plaid trousers, loose-fitting shirts, and sporting shaved heads instilled fear on Moscow streets. The group even gained international attention in Gorbachev's USSR of 1986–87, appearing in U.S. magazines. Under the banner, "We are purifying the capital of hooligans!" ("Otchistim Moskvu ot khuliganov!"), the young toughs gained a reputation for cleaning Moscow's streets of newly emerging 'unwanted' social elements such as the 'punks,' 'rockers,' and 'metal heads,' who dyed their hair various colors, wore leather, and multiple earrings.[26]

After the Law on Cooperatives was passed in 1988, essentially legalizing forms of private business, the weightlifting Lyubers were natural extortionists. The head of an underground factory provided financing for the group. They hired themselves out to other crime groups as muscle for dispute settlements (*razborki*), which frequently turned violent. In 1988–89, several armed clashes erupted between the Lyubers and the Chechens, competing for influence over the automobile market at Southern Port (Yuzhny Port) and several other regions of Moscow. The overall influence of the Lyubers was believed to have been considerable since so many of the people from Lyubertsy were members in several other gangs.[27]

Around 1990, when two of the top Lyuber leaders were released from prison, the group took on a somewhat more organized nature and expanded their activities in robbery, assault, extortion, contract murder, and participation in *razborki*, including those taking place in other regions of Russia. Three Lyubers had accompanied Otari Kvantrishvili's brother, Amiran, when he went to collect a debt in August 1993. They were ambushed and all four of them killed.

Most of the leaders, involved in the group since at least 1981, formed their own legal businesses as part of their money laundering operation. According to law enforcement sources, by the mid-1990s, Lyubers operated in a number of Moscow suburbs including their home town of Lyubertsy, Lutkarino, Dzerzhinsk, Malakhovka, Ramenskoe, Voskresensk, Kolomna, and Zhukovsky. The Lyubers was a fairly typical example of a crime group that developed through the 1980s and took advantage of opportunities presented in the 1990s.

In addition to the activities mentioned above, the illegal manufacture, sale, and distribution of alcohol in the 1980s was another enterprise that helped groups (both the upperworld and underworld 'mafia') accumulate capital and experience.

---

26. Dikselius compared the Lyubertsy to skinheads (*britogolovye*) of the West. M. Dikselius and A. Konstantinov, *Prestupnyi Mir Rossii*, Sankt-Peterburg, Bibliopolis, 1995. I had a close call with them in Gorky Park in 1990.

27. Author conversation with former Moscow police detective Alexander Gorkin, July 1994.

It is little surprise that alcohol, particularly vodka, is closely associated with Russia. After all, as a northern country, the land of potatoes simply acted as other countries in harsh, cold climates: they sought celebration and solace in drink. What might be surprising is that in the late nineteenth century "the per capita consumption of alcohol [in Russia] was amazingly low compared with that of France, Britain, Germany, and Denmark."[28] In fact, for the past two centuries Russian consumption of alcohol has generally been lower than that of many other countries. The main difference was that the Russians made alcohol a centerpiece of social interaction not as a way to enhance an evening of discourse around a dining table for example, but as an extreme method to beat back the weight of oppression, depression, and desperation as well as an overindulgent way to celebrate holidays, birthdays, vacations, weekends, and virtually anything else. And when they marked these events, they did so in volume, by the gallon not the glass. My most recent extreme social interaction with Russian police, in 2006, during an evening around a table covered with food and libation, was a good example of their dangerous attitude toward vodka. In the span of less than two hours, we threw back more shots than I can remember, losing count after 10.

In September 1966, the Soviet newspaper *Izvestia* published what came to be called 'The Drinker's Manifesto.'

> In our country, people drink because of sadness and joy, and because they are on a date. They drink because they have just been paid. They drink because there's a frost, or because a child has just been born. If there are no children who have just been born, they drink anyway. Some people drink because they are still mourning over the last war, some because they feel cold and some because they have just taken a bath. Some drink when relatives gather together, or when a pig has been killed. And some even start the celebration of Women's Day with drinks.[29]

---

28. Ronald Hingley, *The Russian Mind*, New York, Charles Scribner's Sons, 1977, p. 52. The same observation is made by Leonid Vladimirov, *The Russians*, New York, Frederick A. Praeger, 1968, p. 111: "It has long been established, for example, that the average American drinks more liquor in the course of a year than the average Russian."

29. Ibid., Vladimirov, p. 109, and on p. 116: "In Russia, people are likely to do their drinking in a more noticeable way. This lack of calculation and self-restraint is a feature of the Russian character, and under the influence of vodka, the tension spring that has been coiled inside each of us by the pernicious demands of civilized life suddenly starts to unwind. It unwinds more obviously, more openly, in the Russian character, with the result that such a person may do scandalous things."

It's no wonder, then, that when Mikhail Gorbachev introduced his anti-alcohol campaign in 1985, he created the circumstances for the Soviet Union's own kind of Prohibition that would exacerbate black market operations.

There had been other attempts to curb alcohol consumption before 1985. In 1950, pure alcohol was limited to seven liters per inhabitant over the age of 14. But by 1983, this ceiling had crept up to 14.6 liters. Between 1978 and 1983, the price of alcohol nearly trebled.[30] Anti-alcohol policies had come and gone under Brezhnev, Andropov, and Chernenko, all with little effect. But there was good reason for trying. Alcohol consumption had dramatically impacted performance in the workplace. According to Martin McKee, between 75% and 90% of absences from work were attributed to alcohol, and observers estimated that alcohol played a direct role in the decline in productivity, as high as 20%.[31]

The first rules restricting access to alcohol came into effect on June 1, 1985, introducing the kinds of measures that could be implemented quickly for high-visibility impact, "such as banning drinking of alcohol at all workplaces, including formerly legal bars, such as those in higher education establishments; banning sales before 2 p.m.; and banning sales on trains (including dining-cars) and similar establishments." These measures were extended to such things as firing managers who drank too much and reducing the number of places to purchase alcohol. In September 1985, the All-Union Voluntary Society for the Struggle for Sobriety was created and within one year claimed to have 12 million members. In August 1985, prices increased by 25% followed by an increase of 20–25% in August 1986. Cuts in production led to massive shortages.[32]

The consequences of these changes were immediately apparent. Nearly 50% of stores in Moscow that previously sold alcohol now did not. Retail sales of alcoholic beverages in the first half of 1986 were one-third less than they had been in the preceding year.[33] Long lines appeared in front of official alcohol outlets (up to 3,000 people in one case in Moscow).[34] Hardened drinkers resorted to black market moonshine, and the percentage of crimes involving

---

30. Basile Kerblay, *Gorbachev's Russia*, New York, Pantheon Books, 1989, p. 15.

31. Martin McKee, "Alcohol in Russia," *Alcohol and Alcoholism*, vol. 34, no. 6, 1999, pp. 824–829, at http://alcalc.oxfordjournals.org/cgi/content/full/34/6/824.

32. Ibid. See also Stephen White, *Russia Goes Dry: Alcohol, State, and Society*, Cambridge, Cambridge University Press, 1996.

33. Marshall I. Goldman, *Gorbachev's Challenge: Economic Reform in the Age of High Technology*, New York, W.W. Norton & Company, 1987, p. 2.

34. McKee (note 31).

home brew increased by nearly six times between 1977 and 1987. The various upperworld and underworld 'mafias' ran their own production, sale, and distribution of moonshine and even controlled the trade in the sugar necessary for producing moonshine.[35] Sugar had been diverted into the illegal liquor business, resulting in deep shortages in major cities such as Moscow and Kiev.[36]

To give an idea of the scope of moonshine operations across the country, in 1984, official liquor sales had totaled 51 billion rubles, or 16% of consumer spending; by 1987, the figure had fallen to 35 billion rubles. Several billion rubles of that lost revenue had been redistributed to the pockets of the upperworld and underworld 'mafias.' In 1986, officials reportedly confiscated 900,000 illicit stills and convicted more than 200,000 black market dealers or distillers.[37]

Rationing in some parts of the country resulted in taxis venturing hundreds of miles in search of vodka. In some northern regions, helicopter pilots and physicians, who were exempt from restrictions on vodka, became popular overnight. Throughout the Soviet Union vodka was not merely for drinking; it served as a currency, a key item in bartering services, for millions of people. For example, after the restrictions on the sale of vodka were implemented, old peasant women in the countryside were unable to give tractor drivers who came to plow their garden the customary bottle. Illiterate grandmothers in the towns could earn as much as a scientist by lining up to wait for the liquor store to open.[38]

Of course, as throughout Russian history, it was impossible to legislate away problems that were deeply ingrained in attitudes, values, and beliefs of the population.[39] It is tempting to conclude quite easily and neatly that the anti-alcohol campaign was a failure. This may have been true in terms of public policy, but it was clearly beneficial to someone, as Arkady Vaksberg raised that central question we discussed in Chapter 3:

> Who was benefiting from this? Apart from the numberless exporters, arms traders, and other international businessmen, it was the Soviet black market traders once again, who began to supply sugar under

---

35. Galeotti, p. 241 (note 14).
36. Kerblay, p. 107 (note 30).
37. Ibid.
38. Ibid., pp. 46–47, 107.
39. Gorkin shared with me a saying that has been attributed to Catherine the Great: "One must not change with laws that which must be changed by custom." (*Nel'zya peremenyat' zakonami to, chto nadobno peremenyat' obychayami*).

the counter at inflated prices; it was militiamen, closing their eyes (not for free, of course) to the production of home brew; it was the so-called 'people's control' called on to 'be vigilant' and 'mercilessly expose,' but managing very successfully to protect the usual 'offenders.' And who lost out? As usual, it was the unhappy country.[40]

While alcohol might be understandable to us as a product at the center of criminal activity given the U.S. experience with Prohibition, less obvious is the role that computers played in the development of crime groups. It's important to keep several things in mind. First, all of the best technology was channeled into the military. Second, one of the elements that made the Soviet Union successful as a totalitarian government was the strict control of information. And third, even though the USSR was a 'superpower,' this status did not extend to its consumer goods sector, especially electronics. Computers were just another of the many deficit items in the Soviet economy. Consumers wanted products that were either illegal or in short supply and a variety of entities stepped in to satisfy the demand. This is partly why Vaksberg developed such a wide-ranging concept of 'mafia' in the Soviet Union; a large number of products in the USSR were the equivalent of alcohol in the U.S. during Prohibition. There were Al Capones in the alcohol business, furniture, shoes, blue jeans, computers, and countless other products. Some of them were Communist Party officials, some were thugs, and some were enterprising and well-connected college students, who went on to become the top businessmen and criminals in the country. The sudden weakening of the Soviet Union together with the barren computer market created in a short period of time a billion-dollar industry in computers, whether traded, smuggled, or stolen.

Computers were being smuggled into Russia from every direction, on buses, in cars, and on airplanes.[41] For example, personal computers, laptops, terminals, and monitors were being moved into the Soviet Union, with each computer bringing more than 50,000 rubles in profit (at a time when the average Russian monthly salary was less than 1,000 rubles).[42] Interestingly, computers (in some cases the very ones obtained from the West) were being exported from the Soviet Union to Eastern Europe. Numerous groups engaged

---

40. Vaksberg, p. 234 (note 8).
41. A. Craig Copetas, *Bear Hunting with the Politburo: A Gritty First-Hand Account of Russia's Young Entrepreneurs and Why Soviet-Style Capitalism Can't Work*, New York, Simon & Schuster, 1991, p. 97.
42. Vaksberg, p. 229 (note 8).

in smuggling operations to Bulgaria, Czechoslovakia, Austria, Germany, and other countries. Some state officials who were supposed to have been using the computers for work were cooperating with those groups.

It is little surprise that the possibility of excessive profit attracted gangs to this business and helped them to grow and become more organized. As Chebotaryov notes, "According to intelligence estimates, in Moscow alone, operators have earned income in excess of 1 billion rubles by dealing in computers at black market prices. This competition for 'market share' is accompanied by serious clashes between groups."[43]

Those black marketeers used their money from the sale of blue jeans and Russian souvenirs as well as black market currency exchanges to get into other businesses such as computers. But, as in many other aspects of the Russian 'mafia,' we find ourselves harkening back to Vaksberg's concept of a wide-ranging, broadly-defined 'mafia.' In the course of investigating the Russian 'mafia,' Handelman heard the following account regarding the 'mafia' that really ran the underground computer business:

> We started to hear about huge shipments of computers, coming by the planeloads and trainloads. This represented huge sums of money, and it was clear that ordinary businessmen like myself couldn't have entered the business, and it wasn't hard to figure out who was behind them. No one could provide the logistics and protection for transporting so many computers, and arrange the credits, unless he had help from certain official organs.[44]

It's interesting to note that one of the so-called oligarchs got his start by smuggling computers into the Soviet Union. Quite conveniently at that time, while his competition was getting arrested or killed, he and his colleagues appeared to be well protected by the KGB. Despite the 'bad luck' befalling the competition, he continued to rise unscathed through the business world until reaching the pinnacle, where he still resides today.[45]

The need and desire for computers was so great that many institutes, businesses, and state offices were unwittingly concluding agreements with swindlers. The swindlers delivered a small portion of the total number of computers agreed on, demanded the balance of payments before concluding de-

---

43. Gennady Chebotaryov, "Organized Crime in Export-Import Operations," presented at the 20th European Regional Conference of Interpol, London, April 3–5, 1991, p. 4.

44. Stephen Handelman *Comrade Criminal: Russia's New Mafiya*, New Haven, Yale University Press, 1995, p. 157.

45. Author investigative information.

livery, and then disappeared. In one case, a front corporation was registered in the United States with a well-known and influential Westerner listed as president and a Russian as vice president. Although there was no evidence that the president was aware of the scam, the Russian vice president used his credentials as an officer of an American company to defraud small private businesses and research institutes. He opened bank accounts in Moscow and St. Petersburg, got an official stamp and seal (without which nothing happens in Russian business and bureaucracy), and claimed to be the representative of a large American company. He signed contracts to deliver computers from abroad to the small businesses and institutes. It was difficult for the buyers to reject the seller's condition of payment up front. No payment, no computers. This individual made off with millions of rubles. The scope of his activity reportedly included business with high-ranking personnel of the American Embassy in Moscow.[46]

One of the easiest and most effective ways the groups filled their coffers quickly as the Soviet Union faded away was through document fraud and, more specifically, fake payment notices (*falshivoe avizo*). In the early 1990s, document fraud was a pervasive problem in the Russian banking world due in large part to the fact that Russian commercial banks were not connected to SWIFT or any other electronic bank payment system. This meant that in order to conduct bank-to-bank money transfers, Russian commercial banks used *avizo*, which were cleared through the regional payment centers of the Russian Central Bank who then were responsible for verifying the authenticity of an *avizo*.

According to Russian law enforcement sources, most fraudulent transactions involving *avizo* originated in the republics of the North Caucasus, such as Chechnya, Ingushetia, Dagestan, and North Ossetia, all notorious for official corruption and organized crime. The sources believed that the majority of these fraudulent transactions were initiated by ethnic organized crime groups from these republics who had established their own banks or made informal deals with existing Russian commercial banks. While these groups were involved in this activity, it was certainly an exaggeration to claim that they were responsible for the majority of it. Billions of dollars were siphoned out of the economy through the false *avizo* scams.

Here's how it was said to work. A Chechen enterprise, for example, gives a check issued by a Chechen bank to a Russian enterprise. The Russian enterprise passes it to a Russian bank, providing a fake contract as the basis for the

---

46. Case developed by the Organized Crime Control Department.

transaction. The contract shows that the Chechen enterprise was obligated to 'pay' a certain sum of money to the Russian enterprise; the Russian enterprise in turn is to 'supply' certain items to the Chechen enterprise. The Russian bank contacts the Chechen bank for confirmation. A corrupt employee of the bank in on the scam confirms the existence of an account in the bank. The Russian bank credits the account of the Russian enterprise, which then withdraws the funds. The criminals share the money and the Chechen enterprise leaves Russia for Chechnya. The Chechen bank rejects all demands of the Russian bank for payment, denying the existence of an account for the Chechen enterprise. Attempts to get the bank's money back from the Russian enterprise by arbitration fail because the Russian enterprise always 'fails' to supply items according to the 'contract' and instead 'pays' back transferred money to the Chechen enterprise for non-fulfillment of the contract.

In this way, members of a Chechen criminal organization reportedly made off with more than $40 million. One of its members purchased several apartments in Moscow, paying $120–150,000, but the bulk of the money was transferred to Germany. In Hungary, members of the group were caught in possession of $760,000 in cash from this lot.[47]

That story contains everything necessary to be interesting: the further stereotyping of a hated ethnic group, the transfer of large sums of money abroad, the 'penetration' of the European real estate market, and so on. While journalists sounded the alarm about the Chechen 'mafia,' Chebotaryov, the Deputy Chief of the Organized Crime Control Department, adds one critical piece of information making it a more balanced account.

> These illegal activities of the Chechen criminal group had the support of high-ranking Russian military officers and civil servants. According to this evidence, the billions of rubles received by Chechen criminals by means of fake payment orders were ultimately remitted to the foreign bank accounts of Russian officials and businessmen. The criminals received 8% as a commission for having implemented the operation.[48]

As in many other aspects of the 'mafia' landscape, care is needed in the area of false *avizo*. In addition to groups such as the Chechens, Russian banks themselves were, of course, siphoning off billions of dollars for years. According to the Ministry of Internal Affairs, from 1991 to 1993, some 900 banks

---

47. Author conversation with Chebotaryov, December 1994.
48. Ibid.

and 1500 enterprises in 68 regions of Russia had participated in the cashing of these and other fake documents, with most occurring in Moscow and Moscow Region, St. Petersburg, and the Stavropol, Krasnodar, Dagestan, and Tomsk regions.[49]

To give a small example, in the course of several investigations of a major Russian bank between 1996 and 1999, we discovered that the bank had been the 'victim' of several false *avizo* in late 1992 and early 1993, posting 'losses' of millions of dollars. All of the false payment notices came through the same regional payment distribution center in southern Russia. Again there was speculation that the Chechens or Dagestanis were behind these activities. We discovered that all of the false *avizo* were filed by representatives of a single joint venture. Looking further, it turned out that 25% of the joint venture was owned by the 'victim' bank itself and 75% was owned by a Switzerland-based company that had been set up by the 'victim' bank. The company's corporate papers filed in Moscow identified the chairman of the 'victim' bank as the general director of the joint venture. In addition, the joint venture (which supposedly had been victimizing the bank) was also a founder and majority shareholder in at least 9 companies directly and in at least 20 companies indirectly. Some of the money pilfered from the bank by its owners was sent abroad, some of it was used in purchasing Russian industrial concerns at rock-bottom prices. Part of this money was cycled back into bribing officials and used in resolving conflicts surrounding factories. And this was no 'gangster' bank, the kind that was blamed for so much of the looting of the country in the 1990s. Once again, Vaksberg's 'mafia' was the central player; these banks, owned by the Russian 'robber barons,' used their contacts at the very highest levels to steal as much cash and property as possible, just at the time the West was trumpeting their arrival as the future of business in the country.

The story of Viktor covers nearly all the elements of what is referred to by many in the former Soviet Union as 'mafia': he had access to resources and information, partnerships with the traditional criminal world, close relationships with high-ranking bureaucrats, and a criminal record.

Viktor was born in the Soviet Central Asian republic of Uzbekistan, now an independent country. As the son of a high-ranking KGB official in a major Uzbek city in the 1970s, Viktor had an opportunity to study at a prestigious Moscow institute. Many of his classmates went on to become key players in Moscow city and Russian national politics. During his institute years he was known as a talented student but "extremely inclined to opportunism and fraud."[50]

---

49. These scams didn't end in 1993; they continued throughout the decade. See "Rezul'-taty Deyatel'nosti RUOP po Moskve Pri GUOP MVD Rossii za 1993–1998," p. 4.

50. Author investigative information.

After graduating from the institute in Moscow and having served his mandatory two years in the army, he returned to Uzbekistan where his father set him up in a job. All the while he engaged in petty scams.

Among Viktor's friends were junior KGB officers, some of whom were also the sons of high-ranking KGB officials. In the late 1970s, Viktor and the son of a ranking Uzbek KGB officer approached a Jewish army lieutenant and demanded 30,000 rubles to destroy compromising material about the lieutenant that supposedly was being collected by the KGB. Instead of giving in to the threat, the Jewish lieutenant reportedly complained to the KGB, and Viktor and his friend were arrested during the transfer of the money. Viktor was sentenced to eight years in prison for extortion, kidnapping, and torture while his accomplice received four years. (The Uzbek KGB chief saw a political opportunity here and had the accomplice's father—the deputy chief—sacked.)

While serving his sentence, Viktor became acquainted with Igor, a *vor v zakone* who became Victor's protector in prison.[51] After getting out of prison in 1986—nearly two years early (reportedly for good behavior)—Viktor returned to Uzbekistan where he settled in an apartment with the help of Igor but didn't return to 'normal' life. He began engaging in speculation, fraud, and extortion, and also became involved in the underground production of plastic products at a chemical factory together with two police officers.

By the end of 1986, Viktor moved to Moscow and became a leader of the Uzbek diaspora. Any dispute settlements among crime groups (*razborki*) were orchestrated by the *vor v zakone* Igor who by this time was out of prison and operating in Moscow.[52]

---

51. Interestingly, some of the ties in the post-Soviet era between traditional criminal types and major business people were forged in prison during the Soviet period, whether the business people were sentenced for 'Soviet offenses' like possession of foreign currency or 'normal' criminal offenses. For example, a top Russian businessman who did time in a Soviet prison for 'private entrepreneurial activity,' which was a criminal offense in the Soviet Union, became acquainted in prison with one of the future leaders of a Chechen crime group. By the mid-1990s, the businessman was believed to be managing a channel of narcotics to Moscow as well as the transshipment of narcotics to several European countries via Moscow on behalf of the Chechen group. Russian law enforcement believed that the businessman was assisting in the laundering of the illegal drug proceeds through companies he owned in both Russia and Europe.

52. The former Uzbek KGB deputy chief's son who had been imprisoned with Viktor helped Igor get out of the Soviet Union. After failing to obtain a visa at the U.S. Embassy in Moscow, Igor was able to get a visa through the Canadian Embassy in one of the Baltic States. He went from the Baltics through Canada to the U.S. where as of this writing he still operates. He is believed by Russian and U.S. law enforcement sources to be engaged in money laundering on behalf of Russian crime groups and to be part of an extensive in-

In 1987, one of Viktor's scams backfired and he found himself in debt to the now-deceased Sergei Timofeyev, known in the criminal world as 'Sylvester,' and who at the time was the head of the Orekhovsky crime group. Instead of paying Sylvester the 160,000 rubles owed, Viktor reportedly fled to Uzbekistan where through his contacts he became acquainted with two leaders of an Uzbek criminal group involved in narcotics trafficking. These weren't low-level drug dealers but two individuals with close relationships at the highest levels of the Uzbek government and in other Central Asian republics. The two called upon the leaders of the Moscow-based Solntsevo crime group to resolve the conflict. Viktor now found himself beholden to both the Uzbeks and the Solntsevo leaders.

Four years later, Viktor once again found himself in a jam, this time with law enforcement. A criminal case for theft was opened in Moscow against Viktor and two of his associates for allegedly trying to use a bank loan for illegal business dealings. The case was quickly quashed with the help of the KGB, and thereafter the Uzbek KGB put restrictions on access to information related to Viktor. Any attempts to retrieve archived files or transcripts of criminal cases involving Viktor were carefully monitored and immediately reported to the Uzbek KGB. This indicated a high level of protection for Viktor, and attempts to investigate him would have been difficult.[53]

That same year, 1991, Viktor reportedly became acquainted with a powerful foreign businessman who claimed to be connected with one of the Western intelligence agencies and to have had high-level contacts at numerous Soviet governmental agencies in Moscow. Viktor passed this information on to one of the deputy chiefs of the Uzbek KGB. The material regarding the foreigner was sent to KGB headquarters in Moscow and ended up on the desk of a mid-level intelligence officer. Whether the foreign businessman was anybody of consequence is unknown, but the matter brought Viktor to the attention of this officer. The officer, Pyotr, and Viktor eventually became acquainted and developed a relationship which would quickly become a business partnership, cemented by their mutual inclinations to fraud and opportunism.

Pyotr began his career in counter-intelligence but thanks to a close relative who was a high-ranking official in the GRU, the military intelligence agency,

---

ternational criminal network, working with Russian crime bosses in North America, Europe, and the former Soviet Union.

53. It is standard practice for law enforcement and the security services to monitor carefully inquiries for information about certain individuals to the point where sometimes any and all information may be removed from the files. In a number of cases we were informed that the records were sealed or had been removed from the files. In other cases we were politely told not to dig any further.

Pyotr was transferred to foreign intelligence. Originally spotted by the leadership as a talented athlete and active Komsomol (Young Communist League) member with "the makings of a leader," Pyotr's personnel file would later carry the opinions of fellow KGB officers, characterizing him as an ambitious, unprincipled opportunist with "the makings of a criminal."[54]

Perhaps one of the more interesting threads in Pyotr's background was that, according to a report compiled by Russian law enforcement and intelligence analysts, by a secret decision of the Central Committee of the Communist Party of the Soviet Union Pyotr's name was supposedly added to the so-called List Number One. This list reportedly contained the names of those individuals who were supposed to create the 'material-financial base' of the Communist Party in the event the Party 'became the opposition party or an illegal entity.' In essence, this meant that Pyotr would be one of the trusted personnel who would secure funds for the Party's financial stability should it lose its monopoly hold on the state coffers.

Pyotr's presence on the list gave him access to some of the most powerful people in the country. He would prove a most welcome business partner to Viktor. Together they were involved in, among other things, the illegal production of high-quality plastic bags at a factory outside Moscow. While this may not sound particularly impressive or glamorous, don't forget that, unlike in the West, plastic bags were nowhere to be found in the capital. There was considerable money to be made producing this one simple thing.

Viktor also established his own private army of criminals, which provided protection from other crime groups. Soon the illegal plastics production came to the attention of the local police, some believe with the assistance of one of the local crime groups. It was considered illegal production because in the course of their investigation police found that the bags were produced from materials stolen from the plastics factory where they were operating. A criminal case was started against Viktor. Pyotr, lending a helping hand to his partner, introduced him to the leadership of the Moscow region police as a particularly valuable informant and the case was dropped. Viktor got off and was now indebted to Pyotr.

After moving to Moscow, Viktor didn't lose his contacts back in Uzbekistan. According to a report compiled by Russian law enforcement and intelligence analysts, Viktor became the front man for large financial and commercial entities in Uzbekistan closely tied with the criminal world and the clan of a former Secretary of the Central Committee of the Communist Party of

---

54. Author investigative information.

Uzbekistan. The center of a nationwide scandal in the 1980s, the clan was still actively involved in Uzbek gold mining and exporting gold to Switzerland. Viktor also maintained his ties with the two Uzbek drug traffickers as well as other major crime bosses who are currently (2007) based in the Europe and the United States.

One of the Uzbek crime bosses got Viktor involved in smuggling gold and precious gems. These were moved abroad with the assistance of Pyotr's and Viktor's extensive contacts. In addition, Pyotr set up a string of companies, including joint ventures with foreign partners, and through his political contacts he was able to secure customs duties and tax breaks for exporting oil and importing cigarettes. Viktor eventually established other contacts, particularly in banking and precious metals and became a member of the board of several banks.

After the dismantling of the Soviet Union, Pyotr became a consultant to the director of a Russian government enterprise manufacturing military airplanes and quickly gained control over the export activities of the firm. Viktor and one of his highly placed contacts in the Moscow city government came up with the idea to set up a bank to support a variety of export activities including airplanes. Pyotr had meetings with one of Viktor's narcotrafficking contacts from Central Asia to provide protection for the bank. The trafficker supposedly wasn't up to the task, and it was decided to turn to the leaders of the Solntsevo crime group once again. The bank was established in early 1993.

Pyotr was the chairman of the board; the Moscow city official who helped set up the bank was made deputy chairman. High-ranking officials of the Russian Foreign Intelligence Service (SVR) and GRU military intelligence as well as individuals with close ties to the Kremlin also assisted in getting the bank on its feet.

One of the reasons Pyotr pushed to establish the bank was to quickly broker deals of fighter jets abroad. Through his contacts, he obtained licenses allowing him and his colleagues to become independent agents on the international arms market as well as to receive a $40 million credit from the Russian government earmarked for the deal. Other major Russian banks were squeezed out of the deal, at least temporarily.

The bank eventually came to serve Russian intelligence agencies as well as state arms export agency. Crime groups recognized that such heavyweight clients virtually guaranteed the stability of the bank; it wasn't likely to collapse or be looted by its owners, as was so often the case in Russia.

According to Russian law enforcement sources, beginning around the summer of 1995, *obshchak* monies from the Solntsevo group as well as crime groups from the Northern Caucasus were deposited in the bank. The controller of the *obshchak* (*derzhatel' obshchaka*) was the official government representative to Moscow from one of the Northern Caucasus regions and had been both a Party official and a member of the upper house of the Russian legislature. The amount in the crime groups' accounts was reported to be "hundreds of millions of U.S. dollars."[55]

Toward the end of 1996, the intelligence agencies and the state arms export agency began removing their assets from the bank despite Pyotr's attempts to get assistance from his intelligence community contacts. Not even the appointment of one of the KGB/FSB's top people on economic crime as deputy chairman of the bank could keep the intelligence agencies from withdrawing their funds. The bank slipped under the total control of the Solntsevo group.

Viktor began carrying out the orders of the Solntsevo. He didn't have much choice given the overall weakened position of the management as well as Viktor's own indebtedness to the group for assistance years earlier when he ran afoul of Sylvester.

Pyotr and Viktor had a falling out as Viktor took over all management activities of the bank. Although Pyotr himself was in debt to the tune of nearly $25 million ($10 million of which was owed to the Solntsevo group), the urgency of repayment was mitigated somewhat by his appointment to a very powerful government post which the criminal world found particularly useful.

In other activities, Viktor was a member of a group of seven Russian and Uzbek businessmen who acquired a significant share in a major European company around which they created a network of offshore companies and Russian firms. The Europeans had invested tens of millions of dollars in Russia through Viktor, and there was no telling what ultimately became of the money. As was often the case in Russia, Viktor had secretly established a string of companies that would be recipients of at least some of this money. Chapter 10 will explore more of these deep interconnections among government officials, businessmen, and gangsters, as these relationships have come to define the Russian business world.

---

55. Author investigative information.

III

ON THE FRONT LINES

CHAPTER 9

GROUPS

A term [organized crime] that sometimes identifies people and at other times identifies organizations, businesses, or actions is not among the clearest. Furthermore, so comprehensive a term often encompasses activities and people that are not the subjects of consideration. Most professionals have simply stopped explaining what they mean when they use the term.

—Peter Lupsha[1]

A successful fear manager has to fulfill two basic conditions: he must at least provide a credible identification by a smart *naming* of the fear-arousing threat as a first step towards anxiety reduction. And he should never be fully successful: the threat may be reduced, but it still looms somewhere ready to act again. For a religion, the death of the Devil may be worse than the death of God.

—Petrus van Duyne[2]

To this point we have been investigating the context of the rise of criminal groups from a variety of angles. Among the many general observations we can make are: 1) crime groups were nothing new to the Russian landscape and did not emerge only after the dismantling of the Soviet Union; 2) the Soviet economy, among other things, shaped a society that was adept in the ways of what we would call petty crime, fraud, white collar crime, and corruption—they called it survival—and helped create the conditions leading to the rise in crime groups, especially after the disappearance of the Soviet Union; 3) the

---

1. Peter A. Lupsha, "Organized Crime," in William A. Geller (ed.), *Local Government Police Management*, Washington, D.C., International City Management Association, 1991, p. 211.

2. Petrus C. van Duyne, "Fears, Naming and Knowing: An Introduction,' in Petrus C. van Duyne, et al. (eds.), *Threats and Phantoms of Organised Crime, Corruption and Terrorism: Rhetoric and Critical Perspectives*, The Netherlands, Wolf Legal Publishers, 2004.

state was neither omnipotent nor omnipresent as a 'police state' in the sense that there was an officer on every corner, but rather as the ultimate arbiter of arbitrary justice, as the creator of a vast network of informants, as the inspiration for self-censorship by the population, and ultimately as the dispenser of cruel and unusual punishment. At the same time, the police had always been closely connected to the criminal world, easily bought and co-opted or fully participatory; and 4) the media played a central role in defining the threats emerging from Russia and tended toward focusing on the underworld while paying insufficient attention to the role of the upperworld (bureaucracy, oligarchs, MVD/KGB) in the chaos of the 1990s (see Chapter 11).

While it's true that crime groups existed long before the demise of the Soviet Union, clearly they took on a whole new dimension after 1991, particularly as pertains to their levels of organization and influence. And this is where I part company with Melnikov's assertion that the Russian experience of the 1990s was simply a continuation of what had always been (see Chapter 5). He may have been correct in arguing that the elements, the seeds, had always been present—"Russia has always been this way"—but the post-Soviet era was different from what had come before.

The dismantling of the Soviet Union (along with the razing of the Berlin Wall and other events) unleashed a variety of powerful forces virtually simultaneously that created the 'perfect storm' in crime history: 1) international travel both by air and across land borders was suddenly much easier; 2) technology, particularly in the form of personal computers and cellular telephones, flooded the market making global communication easy; 3) banks and other financial institutions could be established simply and inexpensively inside Russia and with easy connectivity around the world; 4) the quantity and firepower of weapons increased dramatically; 5) the population of the former Soviet Union was generally well educated; 6) institutions of control were incapable or unwilling to stem the tide of this criminality and, if anything, were complicit in its intensification throughout the 1990s; and 7) all of this was taking place across an enormous geographic area.

Add to this list the factors we already explored in earlier chapters, such as the legacy of Russian autocracy and Soviet totalitarianism, the formation of the psychology of *Homo Sovieticus*, an economy geared toward rapid militarization and industrialization, vast shortages of consumer goods and the consequent need for sharpening survival tactics, and so on. Crime groups (organized and not-so-organized) grew dramatically in this environment because opportunities presented themselves—the broken system required it. The groups of the anti-society that were largely limited to their own milieu (e.g., prison, underworld) prior to the dismantling of the Soviet Union now influenced to varying degrees many parts of the economy, politics, and society. They became intertwined with the upperworld 'mafia.'

This was all very dramatic for a variety of reasons. First, of course, there was real danger and considerable violence. Second, the 'invading' 'mafia' made great fodder for the media. Third, the Soviet Union—the world's other su-perpower—was now on its knees, having been bested by the West (so the story goes). The story practically wrote itself. Interestingly, though, in some ways the Soviet Union didn't fall quite as far as one might think. Most in the West didn't realize that the 'superpower' status conferred upon the USSR ap-plied largely to the capabilities of certain sectors of the military, especially as related to nuclear weapons. It didn't have the economic development of the West and could never really stand toe to toe with its arch enemies in many cat-egories other than the military (and even that threat was overblown in many ways). It's equally important to realize that Russia was not an anomaly in its vast corruption, lack of rule of law, and widespread criminality. While watch-ing a documentary about Mexico in the late 1990s, it struck me how the video would still be accurate for the most part had I replaced 'Mexico' with 'Russia' throughout the script. Indeed, some contend that, after surviving the so-called Great Mob War of 1992–1994 and the ruble collapse of 1998, Russia was sim-ply becoming

> a 'normal middle-income country': that is, a society with much the same growing prosperity, degrees of political and economic freedom, levels of corruption and inequality, restrictions on the media and controls on the judiciary, consumer choice and contested elections, as can be found in Mexico or Turkey or the Philippines, or anywhere else with a statistical per capita income of some $8,000 a year.[3]

That is to say, while many may have imagined the Soviet Union to have been roughly on par with the United States and the West generally, it never came close to reaching that level of development. In important ways it has al-ways been closer to a middle-income country at best than a world-class econ-omy. Interestingly, the noted American construction engineer Zara Witkin mentioned in Chapter 6 also compared the USSR to Mexico (and to India) back in the 1930s when he was working in Stalin's Soviet Union. It is impor-tant to realize that much of our reaction to the events inside Russia has been driven by our own needs, driven by politics, driven by business, driven by

---

3. Perry Anderson, "Russia's Managed Democracy," *London Review of Books*. vol. 29, no. 2, January 25, 2007, http://www.lrb.co.uk/v29/n02/print/ande01_.html

media, and driven by propaganda. The former Soviet Union has been singled out as being special, unique, and extreme in many ways (some of which is true), but we have to wonder how much of that is real and how much is perception, invention, and wishful thinking.

In previous chapters I raised some questions about the basic nature of the Russian 'mafia' as it had been portrayed by the media, law enforcement, and other interested parties. And here I continue to try to provide food for thought. For example, it was often said that the Russian 'mafia' was ruthless, brutal, and its violence knew no bounds.[4] It had often been heard that the Italians will kill you, but the Russians will kill you and your entire family. This is not to deny that some Russians have been exceedingly violent in the past, but that is not enough proof to necessarily differentiate them from other groups. In other words, these claims of extreme brutality are not exactly based on empirical evidence.

Such linguistic dramatics are, of course, relatively useless as an indicator of the real danger posed by such groups. Several basic questions about the violence of Russians (former Soviets) should come to mind. For example, compared to what? Are there not brutal and vicious Chinese, Vietnamese, Colombian, Italian, and American groups? A Texas gang investigator uttered the very same comment to me about one of the Hispanic gangs capturing media attention these days in the United States: "These guys will kill you and your whole family."[5] I also recall reading an article some years ago about the Jamaican Yardies in London's West End and their propensity for extreme violence at the slightest provocation.

Perhaps it could be demonstrated that certain economic conditions, political and social histories, and psychological patterns lend themselves to greater brutality—a general disregard for human life—in some countries more than others, but this would not necessarily be limited to organized crime or 'mafia' and certainly not limited to Russia or the former Soviet Union. Related to this, from a basic social science research perspective, the question I raised in Chapter 3 regarding media has to be asked again: how do they know that? In other words, who collected data on the frequency of the Russian use of violence to resolve conflict? In how many instances was violence used in cases involving Russians? In how many cases was an entire family killed along with the intended target? And how does this compare with criminal violence in other countries?

---

4. See, for example, Guy Dunn, "Major Mafia Gangs in Russia," in Phil Williams (ed.), *Russian Organized Crime: The New Threat?* London, Frank Cass, 1997, p. 87.

5. Author conversation with Texas gang investigator regarding the Mara Salvatrucha, February 2007.

Another question in all of this is: what is the vantage point of the observer? Over the years I've taken numerous informal surveys of police officers and prosecutors in many cities in the U.S. in an attempt to collect at least some anecdotal material showing that vantage point determines opinion. That is, naturally, many people appear to judge based on their own experience, so if an investigator or prosecutor, for example, has worked primarily Russian cases, Russians may seem exceedingly violent. Ask the same question of an investigator or prosecutor who has handled cases involving a variety of ethnic groups, the answer is likely to be that Nigerians, Colombians, or former Yugoslavians are just as brutal and just as difficult to handle. Again, I have no intention of arguing that groups in or from the former Soviet Union were not violent, but much of the reputation of the Russian 'mafia' was created in an atmosphere of hysteria, about a country that used to be the arch enemy of the U.S., and entailed a relationship that was thick with propaganda, disinformation, and deception. In short, we don't know if groups from the former Soviet Union were any more violent than others.

One last question to ask—one that, to me, is more intriguing than the others: to what extent did we as a nation need to promote the violence of our former arch enemy, as well as other enemies, in order to feel better about ourselves?

In Part I, we discovered that the picture of crime as presented to us was far from certain. It was a kaleidoscope that had an unsettling way of taking on new shapes, new combinations, with each turn. Look at the statistics one way and it seemed the Russian 'mafia' was taking over the world. Look at them another way and it seemed to be a hodgepodge of organized, semi-organized, disorganized, and, in many cases, unorganized gangs of opportunists. Images provided by interested parties (law enforcement, media, and criminals, to name a few) ensured that the sky was falling. But one thing was clear: no one could really say how many groups there were or even what was being counted (gangs, organized crime groups, 'mafia' clans, etc.). And this was understandable. As discussed in Chapter 4, many of the groups were often in flux. Some were better organized and more stable than others. Some shared members so it was difficult to tell where one group ended and another started. They were broken up by police so it was difficult to tell if a group had been disbanded or had been absorbed into another group. They were surrounded by a mystique created and driven by media, law enforcement, and themselves so it was difficult to tell how many crime groups were sophisticated organizations and how many were fly-by-night opportunistic gangs.

Part of the difficulty in all of this finds its roots once again in linguistic considerations. When speaking of 'organized crime' generally, we find ourselves facing similar challenges as we saw with the word 'mafia.' So many definitions have been put forward that the meaning has been diluted if not lost. A quick glance at the website of Prof. Klaus von Lampe reveals more than 75 offerings on the definition of organized crime collected from around the world.[6] Already many years ago Peter Lupsha observed that "unfortunately, because interdisciplinary efforts rarely lead to agreement, the resulting definitions produce as much dissent as accord, and the term 'organized crime' has become a buzzword in criminal justice with its own special meaning for each official who uses it." It can be applied, he says, to 1) a collection of criminals; 2) a type of organizational structure and hierarchy; 3) legal and illegal businesses; and 4) a variety of criminal acts that can build on each other in pyramidal fashion.[7]

Petrus van Duyne joins Lupsha in what is essentially an examination of language in determining the usefulness of the label 'organized crime.' He concludes that the language that has been chosen to describe the phenomenon has created more confusion and produced such a great variety of interpretations as to make it virtually meaningless.

> 'Organized crime' is in many ways a strange concept: it is found in widely diverse contexts, being used as if it denotes a clear and well-defined phenomenon. Nothing is further from the truth. [It] contains all sorts of implicit ideologies and myths, ranging from the 'Mr. Big' to the 'alien conspiracy theory'.... [O]ne has increasing doubts as to the scientific usefulness of the concept. As a matter of fact, it is difficult to relate the popular concepts and theories of 'organized crime' to the existing empirical evidence, which shows a less well-organized, very diversified landscape of organizING criminals.... [I]f one wants to study empirically what organizing criminals actually

---

6. See Definitions of Organized Crime at Klaus von Lampe's website: http://www.organized-crime.de/OCDEF1.htm. As a very small sample of other material on the subject, see also André Standing, *Rival Views of Organised Crime*, Monograph No. 77, February 2003, at http://www.iss.co.za/Pubs/Monographs/No77/Chap1.html; Jay S. Albanese, "The Causes of Organized Crime," *Journal of Contemporary Criminal Justice*, vol. 16, no. 4, November 2000, pp. 409–423; Colin Hayes, "Organized Crime," *The Police Journal*, vol. xlx, no. 1, January 1977, pp. 72–81; James W. Meeker, John Dombrink, and Henry N. Pontell, "White-Collar and Organized Crimes: Questions of Seriousness and Policy," *Justice Quarterly*, vol. 4, no. 1, March 1987, pp. 73–98, and John A. Dellow, "Organized Crime," *The Police Journal*, vol. lx, no. 3, July 1987, pp. 200–204.

7. Lupsha, p. 211 (note 1). For a variety of definitional approaches to organized crime, see C. Fijnaut and J. Jacobs (eds.), *Organized Crime and its Containment: A Transatlantic Initiative*, Deventer, Kluwer Law and Taxation Publishers, 1991.

do, the very words 'organized crime,' let alone mafia, La Cosa Nostra, and the like are not even necessary. I could describe perfectly the findings of our empirical research on 'organized crime' in The Netherlands in terms of the enterprise theory only. A crime-enterprise is a durable market-oriented unlawful cooperative with a hierarchical and spatial organization, whose principal means of making profits is by breaking the law.[8]

After years of debate, the United Nations finally, in 2001, settled on a definition of an organized crime group as part of its Convention against Transnational Organized Crime. It is, says the UN, "a structured group of three or more persons, existing for a period of time and acting in concert with the aim of committing one or more serious crimes or offences established in accordance with this Convention, in order to obtain, directly or indirectly, a financial or other material benefit."[9]

Van Duyne's approach to 'organized crime' may be a more satisfying one when looking at the Russian and former Soviet phenomenon, one that may serve to minimize the sensationalism and focus on the core mission. We may then find ourselves back at Irving Kristol's observation that the Communist Party of the Soviet Union was a 'mafia,' and that the Iron Triangle of bureaucracy, business, and crime was simply an expression of crime-enterprises in a land where most people broke the law in order to survive, and the creation of the traditional organized crime threat was part of the struggle for control over assets in a chaotic free-for-all period of history (see Chapter 10).

In Chapter 7 we saw extreme positions put forward regarding the role and status of *vory v zakone*: some considered the *vory* to be all-powerful "supermen" while others thought they were little more than car thieves. Here, too, with the definition of organized crime, we meet a similar challenge. At one end of the spectrum, Lupsha questions the usefulness of the term while at the other end, Viktor Luneev, a researcher at the Russian Academy of Sciences, provides a staggeringly long list of characteristics of an organized crime group. He says there is an organizer or managing nucleus; a definite hierar-

---

8. Petrus van Duyne, "Crime-Enterprise and the Legitimate Industry," in Fijnaut and Jacobs, ibid., p. 55. See also Petrus C. van Duyne, p. 2 (note 2): "Examples, which are elaborated in this reader, are 'organized crime,' 'financial crime,' and 'corruption.' Judging the clarity of these concepts by the volume of explanatory literature, we cannot maintain that these concepts are really self-evident. They are names, which evoke a variety of associations without crystallizing into a distinct identity."

9. United Nations Convention against Transnational Organized Crime, Fifty-fifth Session, January 8, 2001, http://www.unodc.org/pdf/crime/a_res_55/res5525e.pdf

chical structure separating the leadership from the direct executors of actions; a more or less clear division of roles (functions) realized in fulfilling concrete tasks, duties, or in 'official' behavior; strict discipline in subordination to the hierarchy, based on its own laws and norms, including a code of silence; system of strict punishment; financial means to carry out general tasks; collection of information on profitable and safe areas of criminal activity; neutralization and possible corruption of law enforcement and other state organs to obtain necessary information, aid, or protection; use of important governmental and social and economic institutions through which to legalize their criminal activity; dissemination of frightening rumors as to their power, which brings criminal organizations more benefit than harm, since it demoralizes witnesses, victims, journalists, and law enforcement organs and supports the criminal spirit of rank and file members who execute functions; creation of a management structure which frees the head from the necessity of directly organizing or committing concrete crimes; commission of any crimes primarily for money and control in some sphere or another or some territory or another.[10]

If we lean toward the Luneev interpretation of 'organized crime,' the UN definition seems to resemble more closely 'crime that is organized' rather than 'organized crime.' More important, though, it must be acknowledged that the UN definition addresses 'crime groups' while Luneev is talking about 'organized crime.' Although the two labels are frequently used interchangeably, there is a distinction between the two, which may also shed light on the litany of statistics presented in Chapter 4. In the late Soviet and early post-Soviet era, attention focused primarily on crime groups. The thousands of groups that were said to exist were primarily individual crime groups. Organized crime groups consist of several or even numerous crime groups under some kind of unifying administrative umbrella. In this regard, of course, organized crime groups would number fewer than the crime groups. At least some of the decline in the numbers presented throughout the 1990s was a function of the consolidation of the criminal world, a somewhat more organized environment than what emerged out of the immediate post-Soviet world.

With these varying definitions it becomes easier to appreciate how all manner of groups—organized, semi-organized, and not-so-organized—could be included under that single label. It is unlikely that the Luneev definition would concern itself with the bare minimum requirement of group membership of

---

10. Viktor Luneev, "Crime in the XXth Century—International Criminological Analysis," http://www.american.edu/traccc/resources/publications/luneev03.html

the UN definition, i.e., three people. That is, organized crime hardly could be spoken about in terms of a single, small group. It is the organization of multiple groups under a single leadership structure for the purpose of making money through illegal activities that characterizes organized crime as a concept and phenomenon. Discussing the activities of three individuals seems inadequate as a basis for a consideration of organized crime. Like Luneev above, former Moscow criminal investigator Alexander Gorkin considers that organized crime includes multiple groups each involved in its own criminal specialty, with lines of communication up and down the hierarchy, means to co-opt agents of social control if necessary, maintenance of internal discipline, and a system of known and predictable punishments for rule violators, among other things.[11]

Russian scholar Yakov Gilinskiy offers what strikes me as a reasonable summary of the definitions mentioned here. "Organized crime," he says, "is the functioning of stable, hierarchical associations, engaged in crime as a business, and setting up a system of protection against public control by means of corruption."[12] The notions of stability, hierarchy, and especially the establishment of a system of protection, suggest relatively sophisticated channels of communication, planning, and organization. Gilinskiy delineates three levels of organization among crime entities: 1) a criminal group, 2) a criminal organization or association, and 3) a criminal community.[13] Criminal communities are on par with the syndicates that former Director of the New York State Organized Crime Task Force Ron Goldstock referred to in his definition of organized crime: "The primary purpose of syndicates—and this is what makes organized crime organized—is to serve as a government for the underworld, providing services, allocating resources and territories, and settling disputes."[14]

I think it can be agreed that in the Soviet Union as well as post-Soviet Russia there were thousands of crime groups, those collections of three or more people engaged in criminal activity with some degree of organization and

---

11. Author conversation with Alexander Gorkin, May 2001.

12. Yakov Gilinskiy, "Organized Crime: The Russian and World Perspective," in Kauko Aromaa (ed.), *The Baltic Region: Insights in Crime and Crime Control*, Oslo, Pax Forlag A/S, 1998, pp. 168–182.

13. Ibid.

14. Ronald Goldstock, "Organized Crime and Anti-Organized Crime Efforts in the United States: An Overview" in C. Fijnaut and J. Jacobs (eds.) *Organized Crime and its Containment: A Transatlantic Initiative*, Deventer, Kluwer Law and Taxation Publishers, 1991, p. 7.

planning. How many of these were part of 'organized crime' is anyone's guess, but it would seem, given the fluid nature of the situation, the number of groups that were reportedly broken up, and other factors, that the number was far less than one would have concluded from the screaming headlines.

Law enforcement and the media frequently reported absolute figures for the number of criminal groups in the former Soviet Union, failing to delineate a difference between minor and major groups. We saw in earlier chapters the propensity of observers to neatly compartmentalize the Russian criminal underworld of the 1990s (see Chapters 1, 3, and 4). Russian sociologist Olga Kryshtanovskaya repeats this practice in her 1996 article, "Illegal Structures in Russia," when she says

> …. The Solntsevo gang runs the gambling business; the Kazan gang makes loans; the Chechen mafia is involved in the export of petroleum, petroleum products, and metals, commercial banking operations, and stolen automobiles; the Azerbaijani groups deal in narcotics, gambling, and trade; the Armenian groups specialize in the theft of automobiles, fraud, and bribes; the Georgians are into burglaries, robbery, and hostage taking; the Ingush specialize in procuring gold and trading in precious metals and weapons transactions; and Dagestani groups are into extortion and theft.[15]

Almost all of the article's 30 endnotes—with the exception of one—came from newspaper articles. There is no indication that the information taken from those articles was questioned, challenged, or otherwise investigated for veracity. Moreover, it would seem that the vast majority of that information carried in the press came directly from a single law enforcement report that circulated around Moscow in 1996 (which will be presented in more detail below). Kryshtanovskaya continues,

> The territorial division of Russia into 'zones of influence' has become another characteristic feature of the present stage of development of illegal structures. The Kemerovo group (in Novorossiisk), the Omsk group (in Poberezh'e), the Chechen group and the Abkhazian group (in Krasnodar), and certain others are operating in Krasnodarsk Krai. St. Petersburg has three large groups: the Tam-

---

15. Olga Kryshtanovskaya, "Illegal Structures in Russia," *Sociological Research*, July–August 1996, p. 66.

bov, Chechen, and Kazan groups, which control the entire city. Five large criminal groups operating in Moscow have divided the municipal districts in accordance with their official administrative status. There are forty-nine permanent criminal groups operating in the Moscow suburbs.[16]

I had a difficult time accepting this picture. Phrases like "control the entire city" and "*permanent* criminal groups" (emphasis added) required further explanation and fed into the notion that the situation had become static as opposed to the very flexible and dynamic situation that it was. While groups consolidated throughout the 1990s, particularly after the very bloody period of 1992–1994, the drawing of such neat lines seemed far too simplistic. Surely the Solntsevo weren't the only ones running gambling operations. And while the Armenians may have been involved in "fraud and bribes," so was every other noteworthy group. The commission of fraud and the giving of bribes were the lifelines of most of the groups. Former Moscow City criminal investigator Gorkin says of such depictions, "Every time I read '… the city was divided into …' without mentioning WHO in the hell had done the handy work of 'dividing' and WHO kept the borders secure, and WHO created the transparent areas of mutual interaction and cooperation, I had to take the reporting with a grain of salt."[17]

As we saw in Chapter 4, estimates of the numbers of groups and numbers of individuals reportedly involved varied sharply and fell dramatically toward the end of the century. While part of this was likely the result of the consolidation of the underworld, part of it was also likely a corrective of sorts in the counting of crime groups and their members. As with the overall figures, estimates of the size of the groups themselves were never a good indicator of the strength and influence of criminal groups. With such disarray in the country throughout the 1990s, how did grossly underpaid and widely corrupted police officers learn about and accurately track thousands of criminals? How did these officers depict the relative strength of groups or account for what was occurring inside the groups after each change in leadership, after an internal disagreement, or after a shootout in which several group members were killed?

So here we are with the issue of the size of a group. Of course, the question of what constituted a 'member' would easily cloud the issue. Was it any individual who ever worked for or received payment from the group? Did it

---

16. Ibid.
17. Author conversation with Gorkin, December 2006.

have to be someone who worked for that particular group exclusively? What about the groups that cooperated with each other on a short-term basis, were they being counted as one large group?

The Solntsevo group was one of the best known and most feared groups of the 1990s. The group was believed to have had members in a number of countries including Italy and the United States, and was said to have a close relationship with the *vor v zakone* Vyacheslav Ivankov and high-ranking police officials, among others. Their profile increased even more when one of its alleged leaders, Sergei Mikhailov, was seen in the Russian business newspaper, *Kommersant*, alongside the president of Costa Rica, having presented himself as honorary Russian consul to that country. He gained additional notoriety after having been arrested in Switzerland, put on trial, and acquitted of all charges in 1998.

The Solntsevo group provides an interesting illustration regarding this question of size and membership. In July 2004, an article appeared in *Moscow News* on the state of organized crime in Russia and featured a sidebar on the Solntsevo group. The sidebar said that the group had around 5,000 members. It didn't give any indication of how a group this large functioned, how members communicated, how it was structured, or, for that matter, where the figure came from. One thing in the article cautioned me to take care with that figure. The author writes, "Its leader is believed to be Sergei Mikhailov, known as Mikhas, who is currently being held by the authorities in Switzerland." As noted above, Mikhailov had been acquitted of all charges and had been released in December 1998. This 2004 article carried information from more than six years earlier but did not indicate to the readers that what was being passed off as 'news' was really very dated material.[18]

Compared to the account of former Solntsevo member Iosif Roizis, this figure of 5,000 members was somewhat on the conservative side. Roizis claimed that the group had 9,000 members.[19] Other sources cited a somewhat lesser figure for the size of the group. In an article called, "Major Mafia Gangs in Russia," author Guy Dunn calls the Solntsevo "the largest single gang in the country" and "the best equipped." He goes on to say that the group had 3,500–4,000 members.[20] In her article, sociologist Kryshtanovskaya reports

18. Oleg Liakhovich, "A Mob by Any Other Name," *Moscow News*, July 21–24, 2004, accessed in Johnson's Russia List.

19. Cited in Federico Varese, *The Russian Mafia: Private Protection in a New Market Economy*, Oxford, Oxford University Press, 2001, p. 170.

20. Guy Dunn, "Major Mafia Gangs in Russia," in Phil Williams (ed.), *Russian Organized Crime: The New Threat?* London, Frank Cass, 1997, p. 68.

that the size of the group was 2,000,[21] while Gorkin, the former criminal investigator, said there were more like 700 members in the group.[22] All of these figures derived from sources reporting at essentially the same point in time, 1995–1996. Interestingly, some sources were also claiming in 1995 that the whole of the organized crime world had only 20–25,000 members (see Chapter 4).

According to a document obtained from an FSB (former KGB) agent and labeled 'Secret,' there were 250 members in the group, of which about 180 were active, as well as "a similar number of associated members in small independent brigades (groups) not belonging to Solntsevo but using the reputation of Solntsevo to their advantage."[23] According to the document, the appearance of 'Solntsevo impersonators' had become a serious problem. Presumably, this weakened Solntsevo's ability to manage its reputation or, perhaps more likely, this meant that Solntsevo was not receiving any compensation from those using their name. According to Vadim Volkov, the Solntsevo charged a fee, in a kind of franchising scheme, to smaller groups that wanted to represent themselves as Solntsevo. For the small group it was beneficial as it increased its apparent power—the fear factor—and for the Solntsevo it was beneficial as it disseminated its reputation further than might have otherwise been the case. According to the document received from the FSB, "Most small criminal groups active in Moscow 'subscribed' to the Solntsevo, which could unite no less than 600 people."[24]

According to the vast majority of reports on group size, individual criminal groups themselves (as opposed to 'organized crime groups') were relatively small. According to MVD information from the late 1980s and early 1990s, exposed groups consisted of 7–8 people on average.[25] For example, in 1988, police in Odessa arrested a group of 11 people which in 1986–87 committed crimes dressed as police officers and engaged in theft under the guise of searches of apartments, particularly in Moscow and St. Petersburg (at that time Leningrad). In fact, three of the members were former police officers, having been discharged from the force between 1982 and 1986.[26] In September 1993, it was re-

---

21. Kryshtanovskaya, p. 67 (note 15).

22. Author conversation with Gorkin, June 1996.

23. "Sekretno—Obzornaya Spravka v Otnoshenii t.n. 'Solntsevskoi' Mezhregional'noi Prestupnoi Gruppirovki," p. 1.

24. Ibid., pp. 6–7

25. Vyacheslav Komissarov in G. Min'kovskii (ed.), Bor'ba s Organizovannoi Prestupnost'iu: Problemy Teorii i Praktiki, Moskva, Akademiya Ministerstva Vnutrennykh Del SSSR, 1990, p. 49–50.

26. Ibid., p. 50.

ported that "about 100 major organized criminal groups are now operating in Moscow,"[27] while a year later there was said to be "12 large criminal entities in Moscow, each with about 200–300 members. Another 30 groups with 20–30 members are also on the streets."[28] Many had less than 10 members while the average in 1994 was up to about 20 people, according to Chebotaryov.[29]

In Chapter 4, it was mentioned that a November 1995 *Sevodnya* newspaper article outlined seven ethnic crime communities (*obshchina*) (Georgian, Azeri, Armenian, Chechen, Ingush, Dagestani, Ossetian) consisting of 116 organized crime groups. There were approximately 2,000 active members involved. The article went on to say that for the first nine months of 1995, 101 criminal groups were 'liquidated' in which there were 335 active members. Among the 'liquidated' groups were 16 Chechen (58 people), 12 Georgian (47 people), 12 Armenian (41 people), 11 Dagestani (28 people), and 6 Azeri (14 people).[30] These groups, it would seem, consisted of only 3–5 people, assuming the entire group was 'liquidated.'

As an example closer to the Luneev depiction of an 'organized crime group,' in August 1995, one of the groups within the so-called Vorkutinsky criminal community was broken up. Eleven people were detained, including a 29-year-old subway engineer and a businessman; the rest were unemployed residents of St. Petersburg. One member was accused of the April 1993 attempted murder of a businessman and the murder of his bodyguard. In spring 1994, five members kidnapped a businessman, demanding $32,000 in ransom. In June 1994, the group kidnapped two residents of St. Petersburg and held them for a month in an apartment specially used for that purpose.

By the end of 1995, Moscow Regional Organized Crime Control Department region reportedly registered 189 active criminal groups, 11 of which were based on the ethnic backgrounds of their members, 62 were based on geography, and 23 groups reportedly had international connections. The total number of people involved was 3,500. The notion of organized crime was also illustrated by the 41 crime groups that reportedly united into nine criminal organizations. They were operating primarily in the Moscow suburbs as well as in the city of Moscow, and in Germany, Switzerland, and Israel.[31] Smaller

---

27. *TASS*, "Some 100 Criminal Groups Operate in Moscow," September 16, 1993.

28. Paul Norton, "Crimewise," *Moscow Tribune*, November 10, 1994, p. 8.

29. Author conversation with Gennady Chebotaryov, October 1995.

30. *Sevodnya*, "Kavkazskaya Prestupnost' v Moskve Ustupaet 'Slavianskoi,'" November 16, 1995, p. 6.

31. *Sevodnya*, "Na Territorii Podmoskov'ia Deistvuyet 189 Banditskikh Grupp," February 24, 1996, p. 5.

groups generally tended to operate in a limited geographic area and were self-contained. It was common, however, for larger organizations to coerce these smaller groups into providing a share of their profits in return for permission to conduct their criminal activities, as in the Solntsevo example above. Geographic commonality was also observed in the Tushinsky group in the mid-1990s. Most of the 60–70 members were residents of the northwest administrative region of Moscow.[32]

The Tushinsky group provides an interesting example of the nature of organized crime from a structure and membership perspective. Individual members set up their own companies in order to launder money and they maintained contacts with fellow criminals around the world. One member along with one of the group's leaders coordinated the recruitment of new members in the area, while another member acted as liaison with numerous other Moscow groups and was involved in dispute settlement. The group had direct contact with law enforcement and used the services of a *vor v zakone* to gain access to President Yeltsin's representative in one of the regions of Russia. The *vor*'s younger brother was an advisor to a prominent member of the legislature (Duma) and had connections to other Duma members. A senior member of the Tushinsky crime group was also a leader of the Koptevo group.

While organized crime had gained a reputation for sweeping across the country, it was not a united front engaged in a vast conspiracy. As noted in Chapter 1, it was not the actions of the MVD's Organized Crime Control Department that held in check the formation of a single, massive organization. It was the legacy of distrust built up over centuries, among other factors, that guaranteed the criminal world wouldn't and couldn't work cooperatively on a nationwide scale. Competition over clients and markets spurred violent clashes between groups—the so-called gangland shootouts. According to a member of St. Petersburg's Tambovsky organization, in-fighting among criminal groups in the 1990s had done a lot more to diminish their ranks than any government measures.[33]

It was also easy and perhaps convenient to forget that the groups, like any collection of people, were internally delicate, subject to jealousies, conflicts, and tempers. It didn't help that many of them were drug users and frequently were surrounded by weapons, a lethal combination. Beyond that, groups were

32. *GUVD Moscow*, "Analiticheskaya Spravka, 'Tushinskaya' Organizovannaya Prestupnaya Gruppirovka," 1996.

33. Vsevolod Sokolov, "From Guns to Briefcases: The Evolution of Russian Organized Crime," *World Policy Journal*, spring 2004, vol. 21, no. 1, at http://galenet.galegroup.com/servlet/HistRC.

not exempt from the forces that played on any organization. There were gen-
erational splits both within and between groups that frequently led to different approaches to criminal enterprises. There were ethnic divisions even in
some of the most notorious 'ethnic' groups. (Most of these groups were by no
means 'pure' ethnic groups.) Each shootout involving the death of important
players in the groups led to changing leaderships and shifts in loyalties. There
was little that was static about these groups, particularly given the volatile
times in which they were operating, the shifting markets, the struggle for territory, and other factors.[34] For example, according to an investigator in the
Russian Far East, the powerful *vor v zakone* Evgeny Vasin ('Dzhem') reportedly dismissed his emissary (*polozhenets*) Vladimir Podatiev ('Poodle') from
the group in 1995 and had him thrown out of Khabarovsk. Poodle had been
controlling all of Dzhem's money funds (*obshchaka*) but started to express political ambitions, to Dzhem's dissatisfaction.[35] "Fear was the key. Gangsters
never trusted each other, and their bosses didn't trust them either."[36]

Alexander Gorkin, the former Moscow police detective who spent much of
the 1980s and 1990s investigating some of the best known crime figures in the
former Soviet Union, understood very well the internal workings of the crime
groups as well as the psychology of the players. "As with most other aspects of
life in the Soviet Union," he said, "Every crime boss tried to represent himself
as a 'part' of a unified group, something planned, organized, and highly structured from above and built from the bottom up. But, the 'stability' was really
very fragile, built on dead bodies and glued with blood, and, as we know, these
are not the best construction materials from which to build something good."[37]

Yuri Esin understood the shaky ground his organization was built on. This
Moscow-based "envoy to Rome" of the Solntsevo group made a permanent move
to Italy out of fear of internal conflicts with fellow members of the organization's
leadership.[38] And members of the Orekhovo organization understood it when
their structure disintegrated into smaller warring groups in the early 1990s.[39]

Generally speaking, crime groups ranged from influential, ambitious, and
talented to incompetent, opportunistic, and short-lived. Russia was rife with

---

34. See ibid.

35. Author investigative information.

36. Author conversation with Gorkin, July 2006.

37. Ibid.

38. Federico Varese, "There is No Place like Home: How Mafia Finds it Difficult to Ex-
pand from its Geographical Place," *Times Literary Supplement*, February 23, 2000, http://
www.colbud.hu/honesty-trust/varese/pub02.htm.

39. See Nikolai Modestov, *Moskva Banditskaya: Dokumental'naya Khronika Kriminal'nogo Bespredela 80-90-kh Godov*, Moskva, Tsentrpoligraf, 1996, pp. 176–182.

anecdotal stories of gangs resembling the Keystone Cops: the gangs that kidnapped an individual and released him to make a phone call to arrange payment, or the gangs that drank themselves into oblivion after a kidnapping and the victim simply walked away from the scene. These gangs were legion and dangerous enough in their own ways, but they were not the ones ultimately to be concerned about as part of the fabric of organized crime. The organizations that we think of when we speak of 'organized crime' didn't emerge in their full glory until the dust of The Great Mob War began to settle.

In mid-1996, a document providing the names of major Moscow crime groups, their structures, members, activities, and the location of their headquarters appeared in Russian law enforcement circles. It is important to remember that the organization and presentation of the information was a law enforcement version. From a statistics point of view, some might have counted the first organization mentioned below as a single group; others might have considered it to be thirteen different crime groups. It was a loosely-affiliated criminal association consisting of various groups. According to the original document, which contained the names of the members, there seemed to be some sharing of personnel among the groups and agreements of cooperation among them. Associations were typically dominated by a single nationality or ethnic group, whether Russian, Chechen, Dagestani, Armenian, Georgian, and so on. According to this law enforcement interpretation, the leadership of the association divided Moscow into distinct districts. Police believed that all of the groups in this particular structure shared a common *obshchak* and that one boss oversaw the association.

Southern District
- group of up to 15 people; extortion

Central District
- group of up to 20 people; extortion; main headquarters: offices of a private company;
- group of up to 15 people; drug dealing; main headquarters: major Moscow hotel;
- group of up to 10 people; extortion, weapons dealing; main headquarters: a Moscow restaurant

Southwest District
- group of up to 15 people; involvement in commercial banks; main headquarters: bank and a café;

- group of up to 15 people; sale of stolen foreign cars;
- group of up to 20 people; extortion; main headquarters: foreign car repair center;
- group of up to 40 people; weapons and drug dealing, extortion; main headquarters: café, restaurant, and marketplace;
- group of up to 30 people; armed dispute settlement with other groups, involvement in private companies; main headquarters: a restaurant and a café

Northern District

- group of up to 15 people; auto theft and resale in other Russian cities; main headquarters: two Moscow hotels;
- group of up to 15 people; extortion; main headquarters: restaurant and major Moscow hotel

Northeast District

- group of up to 10 people; extortion, hostage-taking; main headquarters: office of a private company;
- group of up to 30 people; extortion; main headquarters: on territory of southern and northeast districts

Other activities of the structure included debt collection and illegal financial operations, such as using false *avizo* (see Chapter 8). Vast amounts of money made in Russia were sent abroad through their own companies. Some money was returned to Russia in the form of investment or was used to purchase real estate in foreign countries.

In 1995, law enforcement reportedly broke up 12 of these groups. This particular criminal structure had close ties abroad, especially in the United States.

Typically each group within the association had its own name, usually taken from the name of the restaurant, hotel, or geographic district where they were headquartered. Sometimes the name came from the group itself, and sometimes it was assigned by law enforcement in the course of an investigation for identification purposes. Adding up the total number of people involved in the various groups led one to conclude that there were some 250 members in this association.

When examining the full document, which contained the names of all the individuals in the various groups, it quickly became clear that there was sharing of members among groups and occasionally a single individual headed up several groups. This complicated the law enforcement task of accurately identifying relationships within associations or groups. In fact, most groups seemed to have relatively few core members who controlled key elements of the groups such as the flow of information, money, weapons, and contacts. It also illustrated the wide-ranging activities that a single association pursued. Even if law enforcement were to be successful in 'liquidating' or 'neutralizing' five of these groups, eight would still remain to carry on the work of the association.

Another organization was known for its control over the produce, fruit, and consumer goods markets in Moscow. This presence tended to spill over into nearby hotels that the structure also became involved in. The individual groups collected monthly payments from vendors at these markets, which were also convenient locations for drug dealing.

The following is a more detailed look at the group's structure as reported by law enforcement:

Southern District

- group of up to 40 people; narcotics, extortion;
- group of up to 30 people; financial/economic crime (false avizo);
- group of up to 50 people; fencing operations, food trade;
- group of up to 10 people; extortion

Southeast District

- group of up to 20 people; fencing operations, drug dealing;
- group of up to 20 people; active members were registered as officers of private companies;
- group controls sales of all vegetables in a Moscow neighborhood

Western District

- group of up to 50 people; theft and trade in auto transport, spare parts, control trade in vegetables;
- group of up to 30 people; auto theft; main headquarters: major Moscow hotel;
- group of up to 40 people; control major Moscow market, extortion, drug dealing;
- group of up to 20 people; drug dealing, extortion

At the time the information was collected, it was known that an assistant to a state Duma deputy was an *avtoritet* of the group. He was arrested in June 1995 in a cemetery with another member of the group. They had four firearms and a silencer.

In a review of 30 Moscow-based groups, the following characteristics were noted:

- There seemed to be from 1 to 12 leaders depending on the size of the organization and number of groups;
- Group leaders or organization leaders (*avtoritety*) of major crime organizations were also identified as paramount leaders of other, smaller groups;
- Authoritative figures in groups were frequently listed as employees or owners of private companies;
- Leaders actively developed connections with politicians both in Russia and abroad;
- Creation of groups within an organization occurred actively on a wide scale from approximately 1993 to 1997;
- Most major organizations had groups frequently consisting of 5–25 people;
- There was considerable interaction among both groups and organizations, including sharing of personnel, engaging in joint criminal and commercial activities, and assisting each other in *razborki* (violent dispute settlements)
- Internal disagreements frequently resulted in fighting, shooting, explosions, and murder within groups;
- While there were family ties among some members, connections were primarily based on physical proximity (neighborhood, school, work, prison) or based on shared ethnic background;
- Groups frequently used major hotels, restaurants and private companies as headquarters;
- Activities pursued by criminal groups were numerous and diverse;
- Monetary resources were used to promote their own people to positions of real economic power or to influence those already in place;
- A significant portion of financial resources (30–50%) was earmarked for bribing officials and supporting group members and their families;
- In addition to bribing officials, groups actively placed their own members within state agencies such as the police, procuracy, court system, military;
- Groups used a wide range of contacts in the Russian government and vast financial resources to gain access to distribution of quotas, licenses, credit, conversion of hard currency, theft of monetary resources;
- Groups were intimately involved in major infrastructure development projects including real estate development, reconstruction of ports, influence on management of major factories and metallurgical plants, and so on;
- Groups were closely intertwined with banks, companies, and government institutions;

- Groups were well-armed, well-equipped and highly mobile;
- Activity abroad was an increasingly important feature of the most successful and power groups.

We could choose any number of criminal organizations that were active in Russia in the 1990s as an illustration of the general contours of criminal organizations. The Koptevo group formed in the mid-1970s as a small gang without much hierarchical structure to speak of or particularly significant financial interests. Their activities were limited to small local crimes such as petty theft and low-level extortion. The group was a neighborhood gang of sorts begun and controlled by three sets of brothers: the Morozovs, the Deviatkins, and the Naumovs.

As was the case with many crime groups, the Koptevo group developed its network of contacts and expanded its economic interests at the beginning of the Gorbachev period, starting in 1985. One of the first leaders was the *vor v zakone* Viktor Dolzhenikov and an *avtoritet* who went by the nickname 'Potema.' The main part of the group was reportedly composed of representatives of small, local gangs, usually ex-convicts as well as athletes. Koptevo found common cause with the so-called Dolgoprudnensky group, a relationship that would become the basis for the long-term development of the group's structure both vertically and horizontally.

Internal conflict in the late 1980s and early 1990s brought brothers Alexander and Vasily Naumov to the fore of the organization, at a time when the Slavic groups were reportedly clashing with groups from the Caucasus Mountain region (like the Chechens, Ingushetians, and others) as well as Asians. In the early 1990s, groups were moving quickly to legalize the large sums of money they were making from extortion. They set up businesses and created partnerships with former district Communist Party officials to use their influence and contacts. Toward the middle of 1993 the group reportedly counted around 200 people with specific functions and roles delineated.

The Koptevo organization was reportedly divided into 6 smaller groups, each of which controlled its own territory in the northern administrative district and other parts of Moscow. They also worked in cooperation with other groups in the Moscow suburbs where they reportedly had strong, stable, reliable commercial positions and men on the ground. Exemplifying some of Luneev's characteristics, the group had an identifiable structure with separate intelligence and counterintelligence functions. Developing relationships with the power structures at this time was relatively easy as the agencies were under constant reorganization, morale was low, and the economy was experiencing a period more dramatic than the Great Depression of the 1930s. As most other hardcore criminal organizations, the Koptevo group had heavy firepower, including Kalashnikovs that had been stolen from military bases. Members of the Koptevo group were active with the Solntsevo in running enterprises at Sheremetievo 1 & 2, Moscow's international and domestic airports. They also set up charities through which to launder money, which quickly became a common practice around the country. Internationally, they had contacts in Germany, Austria, and Hong Kong where they created a number of trading companies (including both legal and illegal products).

According to law enforcement information, one of the leaders of the Koptevo group, Stepan Murmansky, was in partnership with the leader of the Odintsovsky group in an auto service center, the kind of commercial enterprise organized crime groups were frequently involved in. As an example of the influence of criminal leaders as mentioned in Chapter 7, Murmansky was said to support inmates at Vladimir Central Prison, sending drugs, food, and vodka behind the walls. When the *vor v zakone* by the nickname of 'Tsitska' was released from Vladimir Central, Murmansky reportedly sent a number of foreign luxury cars to escort him from the prison to a local Vladimir restaurant.

In the throes of the so-called Great Mob War, the Koptevo, like many other organizations, were active in staking out their turf and clashing with both police and other groups. In November 1993, several members opened fire with a pump-action shotgun at a police vehicle that was tailing them, injuring one officer.

At the beginning of 1994, police in the local precinct begin to bring pressure to bear on the Koptevo. Activities of the group were severely interrupted and many of the members were arrested. However, the group did not collapse because most of them were eventually set free due to inadequacies in the law, the weak court system, and active assistance by *avtoritety* and corrupt officials (see Chapter 11). For example, during one of the police raids, 20 members were arrested during a meeting (*skhodka*) at which they were planning investment of their criminal proceeds into legitimate businesses. Police seized weapons and 200,000 German marks which were believed to be used for bribes to local officials. Eventually, all 20 members were let go.

Difficulties for the Koptevo would continue throughout the 1990s. In November 1994, the group's *avtoritet*, 'Solovei,' was shot dead. In March 1995, one of the group's leaders, Alexander Naumov, was killed as a result of an ongoing and escalating business dispute with another crime group. In August 1995, two more leaders of the group were gunned down in their car and burned. Shortly thereafter, 'Kornei,' one of the influential members of the group, died from a drug overdose. (The use and abuse of narcotics was a common feature in many criminal organizations.) In December 1996, police found bodies of three Koptevo members buried in the cement floor of a sauna.

After the death of Alexander Naumov, his brother Vasily reportedly took over financial control of the group, overseeing in particular the auto service center and a trade company. According to Polonium-210 poisoning victim and former KGB agent Alexander Litvinenko, and his co-author, the historian Yuri Felshtinsky, Vasily Naumov was one of the many underworld figures who cooperated with the MVD. Part of the reason for the relationship seemed to be attributed to the active gang rivalries of the day. Not only were the Slavic groups engaged in a struggle with the Caucasians, naturally there was tension among many of the Slavic groups. At one point, one group had reportedly gained the confidence of the Koptevo, learned of all their sources of income, and then started murdering the heads of the various crime groups within the Koptevo organization in an effort to take over their interests. Naumov supposedly became a police informant, giving up his rivals in an effort to ensure his group's survival. According to law enforcement sources, the FSB was overseeing the main rival and intervened because its group was in danger of being destroyed and was concerned that news of its involvement with the group would create a scandal. Through its own investigations, the FSB learned that the information was being fed to the police by Naumov. In January 1997, Naumov was gunned down in his car in front of Moscow city police headquarters reportedly while waiting for his contact in the department. As it turns out, all of his bodyguards were members of an elite police commando team called Saturn.

In 1997, the activities of the group fell off dramatically as a result of the murders of the leadership and measures taken by law enforcement against the group. Some of the last reporting on the Koptevo group relates the tension between the group and Slava Ubogii, a former member of the Mazutkinsky group who had been working closely with the Tushinsky group. Apparently, the Koptevo owed Slava a significant amount of money, and he was essentially trying to become a member of the group, pledging his loyalty as a way to forgive the Koptevo debt. The Koptevo used another tried-and-true method of releasing themselves from the debt—they killed Slava Ubogii.

At around the same time, Koptevo members found themselves in desperate straits as 'Zema' landed on the national wanted list, and was believed to have fled to Spain or Austria, where he set up a string of businesses using front people. 'Staryi,' 'Apelsin,' and 'Melz' also found themselves on the list and went into hiding abroad. 'Alex Borodin' was found in a Mercedes with a gunshot to the head. Police moved against two other members of the group who were responsible for several murders in Moscow. During one of the arrests police found a revolver, grenade, and three ampoules of narcotics. This particular individual was a key member who was later tied to a number of other crimes the group had committed.[40]

As in other countries around the world, crime groups in the former Soviet Union grew up in response to conditions in their surrounding environment. In Part II, we looked at general conditions in pre-1917 Russia in order to establish that vast criminality was not an invention of the Communists in the Soviet era. We discussed the Soviet period in order to demonstrate that the underworld did not form as a reaction to the disappearance of the Soviet Union; it existed long before the USSR ceased to exist. But it is also clear that during the period of great confusion, The Great Mob War of 1992–1994, criminal organizations became far more intertwined with the upperworld than previously. Toward the end of the decade, as the country started to find its footing, many of the small crime groups had disappeared or consolidated into larger organizations and the major settling of scores was largely finished. After exposure to the screaming headlines of the 1990s, would it come as a surprise to know that many major crime figures got into business quietly and by invitation rather than by 'gangster methods' and 'gangland shootouts'?

---

40. "Analiticheskaya Spravka o Kharaktere Deyatel'nosti Koptevskoi OPG po Sostoy-aniiu na 30.03.98 (Istoriya, Genezis, Perspektiva Dal'neishei Razrabotki) k Materialam po Meropriyatiyami Svyazannymi s Rasstrelom u Bara 'Dolina' 12.01.98, ul. Novopetrovskaya, 6; Dmitry Kuibyshev, "Vora Podvela Rokovaya Strast' k Oruzhiiu," *Kommersant Daily*, November 10, 1995, p. 14; *The Minnesota Daily Online*, "Gang Leader Shot in Front of Moscow Police Headquarters," January 24, 1997; Mark Galeotti, "Raising the Roof: The Rise of the Russian Private Security Industry," *Crime and Justice International*, vol. 22, no. 95, November/December 2006, p. 11.

CHAPTER 10

BUSINESS

We are an adolescent people. In any culture, adolescents are not very much concerned about moral rules or property and are more prone to base their behavior on force and violence. Force is the main regulator of Russian civilization. The respect for property isn't firmly established here as an important human right.

—Leonid Sedov[1]

We have always lived under market conditions. It never disappeared anywhere, but was only driven into the economic underground by administration methods … thus escaping from any kind of social control. As a result, market relations have acquired quite a barbaric and plundering character, being solely controlled by the corrupted bureaucracy, acting in alliance with the shadow economy bosses.

—V. Arslanov and A. Frolov[2]

In Chapter 6, I laid out some of the features of the Soviet economy as it looked between 1930 and the 1980s. The command economy was the cornerstone to rapidly industrializing the country and maintaining control over the population. A serious consequence of the command economy as it was practiced in the Soviet Union was that in many cases factories were placed great distances from the raw materials. Hundreds of miles came between farms and storage facilities. Stalin's paranoia about virtually anyone else in the country gaining power was absolute. The economy itself was a political and military tool, not a mechanism by which to meet consumer demands. And so we find countless examples of how this contributed to shortages of goods. To give just one simple illustration, hypodermic syringes were produced at one end of the

---

1. Richard C. Paddock, "In Russia, Stealing is a Normal Part of Life," *Los Angeles Times*, September 21, 1998, accessed at Johnson's Russia List.

2. V. Arslanov and A. Frolov, "Are Shadow Dealers Pressurizing Bureaucrats?" *Ekonomika i Zhizn'*, no. 31, 1990, p. 10.

country while needles were produced at the other. "Transportation costs for assembly, then shipment, are exorbitant. Worse yet, the syringes do not fit the needles producing critical shortages."[3]

Whole cities grew up around the manufacture of single products leaving the availability of goods uneven across the economy. For the outer lying regions the dilemma was exacerbated by the cost of transport, an inadequate infrastructure, and the chronic shortage of parts for modes of transport. As Noreena Hertz notes, "There are many settlements and even fair-sized towns that are the socialist equivalent of company towns."[4] Because the economy was held captive to the Five Year Plans and production was highly concentrated, delays or shutdowns at a single factory would produce significant ripple effects throughout that sector of the economy and beyond, strengthening the underground economy. In their book, *Red Tape*, Bill Thomas and Charles Sutherland provide a list of sample items and their production locations to illustrate the point.[5]

Product	Source	Production Percentage
Cigarette filters	Armenia	100
Oil-well pumps	Azerbaijan	100
Electric irons	Kaliningrad	93
Die-casting machines	Moldova	99
Tramway rails	Russia	100
Sewing machines	Russia	100
Forklifts	Ukraine	86
Corn harvesters	Ukraine	100
Cotton harvesters	Uzbekistan	100

When the Soviet Union disappeared, so too did easy access to a wide variety of items produced in the various republics. Whereas the republics listed above had all been part of the same country, by the end of 1991, they were independent. And as the Soviet Union raced toward its final days, state control over industries was weakening dramatically. Individuals—bureaucrats, gangsters, and others—stepped forward to claim ownership. Since Commu-

---

3. Terry F. Buss, "Exporting American Economic Development Practice to Russia," *Policy Studies Review*, Autumn, vol. 18, no. 3, 2001, p. 99.

4. Noreena Hertz, *Russian Business Relationships in the Wake of Reform*, Oxford, St. Anthony Series, 1996, p. 9.

5. Bill Thomas and Charles Sutherland, *Red Tape: Adventure Capitalism in the New Russia*, New York, Dutton, 1992, p. 200.

nist ideology did not, and by definition could not, allow for private ownership of industry, there was little developed legal infrastructure to uphold the
claims of the new owners. These new 'entrepreneurs' were essentially acquiring everything they could get their hands on and calling it their own. Virtually the only way to gain control over these properties, especially the major industrial concerns—and maintain that control—was through Party contacts,
fraud, coercion, and violence. Much of the 'mafia' activity in the late 1980s
and 1990s was obviously part of the larger struggle for property. In some cases,
traditional crime groups were working independently for their own piece of
the pie. In many other cases, though, they were being mobilized by the bu-
reaucrats-cum-businessmen to protect their ill-gotten property. The gangs
provided protection in an ongoing business arrangement rather than engaging in merely short-term extortion; in many cases, they were the front men
hired to do the dirty work of former Communist Party officials. And traditional mechanisms of social control (e.g., MVD, KGB) were themselves choos-
ing sides, fully engaged in the same struggle, lining up their men, their networks, and their guns behind various former Communist Party officials,
bureaucrats, gangsters, and businessmen.

The point is that, first, business has never occupied a central role in society in the same way as in the West, whether in pre-1917 Russia (Chapter 5),
the Soviet period (Chapter 6), or in the present-day Russian Federation. Second, the inadequacy of the Russian infrastructure combined with the highly
centralized and poorly coordinated industries across the country meant that
anyone who could bridge the gaps, anyone who could get access to goods and
deliver them to market, stood to make fantastic sums of money (or die trying). Third, the threats to the business world were coming from every direction, including gangsters, businessmen, bureaucrats, former Communist
Party officials, state security and policing, and others, since all of them in one
way or other were trying to bridge those gaps. In this way, criminal groups
(whether traditional groups or Vaksberg's 'mafia') fought for control over
countless markets (whether for themselves or as proxies), not just alcohol, narcotics, or gambling. Fourth, many foreign businesspeople, whether as single-
person companies or employed by major industries, had little idea how to nav-
igate through the swamp of the Russian commercial world. It must be said
that, in the context of these four points, activities such as gangland shootouts,
contract murders, and so on, were part of the tool kit of businessmen of the
1990s, not the exclusive use of criminal groups that were 'invading' the country. One businessman-bureaucrat pitted against another used the gangsters to
settle their scores. Irving Kristol's 'mafia' (see opening quote in Chapter 1) had
taken over the country in 1917 and Stephen Handelman's Comrade Criminal

in the post-Soviet world had perfected the mutual cooperation between the Communist Party 'mafia' and traditional gangsters in what has been called a 'criminal-syndicalist state.'[6]

Against this backdrop it was interesting to watch in 1998 and 1999 as the former minister of a major Soviet industry continued his decade-long attempts to privatize the entire industrial sector that he previously oversaw as a state official and all of its networks across Russia as well as those in some of the former republics. He successfully convinced, threatened, or otherwise did away with numerous factory directors across the country in his quest to place his own people in these positions. One director was particularly stubborn and refused to capitulate. Their struggle was played out in the newspapers as both sides commissioned journalists to plant biased articles in various publications. The minister called in the tax police to lean on the director. When the situation heated up further, the minister threatened the director's family, who promptly and wisely fled the country. The minister was protected by government officials and a full complement of former KGB agents in the form of a private security company. The director stood fast, gradually securing his position in part through the dramatically improving performance of his factory. He is still director today.[7]

While the former minister was fighting to take over his industry, we in the West were touting the increase in the number of businesses in Russia. The mere number of companies was somehow a key component as proof of the establishment of a free market economy. But thousands of companies actually engaged in no activity whatever and never intended to. Front companies were held in reserve for a convenient moment, used for a single operation, used to smuggle goods across borders, used only to establish joint ventures which did not engage in business or were used as figureheads in auctions for major industrial concerns.

According to Chebotaryov, the former Deputy Chief of the MVD's Organized Crime Control Department, the vast majority of cooperatives and joint ventures at the end of the 1980s and beginning of the 1990s had been established by Communist Party officials and criminals primarily for signing fraudulent contracts with partners both in Russia and abroad as well as for moving massive amounts of both 'dirty' money (money laundering) and 'clean' money (capital flight), whether stolen from the Party, gotten through criminal means, or simply sent abroad to avoid the tax police.[8] And this should have come as

---

6. Jurg Gerber, "On the Relationship between Organized and White-Collar Crime: Government, Business, and Criminal Enterprise in Post-Communist Russia," *European Journal of Crime, Criminal Law and Criminal Justice*, vol. 8, no. 4, 2000, pp. 327–342.

7. Author investigative information.

8. Author conversation with Chebotaryov, November 1992.

no surprise. The upper reaches of the Party had control over virtually all property and commercial entities. They were free to privatize entire industries as Soviet bureaucratic control mechanisms disappeared and no legitimate authority rose to fill the vacuum. Tracking the shareholder list of a major bank established by Party officials in the 1990s, for example, we saw entities owning 10–20% of the bank, which amounted to tens of millions of dollars, simply disappear without a trace. These shareholding entities were owned by the bank itself and used for a variety of activities other than functioning as an actual business. It was difficult to know who was who and what was what.

And for good reason. In a 1997 report, the Center for Strategic and International Studies (CSIS) presented an illustration they called "The 'Iron Triangle' of Contemporary Russia."[9] The triangle depicted the three major groups that dominated Russian society throughout the 1990s: business, bureaucracy, and crime groups.

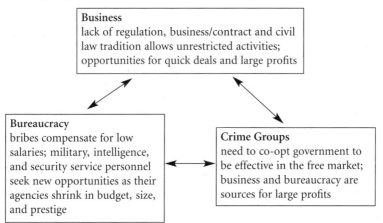

As the CSIS report rightly states, the lines among these three primary actors were frequently blurred, making it difficult to differentiate between the upperworld and underworld. CSIS's point, though, needs to be taken a step further. It's important to note that the very essence of the phenomenon in the 1990s was that these groups were not necessarily fixed in an 'Iron Triangle' arrangement but, rather, frequently merged with each other. Beyond simply blurring, the lines among these three were sometimes erased, so that any two or three of these elements combined and consolidated in a single individual or group. When this occurred, the 'Iron Triangle' collapsed and became a straight line. The members of a crime group were simultaneously business-

9. William H. Webster (ed.), *Russian Organized Crime: Global Organized Crime Project*, Washington, D.C., Center for Strategic and International Studies, 1997, p. 89.

men. Likewise, bureaucrats became members of criminal groups. Instead of a triangle, the various combinations looked as follows:

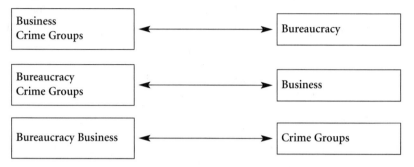

The ultimate merger was the combination of all three in a single individual at which time the 'Iron Triangle' was reduced to a single point.

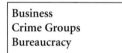

This was the real and lasting impact of the Russian 'mafia.' Russia has not been marching toward democracy since the dismantling of the Soviet Union but rather closer to perfecting the notion of a criminal state. As indicated earlier, crime groups in the Russian context were not necessarily made up of hardened professional criminals. The economic and social dislocations Russia experienced, combined with the historic influences outlined in earlier chapters, encouraged people who would not likely engage in such activity to form criminal enterprises for the purpose of committing crime in the course of pursuing both illegitimate as well as legitimate business goals.

Such crime groups consisted of bureaucrats (loosely defined as agents of the state such as permit and license issuing agencies, criminal justice and state security officials, members of the legislative and executive branches, and others), professionals (lawyers, doctors, engineers), blue-collar workers, and a combination of all three. In addition, there were, of course, criminal groups consisting solely of professional criminals and others that were a mixture of criminals and those bureaucrats and businessmen mentioned above.

Investigations showed that there was considerable movement among these groups. For example, individuals who grew up in families that enjoyed all the privileges of the Communist Party thanks to their parents' elite standing moved easily between worlds, retaining the ability to reach into the elite world for contacts, financing, and government assistance (see, for example, the story of Viktor in Chapter 8). Likewise, career criminals worked closely with businessmen and bureaucrats and in many cases became businessmen or occupied positions in government. There were countless examples of the blurring of the lines, if not the outright merging, of the three actors in the 'Iron Triangle.'

- A long-time economic advisor to the then-Vice President of Russia and himself a member of the legislature had been tried in court four times on fraud charges and was called a particularly dangerous recidivist (*osobo opasnyi retsidivist*) by the court. Despite this, the advisor had a private office in the Kremlin and considerable official authority. Following yet another case of fraud, he fled to Europe.[10]
- One individual who was born in Soviet Georgia worked in the early 1980s as a correspondent for a newspaper specializing in transportation. Beginning in 1985, he worked for a member of the prestigious Council of Writers. At the same time, he was a smuggler of icons and black caviar, working with three other Soviet citizens who were based in West Berlin. In late 1987, he was recruited by the KGB. In exchange for the names of all his contacts and business partners, he was allowed to depart to Europe in 1988. When he returned to Russia, he set up a number of companies, got access to prime real estate through his government contacts, and became one of the wealthiest businessmen in the country and still is today.[11]
- A widely reported case of the lines being blurred among businessmen, bureaucracy, and criminals was that of Vladimir 'The Poodle' Podatiev of Khabarovsk. After spending 17 years in prison camps for theft, armed robbery, and rape, Podatiev emerged as one of the top crime bosses in the Russian Far East and was believed to control much of Khabarovsk's trade. More than that, he formed his own political party, owned a local television station, and reportedly obtained a letter from the Patriarch of the Orthodox Church blessing his charity work. Among the numerous companies he founded, one was a security firm called Svoboda, the Russian word meaning 'freedom,' and even placed an ad in a local newspaper advertising Svoboda's services: "Svoboda is a leading firm in the organization of security and detective services in the Russian Far East. We will help you to collect confidential information about a person or firm of interest to you. We will settle disputes in a fully civilized manner in any region in Russia." He was also reportedly a member of the

---

10. Author investigative information.
11. Author investigative information.

Commission on Human Rights of the Public Chamber of the President of Russia.[12]

- In April 1994, one of the criminal groups under the control of an *avtoritet* and businessman established a political party in Crimea. Official founders were military athletic clubs and associations of Crimea. Presentation of the party's registration was noted with an air show. The President of Crimea, the Minister of Economy of Ukraine, Commander of the Navy, and other influential politicians were on hand. The *avtoritet*-businessman was murdered three months later and one of the President's advisors—also having a criminal background—became the party's leader. Within a month he was murdered. His successor was murdered within a month as well. The activity of the party came to an unceremonious end.[13]

- In one Russian city, a deputy mayor canceled the licenses of the owner of a chain of gas stations although the licenses were fully legitimate and valid. The licenses were divvied up between the private company that was controlled by the deputy mayor and a Chechen crime group. In an unrelated matter, the same deputy mayor threatened to use violence against a businessman unless he sold him a 25% stake in his cellular telephone company.[14]

- Mayors' offices across the country, as well as countless other government agencies, had serious conflicts of interest when it came to business. For example, not only did they hold office overseeing the regulation of business, they were also shareholders in the companies they were regulating. In addition, their relatives and close friends also were entrepreneurs who used the good graces of friends in high office to gain a distinct advantage over their competition. City officials were frequently personally linked to the massive commercial holding structures that provided the city administration with vital services such as insurance policies for public works projects. As city officials, they not only arranged the granting of government loans to private real estate companies under their holding company but naturally ensured that prime real estate was acquired.

---

12. Author investigative information. Olga Kryshtanovskaya, "Illegal Structures in Russia," *Sociological Research*, July–August 1996, pp. 71, 77; David Remnick, *Resurrection: The Struggle for a New Russia*, New York, Random House, 1997, p. 366; Ariel Cohen, "The Purposes of Russian Aid: Supporting Democratic Capitalism," June 22, 1995, at http://www.heritage.org/Research/RussiaandEurasia/BG1041.cfm.

13. Ibid., Kryshtanovskaya, p. 76.

14. Author investigative information.

In Moscow region alone, 22 assistants to deputies of the state legislature and the Moscow City legislature were arrested in 1995 for their criminal activities.[15]

Part of this activity can be explained by pure human greed. But part of it can also be explained by the Russian mentality that grew out of their circumstances over hundreds of years. This was the notion that opportunities must be grabbed immediately because the window of opportunity will close quickly. It was the enduring sense that there was little long-term planning for or faith in the future. It was the age-old survival mentality reasserting itself, this time on an unprecedented scale. Opportunities presented themselves in every sector of the economy and virtually all of the mechanisms of state control and coercion were for sale. The Iron Triangle became impossibly entangled.

For example, Oleg was the founder of an insurance company that, in turn, was the largest shareholder in a regional bank headed by Oleg before 1995 when the bank changed Russian-registered shareholders to off-shore companies. The insurance company was a good example of business affiliations between senior regional industrialists, local government figures, and criminal bosses. Founders of the insurance company were the general director of a commercial entity, three leading crime figures from the strongest crime group in the region, the regional prosecutor, a former deputy minister of transport construction of the Soviet Union, and the deputy chairperson of the regional court who was the wife of the head of the regional criminal investigation department. This type of arrangement was all too common across the country.[16]

Opportunities could be found in every sector of the economy, not the least of which was the oil industry. As illustrated above, this flattened Iron Triangle became prevalent in the last years of the Soviet Union and into the 1990s. In the oil industry, there were no traditional controls to speak of over the export of oil and capital out of the country. The long-existing patterns of corruption spread throughout the bureaucracy and industry, so instead of fulfilling their role of monitoring oil prices established in contracts, the bureaucrats were taking a slice of the pie.[17] Criminal groups were, in many cases, invited to partake in the 'redistribution of state property' while providing a valuable service to their business partners in forcibly removing any ob-

15. Alexander Zhilin, "Russian Organized Crime—A Growth Industry," December 22, 1995, at http://www.amber.ucsf.edu/home/ross/public_html/russia_/ruscrime3.txt

16. Author investigative information.

17. A. Radygin and I. Sidorov, "The Russian Corporate Economy: One Hundred Years of Solitude?" *Russian Social Science Review*, vol. 43, no. 3, May–June 2002, pp. 68–69.

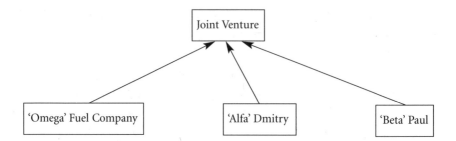

stacles or competition. It was not an invasion by an outside force; the bad guys on the inside were inviting in the bad guys on the outside.

Let's take a look at a simplified version of a complicated situation. In 1989, a joint venture (JV) was established by a Russian company, 'Alfa' (headed up by a Russian citizen, 'Dmitry'), and 'Beta,' based in Liechtenstein (headed up by an Israeli citizen, 'Paul'). The third partner in the JV was 'Omega' Fuel Company.

Paul was an Israeli citizen who had been expelled from Russia for possession of forged passports, visas, and visa invitations. The joint venture itself, involved in the timber industry, was under investigation for fraud. Dmitry moved from Alfa to become a top executive at Omega Fuel Company.

Fast forward three years. In September 1992, 'Money' Financial Company was established. The founders were 'Oil and Gas Bank,' a Moscow-based bank specializing in the oil and gas industry, and a private commercial enterprise, 'National.'

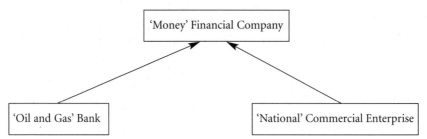

Money underwent several re-registrations and ultimately came under the ownership of 8 individual shareholders, each holding a 12.5% stake. One of the shareholders in Money, Boris, was responsible for implementing the decisions taken by three of the other shareholders. These three other shareholders were the chairman of the board of Oil and Gas Bank who had ties to a major traditional crime group and two other shareholders known by law enforcement agencies to be leading members of another major traditional crime group (CG). These two individuals were tasked with implementing the orders of their leader who was being held in a Moscow detention center on extortion charges in 1993–94.

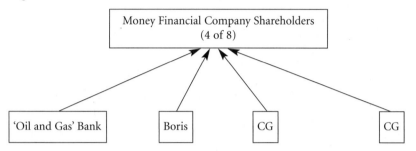

In April 1995, 'Delta' Fuel Company was established by two shareholders: Money (Boris and the crime groups) holding a 65% share and Omega (Dmitry, who had been under investigation for fraud) holding a 35% stake.

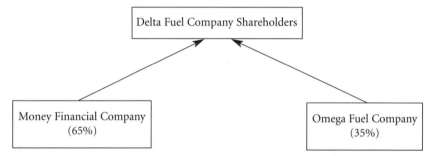

We'll return to these companies in a moment. Back in 1985, the development of oil terminal facilities at a Soviet port city had been declared a strategic goal by the Soviet government. Concrete steps to begin development were finally being taken in 1990. Private commercial enterprises were established to develop the facility. The process was stalled a number of times due, in part, to the dismantling of the USSR.

Ultimately, a decision was made in 1994 that a special joint-stock company should be established to own and manage the terminal facilities which, at the time, were being leased from the Port by a private commercial enterprise, 'Pi,' which had been established in 1990.

Toward the end of 1994, Port and Pi reached an agreement to establish a new joint-stock company by the end of the year. That deadline came and went, and in January 1995, Port managers proposed that Pi extend its already existing lease agreement for a period of three months. Port's contention was that, given the rapid changes in Russian business law and the relatively old age of Pi (four years), Pi would need time to complete all the updates in its company registration in order to proceed with the joint venture. Pi accepted the proposal.

While this was happening a certain 'Ivan' appeared on the scene and, with the help of officials at the local office of the State Property Committee, forced Port and Pi to accept a change of plan and form a new company to manage the port facilities.

At first the shareholders in the new company were: 1) Pi with 65%; 2) Port with 20%; and 3) Dmitry's Omega Fuel Company with 15%.

Apparently, Ivan was lobbying the interests of Omega to ensure its inclusion in the project. At the last moment Omega was removed from the deal and replaced by private limited enterprise 'Zebra'.

A few weeks later, Pi was informed that the new company it was forming with Port and Zebra was having problems with its registration with city authorities and that Ivan was using his influence to speed up the process. Pi, though, was not informed that, at the same time, yet another new company, 'Yankee,' had been registered. Port made a new lease agreement with Yankee, which had gotten the help of the local branch of the State Property Committee. Under this agreement, Yankee became the sole lessee of the port oil terminal facilities. Pi had been squeezed out of the deal.

At the time of incorporation, Yankee had the following shareholders: Port (50%), Omega Fuel Company (30%), and Zebra (20%). As it turned out, Zebra was a company also closely controlled by Ivan, indicating essentially that Ivan and Port had teamed up to oust Pi. Later, the list of shareholders of Yankee changed: Port (30%); Zebra (20%); and yet another new shareholder company appearing on the scene, 'Xanadu' (50%). Both Zebra and Xanadu were controlled by Ivan, giving him 70% control of Yankee, the sole lessee of the port oil terminal facilities. In early 1999, one of the crime figures involved in the deal (who was one of the shareholders in Money Financial Company) was named vice president of Yankee.

This simplified illustration shows a number of things: 1) the lack of recourse by a company like Pi; it was squeezed out of the deal; 2) the importance of being able to harness the power of the local bureaucracy, in this case the State Property Committee; and 3) the introduction of traditional crime groups as partners into major business ventures involving strategic sites important to national security.

The most interesting aspect of the example given above was as an illustration of the blurring of the lines of the Iron Triangle elements. The answer to the question, "Who was Ivan?" pointed to a fairly typical profile of the merging of business, bureaucracy, and criminal groups.

After serving a three-year stint as a low-ranking officer in the Soviet military in the mid-1970s, Ivan took a job as a janitor in a bar and then as a bartender. By the end of the decade, he was the manager of several bars and restaurants and was in the process of developing close contacts with neighborhood bar clientele who would go on to become the leaders of several area criminal groups.

In the early 1980s, Ivan convinced the director of the government agency supervising restaurants in the city to create a special unit that would oversee all waiters and bartenders. (Remember that at this time all restaurants and bars were state-owned enterprises.) Not surprisingly, Ivan himself was put in charge of the unit. He saw in his authority an opportunity to build financial resources for himself.

Every waiter had to pay Ivan 500 rubles per month which, at the time, was more than the average Soviet monthly salary. Ivan used his local contacts, primarily young boxers and martial arts trainees, to enforce his demands. In essence, he created his own group of extortionists. And we can make the assumption that he had good contacts in the local political and law enforcement circles to whom he was kicking back part of his profits. This was the sine qua non of engaging in these kinds of activities in the Soviet Union ... sharing with one's protectors.

According to Soviet law enforcement sources, by the mid-1980s Ivan was also involved in the black market smuggling of antiques out of the Soviet Union, an interest shared by the wife of a high-ranking Party official. A preliminary conclusion that can be drawn from this simple fact is that he likely had good contacts with the MVD and/or the KGB. Numerous black marketeers involved in smuggling, especially those who were physically moving in and out of the country personally, were protected by state security and went on to become some of the top businessmen in the post-Soviet world.

In the early 1990s, when the state no longer had a monopoly on the sale of alcoholic beverages, Ivan used his contacts in city restaurants and bars to set up a beer distribution network. Margins were excellent as demand far outstripped supply. At the time, many Western trading companies were more likely to deal with Soviets who had funding rather than extend credit to those without money. Thanks to his contacts, Ivan secured financing for his operations from the state-owned public food service agency as well as from criminal groups. Businessmen, bureaucrats, and criminal groups had become co-investors in the new post-Soviet business environment.

By the time privatization was picking up steam around 1992, Ivan already had good contacts in the mayor's office and in city government agencies including the State Property Committee, law enforcement, and security agencies. He made his move into the oil business, teaming up with some of the top criminals in the city. The first two organizing board meetings for Ivan's new company were attended by a rather eclectic group including major oil company executives, representatives of a leading insurance company, and local crime figures. From there Ivan moved into his activities with Omega, Yankee, Xanadu, and Zebra.

Generally speaking, there is no such thing as a 'self-made man' in business. And this was no less true in the former Soviet Union. Building an enterprise, accessing financial resources, and creating networks all required a stable of contacts. In the former Soviet Union it was not merely part of building a business but an integral part of circumventing the law, protecting oneself from competition, identifying not only the appropriate decision makers but those who were willing to take bribes, and so on. Part of Ivan's success was quite clearly due to the contacts he managed to collect over the years.

Ivan had five contacts in particular who are worth a look.

1) One of Ivan's closest associates was a former KGB officer from the foreign intelligence department who had become a senior officer of Omega Fuel Company. He used his active contacts in the KGB and MVD to protect Omega and Ivan's other companies from investigation.

2) Another associate had been convicted in December 1974 for rape and sentenced to five years. He was released from prison in April 1978 under a government amnesty. In December 1987, he was convicted of fraud, speculation, and forgery, and sentenced to six years in prison. In 1988, a city court reduced the sentence to four years on the basis of the removal of the speculation article from the criminal code. In September 1989, he was released.

3) One close associate was a boxer who had committed a string of petty offenses but was never convicted of a crime. In 1978, he and his brother opened several black market shops producing counterfeit foreign brand-name shoes and clothing. By the mid-1980s, they had formed a stable criminal enterprise involved in illegal foreign currency trading, protection rackets, running prostitutes and games of chance, and committing fraud in the sale of used cars. By the mid-1990s, the brothers were investing in banks and large trading companies.

4) Ivan had a close associate who had been the head of investigations in the local procurator's office. The official was given a chance by his superiors to resign following accusations of bribery and official corruption. After leaving the procurator's office, he worked as deputy chairman of the city arbitration court from 1985–1990. After resigning from this position, he used his contacts in the arbitration court to assist Ivan's companies win legal disputes.

5) The father-in-law of one of Ivan's contacts was a senior officer in the local police department. Through the father-in-law Ivan gained access to the chief of police. In the early 1990s, the chief and Ivan shared an interest in antiques, mostly their theft and smuggling. The

chief provided protection to, and on occasion attacked the rivals of, Ivan's companies.

It's difficult to deny that Ivan was an ambitious fellow. He took advantage of the opportunities that presented themselves and ultimately carved out a piece of the oil industry for himself—without getting himself killed in the process. No small feat in the always turbulent Russian business world. But compared to Pavel's organizational skill and vast reach, Ivan seemed to be a man of modest ability.

Pavel was a Russian businessman who in the second half of the 1990s managed to build himself into a major industrialist. His various arrangements, simplified below, provide a stark illustration of the Iron Triangle.

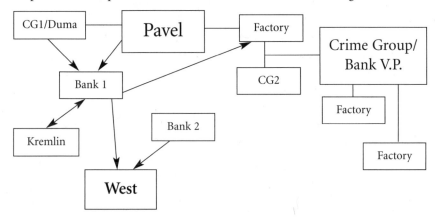

Pavel was a member of the board of directors of Bank 1, whose president was Pavel's nephew. As mentioned in Chapter 4, banks were seldom understood the same way in Russia as in the West, and more often than not they were pocket banks, essentially owned by a single enterprise or group for their private purposes. Frequently, someone in the management of the bank (in this case Pavel's nephew) was the trusted representative of the businessman or industrialist (Pavel) to protect the businessman's interests. Bank 1 had very close ties with the Kremlin and financed regional political campaigns to the tune of some \$10–12 million.

Pavel's cousin was also a member of the board of Bank 1. He also happened to be a member of a major crime group (CG1). Following a common practice in Russia, the cousin had his doctoral dissertation written for him, subsequently rewarding his ghostwriter with a position at the bank. For a mere \$1 million, Pavel's cousin bought his way onto the candidate list of one of the Russia's well-known political parties and became a member of the legislature (Duma). Two deputy chairmen of Bank 1 were also Duma deputies in the same political party and held a 20% stake in Pavel's factory.

Pavel retained the services of a boss of a different crime group to provide security on certain issues surrounding one of his factories. The boss was paid for services with some of the factory product that he could sell on his own. In 1995, the crime boss was squeezed out of the relationship. The police staged a raid on the boss's headquarters and seized half a ton of weapons, machine guns, grenades, launchers, explosives, masks, and various means of communications. The members of his group were reportedly involved in kidnapping, armed robbery, and other crimes in New York, Pennsylvania, and Florida in late 1999. The boss himself was arrested in Europe and later sentenced to more than 14 years in prison.

Pavel also held shares in Bank 2. Together with Bank 1, they moved money obtained through a combination of legitimate and illegitimate means to banks in the West, beyond the reach of Russian tax agencies and, perhaps more importantly, political enemies.

While the criminal groups played an important role and inflicted considerable damage on companies and individuals alike, it is worth repeating Varese and Galeotti's claims that the groups were not the dominant players.[18] I've laid out the simplified illustrations above to give at least a general impression that traditional criminal groups were but one actor and that they grew up with the system, working closely with business, politics, and bureaucracy. By implication, in many cases the violence of the 1990s grew out of competition and disagreement rather than 'invasion' and 'penetration.' In addition, it is useful to keep in mind the environment that foreign businesses were entering at the end of the 1980s and in the 1990s: the 'mafia' was powerful but not invincible and certainly not the only threat. A general discussion of foreign experiences in Russia in the 1990s helps illustrate this point.

By and large, foreign businesspeople (especially U.S. companies) went to the former Soviet Union operating under several assumptions. First, and perhaps the dominant assumption in the early years, they believed that the USSR had no market economy; the Westerners, therefore, could teach the Soviets how to do business and make millions while doing it. Among many there was a sense that it would be 'easy.' Most of the business people I met who went to the former Soviet Union between 1990 and 1995 with dollar signs in their eyes and six-month timetables in their minds lost far more than they anticipated and departed the country confused at why their plan seemed so easy from back home in the West and was so downright confounding once on the ground in Russia.

---

18. See Chapter 1, note 19.

Many business people entering that market assumed that the Soviets were novices at business (and they were in the Western sense). But many Westerners took this to mean naiveté and ignorance. What the Soviets did have was a market sense from an underground economy, survivalist perspective, not a free market economy or capitalism sense. Perhaps most important, as the Rolling Stones song goes, they were 'practiced at the art of deception.' What they didn't know about business or capitalism they made up for by knowing the lay of the land. Remember, they had a thousand years of historical, psychological, and culture formation in a context of facing wave after wave of foreign invaders as well as their own autocratic governments.

The foreigners didn't understand that it took 2–3 times longer to do things in the former Soviet Union than back at home. They didn't appreciate that much of Russian business was part improvisation, part bluff. They didn't understand that the Soviets took a long time to reach a comfort level before doing business. This could mean months of talking and socializing (drinking) while getting to know each other. While all business is about relationships, in the former Soviet Union (as in many other countries) relationships were critical.

Second, and related to this, was the assumption by foreign companies that their goals and the Soviet—and later Russian—goals would be the same. For example, if a contract was signed, the general assumption was that the goal of each party would be to fulfill the contract. While this may have been true in many cases, it was also often true that many Russians stayed engaged in the business relationship only until they got what they wanted. And what they wanted was not necessarily the same as the foreign company. This was a time in the dying Soviet Union that local businessmen didn't have a lot of resources and didn't know how long the opportunities would last. They knew their Russian and Soviet history and moved as hard as they could as quickly as possible to 'cash in,' not knowing when the door of opportunity might slam shut. It was not surprising, then, to hear this reaction by an American businessman from the Midwest who was supplying computers to his Russian partner to start up a newspaper. "He wasn't interested in doing business at all. His only motivation was computers and social profile. Businesswise, he never thought anything through to the end."[19] Actually, the Russian did think things through to the end. His end was to obtain computers. Once he did that, the American

---

19. A. Craig Copetas, *Bear Hunting with the Politburo: A Gritty First-Hand Account of Russia's Young Entrepreneurs and Why Soviet-Style Capitalism Can't Work*, New York, Simon & Schuster, 1991, p. 97.

businessman was no longer needed. The Russian businessman is still in business today and thriving; the American abandoned the country many years ago.

It was understandable behavior from the Russian perspective given what we have discussed throughout the book already. And it was equally understandable that foreigners were not attuned to these realities. Many of them did not study the landscape thoroughly before proceeding. They tried to operate in Russia with a Western mindset. As Michael Mears, the former head of the U.S. Commercial Office in Moscow, observed of Western business practices in the late 1980s and early 1990s:

> There's a big crack between the poor fool who is here trying to do business in this labyrinthine mess and the board of directors and politicians back in the States who are reading perestroika stories.... Virtually all of them had no idea what they were doing. It was an entrepreneurial nightmare. Every one of them had a guaranteed scheme to make a million dollars out of an economy that had no money, no equipment, no convertible currency, and absolutely no idea what to do with or how to make the products people were trying to sell or manufacture in the Soviet Union. But they came anyway.[20]

Westerners assumed that Russians wanted to become more competitive for the sake of their own survival. But here, too, they misinterpreted what steps Russians were willing to take to ensure that survival. It wasn't through the very frightening and extremely uncertain Western notion of risk that Russians would secure the ground under their feet. They reverted to what they knew. As we saw in Chapters 5 and 6, for decades (in the Soviet era and centuries before that) they had been cutting corners, cheating, and stealing. In many ways, theirs was a mentality of state welfare. Working for a living and leaving such important issues as food, money, and housing up to the vagaries of the invisible hand of the free market was not the Russian way. Soviet factories and other production units, for example, were usually very closely tied to the surrounding neighborhood in terms of education, health care, dining facilities, recreation, housing, and so on. This meant that there were far more people dependent on the factory than just the employees. And since the state had subsidized everything during the Soviet era, the Russians would continue that practice after the disappearance of the Soviet Union. Instead of relying on business competition to spur them to survive, the large factories remained tied

---

20. Ibid., pp. 50, 99.

to these neighborhood organizations and functions so that the state would prop up the company if it were in danger of failing.[21]

Third, in this context, foreign companies, especially large ones investing in factories, were not prepared for the lengths to which Russians would go to undermine the investment, if necessary. In the case of a factory, for example, the Western mentality would expect to purchase a factory, create conditions for work to continue, give vendors an opportunity to compete for the factory's business, and get on with the business of making money. If, in the process, people had to be 'downsized,' so be it. If there were to be accountability measures (no conflict of interest, no double dipping), so be it. There would be rules of the game. What the foreign business didn't expect was essentially extortion by crime groups, city and regional officials, suppliers, and others—not a typical low-level extortion but a more ambitious operation to drive the foreigners out of their investments. Once the factory had been bought or an investment had been made, it was a relatively easy task by a Russian competitor, crime group, or state official to get the suppliers to stop delivering raw materials to the factory. The Russian interest was to retain control over the factory and employ as many people as possible. The Russian attitude essentially was, Fine, let the Americans invest $100 million dollars in the factory, but when we want to drive them out, all we have to do is shut down electricity, water, and supply lines. The Russians understood this game very well, which was one of the reasons Russian companies "seek to buy up all links in their production chain. They hope to be able to control every aspect of their business, from the early production stages to delivery of the final product to the customer."[22]

And finally, Westerners took quite literally claims that Russia was a 'lawless' land, interpreting that to mean anarchic, anything goes. They failed to appreciate the notion of the 'hook'—that everyone was vulnerable not for lack of law but for the sheer volume of it and the arbitrary and frequently contradictory way it could be wielded. Russia had more law than it knew what to do with, but its primary purpose was to protect the state and keep the population in line. Complicating matters, beyond the formalistic, legalistic laws, there were customs, traditions, political clan rules, ethnic clan rules, and collectivist behavioral norms to be observed. We would like to speak of Russia in terms of democracy, capitalism, and rule of law—or at least as a country that

---

21. Buss, p. 98 (note 3).

22. Robert Orttung, "The Role of Business in Russian Foreign and Security Relations," PONARS Policy Memo 351, November 2004, p. 3.

is moving in that direction—but it's not and, with only the most minor exceptions in its history, it never has.

This assumption of lawlessness carried serious implications. One line of Western business logic in the early 1990s went as follows: since the 'mafia' (traditional crime groups) control everything and more than 90% of the cops are corrupt, it makes better sense to hire a crime group. Some businessmen did their homework, collecting information on the local gangs, deciding who had the best reputation, and turned to them for assistance. The only problem was, as former Moscow criminal investigator Alex Gorkin points out, "The cops may be corrupt, but the criminals are criminals 100% of the time."[23] Once on their hook, it was difficult—not to mention dangerous and expensive—to get off.

Here, too, was another of the many misconceptions in business throughout the 1990s: because of the way the 'mafia' was portrayed, few people understood that there were ways to counter it. They failed to realize that most crime groups had no interest in coming under the scrutiny of law enforcement or state security. In the case of an extortion attempt or the offer of ongoing 'protection,' such as a *krysha* (roof), a 'mafia' sit-down would be arranged: the underworld 'mafia' on one side of the table and the state 'mafia' on the other side. Once it was explained by, for example, a KGB colonel that he was already providing protection to the target company, invariably the traditional gangsters would apologize and leave. Period. End of story. As in any power relationships, dealing with 'mafia' advances required determining their strength and countering with a greater force. The media seldom gave the impression that the shootouts, kidnappings, bombings, and contract murders were the end result of what was usually a failed negotiation and escalation in tension that occurred over time. That is, there was little that was fully spontaneous or irrational about what was happening. In most cases, the chaos had its own internal logic, which matured and became less violent within just a few years.

Long after the ruble collapse of 1998 and the apparent stabilization of the economy, a number of articles appeared in 2003 in both the Russian and Western press that once again highlighted the confusion and uncertainty about operating in Russia. For example, on February 15, 2003, *The New York Times* carried the headline, "Glimmers of an Investor-Friendly Russia." Three days later, *Pravda.ru* announced this headline: "Russian Business Ethic: Give Your Money and Get Out!" which sounded remarkably similar to the account of the Midwestern businessman investing in the Russian newspaper some fifteen

---

23. Author conversation with Gorkin, July 1994.

years earlier mentioned above. A week later, on February 24, a *Chicago Tribune* headline declared, "Despite Risks, Russia again Tempting World's Investors." A month later, on March 24, the assessments continued. *The Financial Times* (UK) revealed in its headline, "Fighting its Risky Reputation: A new business survey shows that Russia still has a long way to go to put itself on the investment map." Three days later, *Pravda.ru* concluded that "Foreign Investors Forget about Russia." In a jolt of optimism, on May 18, 2003, a *Sunday Times* (UK) headline trumpeted, "Investors Pile in to Russia." On December 18, 2006, a *Bloomberg* article swung the pendulum back the other way: "Global Investors Should Think Again About Russia." "It is time," the author writes, "[western companies] wised up. Sure, you can make a quick buck in Russia. The trouble is that you can lose it just as fast if the government bullies you out of what you have created. Until Russia starts playing by the rules as part of the global economy, foreign investment should be shifted elsewhere."[24] Much investor concern was based on numerous factors in post-Soviet reality, very little of which had anything to do with the traditional 'mafia.' It had much more to do with Vaksberg's 'mafia' and the continuing influence it has on the psychology and culture and the conduct of business.

In the 1990s, of course, Vaksberg's 'mafia'—the all-encompassing state 'mafia'—functioned largely the way it always had. As absolute rulers, they took what they wanted. One of the major differences, though, was that the state used the rules of the underworld even more actively than during the Soviet era since many societal institutions had collapsed after the dismantling of the USSR. One foreign businessman, feeling much like the English merchants of the 16th century, hissed, "Government officials operate in the same pattern as the mafia here: They stick their fat paws wherever they suspect there's big money, with no regard whatsoever for the elementary laws of the marketplace."[25]

In 1992, a major foreign company producing plastic cups and utensils for the airline and hotel industries pulled out of the former Soviet Union after spending four years and $50 million. As was the case with many other foreign companies, it made an initial investment believing it was operating in a tax-free zone and was promised a five-year tax holiday. The promise, made by Gorbachev, was later repealed by Yeltsin who issued hundreds of presidential

---

24. Matthew Lynn, "Global Investors Should Think Again About Russia," *Bloomberg*, December 18, 2006.

25. Broder Drees in Tim Obojsky, "Pioneer Joint Venture Foiled by Crime, Red Tape," *The Moscow Times*, August 19, 1994, p. 12.

decrees affecting businesses.[26] A common refrain of the time was sounded by a Western businessman: "The Russians cry for Western investors but do everything suited to scare them off."[27] Countless examples of this were available throughout the 1990s.

Years later, in October 2006, Carlos Gutierrez, U.S. Secretary of Commerce, commented that American companies have complained of a "soft nationalization" taking place in some sectors of the Russian economy. "American companies are anxious to invest in Russia, but many remain hesitant to do so. Some have invested tens of millions in a production facility only to be faced with a competitor backed with preferences in the form of government ownership or capital."[28]

Earlier in the year, in an episode reported in the British press, the Russian joint venture factory of General Motors and Russian carmaker Avtovaz ground to a halt after the new management team forced on Avtovaz by the state halted component supplies. The Russian arms export agency, Rosoboronexport, reportedly close to the Russian president, seized control. The Russians claimed that the GM joint venture was profitable but that Avtovaz lost money on it and that the joint venture only made money because Avtovaz sold components at a loss. Analysts speculated that one of the possibilities was that the Russian side was trying to raise prices so high as to make it unprofitable and then the Russian side would take over. This was a pattern long repeated across time. "It's the typical Russian story. They let the American partners in and then start squeezing them out."[29] This is not to say that the foreign businesses were always innocent victims. The point here is that there were many other forces at work in the 1990s in the business environment that had more to do with the Russian way of doing things than with the traditional 'mafia.'

Many of the problems that businesses faced in the 1990s were attributed to 'mafia' or organized crime groups. The media highlighted individual cases— some with hyperbole, others with inaccuracies—leaving the impression that the 'mafia' was steamrolling over all sectors of society. However, in reality, while criminal organizations were active and guilty of contributing to the chaos, part of the threat sprang forth from the fabric of Russian society and

---

26. *The Moscow Times*, "American Industrialist Pulling Out of Russia," September 13, 1994.

27. Drees in Obojsky, p. 12 (note 25).

28. *RIA Novosti*, "U.S. Commerce Chief Voices Concerns over Investments in Russia," October 12, 2006.

29. James Mackintosh and Neil Buckley, "GM Russian Joint Venture Halts Production," *FT.com*, February 17, 2006.

culture, the environment of survival we addressed in Chapters 5 and 6. It came from the bureaucracy, from business, and from politics. It came from the atomized nature of society, the ad hoc opportunism that helped define the system rather than a concerted effort by large, well-organized criminal empires. It's worth bearing in mind something that Lenin said at the Eleventh Party Congress in March 1922. "The point is that the responsible Communist—even the best, who is certainly honest and devoted, who in the past endured imprisonment and did not fear death—does not know how to carry on trade, because he is not a businessman. He did not learn to trade, does not want to learn, and does not understand that he must start learning from the beginning."[30] In the context of this mentality, which has survived to this day, shortcuts to success and the use of force by virtually anyone in a position to use it were the key devices employed in the business world.

The 2006 experience of an American dentist who abandoned his dental practice in Moscow after being threatened by thugs is a typical example of what has occurred for the past twenty years and for at least five hundred years before that. When his clinic began to show a healthy profit, his Russian partner, true to Lenin's characterization, took a shortcut and started to squeeze him out. Typical of stories like this, the Russian partner had set up the accounts and controlled the paperwork, making the takeover a relatively easy undertaking. The dentist concluded, "If you go into partnership with somebody and the company is losing money, it's your company. If you make money, it's theirs and they'll find a way to get it from you."[31]

30. Alan Ball, *Russia's Last Capitalists: The NEPmen, 1921–1929*, Berkeley, University of California Press, 1987, p. 19.

31. *National Public Radio*, "Like Pulling Teeth," August 21, 2006, accessed at Johnson's Russia List.

CHAPTER 11

LAW ENFORCEMENT

Sometimes it is enough to mention the name of a relative in governmental spheres for the trembling bureaucrat to give you the favor you require. Sometimes one has to slip a ruble, or two rubles, into the hand which is held carelessly open on the edge of the table. And sometimes, if it is an official of top rank, it is a good thing to prepare a well-filled envelope in advance. So you see, with us the law is rigid, but man is supple. That is the secret of our organization. Seen from outside it appears to be uncompromising, but from within you can see there are innumerable adjustments to the most terrible regulations.

—Alexander Vassilievitch[1]

I consider, as a lawyer, that today Russia, as in the past, remains a totalitarian state. In my opinion, the primary indicator in the development of a democratic society is legality, real—not merely declared—equality of all citizens before the law in any and all spheres of social relations. However, in our country, the law always fell victim to politics.

—Anatoly Volobuyev[2]

As the Soviet Union declined during the 1980s, law enforcement was slowly coming to recognize officially what it had known for years unofficially—that criminal groups were alive and well and living in the land of Communism. In 1985, an order (*prikaz*) of the MVD USSR spoke of the merging of shopkeepers with the elite of the criminal world, the increasing visibility of the *vory v zakone*, and the attraction of athletes and former police officers into criminal groups, but as of yet no mention of 'organized

---

1. Alexander Vassilievitch is a fictional character in Henri Troyat's *Daily Life in Russia Under the Last Tsar*, Stanford, Stanford University Press, 1979, p. 136.
2. Anatoly Volobuyev, "Edinstvennaya Nadezhnaya Upravlencheskaya Struktura v Rossii: Organizovannaya Prestupnost,'" unpublished article, 1993, p. 18.

crime,' only the 'appearance of organization in crime' (*proyavleniye organizo-vannosti v prestupnosti*).[3]

An organized crime control unit with 25 personnel was quietly formed in 1986 as part of the Criminal Investigation Department (MUR) of Moscow City police (GUVD).[4] In 1988, the Ministry of Internal Affairs established the Sixth Directorate for Organized Crime Control (*Shestoe Upravleniye po Bor'be s Organizovannoi Prestupnost'iu*). Finally, in December 1989, at the Second Congress of People's Deputies, Vadim Bakatin, then-Minister of Internal Affairs, officially acknowledged the existence of organized crime in the Soviet Union.[5]

In 1990, shortly after Bakatin's speech to the Second Congress, there was a total of 1200 members in organized crime control departments nationwide,[6] including 85 personnel in the Sixth Directorate based at MVD headquarters in Moscow.[7] By 1991, this figure had more than doubled, to 3,000, around the country.[8] Heading into 1993, manpower in organized crime control units reportedly increased by 15,000, which also included the formation of rapid deployment units and the acquisition of special equipment, ammunition, and weapons. From 1993 to 1995, Regional Units for Organized Crime Control (RUOP) were being established around the country.[9]

With the increase in the number of people searching for organized crime, it was easy to see how the threat of organized crime—at least from the point

---

3. Author conversation with Volobuyev, March 1991.

4. In 1992, the organized crime unit was removed from the Moscow Criminal Investigation Department and transformed into a department. According to the Pronouncement of the Government of the Russian Federation, November 29, 1992, no. 914–63 "Ob Organizatsionnykh Merakh po Obespecheniiu Borby s Organizovannoi Prestupnost'iu" passed in fulfillment of Presidential Decree of October 8, 1992, no. 1189, O Merakh po Zashchite Prav Grazhdan, Okhrane Pravoporiadka i Usileniiu Borby s Prestupnost'iu, the department was transformed into the Regional Unit for Organized Crime Control. At the end of 1996, RUOP was moved to direct subordination of GUOP MVD.

5. See the subsequently adopted Decision of the Congress of People's Deputies of the Union of Soviet Socialist Republics, "Ob Usilenii Borby s Organizovannoi Prestupnost'iu" signed by Mikhail Gorbachev, December 23, 1989. See also the Resolution of the Council of Ministers, No. 86-26, January 25, 1989.

6. Cited by Yuri Shchekochikhin in "Lion Hunting or Shadow Boxing: Is the Mafia also Ready for Reform?' *Literaturnaya Gazeta*, p. 12, no. 21, May 23, 1990.

7. Joseph D. Serio, "Law and Order Crisis Fosters Upheaval and Confusion," *CJ International*, 7(3): 1–7, 1991.

8. N. Zhelnorova, "Those who have Joined the Gang ... are Sentenced," *Argumenty i Fakty*, no. 50, p. 4, 1991, interview with M. K. Yegorov.

9. Author conversation with Gennady Chebotaryov, November 1993.

of view of statistics—could have worsened. We saw the figures for 'crime groups' in Chapter 4. From 1993–95, the number of registered crimes in Moscow alone increased by 12.3%[10] and the number of serious offenses increased 2.4 times.[11] While there was a reported decrease in registered crimes by 19.1% in 1996,[12] the numbers for 'banditry' increased from 18 in 1996 to 33 in 1997, and the number of contract murders increased from 5 in 1996 to 15 in 1997. Crimes involving narcotics trafficking nearly doubled between 1996 and 1997[13] and illegal possession of weapons increased by 15.4%.[14] The number of people arrested for committing a crime as a member of an organized crime group increased from 802 in 1996 to 1,061 the following year. From 1993–1998, the Moscow RUOP reportedly broke up 2,827 organized crime groups which included 9,511 people. These groups committed 4,130 crimes. Seizures in the capital from 1993–98 included 4,209 firearms, 8,562 knives, 1,488 grenades, around 81,000 bullets, 1,053 kilograms of explosive material; 571 kilograms of narcotics; cash and valuables amounting to 300 billion rubles; hard currency in the equivalent of US$75,000; 106 kilos of gold and silver, and 178 carats of diamonds and gems.[15]

Despite this apparent progress in uncovering crime and confiscating weapons and valuables, it was believed by many that law enforcement didn't stand a chance; in essence, the 'fight against organized crime' was over long before it ever began. As we saw in preceding chapters, and particularly in Chapter 10, crime groups, businessmen, and bureaucrats had become deeply entangled. The statistics cited above were virtually meaningless as an indicator of the success of law enforcement against organized crime. What could law enforcement agencies do against a phenomenon that was not only ill-defined but that was an organic part of the social and economic roots of the system? What chance did they stand of uprooting the groups when the most powerful of them were deeply intertwined in the system, when the plunderers of the state coffers included some of the most powerful politicians, bureaucrats, and businessmen? What more could police do than go after the small fry?

In a Memorandum dated November 22, 1990—even before the demise of the Soviet Union—the director of the MVD's All-Union Scientific Research

---

10. 1993—82,556; 1995—92,675
11. 1993—19,590; 1995—47,531
12. 1996—38,362; 1997—32,929
13. From 4,625 to 8,720.
14. 1996—2,766; 1997—3193
15. All of the statistics in this paragraph come from "Rezultaty Deyatel'nosti RUOP po Moskvy pri GUOP MVD Rossii za 1993–1998," pp. 1–2.

Institute concluded that "organized crime has in fact slipped from under the control of law enforcement agencies." The serious shortcomings in the fight against organized crime, he wrote, included 1) the absence of a single approach to fighting organized crime; 2) the lack of coordination among law enforcement agencies such as the MVD, KGB, the Procurator's office, and the Supreme Court; 3) the ineffectiveness of tax collection agencies and other forms of financial control, and 4) serious limitations in the legal toolbox of law enforcement officials, in particular detectives of the MVD. As a result, only the lowest levels of organized crime were being addressed. There was no effective mechanism for fighting corruption at the highest level of power.[16]

Anatoly Volobuyev, one of the MVD's pioneers in the study of organized crime in the Soviet Union, agreed, calling the government's fight against organized crime "purely declarative." In an article in *Komsomolskaya Pravda* in 1991, Volobuyev criticizes his own agency, saying, "Pinning all hopes on the MVD is as useless as pretending that the KGB can significantly contribute in this pursuit. The MVD (just as the KGB) has been adapted by the power structures to handling quite different tasks. In the best case it is ready for the struggle against traditional (elementary) crime." In one last swipe, Volobuyev dismisses the Organized Crime Control Department as a political tool of the Soviet Union to discredit the government of the Russian Republic as the USSR gasped its last breaths.[17]

Politics of a dying empire aside, a Russian judge presiding over a racketeering trial in 1991 summed up one of the main reasons enforcement mechanisms would ultimately remain toothless in the so-called fight against organized crime:

> The law is absolutely unprepared to combat organized crime, and this is the reason why one case after another fizzles out. Even in Moscow. Here, intimidated witnesses failed to appear in court; the Zavolzhsky district police had no cars to bring witnesses to court. Defendants broke the bars to disrupt the trial. What could I have done? Fine them? As the trial proceeded, it became obvious that the code of criminal process has long been obsolete.[18]

---

16. Memo from the head of the All-Union Scientific Research Institute of the MVD, Vladimir Rezvykh, to Alexander Gurov, the Chief of the 6th Department for Organized Crime Control, "Recommendations Regarding Measures to Fight Organized Crime," November 22, 1990.

17. Anatoly Volobuyev, "A Separate Scientific Battalion," *Komsomolskaya Pravda*, May 3, 1991, p. 2.

18. Mikhail Gurtovoi, " 'Godfathers' End Up in a Clink," *Moscow News*, no. 19, 1991, p. 15.

It was a theme that emerged time and time again. What the judge alluded to the president of an 'anti-mafia private foundation' stated quite unequivocally: "They proclaimed war but forgot to equip and mobilize the army.... [H]ow can we speak about a struggle if there are no actual sanctions?"[19] Not only were the soldiers in this war ill-equipped for battle, some of the generals back at headquarters weren't even taking up the cause. The Procurator's office was notorious for failing to pursue any meaningful cases under the existing 'gangsterism' and 'banditry' legislation of the day. "The Procurator has never done anything, before [Yeltsin's] decree or after it. There are approximately 2,600 organized criminal groups in Russia; 485 of them have well-placed connections in state structures. But that's just the tip of the iceberg. What we mean by the term 'organized crime' is a symbiosis of entrepreneurs, gangsters, and clerks."[20] Gennady Chebotaryov, the Deputy Chief of the Organized Crime Control Department at that time, essentially agreed with the assessment. "Since those long-ago years when the Party declared that 'gangsterism is finished in the USSR,' the Procurator's office has continued to err with respect to this phenomenon. We hope that the new leadership of Russia's General Procurator's Office, as well as the Supreme Court, will finally turn their attention to the problem."[21]

From the very beginning, then, Soviet and post-Soviet law enforcement was totally unprepared or unwilling to deal with organized crime.

First, the Soviet and later Russian agencies suffered from a laundry list of daunting challenges: excessive caseloads; lack of motivation; lack of adequate equipment (including vehicles and gasoline); a delicate political climate; ridiculously low salaries; pervasive corruption; the necessity to observe unreasonable time limits in the course of an investigation; the complex nature of some of the

---

19. Yevgeny Myslovsky quoted in Yekaterina Barabash, "The Mafia Symbiosis: Dealers, Gangsters, Clerks," *Megapolis-Express*, no. 43, November 1992.

20. Ibid.

21. Gennady Chebotaryov quoted in FBIS-USR-93-144, November 10, 1993. After the arrest of Mikhas, the reputed leader of the Solntsevo group, by the Swiss police in November 1996, the Swiss prosecutor general's office contacted the Russian MVD's Organized Crime Control Department and the Russian prosecutor general's office with a request to provide information about Mikhas. The Organized Crime Control Department responded with a document describing Mikhas as the leader of the Solntsevo group who had a criminal conviction in 1984 and faced criminal charges in 1989 and 1993. The district prosecutor from the criminal's neighborhood responded on behalf of the prosecutor general's office that neither his agency nor the MVD knew Mikhas as a criminal or in any capacity and that there was no information regarding his convictions or criminal charges against him.

criminal groups; the lack of investigative experience concerning organized crime, financial crime, money laundering, and so on; the absence of appropriate legislation to guide investigations and the collection of evidence, and the lack of cooperation among law enforcement agencies, among other things.[22]

To give one simple example, the ability to safeguard witnesses in the course of an organized crime investigation is a key function of law enforcement. Understandably, the Soviet Union had little ideological ground on which to build a witness protection program prior to the demise of the country for the purpose of fighting organized crime. Despite the lip service the Soviet law paid to requiring the police, investigators, procurators, and courts to adopt measures to protect the "life, health, honor, valuables, and property of victims, witnesses, or other participants in a case, as well as members of their families or close relatives, on sufficient evidence that they are threatened by murder, violence, destruction or damage to property, or other illegal acts," in reality the conditions needed to satisfy those requirements were never met. Moreover, these protective measures did not extend to informants.[23]

Second, the mindset of the people toward law enforcement was changing rapidly. There was never much respect for the police force—a national, centralized agency that played a key role in the development of the gulag system— and now whatever fear existed was quickly evaporating. In 1990, veteran police officers complained that whereas in the past they could arrest three, four, or five criminals without even having a weapon, now they were likely to be fired upon in the course of executing their duties.[24] In 1992, 317 policemen were killed while on duty and 586 were wounded, enormous figures at the dawn of the post-Soviet era. Many officers didn't stay around to complain about the deteriorating conditions. In 1992, the number of police who left the service in search of greener pastures increased by 19% over the previous year.[25] Some joined the staff of banks, hotels, private security firms, or the ranks of crime groups, among other things. Those who remained on the force found extra money through moonlighting or bribe taking.[26]

---

22. "Organized Crime Survey Response" prepared by the Sixth Department for Organized Crime Control of the Ministry of Internal Affairs of the USSR, 1991, for the United Nations-MVD Conference on International Organized Crime Control, October 21–25, 1991, held in Suzdal, Russia, pp. 12–13.

23. Ibid., p. 8.

24. Author conversation with MVD detective, Igor Ratsep, September 1990.

25. Author conversation with Gennady Chebotaryov, November 1993.

26. Mark Galeotti, "Perestroika, Perestrelka, Pereborka: Policing Russia in a Time of Change," *Europe-Asia Studies*, vol. 45, no. 5, 1993, p. 769. See also Louise Shelley, *Policing Soviet Society: The Evolution of State Control*, New York, Routledge, 1996.

Finally, and as stated numerous times throughout this book, law enforcement and traditional crime groups were of the same environment. Contrary to the image of gangsters bearing down on the police like an invading force, in many cases the relationships between thug and cop had developed through the normal course of life. They'd met each other in grade school or high school or in the neighborhood. They lived in the same places and traveled in the same circles. They were friends. (Recall Ivan's story in Chapter 10.) What devotion were the police going to have to the state in return for a salary of $50–$100 a month? While salaries have increased in the past decade to perhaps $500–$700 a month, the increase in the price of goods has far outstripped their salary increase. There has always been great incentive to find supplemental forms of income. After all, they had families to feed and friends to protect.

Consider this story that Anatoly Volobuyev, the MVD pioneering researcher on organized crime, relates about the reality of policing organized crime in Russia. A former lieutenant colonel working in the prison system had a friend who was the director of a large company dealing in oil and oil products. The firm was under the 'protection' of both the Dagestani and the Podolsk crime groups simultaneously, demanding regular payments. Meeting the demands was physically impossible. The director didn't have the money, as a result of which the gangsters beat him regularly and threatened to kill him. The director turned to the lieutenant colonel for help who in turn called upon the Regional Unit for Organized Crime Control (RUOP), hoping they would resolve the matter. One of the chief's assistants promised to come to the company's office the next time the gangsters returned. On that occasion no police appeared and the gangsters once again beat the director. The lieutenant colonel went from office to office at RUOP looking for help. He found one ranking officer who referred him to another officer. Unfortunately for the director of the company, the officer who was offered up to assist him was the same person the Dagestanis had on their payroll.[27]

In another case, organized crime control officers in a region learned that the daughter of the deputy chief of the local police precinct (who was also the head of the criminal investigation division) was working as the chief accountant at a firm set up by a criminal group. Another thing surprised the police: the permits for the ten firearms that were seized from the organized crime group in the course of the investigation had been signed by the deputy chief of the precinct.[28]

By the end of the 1990s, the state finally said publicly what had been noted in memos nearly a decade earlier: the war was over and law enforcement had

---

27. Author conversation with Anatoly Volobuyev, August 1995.
28. Volobuyev, p. 8 (note 2).

lost. Or at least this was the stated opinion. On January 15, 1999, then-Minister of Internal Affairs Sergei Stepashin admitted that "despite adopted measures, the police failed in its fight against organized crime which undermines Russia's foundation by crawling into all levels of the power structure."[29] From a certain perspective, this seemed another example of the portrayal of organized crime as an 'invading' force taking over the state. We've seen in earlier chapters, though, that the relationship was not one of organized crime dominance over the state but rather one of mutual benefit. There was no way to beat organized crime because it was in the interest of various elements of the state and business to maintain it. (Recall Pavel's reliance on organized crime in Chapter 10.) Former Moscow criminal investigator Alexander Gorkin provides an interpretation that is slightly different than Stephashin's when he notes,

> Organized crime was heavily politicized and there was no way we could get a handle on those 'goodfellas' who were supported by the regime—which needed organized crime to exist as a special tool in the 'real world' to cover up governmental wrongdoing and other nefarious activities … in order to give the world the impression that all bad things happened because of organized crime.[30]

While some of the details may have changed, many of the legal shortcomings of the early 1990s in the 'fight against organized crime' remained years later, in large part because it was in the interest of elements of the state, business, and the legislature to ensure that effective enforcement mechanisms were not instituted. There were still problems defining the concept of 'organized crime' and what constituted an 'organized crime group.' Robert Orttung rightly notes that "existing legislation is poorly worded and in places contradictory. Some types of crime groups do not fall within the current legal definition. For example, some critics question the Russian Supreme Court's decision that only a 'stable' group can be considered an organized crime group."[31]

Tom Firestone, a lawyer in the U.S. Attorney's Office, spent two years in Russia, from 2002–2004, working with law enforcement authorities on the

---

29. *AFP*, "Russia Admits It Failed in Fighting Organised Crime," January 15, 1999.

30. Author conversation with Alexander Gorkin, June 2006. Volobuyev seems to agree with this assessment when he says, "Political figures who act in their own interests rather than in the interests of society are trying to pass off the lowest level of organized crime as the whole of it and drown the essence of the problem in such verbiage as 'economic sabotage,' etc." See Volobuyev (note 17).

31. Robert Orttung's report of a conference of criminologists at Yaroslavl State University on January 20–21, 2004. Russian Regional Report, Vol. 9, No. 1, February 3, 2004, accessed at Johnson's Russia List.

legal foundation for organized crime control. Like Orttung, he raises the issue of insufficient definitional base in the criminal code, and the unclear and circular reasoning within the understanding of 'criminal society,' 'criminal organization,' 'band,' and other entities.

Article 209 concerning 'banditism,' with its roots in the Criminal Code of 1922, criminalizes the "creation of an ongoing armed group (band) for the purpose of attacking citizens or organizations ..." "It is hard to imagine," Firestone says, "that any armed criminal group formed 'for the purpose of attacking citizens or organizations' would not also qualify as a 'criminal society' under Article 210." Unfortunately, as he notes, Article 210, which speaks of criminal societies, provides no definition of a 'criminal society.' Article 35 in the general definitional section of the Russian Criminal Code states only that "a crime is considered to have been committed by a criminal society ('criminal organization') if it is committed by a unified criminal group (organization), which has been created for the commission of serious or especially serious crimes ..." "In other words," says Firestone, "the Russian Criminal Code's definition of 'criminal society' is entirely circular and it is no wonder that the statute is difficult to use."[32]

It has been noted by U.S. specialists that in order to create an effective organized crime control program, five elements are needed. First, criminal statutes which allow for the prosecution of a criminal enterprise as a whole must be in place. Second, there need to be laws which allow for the use of confidential informants and undercover operations. Third, the use of cooperating witness testimony in court proceedings is critical for the successful prosecution of organized crime cases. Fourth, the legal base must permit electronic surveillance and the use of wiretap evidence in court proceedings. And fifth, an effective witness protection program must be in place.[33] Virtually none of these tools are in place in Russia in a meaningful way in the 'fight against organized crime.'

Russian investigators do not have the long-term tools necessary to investigate organized crime activities. For example, according to Article 162 of the Criminal Procedure Code, investigations can't be extended longer than 12 months, and, as Firestone points out, this is far shorter than most effective organized crime investigators need in order to obtain adequate evidence.[34] Also, nothing in legislation protects undercover agents from criminal prosecution. For example, Article 304 of the Criminal Code criminalizes the giv-

---

32. Tom Firestone in his draft article, "What Russia Must Do To Fight Organized Crime," presentation at the International Law Enforcement Academy, April 2004.

33. Kenneth Lowrie, Deputy Chief of the United States Department of Justice Organized Crime and Racketeering Section, presented in ibid.

34. Firestone (note 32).

ing of a bribe in connection with setting up a prosecution of the recipient. But in the event the bribe is refused it creates the possibility of the criminal prosecution of the bribe giver even if the duties were executed in the course of a sting operation.

Article 12 of the Law on Operational-Search Activity defines the identity of informants and undercover agents and the information they provide as 'state secrets,' the disclosure of which can be criminally prosecuted under Article 283 of the Criminal Code. The law prohibits the use in court of information provided by confidential informants and undercover agents unless the individual gives written consent. Article 12 provides that the results of 'operational-search activity' can be disclosed upon application of the director of the law enforcement agency responsible for conducting the investigation. In Firestone's observations, "Such applications are almost never made because most law enforcement officials are unfamiliar with the necessary procedures and fear being accused of disclosing secret information."[35] Wiretap evidence is admissible so long as the evidence was not obtained in violation of the Criminal Procedure Code. Article 12 defines wiretap evidence, like information provided by confidential informants and undercover agents, as a "state secret." Wiretap evidence, like cooperating witness testimony, is rarely used in Russian criminal prosecutions.[36]

New witness protection legislation went into effect in January 2005. The "Federal Law on Government Protection of Victims, Witnesses, and Other Participants" provides for the protection of home and property, individual protection, communication and security alarm devices, relocation, issuance of new documents, change of appearance, transfer to a new job or educational institution, and temporary relocation to a secured shelter. As in the past, though, there is insignificant funding and, more importantly, there is little trust on the part of potential witnesses that it will effectively protect them.

Interestingly, when it comes to pursuing penalties against criminal groups, amendments to the Criminal Code adopted in December 2003 essentially turned a potentially painful punishment into a slap on the wrist. Among other things, these amendments replaced the penalty of confiscation of property with fines of up to one million rubles. Criminal profit, however, is often far in excess of a million rubles. According to Orttung, some experts defend reliance on fines on the grounds that property confiscation is unenforceable.[37]

Legislators who became criminals, criminals who became legislators, corrupt bureaucrats, and the realities of the environment have combined to cre-

---

35. Ibid., p. 5.
36. Ibid., p. 6.
37. Orttung (note 31).

ate a powerful force to prevent the creation of any truly effective means to deal with organized crime. Chebotaryov's desire declared in 1993 to see procurators pursue more organized crime cases would appear to have fallen on deaf ears. To this day, very few cases have been prosecuted across the country. For example, the Deputy Chief of the Organized Crime Control Department in one of the regions reported that they had not had a major crime case for about three years despite the presence of ten functioning organized crime groups there.[38]

This quick glimpse at some recent legislation is merely to illustrate the point that in many ways little has changed in the formal mechanisms that could potentially be used against organized crime. In addition, the public by and large questions law enforcement's ability to get the job done. If public opinion polls are to be taken at face value, the estimation of law enforcement in the eyes of the public has not improved much in the fifteen years since the dismantling of the Soviet Union. A 2005 poll showed that 80% of the respondents believe they could become victims of abuse by the police, the Procurator's office, or the courts. Only 1% responded with any degree of trust toward law enforcement agencies.[39] In another poll, posted on the website of Transparency International, Russia's police received 4.2 points out of a possible 5.0 for corruption.[40] In an August 2005 poll, the Yuri Levada Center found that "the public associates the police with crime to a greater extent than any other organization...."[41] The respondents of this last poll might have been seen as prophetic if corruption weren't already such a pervasive part of Russian life. A month after the August poll, an article appeared in the Russian press featuring a story of police involvement in the underworld.

> The main news yesterday (September 28) was the arrest in Moscow of another large gang of 'bad cops' who had organized contract killings. There was far more conjecture and rumor about this latest in a long line of gangs than there was fact about it. Perhaps because everyone is still hearing about the arrest two years ago of Vladimir Ganeyev, a general in the Ministry for Affairs of Civil Defense, Emergency Situations, and Elimination of Natural Disasters, and of six

---

38. Ibid. This last point is one widely shared by police around the world.

39. *Vedomosti*, "One Percent Confidence," November 3, 2005, accessed at Johnson's Russia List.

40. *Mosnews.com*, "Russian Police, Politicians Most Corrupt—Poll Results," December 9, 2005, accessed at Johnson's Russia List.

41. *Vedomosti*, "Police and State Officials Seem More Frightening than Criminals," August 11, 2005, accessed at Johnson's Russia List.

high-ranking officers of the Moscow Criminal Investigations Department who were acquaintances of his.[42]

By themselves, the polls simply indicate behaviors and sentiments that seem eternal in Russia. The significant change in the post-Soviet world was that the law of the jungle filled the vacuum left by the disappearance of the Communist Party and the abdication of many state institutions in fulfilling their traditional functions. (As the Russians are fond of saying, Nature abhors a vacuum. *Svyatoe mesto pusto ne byvayet.*) After 1991, Russia needed new laws, new law enforcement, and indeed a whole new legislative system. Many ex-convicts (which doesn't mean ex-criminals) became 'noble citizens' and made their way into the legislature of the new country bringing with them their criminal mentality, part of the reason for the failure to institute new and effective measures against organized crime. Eventually, the country became 'stabilized' in such a way that traditional criminals became lawmakers as well as law enforcers or protectors. As the former police detective Alexander Gorkin notes, "The only substitute for the old legal system was the 'common law,' which in Russia, due to decades of living under an oppressive regime, could be nothing but the 'law of the underworld,' with the corresponding criminal law enforcement structure."[43] In essence, this meant that the *vory v zakone* could come out from the shadows of the prison world they ruled and criminal groups could enjoy unprecedented opportunities; it meant that the rough and tumble methods used by the Communist Party and KGB in their ongoing struggle for power throughout the Soviet era would now be used in a much bigger and more visible contest for property rights; it meant that there would be little to distinguish bureaucrats, businessmen, and criminals.

While the Communist Party had long been portrayed as a monolithic, strictly hierarchical organization, within that hierarchy there was a constant struggle for power where the police, KGB, and other agencies were essentially used as henchmen, as Arkady Vaksberg details in his book, *The Soviet Mafia*. Recall from Chapter 1 the three characterizations of 'mafia' by Shchekochikhin, Zaslavskaya, and Simis, contending that traditional groups barely figured, even as minor players, in the game. By the 1990s, they had risen to become in some cases partners with (and in other cases useful pawns of) the former political bosses as the struggle for power among the kingpins of the disintegrated Com-

---

42. Natalya Kozlova, "Faceless 'Bad' Cops. Another Gang of Policemen Detained in Moscow. As Yet They Remain Anonymous," *Rossiiskaya Gazeta*, September 30, 2005, accessed at Johnson's Russia List.

43. Author conversation with Gorkin, December 2006.

munist Party became increasingly violent. The process was a redistribution of property rights writ large. If before, in order to maintain position, the various factions of the Communist Party relied on a monopoly of coercion as wielded by squads of KGB and MVD agents, now the 'means of coercion' were available to a much wider group of people. The state wasn't squeezed out by the traditional groups. Rather, the two became more closely entangled. Remember Chebotaryov's assessment in Chapter 8 that the massive Chechen banking frauds were actually undertaken on behalf of bureaucrats, officials, and politicians. As scholar Serguey Braguinsky notes,

> [T]he salient features of the old Soviet order were its highly politicized and insider-serving property rights system, and high discriminatory barriers against outsiders.... As the Communist system gradually decayed following the death of Stalin, the privileged *nomenklatura* class gained more independence in economic decisions and increasingly exploited their positions for personal gain, in particular by teaming up with parallel economy businesses in what became known as the 'Soviet mafia.'[44]

This relationship among the Party elite and a variety of underground businessmen as well as traditional criminal elements had been simmering for decades. The decline and dismantling of the Soviet Union, within a context of inept leadership personified by Mikhail Gorbachev and Boris Yeltsin, meant that there were no longer any checks against the law of the jungle.

In their book, *Blowing-Up Russia: The Secret Plot to Bring Back KGB Terror*, Polonium-210 poisoning victim and former KGB agent Alexander Litvinenko, and his co-author, the historian Yuri Felshtinsky, talk about cases in which KGB/FSB agents were asked by police officials to create and lead criminal gangs. When asked why, the police officials reportedly replied that it would help them clamp down on businessmen who had "gone loose" and refused to pay their dues. In this game, the agents' role was to intimidate and threaten disobedient businessmen, while the police role was to feign protection and squeeze money out of them. Part of the money then went to the agents as a reward.[45]

---

44. Serguey Braguinsky, "The Rise and Fall of Post-Communist Oligarchs: Legitimate and Illegitimate Children of Praetorian Communism," April 2007, p. 4, http://pluto.fss.buffalo.edu/classes/eco/sb56/OligarchsRus411.pdf.

45. Andrei Antonov, "The FSB as a Criminal Grouping," radicalparty.org (Italy), *Prima News*, February 4, 2003. The complexity of the relationships among criminal groups, politicians, bureaucrats, law enforcement, and businessmen was masterfully illustrated in the Russian television series, *Brigada*.

In an August 2002 email, the lawyer Tom Firestone reports a conversation he had with a cab driver in Moscow about the state of organized crime. "He insists that it is all in the hands of the police and government now and that they provide all the *kryshas* (lit. 'roof,' i.e. 'protection') to small businesses and that the gangsters have moved on to bigger business. This is consistent with everything else I have heard on this subject, including from the Procuracy." This was something I'd come across numerous times in the course of investigations throughout the second half of the 1990s. Actually, the gangsters moved on to a variety of places: some to big business, some to security firms, some overseas, some to prison, and some to the cemetery. But the point remains: the police and other agencies displaced the local gangsters and took control over the protection business. There should be nothing surprising in this. In fact, I would argue that the process as characterized by the cab driver had been going on for some time. It was well known in informed circles that the police as well as local government officials had an active role in running prostitution, for example, long before 2002.

In December 2006, Russian journalist Yulia Latynina supports the observations of the cab driver when she notes that state agencies have taken over from the gangsters to such an extent that they are now essentially facing off against each other as they each control various aspects of both business and the protection industry.

> Two factions of highly placed Russian secret service agents divide up the customs business and then go after each other with riot police; regular government housecleaning occurs, including decrees coming down from on high firing senior deputies to the foreign minister and in the Federal Security Service, but these same officials continue to work, inconspicuously, in the same offices.[46]

Like much else in this Russian 'mafia' scenario, the notion of agencies squaring off against each other was not new, as Melnikov suggested in his remark that the West is only now learning how Russia has always been. MVD intelligence reports I'd come across over the years indicated that officers from various police precincts in Moscow had been involved in shootouts against each other in the 1970s and 1980s fighting over the spoils of criminal activity.[47]

The notion of the KGB (later the FSB) and other agencies being in the middle of the struggle for power and property comes as no surprise given all we've

---

46. Yulia Latynina, "Tougher to Call than in the Old Days," *The Moscow Times*, December 6, 2006, accessed at Johnson's Russia List.

47. Author investigative information.

said about the nature of Russia at that point in history, the nature of information, the nature of business in the transition period, and the nature of the Communist Party's monopoly on the levers of power. It also comes as no surprise, then, that a Russian intelligence report appeared on my desk one day in 1999 titled, "On Participation of Representatives of the Russian Special Services in Business Activity of Commercial Structures Associated with the Aluminum Business," enumerating the names and positions of senior officials from the KGB/FSB, Customs, and Tax Police, both retired and active duty, who were "involved in securing the interests of tycoons of the aluminum business of this country." As these officials became more rooted in the post-Soviet business world, gangsters involved in the aluminum business met the same fate as many others: some were squeezed out and fled the country, others were arrested, and yet others were killed. Some, of course, were retained to handle the dirty work.[48]

According to the report, these 'Representatives of the Russian Special Services' were the First Deputy Director of the former KGB; the Chief and Deputy Chief of the Economic Counterintelligence Department; the Director of the Federal Tax Police, and the Deputy Director of the Federal Customs Department, among others. This collection of officials was referred to as the Firm, whose function "first and foremost is aimed at conducting a whole range of activities including investigative services that serve to minimize financial risks of the illegal import of raw materials for the aluminum industry into Russia as well as 'pumping' hard currency assets abroad." In the course of pursuing these activities, according to the report, the Firm "utilizes existing contacts with leaders of certain organized crime groups to resolve these issues."[49]

According to the report, these active officials along with their retired colleagues maintained their own businesses to generate income to put toward their larger goals in the aluminum industry. One official was deeply involved in the murky deals involving assets of the former Soviet military contingent in Germany. Another helped his brother privatize entities at several Russian airports and seaports. The key individual in this group had direct contacts in Yeltsin's inner circle to facilitate his own interests.

As one example, through the bank he worked with, the key player in the group purchased an apartment for a KGB/FSB officer based in one of the regions. This individual was able to create a system of funneling metals through the port in the region where he was stationed and send them abroad. Later

---

48. "Ob Uchastii Predstavitelei Rossiiskikh Spetssluzhb v Deyatel'nosti Kommercheskikh Struktur, Sviazannykh s Aliuminievym Biznesom," received from former KGB sources in the course of an investigation.

49. Ibid.

he was transferred to the main FSB office in Moscow, then promoted as an officer of the State Customs Committee, and later was moved to the security service of the aluminum company where other top retired FSB officers were employed.

Authors Litvinenko and Felshtinsky go a step beyond the intelligence report and name virtually the entire state power structure as the winners of the game, contrary to Stepashin's contention in January 1999 that the fight against organized crime had been lost. It would seem that, according to the authors, both the 'oligarchs' and the traditional criminals were ultimately the losers in this massive struggle. Perhaps one can consider The Great Mob War of 1992–1994 a kind of reorganization period. The aftermath, particularly after Yeltsin's selection of Vladimir Putin as President of the Russian Federation, featured the reemergence of old guard elements guided by KGB values and principles. Meet the new boss, same as the old boss. According to Litvinenko and Felshtinsky,

> Gradually, with the help of journalists who were operatives or agents of the FSB and SBP and an entire army of unscrupulous writers eager for easy, sensational material, the small number of 'oligarchs' in Russian business came to be declared thieves, swindlers, and even murderers. Meanwhile the really serious criminals, who had acquired genuine oligarchic power and pocketed billions in money that had never been listed in any accounts, were sitting behind their managers' desks at the Russian state's agencies of coercion: the FSB, the SBP, the FSO, the SVR, the Central Intelligence Department (GRU), the General Public Prosecutor's Office, the Ministry of Defense (MO), the Ministry of Internal Affairs (MVD), the customs service, the tax police, and so on.[50]

Litvinenko and Felshtinsky rightly distinguish between the 'oligarchs' as criminals on the one hand, and the "really serious criminals" on the other. Of course, the 'oligarchs' were guilty of a variety of crimes and it couldn't have been otherwise in a country where the law of the jungle ruled. As much as the outside world may have wanted to believe that they represented a sort of 19th century robber baron elite paving the way to the future, the 'oligarchs' reacted in a fairly predictable way. They grew up in the environment and had little interest or ability to change it. In his study of the Russian 'oligarchs,' Serguey Braguinsky concludes that "most of the new ['oligarchs'] could not or perhaps would not change the rules and the reward structure of the socio-economic

---

50. Alexander Litvinenko and Yuri Felshtinsky, *Blowing-Up Russia: The Secret Plot to Bring Back KGB Terror*, New York, Encounter Books, 2007.

game established by the 'Soviet Mafia' and ended up embracing those [rules] themselves."[51]

But like other players in this complex game, the 'oligarchs' in many ways were convenient tools to parade in front of the world as a symbol of a new business era in post-Soviet Russia, while the arms of the state regained their strength. And the arms of the state indeed regained their strength, primarily the KGB in the form of its successor, the FSB. More than any other single agency, the FSB was in a position to capitalize on its vast resources and highly trained staff to squeeze out the gangsters when necessary and to monitor the business world. And with a former KGB agent as President of the country, their task became considerably easier.

> [M]ost FSB staff who are meant to be monitoring private companies actually spend entire days at those companies, planning financial transactions at their offices, and reaching agreements with their colleagues about joint financial operations. They can make money by finding out the address of a potential business partner, collecting information about the person, and checking whether that person is a secret service agent.... But the main problem is the alarming rise in corruption within the FSB. Money is all. Entire groups of FSB staff work for companies in the private sector, sometimes even from their FSB offices.... It is also known that business owners and managers of state agencies actively 'feed' the bosses at the FSB, especially on such occasions as birthdays or holidays. Usually they give money—from $50,000 to $100,000.[52]

The war against organized crime in Russia was indeed over—not because law enforcement lost, as Stephashin claimed, but because the state actually won. Organized crime groups, *as we knew them in the 1990s*, particularly in cities like Moscow and St. Petersburg, have largely become a thing of the past. Some have been squeezed out by state competition. Some have become 'legitimate,' taking the form of private security companies and business owners. Still others remain. Much of their low-level operations have been taken over by state agencies, while the most powerful crime groups continue to legitimize their holdings. This doesn't mean, however, that they've abandoned 'mafia' tactics; contract killings and other forms of coercion continue as a normal tool

---

51. Braguinsky (note 44), p. 4.

52. *Novaya Gazeta*, "Corruption is Among the Main Problems for Russia's Secret Services," no. 6, February 2001, accessed in Johnson's Russia List (February 8, 2001). See also WPS Monitoring Agency www.wps.ru/e_index.html.

in the toolbox of business, politics, and crime. But as noted earlier, the organized crime groups have not taken over the country. In many ways, they simply joined the 'mafia' that existed prior to the dismantling of the Soviet Union (or died trying). We have come full circle. The Communist Party 'mafia'—that network of competing political and economic clans in the guise of a monolithic hierarchy—has adapted and reorganized itself. Kristol's quote at the beginning of Chapter 1 portraying the Communist Party as 'mafia' is now apropos once again. My friends who used to point to the Kremlin in the late 1980s and say, "But, of course, that's where the real mafia resides," are now right once again. Meet the new boss, same as the old boss.

* * *

While the international aspects of organized crime from the former Soviet Union and the law enforcement response to it in the United States and Europe are the subject of a future book, it's interesting to outline some of the dynamics underway in the 1990s. The USSR's membership in Interpol, the international police organization based in Lyon, France, was accepted in September 1990, enabling the Soviet Union to widen its base of resources in fighting organized and transnational crime. And cooperation with the United Nations had increased dramatically, with the USSR taking a lead role in hosting UN conferences on international organized crime and narcotics trafficking.[53] Numerous other initiatives of this sort were undertaken in the initial excitement and hopefulness of the post-Soviet years.

This may have sounded very promising back in the early 1990s to outsiders, but the fact was that Interpol at that time was generally considered slow and unreliable. National Central Bureaus (NCB), the Interpol representative offices in each member state, were not firmly established in Eastern Europe, and getting information from places like Central Asia was slow if it arrived at all. In a region of the world that built trust through personal contacts, it was psychologically difficult for officers to rely on that formalistic, bureaucratic mechanism. Moreover, there was high personnel turnover in the offices, complicating already delicate relationships.[54]

---

53. Joseph D. Serio, "Organized Crime in the Former Soviet Union," Masters Thesis. University of Illinois at Chicago, 1993, p. 100.

54. H.L. Zachert, "The Threats Posed by East European Organized Crime: Statement Presented to the Permanent Subcommittee on Investigations of the Committee on Governmental Affairs," United States Senate, p. 20. Also, author conversations with personnel of Russia's National Central Bureau in Moscow, especially Alexander Safronnov, and in-

Generally speaking, Soviet and later Russian police lacked operational contacts abroad, particularly with Western Europe and the United States. There
was little way for police officials to reach out to counterparts in other countries without going through their embassies or Interpol, contributing to a general sense of frustration among those who wanted to get things done. This was
all perfectly understandable. For its part, the West had an abiding suspicion
of former Soviet officials, and for the most part Soviet police had little idea of
the realities of the West. And they both had their own formidable bureaucracies to face. The following examples illustrate how both the United States and
the Russian Federation needed to overcome significant challenges in order to
move the relationship forward to fight the 'Russian mafia' in the international
arena. In many ways, they still haven't succeeded.

In several places in this book we've met Gennady Chebotaryov and Anatoly Volobuyev. In the late 1980s and early 1990s, Chebotaryov was an MVD
colonel (later general) and Deputy Chief of the Organized Crime Control Department for the Soviet Union and the post-Soviet Russian Federation.
Volobuyev was also a colonel and a leading MVD researcher on organized
crime. In August 1989, before the Western media began trumpeting the rise
of the 'Russian mafia,' Chebotaryov and Volobuyev visited the University of
Illinois at Chicago, where I was working at the Office of International Criminal Justice, to present conference papers on the state of organized crime in
the USSR. Their two-fold bottom-line message was clear and concise: 1) we
have an organized crime problem we're not prepared to handle and need the
help of the U.S., and 2) sooner or later our organized crime problem will be
your organized crime problem.

They asked our assistance in setting up a meeting with the FBI in Chicago.
Unfortunately, though perhaps understandably, the FBI refused their request.
According to FBI sources, there was a major firestorm raging inside the Bureau
between the law enforcement division and the counterintelligence side of the
house. Long-time counterintelligence agents who had spent a fair portion of
the 1970s and 1980s monitoring Soviets in and around New York City, Los Angeles, San Francisco, and other cities, were outraged by even the mention of
opening the door to the very people they had been laboring to keep out. They
were concerned that, among other things, the Soviets would attempt to compromise the counterintelligence and organized crime control agents who would
become known to them in the event of a working relationship. One of the Bu-

---

vestigators in the MVD's Organized Crime Control Department, especially Leonid Se-
leznyov.

reau agents in the Chicago Field Office noted the FBI's fear that these officers could have been KGB agents acting as a Trojan horse, extending a hand of cooperation and friendship while harboring less gracious motives. According to sources inside the Bureau, the law enforcement arm appreciated the need for cooperation but was outgunned by the old guard. Chebotaryov and Volobuyev left at the end of their stay without having seen a Bureau representative.

The following year, in May 1990, Chebotarev returned to Chicago with two generals, a colonel, major, and captain to explore the possibility of establishing an exchange program between the University of Illinois (since the Bureau wasn't interested) and the MVD. During the visit, the group was briefed by the IRS, the U.S. Marshal Service, and other agencies, and met with fellow practitioners from the Chicago Police Department. This time, the Bureau did take five minutes to say a guarded 'hello' to the Soviets but no meaningful inroads were made. As a result of the Soviets' visit it was agreed that I would be sent to Moscow for one year and two officers from Chebotaryov's department would go to Chicago.

As far as I can tell, one of the earliest 'recon' visits of the FBI to Moscow took place in April 1991. At the time I was working in the MVD's Organized Crime Control Department, supervised by Chebotaryov. He asked me to be the interpreter in a meeting between him and the Bureau's international representative who was visiting Moscow. As might have been expected, the representative was totally unaware of reality on the ground in the Soviet Union, and I had the impression that if this was the Bureau's first line of interaction it would be a long time before the two sides started to understand each other.

In October that year, together with the United Nations, the MVD sponsored an international conference on organized crime control, attended by representatives from some 25 countries. The United States was represented by Jim Moody, then-head of the FBI's Organized Crime Control Department, and Michael DeFeo, a lawyer from the Racketeering and Organized Crime Section of the Department of Justice. The conference was closed to the public with only five outside observers present. Perhaps to reduce distractions or to keep out the 'mafia,' the conference was held in Suzdal, some 130 miles from Moscow. In any case, to get U.S. practitioners on the ground in the USSR— and beyond Moscow city limits—I thought was a positive step. Trying to judge or even to imagine conditions in the Soviet Union without ever having visited was rife with pitfalls.

As Moody's interpreter for a number of informal conversations with local law enforcement and KGB officials, I know he heard things that sent him into a mild state of shock: Eighty percent corruption in the local police departments, lack of equipment, vehicles, and even gasoline, and unbelievably low salaries. After one day of conference sessions, several of us were invited to dinner by the Chief of the KGB's Organized Crime Control Department. Jim Moody and Michael DeFeo, along with Dick Ward, then Vice Chancellor of the University of Illinois at Chicago and Director of the Office of International Criminal Justice, and I were taken by jeep to a secluded hunting lodge protected by a tall wooden fence. Our host was said to be the chief of environmental conservation. Ironically, the rooms and corridors were adorned with stuffed animals that had once roamed the hundreds of acres surrounding the house. The conservation chief boasted that just a few hours earlier our dinner had been enjoying the great outdoors.

The Soviet side was represented by the chiefs of the Soviet, Russian, Suzdal, and Vladimir organized crime control departments of the KGB as well as Evgeny, a junior KGB officer who served as interpreter. Although his English was very good, at some point in the evening we developed a tag-team style of interpretation when he came up short on his English. After the conversation had turned serious, the senior KGB general suggested that his organization and the FBI establish a joint training program. Moody seemed somewhat taken aback by the straightforward way and seriousness with which the general made his proposal. The only response Moody could give seemed obvious: the timing was not right to hurry into a close partnership particularly given the history of relations between our two countries and especially given the nature of the KGB. Moody chose his words with great care, diplomatically telling the general that he shouldn't hold his breath waiting for such a relationship to develop. But the general did not miss a beat, claiming that the KGB of old was dead and what remained had been reformed. "That was then; we're a different organization now. We're new…." The only problem with the general's claim was that, by the time of our dinner, the spy agency had been dead for all of six hours.

Moody returned to Washington with a more urgent message than the international representative who preceded him. Shortly thereafter, of course, the Soviet Union was thrown into the dustbin of history. The Bureau then found itself in a position to wait for the dust to settle, re-identify the real decision makers, and continue to do battle with Russian bureaucratic uncertainty and lingering Cold War suspicions. This waiting game was a source of frustration for Chebotaryov who was now Deputy Chief of the Organized Crime Control Department for the Russian Federation. He noted in 1992 that any sense of cooperation that had been generated by Moody's visit and subsequent mutual assistance was quickly evaporating. Part of this certainly was due to the FBI's own internal complexities. But even basic communication seemed to be failing. When Chebotaryov provided information on a hit man who had entered the United States and was operating out of New York, there no response, no feedback. Other cases that Chebotaryov asked me to forward to law enforcement fell on deaf ears. In the meantime, the subjects of those cases went on to become some of the most powerful ex-Soviet gangster-businessmen operating in the United States and continue to operate in the U.S. and in a number of other countries to this day.

At the same time, the FBI had legitimate concerns of its own. In the early 1990s, the Western media was exploding with stories about the Russian 'mafia' and the corruption endemic to the Russian police. Whom to trust? There had already been indications that information shared with the Russians had been passed on or sold to the subjects of the investigations.

In February 1993, then-Chief of the Russian Federation's Organized Crime Control Department, Mikhail Yegorov, traveled to the U.S. for meetings with the Bureau to move the relationship forward. This was a moment of absolute commitment by the Russians, according to one of the Russians involved in developing the relationship. However, their frustration with the U.S. was deepening at this point. The Bureau was facing its own bureaucratic morass, as permission to open an office overseas inside the U.S. Embassy in Moscow would require the assistance of the State Department and the approval of Congress. That couldn't have been an easy process. According to sources in Moscow, once the liaison office was finally approved, relations between some U.S. Embassy staff and the FBI were slow to get off the ground. After its own bureaucratic hurdles were cleared, the FBI eventually developed an ongoing if difficult line of communication with Russian authorities.

Here in the United States, one of the few major, widely-publicized, apparent victories the FBI scored was the 1995 arrest of the *vor v zakone* Vyacheslav Ivankov in New York City. The case was splashed across newspapers around the world, heralding international cooperation while giving the Russian 'mafia' a face. A more balanced account with the ring of truth to it, according to insiders, might speak of the dramatic fumbling of the case due to interagency jealousies on the U.S. side. The slam-dunk case nearly slipped through their fingers.

Since that time, the only high profile case of the Russian 'mafia' in the U.S. was the Bank of New York 'scandal' in which Russians and other former Soviets were caught laundering billions of dollars through BoNY. Of course, the real scandal wasn't the movement of such large sums of money, but that anyone was surprised that it happened. With billions of dollars moving out of Russia every year for more than 15 years, banks around the world were making tremendous amounts of money. In actuality, few had a real interest in stopping the Russian 'mafia' cold in its tracks. There was too much money to be made and too much bureaucratic mileage to get out of it. But September 11 wiped the Russian 'mafia' off the map. There is currently comparatively little attention being paid to it, and many of the law enforcement officers assigned to the task, particularly at the federal level, have little experience in dealing with the Russians and former Soviets in general. Terrorism is the crisis du jour, and there is far more money to be made from it. But given everything we've said about Russia and the Russia 'mafia,' I have a sneaking suspicion that its heyday in the U.S. and Europe has yet to come.

Why Should You Care?

One of the goals of this book was to present a critical examination of the information produced in the 1990s about the so-called Russian 'mafia.' When dissecting mountains of data from the media, law enforcement, and other sources, one finds that the contours of the problem become far more nebulous than they may have once seemed. Rather than a cut and dried, good guy/bad guy scenario, we see that the players were hopelessly entangled in a game where the line between legality and illegality was far from clear, where the labels given to the players were subjective and constantly shifting, and where our impressions of the situation were manufactured and manipulated by parties that had a direct interest in the outcome.

The analysis points us toward a far less monolithic phenomenon than what many had assumed and an apparently less dramatic growth in the number of crime groups throughout the decade in the former Soviet Union. As I have been careful to indicate throughout the book, this is not to say that organized crime (or, organizING crime, as Petrus van Duyne would say) wasn't real and wasn't responsible for vast damage and suffering. It is not my intention to downplay the seriousness or minimize anyone's loss.

For the student readers, I am far less interested in reporting the minute details of the story than creating an overarching exercise of questioning sources. I am also hoping to instill a sense in student readers that conducting research at the undergraduate and graduate levels is an investigation and requires examining assumptions, putting ourselves in other people's shoes, and coming up with conclusions that have the ring of truth to them, not simply reaching the most convenient, expedient end to a search. All too often, students cut and paste material wholesale with the goal of completing a project and getting a grade rather than questioning the assumptions behind the arguments and the methods with which information was collected and presented. With any luck, this book has encouraged some readers to be less accepting of media versions or official pronouncements, whether addressing the so-called Russian 'mafia' or any other subject for that matter.

The problem of organized criminality in the former Soviet Union generally and in Russia in particular is complex and emerged from a rich and varied—and in many ways tragic—social, political, and economic history. I find
it impossible to look at Russia without fascination, awe, and perhaps a certain degree of pity. At the same time, it is important to remember that in
many ways the former Soviet Union was little more than a developing country with nuclear weapons. Perhaps we came to expect too much from her,
more than she had to give. Much of the story of crime in Russia in the late
1980s and 1990s had to do with our own ignorance of the place. As Yuri Melnikov noted, Russia has always been this way.

Doubtless these points may be debated endlessly. There seems little consensus on what Russia is and what the 1990s will mean for her over the long
term. It will be left to criminologists, historians, political scientists, and others to decide years from now the implications of that period of the so-called
criminal revolution. However, there are final questions to consider as we come
to the end of this book. The major questions that a work of this nature should
at least try to answer, ones that are pertinent to us today, now take center
stage: "Why should I care?" "Why is this important to me?" "How does this
issue impact me?" These questions actually determined the form of this book.

If we read the Russian 'mafia' story as simply one of gangsters of the 1990s,
we might be tempted to conclude that the threat has disappeared, particularly
since the media has largely stopped talking about it. If we orient ourselves toward an examination of Russia more generally and regard the 'mafia' story as
merely one facet in a complex history, we might be inclined to view potential
threats far more broadly. For this reason, Chapter 5 attempted to provide a
longer view—albeit a rather general, introductory perspective—of some of
the long-standing realities of Russian life. Chapter 6 endeavored to provide a
snapshot of the economic system and its impact on the psychology of a country. The story of the Russian 'mafia' as told by most will be limited in scope to
the late 1980s and 1990s, but it may be that, ultimately, the more important
story is the organized, semi-organized, and disorganized fraud engendered by
the system, a legacy received, as Andrei Dmitriev said, "with our mother's
milk."

That fraud touches us in numerous ways, for many from the Russian Federation (as well as the former Soviet Union) have taken what they've learned
in their warped political and economic system and exported it to numerous
countries around the world. It is true, as I noted in several places, that most
former Soviets coming to our shores want nothing more than to live good,
productive lives, and steer well clear of breaking the law. Others, though,
while not necessarily gangsters, thugs, or members of any 'mafia,' frequently

use well-developed skills in manipulating systems in order to make money out of thin air, in much the same way as we saw throughout Russian and Soviet history.

For example, in 1983, a group of about two dozen people organized by two Soviet-trained doctors established 'rolling medical laboratories' offering free or low-cost medical testing around the United States. The group worked the system thoroughly, filing countless fraudulent medical insurance claims for services supposedly rendered. Because most insurance programs covered only testing and treatment that was medically necessary, the group falsified the diagnosis on bills and patient medical records so as to create the false impression that the patient was suffering from an illness or injury and that the doctor had prescribed the medical testing as a medically necessary treatment. In fact, most of the patients were in normal physical health and had no need for extensive testing; the patients had come to the lab sites only to receive 'free exams,' for which they had been solicited by telephone. Over the course of almost ten years, the group ran up $1 billion in fraudulent medical billings and raked in more than $80 million, perpetrating "the largest health insurance fraud ever prosecuted in the United States.... More than 800 government programs, health insurance companies, and employee benefit plans were victimized by the scheme."[1] They were finally stopped in 1993 by the U.S. Postal Inspection Service working in concert with no less than seven other major law-enforcement and health-related agencies.

Likewise, profits were generated by others through staged auto accidents. In one U.S. city alone, about 200 staged crashes were organized by one former Soviet to collect insurance money for 'soft tissue' injuries. Lieutenants of the ringleader would recruit accomplices—often recent immigrants with poor language skills and a need for quick cash—to help stage their crashes. In the scam, as many as three cars would box in a late model car that was likely to have good insurance coverage. One car pulls in front of the target, one behind, and sometimes one to the side, leaving no escape. The lead driver slams on the brakes, forcing the victim to hit him. The driver and the passengers then file injury claims against the victim's insurer, claiming an array of soft-tissue injuries. Claims per accident reportedly averaged about $50,000, although the conspirators typically received about a third of that. The leader of this particular network was found with a suitcase containing $263,000 in cash, and law enforcement documented at least $4 million in false claims. He had

---

1. Letter from the U.S. Postal Inspection Service official in charge of the case to Gennady Chebotaryov, then Deputy Chief of the Organized Crime Control Department of the MVD of the Russian Federation, October 13, 1994.

set up a string of chiropractic clinics and law offices to help bill for the fraudulent injury claims. This may not seem like much but consider that there are groups filing thousands of claims of this type.[2]

In a presentation prepared by the Coordinated Law Enforcement Unit of British Columbia for a three-day closed-door law enforcement conference on Russian organized crime in April 1999, the representative presented the Unit's research findings on the extent and impact of Eastern European Organized Crime (EEOC) in British Columbia. The material noted a noticeable growth of EEOC activities of a transnational nature that were increasingly sophisticated and diverse, and involved previously unknown groups and individuals. Groups from the former Soviet Union were entering Canada using the country's business entrepreneur/investment program. As in other parts of the world, these groups were believed to be engaged in money laundering, drug trafficking, extortion/protection, smuggling, gaming, credit card fraud, prostitution, auto theft, weapons trafficking, and securities fraud. Remember that they go where the money is and will engage in virtually any activity in which money can be made. It's not surprising to find drug traffickers engaging in insurance fraud.

In 1997, I gave a presentation in North Carolina about the Russian 'mafia' to an audience of more than 500 insurance investigators from around the country. At the end of my session, I was approached by a number of audience members with their own tales to tell. Each of them, regardless of the part of the country they came from, made the same statements. "I'm from Baltimore and I have a problem with Russians," "I'm from Washington, D.C. and I have a problem with Russians." I wasn't too surprised to hear such things from these locations. Many major cities, such as New York, Los Angeles, Chicago, and Miami, could claim a reasonably large population of former Soviets, and their activity in fraud was a well-established reality in these places. What took me aback were the next two comments. "I'm from Alabama and I have a problem with Russians." "I'm from Louisiana and I have a problem with Russians." Their references really were to 'Soviets' of course, but the point was taken: former Soviets were active in various parts of the country perpetrating frauds using much of the homegrown knowledge derived during the Communist era. In a private conversation during the conference, an FBI agent showed me a map marking the U.S. states that had reported a 'problem with Russians.' Nearly every state was shaded, leaving less than a handful blank. Of course,

---

2. Author access to insurance company files pertaining to the case. See also Mark Potok, "Russian Mob Linked to U.S. Scam," *USA Today*, August 23, 1996.

the claim shouldn't be taken at face value. There was no indication of the concentrations of former Soviet citizens in each of the states. There was no sense of how many people or how many crimes constituted 'a problem.' Far more research would have to be conducted to get a sense of what is occurring around the country. But the point was made: there seemed to be a fairly widespread occurrence of fraud by former Soviets across the country.

These examples may strike some as ancient history, but do not be lulled into thinking that they are anomalies or that such activity has ceased to exist because the media generally has moved past this story. Consider that the behaviors we're talking about existed in Russia and the former Soviet Union for hundreds of years. Are they likely to stop now? In the post-9/11 world, with the attention of federal law enforcement primarily directed toward terrorism, this very well may be the golden age of fraud. (Just ask the insurance companies who are at a loss about how to address these issues.) The FBI did issue an unclassified information bulletin in June 2007 to all FBI field offices indicating a Massachusetts-based Russian physical therapist engaged in billing fraud and staged automobile accidents through his clinic. His colleagues previously had been convicted of health care fraud, mail fraud, wire fraud, and money laundering. They were also said by the FBI to have ties to Russian organized crime. The point that needs to be appreciated is that such activity is happening across the United States.

The questions, as always, remain: are groups from the former Soviet Union a different breed or have they simply joined the numerous other national and ethnic groups involved in defrauding the system? Do they seem worse than the others because of the media attention focused on them in the 1990s or are they in fact ultimately worse because of the manipulative ways they internalized back in the former Soviet Union?

New Jersey-based police investigator, Eugene Troyansky, gives a piece of advice to his law enforcement colleagues: "In deciding whether to indict or investigate a particular Russian businessman for tax evasion, racketeering, and so on, the law enforcement official has to ask himself: 'Would I do it if he were Irish or black or Chinese?'" In discussing the nature of the threat in the U.S., Troyansky indeed echoes the fraud point made in many parts of the book. "They set up companies and run financial schemes. When stakes become too big and you can't bribe someone, well, then it [violence] becomes unavoidable. [But] in his mind, he didn't commit a crime."[3]

This is a point that law enforcement needs to take to heart. If the vast majority of their activity is financial and their activities are entwined in legal and

---

3. Author conversation with Eugene Troyansky, May 2000.

illegal businesses, the law enforcement tools needed to counter them go well beyond search warrants, handcuffs, and guns. Forensic accountants, specialists in finance, and computer experts are more appropriate weapons in this fight. Beyond that, cultural intelligence may be the most critical element. Knowing the history of the Gulag and Soviet prisons generally may give police interrogators a clue that threats of incarceration may not yield much information. The good cop/bad cop approach to eliciting information also frequently produces little. While detailed prescriptions for dealing with informants, suspects, and criminals from the former Soviet Union are subjects for a different book, suffice to say that former Soviets have seen far worse circumstances and far tougher law enforcement approaches than we could deliver in the United States.

It comes as little surprise that the Russian 'mafia' story of the 1990s in the United States was misinterpreted by some. For example, then Director of the FBI's Russian Organized Crime Squad in New York, Raymond Kerr, noted that Russian organized criminals "have not managed to institutionalize themselves in America. Big organizations like Cosa Nostra don't exist. It has not taken off the way that many feared."[4] This perception was based on the mistaken assumption that the violence being perpetrated in the former Soviet Union and the vast organizations that *seemed* to exist over there were somehow normal features of post-Soviet organized crime. In reality, there was no reason whatever for that behavior to transfer to places like the U.S.; the environment of the former Soviet Union in the 1990s dictated the mode of behavior. That is, virtually the entire economy was up for grabs in a period of dramatically declining social and political control. There was no need to transfer these activities to the U.S. because fraud, deception, counterfeiting, forging, and a host of other activities in a stable economy were quite satisfactory to reach the ultimate goal: make money out of thin air. This is a Russian criminal's dream come true.

While the threat the FBI was anticipating may not have "taken off the way that many feared," it has indeed taken off in other, more subtle, more insidious ways. The lessons of Chapters 5-8 underscored the Russian and Soviet need to and penchant for manipulating systems, whether it was through the black market production of goods, diversion of consumer goods, or sleight of hand with documents. (Remember, many state workers received bonuses based on the *reported* fulfillment of the plan.) This is not about to end in the foreseeable future.

---

4. *The New York Times*, August 19, 2002, cited in the newsletter of the International Association for the Study of Organized Crime, www.iasoc.net/htm.

Index

A

Abkhazian group, 214
Afghan War, 176
agriculture, 101, 112–13, 125, 126–27, 129
airfields, 40–41, 226
Aizderdzis, Andrei, 15–16
alcohol, 241
    consumption of, 189
    criminal groups and, 188–92
    during NEP era, 118
    restrictions on, 190
Aleksanian, Rafail, 167
'Alex Borodin' (Koptevo group member), 227
All-Union Voluntary Society for the Struggle for Sobriety, 190
aluminum industry, 40, 41, 267–68
American Medical Center, 64
amnesties, 135
Analytical Center for Socio-Economic Policy (Analyticheskii Tsentr po Sotsialno-Ekonomicheskoi Politike pri Prezidenta Rossiiskoi Federatsii), 75–78, 81
And Now My Soul Is Hardened (Ball), 119–22
Anderson, Scott, 62
Andropov, Yuri, 190
Anna, Empress, 121n.93
anti-capitalism, 103
anti-society, 107, 119–20, 154, 162, 173
Antonyan, Yuri M., 157
'Apelsin' (Koptevo group member), 227
argot, criminal, 104, 164–65
Armenian groups, 214, 215, 218

arrests, 133–34
autocracy, 35–36, 37, 101, 108, 206
automobiles
    Five Year Plans and, 128–29
    markets, 188
    repair, 222
    selling of, 222
    service centres, 226
    spare parts, 223
    staged accidents, 279–80, 281
    theft of, 222, 223
aviso (payment notice), 194–96, 222, 223
avtoritety, 85, 89, 145, 159–60, 225, 226
Avtovaz, 250
Azerbaijani group, 60n.30, 214, 218

B

Babunashvili, M., 23
Bagdasarian, Rafik ('Svo,' 'Rafik-Svo'), 167–68
Bakatin, Vadim, 146, 254
Baku Juvenile Affairs Commission, 122
Balashikhinsky criminal group, 186
Ball, Alan, 115, 120
    And Now My Soul Is Hardened, 119–22
banditism, 261
banditry, 88, 103–4, 105, 106, 122, 150n.6, 255, 257
Bank of New York, 274
bankers, murders of, 71–75
banking and banks
    control of, 77, 79
    criminal groups and, 71–75, 221
    document fraud and, 194–96

establishment of, 74, 206
extortion and, 81
loans to entrepreneurs, 75
private, 74
shareholders of, 233
state, 74–75
Barannikov, Viktor, 88
Baranov, Viktor, 176
barter, 12, 13, 109, 113, 139n.48, 191
Bennett, Venora, 64–65
Berezovsky, Boris, 49–51
Beriozka stores, 187
Berlin Wall, 206
Bernstam, Michael C. *Fixing Russia's Banks*, 75
Bernstein, Laurie, 121n.93
besprizorniki, 119–22
bitches *(suki)*, 153
bitches' war *(such'ya voina)*, 153
'Black Cat' gang *(Chyornaya Koshka)*, 176
black market
    in computers, 193–94
    criminal world-upperworld interaction and, 145
    deficit goods for, 177
    Five Year Plans and, 128, 129, 130
    and hotels, 182
    in items stolen from dormitories, 180
    'mafia,' 22–23
    moonshine, 190–91
    and smuggling, 241
    in Tbilisi, 143
    Western goods on, 139
Blasi, Joseph, et al. *Kremlin Capitalism*, 80–81
Blowing-Up Russia (Litvinenko, Felshtinsky), 265, 268
Bolsheviks, 5, 112–13
bonuses, 85, 130, 282
bosses, criminal. *See* crime leaders
Braguinsky, Serguey, 265, 268–69
Brezhnev, Leonid, 142, 190
bribery
    big businessmen and, 25
    in coal factory, 140
    command economy and, 137

Koptevo group and, 226
and 'mafia' concept, 14
during NEP era, 116, 117
Peter the Great and, 109–10
police and, 110–11, 258
predictability *vs.* unpredictability of, 111–12
state as 'mafia' and, 17
in sting operations, 262
taxation *vs.*, 108
in Tsarist era, 108–9
and violence, 281
voevoda system of *kormlenie* and, 108
Brokhin, Yuri, 18, 144–45
    Hustling on Gorky Street, 140
Brown, Guy, 60n.31
bureaucrats/bureaucracy
    anti-capitalism of, 103
    banking frauds and, 265
    as businessmen, 230, 231
    collectives and, 127
    corruption among, 12, 18, 39, 229, 237
    criminal groups and, 244, 255
    in criminal pyramid, 19
    excess of, 100
    under Five Year Plans, 136
    ideology *vs.* reality among, 85
    in Iron Triangle, 211, 233, 234, 235, 255
    law enforcement and, 271, 273, 274, 275
    'mafia' and, 196
    in Muscovy, 108
    Nepmen and, 117
    as part of Iron Triangle, 233–37, 244
    politics and, 48
    production and, 130, 136
    salaries, 108
    in 17th century, 100, 108–9
    See also officials
business(es)
    attitudes toward, 17, 103
    Catherine the Great and, 101
    Communists and, 103
    control of, 77–80, 79, 83
    employees' actions, 25

extortion and, 81
goals of, 245–46
lack of environmental development,
    100–101
negative forces, 103
numbers of, 232
as part of Iron Triangle, 233–37, 244
Peter the Great and, 101
as players in crime world, 27
self-made man in, 242
and stereotypical gangsters, 81–82
style of, 245
training in, 185–86
types of actors in, 181
Western practices compared to Soviet,
    231–32, 246.
See also foreign businesses/
    businessmen; private business
businessmen
    big, 25
    black marketeers as, 241
    and bribery, 25
    corruption among, 24
    and criminal groups, 11, 231, 234–35,
        248, 255
    as criminals, xviii, 19, 27–28
    foreign companies and, 245–46
    law enforcement and, 255, 265
    as 'mafia,' 17, 25, 26
    negative forces against, 103
    organized crime groups as, 269
    protection for, 178
    small, 25
    use of underworld methods, 146,
        231–32
    See also entrepreneurs; 'oligarchs'
Butyrski Central prison, 158n.29

C

Campanella, Joel, 58
capital flight, 232
capitalism
    on eve of World War I, 102–3
    and organized crime, 46
Carstensen, Fred, 102
casinos, 118
Catherine the Great, 101

Center for Strategic and International
    Studies (CSIS). "The 'Iron Triangle'
    of Contemporary Russia," 233–34
Central Bank of Russia, 74, 75
Central Commission in the Struggle
    against Contraband, 117
central planning
    Bolsheviks and, 112
    Five Year Plans and, 127
    Gosbank and, 74
    War Communism and, 112
Chalidze, Valery, 164
chambermaids, 181–82, 183
Chancellor, Richard, 98
Charles I, King, 99–100
Chebotaryov, Gennady
    and black market computers, 193
    on Chechen 'mafia,' 195
    credit card fraud and, 185
    on criminal groups, 11
    on establishment of joint ventures and
        cooperatives, 232, 265
    and FBI cooperation, 273–74
    and Ivankov, 170
    and 'mafia' as on inside, 7–8
    on meaning of 'control,' 78–79
    on *obshchak* funds for bribery, 161
    and Organized Crime Control
        Department, 6n.3, 7–8, 48
    on Procurator's office, 257, 263
    respect for, 48n.9
    on size of criminal groups, 218
    visit to U.S., 271–72
Chechen group, 184, 188, 214, 215, 218
Chechen-Ingush Republic, 183
Chechen 'mafia,' 56–60, 180, 214
Chechnya
    organized crime in, 194
    secession from Russian Federation, 57
Cheka, 122
Chernenko, Konstantin, 190
children
    prostitution, 120–21
    See also besprizorniki
churches, 112
CIA, 73
Civil War, 5, 112

codes
  idealistic/ideological *vs.* survival, 141
  repressive regimes and, 170
  social changes and, 171
  survival and, 171
  of *vory v zakone*, 155–56, 170–73
  See also laws
Cold War, 9, 32, 176
collective farm system *(kolkhoz)*, 126–27
collectivization, 132, 134
The Coming Russian Boom (Layard,
  Parker), 25–27, 60n.30
command economy, 42, 137, 175, 180,
  229
Communist Party (CPSU)
  Central Committee, 140, 184, 199
  code of devotion to building
    Communism, 141
  coercion applied by, 265
  control over property and businesses,
    233
  and corruption, 143–44
  and criminal organizations, 265
  foreign businesses and, 6
  legal vacuum left by disappearance, 264
  as 'mafia,' 18–21, 211, 232, 270
  power struggle within, 264–65
  racketeering by, 19
  and underworld, 265
Communist Party of Uzbekistan, Central
  Committee, 199–200
companies/corporations
  chartering of, 101, 102
  dormant, 80
  during 18th century, 101–2
  fake, 27
  life spans of, 101
  during 19th century, 102
  numbers of, 232
  profitability, 80
  shell, 80
  stand-by, 80
  types of, 232
  See also business(es)
computers, 192–94, 245–46
Comrade Criminal (Handelman), 28,
  46–48

connections. *See* personal contacts
construction sector, Five Year Plans and,
  128
consumer goods
  criminal groups and, 223
  personal contacts and, 12–13
  shortages of, 132, 177, 192, 206,
    229–30
contacts. *See* personal contacts
contract murders, 56, 71–72, 73–74, 263
control
  of businesses, 77–81, 83
  meaning of, 78–81
convictions, 134–35
cooperatives, 232
Coordinated Law Enforcement Unit
  (British Columbia), 280
coronation ceremonies, 165
*The Corporation Under Russian Law,
  1800–1917* (Owen), 100–101
corruption
  among businessmen, 24
  within bureaucracy, 12, 18, 39, 229,
    237
  Communist Party and, 143–44
  and crime, 180
  in Dagestan, 194
  extent of, 24
  as ingrained and systemic, 20
  in Ingushetia, 194
  in Kazakhstan, 78
  lacks in administration system and,
    109
  in Mexico, 207
  in North Ossetia, 194
  in oil industry, 237–38
  Peter the Great and, 109–10
  police, 53, 273
  state and, 25
Cosa Nostra, 16
Council of Ministers of the USSR,
  139–40
credit card fraud, 185
crime
  during Civil War, 112
  economy and, 205
  eradication of, 145

fear of, 45–46
hierarchy and, 106
meaning of, 107
as non-existent, 139
omnipresence of, 103–4
peasants and, 106–7
prisons and, 135
rates, 45–46, 255
in 16th and 17th centuries, 103–4
socialism and, 145
state measures to fight, 139–40
crime leaders
 avtoritety (*see avtoritety*)
 emergence of, 106
 as high profile bosses, 145
 of 1920s gangs, 120
 vory v zakone (*see vory v zakone*)
criminal activities
 gangs and, 176
 and 'mafia' concept, 24, 25–27
 numbers by Tashkent 'bandit' group,
 179
 by organized crime groups, 179
criminal associations/organizations,
 221–22, 223
 Communist Party and, 265
 crime groups united to form, 218–19,
 221–22
 and oil industry, 40
 as reflection of larger environment,
 173
Criminal Code
 of 1922, 261
 Article 35, 261
 Article 209, 261
 Article 210, 261
 Article 283, 262
 Article 304, 261–62
criminal gangs
 activities, 176
 during Civil War, 112
 during 18th century, 104–6
 leaders of (*vozhak/glavar*), 120
 length of time of existence, 179–80
 during NEP era, 118
 during 1950s, 140
 during 1970s and 1980s, 176

in Tashkent, 178–79
and *tsekhoviki*, 177
criminal groups
 and alcohol, 188–92
 arrests of, 92–93
 within associations, 218–19, 221–22
 and banking sector, 73
 breaking up of, 93, 222
 bureaucracy and, 244, 255
 businessmen in, 11, 231, 234–35, 248,
 255
 in Canada, 280
 characteristics of, 223–25
 and computers, 192–93, 193
 consolidation of, 94, 228
 control of enterprises, 77–80
 cooperation among, 221
 disappearance of, 228
 dismantling of Soviet Union and, 35,
 86, 93, 206–7
 distinguishing of one from another,
 93–94
 and dormitories, 180
 ethnic divisions within, 220
 fluidity of, 90
 foreign businesspeople and, 248
 growth in response to environment,
 228
 in-fighting among, 219
 interconnected, 179
 internal dynamics of, 219–20
 KGB/FSB and, 265
 labels attached to, 86, 89
 lack of coordination of, 10, 11
 liquidation of, 92, 93, 218
 as 'mafia,' 15–16
 market control, 15, 231
 membership, 89, 91–92, 215–16,
 221–22
 in Moscow, 215, 221–25
 move into legitimate business, 93
 names of, 222
 'neutralization' of, 93
 numbers of, 11, 15, 71, 75, 85–92,
 213–14, 215, 218, 255, 257
 numbers of people involved, 89,
 91–92, 221–22

organized crime groups *vs.*, 212
as part of Iron Triangle, 233–37, 244
partnerships with, 74, 81
penalties against, 262
as private companies, 94
and property ownership, 231
prosecution of, 263
and redistribution of state property,
    237–38
sharing of personnel among, 221,
    222–23
with 'signs of organization,' 86, 254
sizes of, 90, 215–17
during Soviet era, 86
Spanish operations targeting, 11
in St. Petersburg, 214–15
state and, 264–65
and survival, 205
types of people involved in, 234
and UN definition of organized crime,
    212
and upperworld, 228
varieties of, 220–21
violence of, 208
vory v zakone and, 172
See also ethnic crime groups;
        organized crime groups
criminal justice system
arbitrariness of, 114–15
disappearance of crime and, 145–46
improvement of, 146
Criminal Procedure Code
Article 162, 261
and wiretap evidence, 262
currency
changers, 182, 183
foreign, 139, 187
foreign goods as, 139
fraud, 186

D

Dagestan, corruption in, 194
Dagestani group, 183, 218, 259
Davies, R.W., 113
debt collection, 222
deception, 245;
bonuses and, 130

dismantling of Soviet Union and, 116
under NEP, 115–16
for survival, 138
decree *(ukaz)*, 111
DeFeo, Michael, 272, 273
dekulakization, 126, 132, 134
Dementiev, Alexander, 10–11
democracy, 35–36, 75, 234
den owners *(pristanoderzhateli)*, 106
Derluguian, George, 149, 161, 168, 170
Deviatkin brothers, 225
Dikselius, M., 188n.26
dismantling of Soviet Union
and attitudes toward business, 17
and criminal groups, 35, 86, 93,
    206–7
and criminal state, 234
and deceptive practices, 116
and FBI, 273
foreign businesses and, 244
and FSB, 168
and KGB, 168
and law, 264–65
and law enforcement, 35
and law of jungle, 147, 264, 265, 268
and 'mafia,' 26
and MVD, 10–11, 168
NEP era compared to, 116, 118
and ownership of industries, 230–31
and 'perfect storm' in crime history,
    206
and property, 231
and survival mentality, 237
and underworld hierarchy, 65
and *vory v zakone,* 168–73
See also post-Soviet era
dispute settlements *(razborki)*, 45, 74,
    188, 197, 222, 224, 235
distribution system, 42, 129
Dmitriev, Andrei, 98, 111, 278
documents
fraud, 116, 194–96
as information, 52–53
Dolgoprudnensky group, 60n.30, 225
Dolzhenikov, Viktor, 225
Domodedovsky criminal group, 186
dormitories, 180

downcasts, 159
Dr. Zhivago, 34
drugs
    dealing, 41, 60n.30, 145, 221, 222, 223
    during NEP era, 118
    subculture, 176–77
    See also narcotics
Duma, 219, 223
Dunn, Guy, 216
Duranty, Walter, 117, 118
Duyne, Petrus van, 210–11, 277
Dynamo, 167
'Dzhem.' *See* Vasin, Evgeny

E

Eastern European Organized Crime (EEOC), 280
Economic Crime and Drug Enforcement Units, 93
electronic surveillance, 261
embezzlement, 109, 110, 141
empire building, 34–36
English Muscovy Company, 98–99
English traders, 98–100
entrepreneurs
    bank loans to, 75
    murders of, 71–75
    russkii vs. rossiiskii and, 37
    'violent,' 82
    See also businessmen
epidemics, 113
Epifan, Tamara, 138
Esin, Yuri, 220
Esipov, V., 103–4
ethnic crime groups, 90, 218–19, 220, 221
ethnic groups, 10, 14–15, 35, 58. *See also names of specific groups*
evidence
    documents and reports as, 52
    journalism and, 55, 61
    in law enforcement, 258, 261–62
    tape recorded interviews as, 51–52
extortion
    and banks, 81
    foreign businesspeople and, 247
    frequency and scale of, 45
    and hotel guests, 182
    Kain and, 105
    Koptevo group and, 225
    media and, 63–64
    by Moscow criminal groups, 221, 222, 223
    and privatized businesses, 81
    protection *vs.,* 231
    resistance to, 74

F

factories
    distance from raw materials, 229
    ties to surrounding neighbourhood, 246–47
famines
    of 1921–22, 113
    of 1930s, 129
    in Ukraine, 127
FBI
    on Chechens, 59–60
    dismantling of Soviet Union and, 273
    and Ivankov, 172, 274
    and KGB, 273
    law enforcement division *vs.* counter-intelligence, 271–72
    MVD and, 53
    and police corruption in Russia, 273
    refusal to meet Chebotaryov and Volobuyev, 271–72
    reports, 52
    and Russian 'mafia,' 62, 273
"Federal Law on Government Protection of Victims, Witnesses, and Other Participants," 262
Felshtinsky, Yuri, 227
    Blowing-Up Russia, 265, 268
fencing operations, 223
fenia, 104, 164–65
financial operations, 73, 222, 223. *See also* currency; money laundering
Finckenhauer, James O., 57n.27, 62–63
    Russian Mafia in America, 24, 59
Firestone, Tom, 260–61, 266
Firm, the, 267–68
fish industry, 22, 40, 41

Fitzpatrick, Sheila, 136
Five Year Plans, 125, 127–33, 136, 230
Fixing Russia's Banks (Bernstam, Rabushka), 75
Fletcher, Giles. *Of the Rus Commonwealth,* 99
food
    criminal groups in trade, 223
    search for, 13.
    See also famines; produce market; restaurants
foreign businesses/businessmen
    assumptions of, 244–48
    costs for, 102
    and criminal groups, 248
    dismantling of Soviet Union and, 244
    extortion and, 247
    KGB and, 6
    and 'lawlessness' of Russia, 247–48
    media and, 248–49
    in 1990s Russian Federation, 231–32
    relationships with Soviet enterprises, 82–83
    and state 'mafia,' 249–50
    survival mentality and, 250–51
    takeovers of, 251
    and tax collectors, 6
    in Tsarist era, 98, 102
Foreign Ministry, 11
foreigners
    control of movement of, 176
    targeted for violence, 64
    tourism, and perception of danger, 45
    as visitors, 139
fraud
    bonuses and, 130
    in business contracts, 232
    credit card, 185
    currency, 186
    document, 194–96
    by former Soviets in North America, 278–81
    golden age of, 281
    medical insurance claims, 279–80, 281
    NEP and, 115
    state measures against, 140
    as widespread, 138–39
frayer, 159
Friedman, Robert. *Red Mafiya,* 49, 53, 54n.20, 55–56
FSB, 53, 168, 227, 269. *See also* KGB

G
Gachev, Georgii, 34
Galeotti, Mark, 79–80n.23, 88, 244
gambling, 118–19, 144–45
Gamsakhurdia, Zviad, 17
Ganeyev, Vladimir, 263–64
gatekeepers, 14
Gathman, Roger, 56
General Motors, 250
Georgian group, 214, 218
Gilinskiy, Yakov, 213
Gilyarovsky, Vladimir, 107, 119, 154
glasnost', 9, 18–19, 87, 166
globalization, 173
Godfather of the Kremlin (Klebnikov), 49–51
Goldman, Marshall, 129
Goldstock, Ronald, 213
Golianov group, 94
Gorbachev, Mikhail, 85, 146, 185, 186, 265
    anti-alcohol campaign, 190
    and foreign businesses, 249
    reform policies, 23
Gorkin, Alexander
    on beneficiaries of crime, 61
    and businessmen's use of criminal groups, 248
    on changes made by law *vs.* custom, 191n.39
    on 'common law' as law of underworld, 264
    on internal workings of crime groups, 220
    on Lyubers, 187
    on media coverage of organized crime, 215
    on *obshchak* funds, 161
    on organized crime, 213
    on politicization of organized crime, 260

on psychology of players, 220
on Solnetsevo group, 217
on *vory,* 172
Gosbank, 74
Gostorg (store), 115–16
GPU (secret police), 114, 118
Granville, Johanna, 55, 56
Great Mob War, 161, 207
    and criminal organization-upperworld
        relationship, 228
    doubling of numbers of crime groups
        during, 71
    Koptevo group and, 226
    media coverage of, 75, 77
    and organized crime concept, 221
    as reorganization period, 268
    struggle for power during, 169
Gregory, Johann Gottfried, 109
Grigorii (wrestler), 185–86
Grinenko, Peter, 170
GRU (military intelligence), 198, 200
gruppa bezopasnosti, 158
gruppa obespecheniye, 158
Gulag system, 132–36, 258
Gurov, Alexander
    Handelman and, 46–48
    and 'mafia,' 8
    and Organized Crime Control
        Department, 7, 46, 47
    Professional Criminality, 46
    in Russian Institute of Security
        Problems, 48
    on *vory,* 151, 156–57, 165, 169, 170
    working in Lubyanka, 47–48
Gutierrez, Carlos, 250

H
Hammer and Sickle Metal Works, 84
Handelman, Stephen, 23, 169–70, 193,
    231–32
    Comrade Criminal, 28, 46–48
Hartley, Janet, 109
Hersh, Seymour, 55
Herspring, Dale, 68–69
Hertz, Noreena, 230
hierarchy
    in anti-society of 1890s, 107

crime and, 106
    of criminality, 19–20
    organized crime and, 213
    in prisons, 158–59
    vory v zakone in criminal, 157–59
hoarding, 131, 137
Hoffmann, Erik, 31–32, 36
Homo Sovieticus, 125, 136, 206
hostage-taking, 222
hotels, 13–14, 22, 180–85, 181, 223
housing, for industrial employees,
    130–31
hustlers' brigades, 144–45
Hustling on Gorky Street (Brokhin), 140
Huyn, Hans Graf, 77n.16

I
industrialization, 125, 127–29, 136, 206,
    229
industries
    concentration of, 231
    ownership, 230–31
    privatization, 232, 233
    state control over, 230.
    See also production
informants
    in crime control programs, 261, 262
    KGB, 138
    neighbors as, 84
    state as creator of network of, 206
information
    additional, 55, 56
    age, 43–44
    assessment of, 55–56
    dissemination of, 60
    documents and reports, 52–53
    and knowledge of 'mafia,' 44
    layers of interpretation of, 65
    media as source of, 63–69
    multiple sources of, 53–54
    reports as sources of, 52–53
    snapshots as, 44–45, 49
    tape recorded interviews and, 51–52
    unnamed sources of, 55
    versions of, 49, 61
infrastructure
    inadequate development of, 42, 230

legal, 231
  urbanization and, 126
Ingush group, 214, 218
Ingushetia, corruption in, 194
intelligentsia, 37
International Harvester, 98, 102
Interpol, 10, 270
invasion, xviii
Iron Triangle, 211, 233–37, 240, 243
Ivan the Terrible, 34, 98–99
Ivankov, Vyacheslav ('Yaponchik'), 55–56,
  62–63, 145, 169–70, 172, 216, 274
Izmailovo group, 94

J

Jakobson, Michael, 134
jargon. *See* argot, criminal
Jasper, William F., 77n.16
Johnson's Russia List, 61
joint-stock companies, 239
joint ventures, 77, 79, 232, 238, 250
journalists, 62, 65–69
justice
  arbitrariness of, 206
  during 19th century, 107

K

Kadar, Janos, 150
Kain, Vanka, 104–5, 122
Kamchatka. *See* Romanov, Pyotr
  ('Kamchatka')
Kazakhstan, corruption in, 78
Kazan group, 214, 215
Kemerovo group, 214
Kerr, Raymond, 282
Kesselman, Leonid, 123
KGB
  creation of unit to focus on organized
    crime, 93
  and criminal gangs, 265, 269
  dismantling of Soviet Union and, 168
  and FBI, 273
  and foreign businesses, 6
  Gurov working for, 47, 48
  informants in hotels, 180
  and lack of cooperation among law
    enforcement agencies, 256

MVD compared to, 6
  relationships with, 27
  See also FSB
Kharkov, Gennady ('Mongol'), 145
Kharkov Tractor Plant, 130–31, 136
Khlevniuk, Oleg, 136–37
Khrushchev, Nikita, 18, 114, 135, 142
kiosks, 25, 26
Kislinskaya, Larisa, 89
Kitaigorod, Moscow, 104, 119
Klebnikov, Paul, 61
  Godfather of the Kremlin, 49–51
kolkhoz. See collective farm system
  (*kolkhoz*)
Komissarov, Vyacheslav, 23, 86, 161
Kommersant, 60
Komsomol (Young Communist League),
  199
Koptevo group, 219, 225–28
kormlenie, 108–9
'Kornei' (Koptevo group member), 226
Krajicek, David, 67–68, 69
Krasfina, Lydia, 77n.16
Krasnodarsk Krai, groups in, 214
Kremlin Capitalism (Blasi et al.), 80–81
Kristol, Irving, 5, 211, 231, 270
Krokodil, 12–13
krysha (roof), 178, 248, 266. *See also*
  protection
Kryshtanovskaya, Olga, 77n.16, 214–15,
  216–17
Kuchuloria *(vor)*, 167
kulaks, 126
Kultyapnyi, Misha, 122
Kuntsevo group, 87
Kvantrishvili, Amiran, 188
Kvantrishvili, Otari, 145, 186–87, 188
Kyrgyzstan, opium in, 177

L

labor camps, 126, 132–33, 152
Lampe, Klaus von, 210
Latynina, Yulia, 266
Law Code of 1649, 121n.93
law enforcement
  as beneficiary of existence of 'mafia,' 61
  breaking up of groups, 222

challenges facing, 257–58
criminal groups and, 179, 214,
    221–25, 255–56, 259
criminal hierarchy and, 20n.26, 256
dismantling of Soviet Union and, 35
ethnic diversity and, 39
as having lost battle against organized
    cime, 259–60, 268
lack of coordination in, 256
limitations in legal toolbox, 256
MVD and, 6
and nature of Russian 'mafia,' 208
and official disappearance of crime,
    145–46
and organizational charts, 58–59
public opinion of, 263–64
as "purely declarative," 256
recognition of criminal groups, 253
as source of information, 56–60
and speculation, 114
and tattoos, 164
and terrorism, 281
as toothless, 256–57
totalitarianism and, 9
in U.S., 163–64
and *vory v zakone,* 155
and *vory vs.* crime groups, 172
Law on Cooperatives, 188
Law on Operational Search Activity,
    Article 12, 262
'lawlessness' of Russia, 46, 247–48
law(s)
    administrative ruling *(razporyazhenie),*
        111
    'common,' 264
    dismantling of Soviet Union and,
        264–65
    and Five Year Plans, 132
    Khrushchev on, 142
    narcotics, 176–77
    during 19th century, 107
    and property ownership, 231
    regulations, 111
    rules *(pravila),* 162
    varieties of, 247–48
    zakony, 111, 162
    of *zhigani,* 151–52

See also rule of law
Layard, Richard. *The Coming Russian
    Boom,* 25–27, 60n.30
Lebedev, S. Ya., 161–62, 164
Lee, Rens, 177
Lenin, V.I., 5–6, 112, 113, 163, 251
Leningrad
    naval yard, 116, 130n.14
    See also St. Petersburg
Lewin, Moshe, 136
Lichfield, Gideon, 61
Likhachev, D.S., 152, 164
liquor. *See* alcohol
Litvinenko, Alexander, 227
    Blowing-Up Russia, 265, 268
livestock, 126
London, crime epidemic of 1720s, 174
Lubyanka, 47–48
Luneev, Viktor, 211–13, 218
Lupsha, Peter, 210, 211
'Lyonka the Lucky.' *See* Pantelkin,
    Leonid
Lyuberetsky criminal groups, 186
Lyubers, 187–88
Lyubertsy group, 60n.30

M
machinery, 127, 129
'mafia'
    as access, 12
    activities and concept of, 25–27
    avoidance of label, 28–29
    beneficiaries of existence of, 61–63
    Communist Party as, 18–21, 211, 232,
        270
    criminal groups as, 15–16
    definitions of, xvii, 15, 24, 25–26,
        27–28, 29
    denial of existence of, 8–12
    diminishment of, 94
    dismantling of Soviet Union and, 26
    ethnic composition of, 37–38
    and ethnic Russians, 15
    FBI and, 273
    as gatekeepers, 12–15
    implications of word, 8
    information processing and, 69

information sources and knowledge
    about, 44
as invading force, xviii, 8, 15, 25, 71,
    73, 77, 83, 94
as Italian phenomenon, 9, 10
Ivankov as example of godfather,
    62–63
media and, 9–10, 11–12
as modus operandi, 24
MVD and, 7–8, 9–10
and 'new democracy,' 75
political regime as, 21
and protection, 16
robber baron concept of, 25, 26–27
September 11 and, 275
service providers as, 14–15
Sicilian, 16, 24
Soviet-type, 24
Soviet view of, 21–23
state, 17, 25, 249
substitute words for, 28
tactics, 269–70
thugs as, 16, 25, 27–28
totalitarianism and, 21
traditional, 10, 16
typical activities of, 24
varieties of groups comprising, 25–27
Western perception of, 26, 27–28,
    31–32
'mafiya,' 23, 28
Magnitogorsk, 127
market economy, 98, 232, 244–45
markets
    besprizorniki and, 119, 121
    during Civil War, 112, 113
    control of, 231
    criminal groups and, 15, 223
    ethnic merchants and, 14–15
    private, 112, 113
    smuggling and, 117
Mayakovsky, Vladimir, 115, 116
mayors' offices, 236–37
Mazutinsky group, 227
McKee, Martin, 190
Mears, Michael, 246
media
    as beneficiary of existence of 'mafia,' 61

characteristics of people in, 67–68
competition within, 67
exposure, 66–67
and foreign investment, 248–49
headlines, 63, 64–65, 72
and invading 'mafia,' 207
and layers of interpretation in stories,
    65
and 'mafia,' 9–10, 11–12
and nature of Russian 'mafia,' 208
and numbers of crime groups, 214
over-emphasis on organized crime,
    69
as source of information, 63–69, 208
telling of stories, 65
and underworld vs. upperworld, 206
Melnikov, I.G., 105
Melnikov, Yuri, 10, 38, 97, 146, 173, 206,
    266
'Melz' (Koptevo group member), 227
merchants
    American, 102
    argot used by, 164
    elite, 102
    English, 98–99, 102, 249
    in municipal service, 110
    in NEP period, 117
    from republics, 14–15
    of Tsarist Russia, 100, 102, 103
Mesto Vstrechi Izmenit' Nel'zya (movie),
    176
Mexico, corruption in, 207
middle class, 37
Mikhailov, Sergei, 216
Mikhas, 257n.21
militarization, 34–35, 127, 206
minerals, 40
Ministry of Foreign Affairs, Chechens
    and, 184
Mogilevich, Semion, 55, 56
money laundering, 188, 219, 226, 232,
    274
'Mongol.' See Kharkov, Gennady
    ('Mongol')
Moody, Jim, 272–73
moonshine, 190–91
moral climate, 140–42

'The Morals and Ethics of Trade,' 141, 142
Morozov brothers, 225
Moscow, 41
    as crime center during 17th and
        centuries, 104
    criminal groups in, 90, 215, 221–25
    Criminal Investigation Department,
        176, 254
    districts of, 221–22
    hotels in, 184
    population, 113
    Regional Organized Crime Control
        Department, 93, 218
    Sheremetievo airport, 226
movement, restrictions on, 14, 176, 181
Murmansky, Stepan, 226
Muscovy Company, 98, 100
muzhiki, 159
MVD (Ministry of Internal Affairs), 6–7,
    9–10, 256
    on Chechens, 57
    on control of enterprises by criminal
        groups, 78
    dismantling of Soviet Union and,
        10–11, 168
    exchange program with University of
        Illinois, 272
    FBI and, 53
    instability of, 87
    Internal Troops branch (Vnutrennaya
        Voiska), 7
    international conference on organized
        crime control, 149–50, 272–74
    and 'mafia,' 7–8, 9–10
    and media, 9–10
    on numbers of criminal groups, 75,
        79, 85–88
    and organized crime, 253–54
    Organized Crime Control Department
        (see Organized Crime Control
        Department (MVD))
    production by, 133
    relationships with, 27
    Sixth Directorate for Organized Crime
        Control (Shestoe Upravleniye po
        Bor'be s Organizovannoi
        Prestupnost'iu), 254

    as source of information in FBI
        documents, 52–53
Mzhavanadze, Vasily, 143

N
narcotics, 145, 223, 226, 255, 270. See
    also drugs
nation-states, 36
national identity, 36–37
nationhood
    civic aspect of, 35–36
    empire building vs., 36
    ethnic aspect of, 35
natural gas, 40, 41
natural resources, 39–41
Naumov, Alexander, 225, 226–27
Naumov, Vasily, 225, 227
Nepmen, 114, 116, 117, 118, 122, 125
New Economic Policy (NEP), 113–18
New York
    crime during 1870s and 1880s, 174
    Ivankov and, 167, 170, 172
    Russian 'mafia' in, 58, 271, 274
Nicholas I, Tsar, 102
North Ossetia, corruption in, 194
Novorossiisk, Kemerovo group in, 214
novye vory v zakone, 166–67

O
oath of initiation, 165
obshchak, 158, 160–61, 167, 179,
    200–201, 220
obshchina (ethnic crime communities),
    218–19
Odintsovsky group, 226
Of the Rus Commonwealth (Fletcher),
    99
officials
    as Firm, 267–68
    power struggles among, 266–67
    in Prussia, 109
    in Russia, 109
    See also bureaucracy
oil industry, 39–40, 237
Oil Industry Bank (Neftprombank),
    75
Oktyabrskaya Hotel, 184–85

'oligarchs,' 6, 26–27, 268
 activities of, 51
 Berezovsky as, 49–50, 51
 control of economy, 80, 81
 as criminals, compared to serious
  criminals, 268–69
 FBS and, 53
 fight against organized crime and, 268
 journalists and, 69
 'mafia' compared to, 16
 Moscow Institute of Metals and Alloys
  and, 6
 See also businessmen
Omsk group, 214
opium, 177
Orda group, 87
Orekhovo group, 198, 220
organizational charts, 58–59
organized crime, 205
 acknowledgment of existence of, 46,
  178, 254
 capitalism and, 46
 as crime groups united into criminal
  organizations, 218–19
 definitions of, 87, 209–14, 260–61
 diminishment of, 94
 elements of control programs, 261
 Great Mob War and, 221
 group membership, 212–13
 lack of cooperation within, 219
 levels of, 256
 media emphasis on, 69
 MVD and, 253–54
 natural resources and, 39–41
 numbers of members, 217
 as politicized, 260
 and state, 260
 syndicates, 58
 war against, 259–60, 268, 269–70
Organized Crime and Its Control in
  Central Asia (Redo), 78
"Organized Crime and the Prospect of
  National-Socialists Coming to Power
  in Russia" (Analytical Center for
  Socio-Economic Policy of the
  President of the Russian Federation),
  76–78

Organized Crime Control Department
  (MVD)
 anti-Chechen unit, 58
 Chebotaryov and, 7
 and cooperation within organized
  crime, 219
 creation of, 87
 definition of organized crime, 87
 dormitory, 180
 Gurov and, 46, 47
 increase in resources to fight crime
  groups, 93
 information collection by, 87–88
 and KGB bank accounts in West, 6n.3
 on Mikhas as leader of Solntsevo
  group, 257n.21
 on number of criminal groups, 86,
  87–88
 and osobo opasniye retsidivisty, 169
 as political tool, 256
 and vory v zakone, 169
 Yegorov and, 48
organized crime groups
 breaking up of, 218, 255
 as businessmen, 269
 criminal activities, 179
 criminal groups vs., 212
 definition of, 260–61
 diminishment of, 269–70
 length of time of existence, 179–80
 'mafia' tactics, 269–70
 numbers of, 255
 numbers of members in, 217–18
 as private security companies, 269
 See also criminal groups
Orttung, Robert, 260, 262
osobo opasniye retsidivisty (especially
  dangerous recidivists), 150, 169, 235
Ossetian group, 218
otkoloty, 153–54
Ovchinskii, V.S., 19n.22
Owen, Thomas, 102
 The Corporation Under Russian Law,
  1800–1917, 100–101

P
Palmer, Richard L., 79n.21

Palmer, Rick, 77n.16
Pantelkin, Leonid ('Lyonka the Lucky'),
    122–23
Parker, John. *The Coming Russian Boom,*
    25–27, 60n.30
passports
    multiple, 167
    prostitution for, 184
peasants
    and crime, 106–7
    marketing of goods, 113, 114
    War Communism and, 112–13
    See also kulaks
Penal Code, Article 58, 134
Perov group, 94
personal contacts, 137–38
    and building businesses, 242
    consumer goods and, 12–13
    and cooperation with international
        organizations, 270
    as 'mafia,' 14
    under NEP, 114–16
    and state as 'mafia,' 17
Peter the Great, 34, 99n.6, 100, 101, 104,
    108–9, 119, 121n.93
Poberezh'e, Omsk group in, 214
Podatiev, Vladimir ('Poodle'), 220, 235
Podolsk group, 59, 259
police
    and bribery, 110–11, 258
    and businesses, 265
    contacts in U.S., 271
    corruption, 53, 273
    and criminal world, 206
    dangers facing, 258
    displacement of local gangsters, 266
    intelligence documents, 52
    international cooperation by, 271
    involvement in underworld, 263
    and Koptevo group, 226, 227–28
    and 'mafia,' 8, 9, 11
    personnel leaving, 258
    and prostitution, 266
    protection by, 265, 266
    respect for, 258
    salaries, 110, 259
    shootouts, 266

sources of income, 110–11
    and speculation, 114
    state, 3, 97, 108, 206
    through 19th century, 110–11
    turnover rate, 110
    understaffing of, 110
    See also FSB; GPU; KGB
political prisoners, 134, 150
polozhentsy, 160–61, 220
population, 113
porters, hotel, 181–82, 183
ports, 40
post-Soviet era
    businesses, 79, 80, 117, 241
    businessmen, 26–27
    criminal groups in, 11, 73, 75, 86, 92,
        176, 212–14
    criminal-syndicalist state in, 232
    criminals-business people relationship,
        197n.51
    empire building in, 34
    historic similarities to, 123
    law enforcement in, 11, 87–88,
        257–60, 270
    law in, 264–65
    law of jungle in, 146–47, 264
    'mafia' concept and, 15, 20, 23, 24,
        28, 98, 249
    monetary foundation of, 171
    obshchak in, 160–61
    organized crime in, 38, 282
    police in, 258
    state 'mafia' in, 17
    statistics in, 75
    vory in, 166–68
    workshops in, 177
'Potema' *(avtoritet),* 225
Powers, Francis Gary, 150–51
Powers, William, 67
pravila (rules), 162
prestupniki na gastroli (roving criminals),
    181
prices, 113
prisoners
    in Gulags, 134–35
    mentality, 136
    return of, 135

tattoos, 162–64
team leaders in, 153
prisons
    barbers in, 153
    bitches' war in, 153
    hierarchy in, 158–59
    vory v zakone and, 154–55, 168, 171
private business, criminal groups and,
    222, 223, 225
in NEP era, 113, 114, 117
speculation and, 113–14
Stalinist era and, 125
state *vs.*, 114, 117
taxes and, 117
privatization
    of industrial sector, 232, 233
    as 'mafia' behavior, 17
    of state property, 142
procurators, 256, 257, 263, 266
produce markets, 223
production
    bonuses, 130
    concentration of, 230
    under Five Year Plans, 128–29, 130
    labor camps and, 132–33
    manipulation of output figures, 136
    by Ministry of Internal Affairs, 133
    reports, 130, 136
productivity, 131
    alcohol and, 190
    economic policies and, 37, 127
    Homo Sovieticus and, 136
    illegal business activities and, 131
    in labor camps, 133
    in prisons, 158
Professional Criminality (Gurov), 46
The Professional Thief (Sutherland), 173
property
    criminal groups, and redistribution of,
        237–38
    dismantling of Soviet Union and, 231
    state, 116, 142–43
propiski (residence permits), 181
prostitution
    chambermaids and, 183
    Chechens and, 60
    child, 120–21

and hotels, 182, 183
in media, 64
for passports, 184
places of, 121n.95
police and, 266
during Tsarist era, 121n.93
protection
    bankers-entrepreneurs-criminal
        groups relationship and, 74
    control as, 81
    criminal gangs and, 231
    'mafia' and, 16
    by police, 265, 266
    rackets, 60n.30
Pugachev, Emilian, 172–73
Pugo, Boris, 185
punishments
    of criminal groups, 262
    Five Year Plans and, 132
    in labor camps, 133
    in prisons, 154
    state and, 206
Pushkin, Alexander, 172–73
Putin, Vladimir, 268

Q
queues, 131

R
Rabushka, Alvin. *Fixing Russia's Banks*, 75
racketeering, 19, 75–76, 81
Red Mafiya (Friedman), 49, 53, 54n.20,
    55–56
Red Tape (Thomas, Sutherland), 230
Redo, Slawomir. *Organized Crime and Its
    Control in Central Asia*, 78
republics, 32, 33
    merchants from, 14–15
    products from, 230
    See also ethnic groups
restaurants, 13–14, 63–64, 241
Riasanovsky, Nicholas, 126
roadways, 129
robber barons, 25, 26–27, 268
Robinson, Matthew, 66n.43
Roizis, Iosif, 216
Romanov, Pyotr ('Kamchatka'), 104–5

Rosner, Lydia, 66
Rosoboronexport, 250
Rossi, Jacques, 135, 150, 158n.30
Rossiiskaya 'mafia,' 37–38
rossiiskii, 34, 36, 37
Rossiya, 34, 36
Rossiya Hotel, 13–14
ruble, collapse of, 207, 248
rule of law
    arrests and, 133–34
    civil society and, 37
    under NEP, 114–15
    state and, 133–34
    survival and, 141–42
RUOP (Regional Units for Organized
    Crime Control), 93, 254, 259
Rus, 33–34, 36
Rushailo, Vladimir, 81
Russia
    compared to other middle-income
        countries, 207
    criticism of, 38–39
    difference between Soviet Union and,
        32–33
    Western perception of, 31–32
Russia Company, 100
'Russian'
    meaning of, 33–34
    'Soviet' *vs.,* 10
Russian Federation, 32
    ethnic composition of, 38
    nation-statehood compared to, 36
Russian Foreign Intelligence Service
    (SVR), 200
Russian Institute of Security Problems, 48
Russian language, 33, 35
Russian Livestock Insurance Company,
    101
Russian Mafia in America (Finckenhauer,
    Waring), 24, 59
The Russian Mafia (Varese), 16, 165–66
Russian Revolution, 112
Russian Soviet Federated Socialist Repub-
    lic (Rossiiskii Sovetskii Federativnyi
    Sotsialisticheskii Respublik), 32
Russian State Agriculture Bank
    (Rosselkhozbank), 75

Russkaya 'mafia,' 37–38
russkii, 33–34, 36, 37

S
salaries, 137–38
    delayed payment of, 109
    inadequacy of, 137–38, 139
    police, 139, 259
Sanford, Tawnia, 61
'Sasha' *(vory v zakone),* 151
Saturn (police commando team), 227
security companies, 235
    as beneficiaries of existence of 'mafia,'
        62
    organized crime groups as, 269
seizures, 255
Serge, Victor, 118
sertifikaty (vouchers), 187
shadow economy
    accounting for nearly half national
        economy, 137
    bureaucracy and, 229
    Chechens and, 59
    concentration of production and,
        230
    and crime, 180
    and market sense, 229, 245
    operators *(teniviki),* 145, 177
    Western goods and, 178
Shalamov, Varlam, 135
Shanker, Thom, 48n.9, 66
Shchekochikhin, Yuri, 13, 19, 264
Shchransky, Anatoly, 150
shesterit', 158n.30
shestiorka, 158
shootouts, 45, 187, 215, 219, 220, 231,
    248, 266
shopkeepers, 177, 253
shortages
    of alcohol, 190–91
    command economy and, 137
    of consumer goods, 206, 229–30
    and crime, 180
    of hotel rooms, 181
    and personal contacts, 138
    of sugar, 191
    and survival, 206

Simis, Konstantin, 20, 143, 264
  USSR: The Corrupt Society, 178
Singer Sewing Company, 98, 102
Sixth Directorate for Organized Crime
  Control *(Shestoe Upravleniye po
  Bor'be s Orgaizovannoi Prestupnos-
  t'iu): See* MVD (Ministry of Internal
  Affairs): Sixth Directorate for
  Organized Crime Control *(Shestoe
  Upravleniye po Bor'be s Organizovan-
  noi Prestupnost'iu)*
slave labor, 133
Slavic groups, 225, 227
sledit' za poriadkom, 157–58
smotriashchyi, 157–58
smuggling, 235
  of antiques, 241
  of computers, 192–93
  Ingush and, 60n.30
  during NEP era, 117
  of tobacco, 100
Sogomonian, Rafail, 167
Sokolov, Yuri, 143–44
Soldatov, Alex, 58
Solntsevo group, 183, 198, 200–201, 219
  Chechens and, 59
  Esin and, 220
  and gambling business, 214, 215
  Ismailovo group and, 94
  Koptevo group and, 226
  Mikhas and, 257n.21
  size and influence of, 216–17
'Solovei' *(avtoritet),* 226
Solovki camp, 133
Solzhenitsyn, Alexander, 37, 134
sovetnik, 157–58
Sovetskaya Hotel, Moscow, 186
Soviet 'mafia'
  and criminal groups, 175
  relationship with criminal world, 94,
    123, 131
The Soviet Mafia (Vaksberg), 21–23, 49,
    183, 264
'Soviet,' 'Russian' *vs.,* 10
Soviet Union. *See* USSR (Union of Soviet
  Socialist Republics)
sovkhoz. See state farm structure *(sovkhoz)*

Spain, operations targeting criminal
  groups, 11
speculation/speculators
  hotels and, 182, 183
  NEP and, 113–14
Sports Academy, 186
St. Petersburg, 41
  criminal groups in, 214–15
  population, 113
  See also Leningrad
Stalin, Josef
  and agricultural collectivization, 126
  and Chechens, 57
  death of, 18
  and forced labor camps, 132
  and growth in illegal businesses, 139
  Khrushchev and, 142
  paranoia regarding power of others,
    229
  Solzhenitsyn and, 134
  succession following Lenin's death, 125
  tattoos of, 163
starye vory v zakone, 166
'Staryi' (Koptevo group member), 227
state
  as beneficiary of existence of 'mafia,'
    61
  and corruption, 25
  and criminal groups, 264–65
  and hotels, 180
  institutions and, 35
  'mafia,' 17, 25, 249
  under NEP, 113, 117
  organized crime and, 260
  people *vs.,* 36
  as police state, 206
  private business *vs.,* 113, 114, 117
  property, 116, 142–43
  subsidization by, 246–47
  thieves' code and, 152
  and *tsekhoviki,* 177
state farm structure *(sovkhoz),* 126–27
State Planning Agency (Gosplan), 128
statistics
  and changes in picture of crime, 209
  crime groups *vs.* organized crime
    groups and, 212

criminal groups and, 221
distrust of, 75
economy and, 85
industrial, 84, 130
and 'mafia,' 83
malleability of, 85
and numbers of crime groups, 85–88,
    90–93, 94
of organized crime, 254–55
steel production, 40
Stepashin, Sergei, 260, 268, 269
Sterling, Claire, 150n.4
    Thieves' World, 170
stores
alcohol and, 190
Beriozka, 187
Communist Party and, 19
private, 116
sale of goods in, 12–13
street crime, 45–46
sugar, 191
Supreme Court, 256, 257, 260
survival, 132
autocracy and, 101
Bolshevism and, 112
codes and, 171
competitiveness and, 246–47
crime groups and, 205
deal making for, 138
illicit financial transactions and, 73
mentality, 107, 237
personal contact and, xvii
in prison, 153
rule of law and, 141–42
shortages and, 206
underground economy and, 245
Sutherland, Charles. *Red Tape,* 230
Sutherland, Edwin. *The Professional Thief,*
    173
Suzdal conference, 149–50
Svinarenko, Igor, 60
Svo. *See* Bagdasarian, Rafik ('Svo,' 'Rafik-
    Svo')
Svoboda (security firm), 235
'Sylvester.' *See* Timofeyev, Sergei
syndicates, 213. *See also* criminal
    associations/organizations

T

Tambov group, 214–15, 219
tape recorded interviews, 51–52
Tashkent, criminal gangs in, 178–79
tattoos, 162–64, 168
taxes
bribes *vs.,* 108
foreign businesses and, 6
ineffectiveness of collection agencies,
    256
and private business, 117
telephones, 131, 132
teniviki (shadow economy workers), 177
terrorism, 275, 281
theft(s)
of automobiles, 222, 223
command economy and, 137
Five Year Plans and, 130
from hotels, 182, 183
during 19th century, 106
profession of, 173
of state property, 116, 143
for survival, 138
unwritten rules of, 140
Thieves' World (Sterling), 170
Thomas, Bill. *Red Tape,* 230
timber, 40, 41, 160, 186, 238
Timofeyev, Sergei ('Sylvester'), 198
tobacco trade, 100
Tolz, Vera, 36
totalitarianism, 9, 21, 32, 36, 206
trade
arbitrariness in, 100
hoarding and, 138
'mafia,' 22
speculation and, 113–14
See also barter
transport
cost of, 230
'mafia,' 22
Transtorg, 115–16
travel, international, 206
Troyansky, Eugene, 281
Tsarist Russia: administration in,
    108–11
central planning policies, 112
law in, 107, 111

peasants in, 106–7
robber gangs in, 105
tsekhoviki, 145, 177
'Tsitska' *(vor v zakone)*, 226
Tushinsky group, 219, 227

U

Ubogii, Slava, 227
Ukraine, famine in, 127
undercover operations, 261–62
underground economy. *See* shadow
    economy
underworld
    Communist Party and, 265
    as hodge-podge of groups, 94
    and hotels, 180–81
    merged with upperworld, 186
    during NEP era, 119
    police involvement in, 263
    relations with upperworld, 178
    during Soviet era, 144
    state 'mafia' and, 249
    upperworld and, 19, 173, 175
United Nations
    Convention against Transnational
        Organized Crime, 211, 212
    cooperation with, 270
United States
    Border Patrol, 163–64
    and breaking up of criminal groups,
        222
    Canadian border, 164
    Cold War and relations with USSR,
        176
    Department of State, 163
    former Soviets living in, 278–81
    government as beneficiary of existence
        of 'mafia,' 61
    law enforcement in, 163–64
    Permanent Subcommittee on
        Investigations, 88
    police contacts in, 271
    Prohibition in, 192
    Russian 'mafia' in, 53, 58, 274, 282
    vory in, 169–70, 170
upperworld
    and alcohol, 191

criminal groups and, 228
'mafia,' 191, 207
underworld merging with, 19, 275
urbanization, industrialization and, 126
urki, 152
USSR: The Corrupt Society (Simis), 178
USSR (Union of Soviet Socialist
    Republics), 32
    difference between Russia and, 32–33
    economy of, 207
    ethnic composition of, 38, 39
    institutions in, 35
    journalists in, 66
    population, 113
    size of, 41
    superpower status, 41–42, 207
    Western development compared to,
        35
    Western perception of, 31–32
Uzbeks, 197–98

V

Vaksberg, Arkady
    on alcohol restrictions, 191–92
    'mafia,' 196
    on politician-criminal relationship,
        28n.43
    The Soviet Mafia, 21–23, 49, 183, 264
    and state 'mafia,' 249
    wide-ranging concept of 'mafia,' 192,
        193
Varese, Federico, 24, 244
    The Russian Mafia, 16, 165–66
Vasin, Evgeny ('Dzhem'), 156, 160–61,
    220
violence, 207, 208
    bribery and, 281
    Communist Party and, 21
    data on, 208
    entrepreneurship and, 23
    failed negotiations and, 248
    foreigners targeted for, 64
Violent Entrepreneurs (Volkov), 23
Vishinsky, Andrei, 134
Vladimir Central Prison, 150–51, 226
Vladimirov, Leonid, 128
vodka, 189

voevoda, 108
Volkov, Vadim, 81, 82, 217
  Violent Entrepreneurs, 23
Volobuyev, Anatoly
  on criminal groups as unskilled
    workers, 20n.26
  on fight against organized crime as
    "declarative," 256
  and ideological stance on organized
    crime, 146
  on numbers of crime leaders, 85
  on politicization of crime levels,
    260n.30
  and relationship between RUOP and
    criminal groups, 259
  on Soviet 'mafia' system, 21
  visit to U.S., 271–72
Vorkutinsky criminal community, 218
vorovskoi mir (culture of thieves' world),
  173
vory v zakone
  ages of, 168–69
  as caste-like rank, 149
  characteristics of, 120
  code of, 155–56, 170–73
  compared to Communist Party elite,
    170
  and crime groups, 172
  in criminal hierarchy, 157–59
  departure from criminal traditions,
    153–54
  dismantling of Soviet Union and,
    168–73
  functions of, 157, 159–60, 211
  gang leaders of 1920s compared to, 120
  as high-profile bosses, 145
  intermingling into "respectable
    society," 107
  international spread of, 170
  law enforcement and, 155
  new, 166–67, 171
  numbers of, 89, 168–69
  old, 166
  parasitism of, 156–57
  predecessors to, 151–52
  and prisons, 151, 152, 154–55, 168,
    171
    regional influence, 159
    as rulers of anti-society, 154
    'Sasha,' 150–51
    skhodki, 154, 165
    special meetings held by, 154
    status of, 169–73, 211
    and Tashkent criminal clans, 179
    and tattoos, 162–64, 168
    as 'thieves in law,' 152
    and *tsekhoviki,* 177
    in U.S., 169–70, 170
    visibility of, 253
    World War II and, 152–53

W

Wallenberg, Raoul, 150
War Communism, 112–13
Ward, Dick, 150n.4, 273
Waring, Elin J., 57n.27, 62–63
  Russian Mafia in America, 24, 59
weapons
  dealing in, 221, 222
  dismantling of Soviet Union and,
    206
  Koptevo group and, 226
  police and, 258
  seizures of, 255
Wild, Jonathan, 174
wiretap evidence, 261, 262
Witkin, Zara, 127–28, 130–32, 207
witnesses
  cooperation of, 261
  protection programs for, 258, 261
Woolsey, James, 73, 77n.16
Wooster, Martin Morse, 55
World War I, 112
World War II
  Chechens and, 57
  excavation of ordnance from, 176n.3
  and *vory v zakone,* 152–53
Worth, Adam, 174

Y

Yaponchik. *See* Ivankov, Vyacheslav
Yegorov, Mikhail, 48, 88, 89, 274
Yelisayevsky's (store), 143–44
Yeltsin, Boris

and Analytical Center report on
    organized crime, 76
the Firm and, 267
and incentives for foreign businesses,
    249–50
ineptness of leadership, 265
on national identity for Russia, 36
and Procurator's office, 257
reform policies, 23
selection of Putin as successor, 268
and Sports Academy, 186
Yudin, Igor V., 181–82
Yuri Levada Center, 263

Z

Zakharov, Alexander, 157–58n.29
zakony, 162
Zariad'e, Moscow, 104
Zaslavskaya, Tatyana, 19–20, 264
Zavadski, Leonid, 157–58n.29
'Zema' (Koptevo group member), 227
zhigani, 151–52
Zhirinovsky, Vladimir, 76
Zhoglo, Anatoly, 171–72
Zhora 'the Engineer,' 170–71